Circular
Economy

for
dummies®
A Wiley Brand

Circular Economy

by Kyle J. Ritchie & Eric Corey Freed

Circular Economy For Dummies®

Published by: **John Wiley & Sons, Inc.,** 111 River Street, Hoboken, NJ 07030-5774, www.wiley.com

Copyright © 2021 by John Wiley & Sons, Inc., Hoboken, New Jersey

Published simultaneously in Canada

For general information on our other products and services, please contact our Customer Care Department within the U.S. at 877-762-2974, outside the U.S. at 317-572-3993, or fax 317-572-4002. For technical support, please visit https://hub.wiley.com/community/support/dummies.

Wiley publishes in a variety of print and electronic formats and by print-on-demand. Some material included with standard print versions of this book may not be included in e-books or in print-on-demand. If this book refers to media such as a CD or DVD that is not included in the version you purchased, you may download this material at http://booksupport.wiley.com. For more information about Wiley products, visit www.wiley.com.

Library of Congress Control Number: 2021934617

ISBN: 978-1-119-71638-9; 978-1-119-71639-6 (ebk); 978-1-119-71640-2 (ebk)

Manufactured in the United States of America

SKY10025917_033021

Contents at a Glance

Table of Contents

Introduction

Welcome to *Circular Economy For Dummies!*

This is a book about materials and waste, but it's also a book about design and business and how these elements are connected. At its heart, this book is about rethinking how we humans can create food, buildings, fashion, and other products without destroying Planet Earth and burying the world in waste.

To safely provide for the needs of billions of people in an ever-warming world, we need to change the situation dramatically. Every manufacturer, designer, and producer of goods needs to rethink their industrial approach to how products are made. Instead of the old take-make-waste approach to manufacturing, where natural resources are extracted from the earth to make stuff that ends up rotting in a landfill, we need to explore a new model. That's the definition of the circular economy.

Although you'll find a lot of information about the impact of waste in this book, it isn't a book about trash. Nor does the book focus only on how to reduce plastic, even though that's a part of the story. At its core, the circular economy focuses on how to redesign everything so it can be made and remade over and over again. It turns out that doing good can also be beneficial to a business's bottom line.

The planet is swimming in trash. Though the industrial revolution transformed the quality of life for everyone, it also produced billions of tons of plastic waste, nearly all of which ends up in the oceans or in a landfill. At this rate, the oceans will contain more plastic than fish by 2050. If we want to save the planet from a terrible waste, resource, and climate crisis, we have to transform our way of making things.

REMEMBER

The environmental problems we humans need to solve aren't trivial or easy to fix. Though it's true that we understand far better the impact that humans have had on the environment, we still have a long way to go to be truly circular in terms of the entire economy. Rethinking our approach, reimagining our businesses, and redesigning our products is a huge challenge, but it's also a huge opportunity.

We wrote this book to be the definitive guide to the circular economy. Though the circular economy has been gaining mainstream adoption in Europe and the United Kingdom, it's still largely a new concept in North America. This book is for anyone who runs a business and has an interest in making better products, services, or approaches for their customers. It's also intended for anyone who wants a clear framework for how to create a truly sustainable product or material.

In our daily lives, we both work on improving the sustainability, health, and impact of buildings, and we're driven to help show people how to have a positive impact on the planet. This book — which reflects our hope for a better and brighter future — shares the lessons we've learned from working with thousands of businesses, institutions, and government agencies to help them create vibrant, healthy, and waste-free buildings.

Circular Economy For Dummies is the first comprehensive reference and how-to book that gives you the knowledge and tools you need to transform your business from a linear (wasteful) model to a circular (sustainable) one — and to impact the lives of everyone in the world for the better.

About This Book

This practical, action-oriented book is about manufacturing and design. It doesn't dwell on theory or abstract concepts. Nor do you need a PhD in supply chain management. Throughout, we focus on asking the right questions and figuring out how to radically rethink materials so that you can make a true impact. The book includes a diverse set of case studies, interviews, and examples to inspire and guide you.

Transforming how everything is made is no easy task. Trying to improve the environmental impact of your product might require you to study dozens of books. Who has time for all that? Instead, we've distilled and condensed only the parts that truly matter so that you can delve directly into the heart of what's important. This book is detailed, but we didn't include long-winded passages or unnecessary content. You get everything you need in order to be successful in creating and implementing a complete circular strategy.

Our hope is that this book inspires you to take action to envision a better approach to manufacturing, materials, and waste — full of new possibilities. Unlike some other topics, the circular economy is quite complex, with layers of meaning and understanding to it. Luckily, we've written this book so that anyone can find an aspect that will grab them and motivate them to make a positive change. The circular economy addresses biodiversity, climate change, energy use, natural resources, and so much more. This book focuses on materials and products, but covers hundreds of interconnected subjects.

REMEMBER

The future success of humanity is tied to figuring out how to achieve the ideas outlined in this book. If we're going to be able to house, clothe, and feed a global population of 9 billion (and counting), we need new ideas and new approaches to making durable, reusable, and recyclable materials of tomorrow. This book can make that future possible.

Whether your job is linked to manufacturing, design, or materials — or if you're just a curious soul looking to make the world a better place — you'll find *Circular Economy For Dummies* to be a fun, inspiring, and helpful guidebook on your journey.

Foolish Assumptions

Throughout the writing of this book, we had only you (our gentle reader) in mind. Don't panic, but here's the information we assumed about you so that you can get the maximum benefit from this book:

» You're seeking a comprehensive but condensed and easy-to-follow guide to implementing a circular economy strategy.

» You've already heard about sustainability and you're interested enough to buy this book.

» You're not a treehugger, but you're concerned about climate change and waste.

» You lack the time or patience for tracking down the meaning of unnecessary buzzwords or jargon — you want to get only the essential knowledge you need in order to get stuff done.

» You recognize that the old "take-make-waste" approach to industrial manufacturing is less than perfect and that you might be able to find opportunities to save money and do the right thing at the same time.

» You recognize that the field of circular economy is still a nascent and emerging topic and that, as more companies embrace these ideas, it will continue to evolve and change.

» You realize that transforming and innovating a business requires careful planning and research.

» You understand that this book is ultimately about people and the future of the planet.

Icons Used in This Book

Throughout this book, you see these little graphical icons to identify useful paragraphs:

The Tip icon highlights expert advice and real-world experience to provide ways to save you time and money — and preserve your sanity!

The Remember icon marks information that's so important you'll want to remember it for later use. To grab the most important points in each chapter, just skim these paragraphs.

The Technical Stuff icon marks information that's technically oriented but not critical to your understanding, so you can safely skip over them without harm.

The Warning icon highlights some sage advice to follow so that you can avoid costly mistakes or missteps. *Warning:* Don't skip over these warnings!

How This Book Is Organized

This book is divided into six main parts — feel free to jump to any part you want. Each part is written in a way to tell you everything you need to know about a single topic inside each chapter. The following sections explain what you'll find, and where:

Part 1: Linear Is Out, Circular Is In: An Economic Revolution

The early chapters in Part 1 help you understand the problem behind the traditional approach to making products. It starts with an overview of the damage that industrial manufacturing has created and explains that it cannot continue in its current state. Then you'll see how the circular economy has emerged as a new model that corrects these issues. Finally, you'll read how the traditional approach compares to a circular approach in order to identify new ways to discuss and understand both approaches.

Part 2: Rethinking Business for a Circular Economy

In Part 2, you'll look at business in a new way that will help you identify and uncover the issues in your current business approach. You'll quickly understand how actions that you previously assumed were "just a part of doing business" (like creating waste and using toxic chemical processes) are actually costing you money. From there, you'll find out how to structure a new business model based on simple pillars that will improve your relationship with your customers and your suppliers — and improve your profits. Think of this book as a crash course in strategic business planning for a new, circular world.

This part concludes with an extended look into waste products for what they really are — valuable resources to be reused.

Part 3: Rethinking Material Lifecycles — The Circular Perspective

In the chapters in Part 3, you discover the bold, new concept, called lifecycle, that will help you map and understand all aspects of your products. This becomes a foundational strategy that you can use to bend and convert those old, manufacturing pathways into circular loops of sustainable goodness.

You'll see materials in an entirely new light and make better-informed decisions about sourcing, supplying, and processing materials. Part 3 gives you a comprehensive list of case studies showing how dozens of companies are innovating their way to more profits.

The final chapter in Part 3 explores how this all comes together to encompass the packaging and reuse of these materials.

Part 4: Redesigning the Future to Be Circular

The circular economy is looking toward the future. In Part 4, you get to see the vision of what a true circular design strategy looks like for food production, product design, architecture and construction, and fashion and clothing. You'll be inspired and excited about the innovations to come with this circular future.

Each chapter in this part covers practical examples and steps you can apply immediately to your own work in these fields. You'll discover what's possible in the circular designs of tomorrow, such as shoes made from plastic waste that's harvested from the ocean or alternative wall panels made from plants.

Part 5: Creating a Circular Economy for All

A true circular economy should be equitable, accessible, and available to everyone. In this part, you'll read about the role that each individual person plays in making this future a reality, and you'll discover the various career opportunities that await you. We close out Part 5 with a big vision of a worldwide circular economy and what that might mean for everyone.

Part 6: The Part of Tens

This wouldn't be a *For Dummies* book without these handy lists of the top ten key discussion topics. The Part of Tens is a collection of important advice and suggestions about implementing a circular approach to materials, waste, and supply chains. We wrap up the book with the best questions to ask to help get you and your team thinking in innovative ways so that you can start putting these ideas into practice.

Beyond the Book

Although this book covers the essentials of the circular economy, there's only so much that can be covered! You might reach the end of this book and find yourself thinking, "Gosh, that was incredible. Where can I learn more about the circular economy?" If that's the case, head over to www.dummies.com for more resources.

If you're looking for that helpful *For Dummies* Cheat Sheet, visit www.dummies.com and type **circular economy for dummies cheat sheet** in the Search box.

The circular economy field is evolving quickly. The day after this book is printed, some company will come along and introduce a cool, innovative product with a circular design. We'll keep up with this product and include it in future revisions of this book. We've also created a site at www.circulareconomyfordummies.com with extended interviews and bonus content that just didn't fit into the book.

Luckily, other books in the *For Dummies* series cover some of the more technical topics in this book. For example, you might want to learn more about climate change, supply chain management, or sustainability. Experts who specialize in these areas comprehensively cover all the subject details.

We both speak regularly on the topic of sustainability and the circular economy at dozens of events a year, both online and in-person at conferences around the world. If you're looking for a fun, entertaining, and inspirational talk, we invite you to attend our sessions and to come up and say hello. We love meeting anyone working to make the world a better place and hearing about your adventures.

You can keep up with our work and ideas by following us on Twitter (@EricCorey-Freed and @RitchieRevo), on LinkedIn (by name), or at our personal websites: www.organicarchitect.com and www.circulareconomy.studio.

We encourage you to share the topics and examples used in this book, and we ask you to include the hashtag #circulareconomyfordummies. We'll follow and share your interesting posts!

Where to Go from Here

You don't need to read this book from cover to cover. Each chapter is organized as a stand-alone topic so that you can go directly to the info you want. If you're interested in food, jump ahead to Chapter 15. If business strategy is your thing, flip over to Chapter 7. Just want some quick tips? Chapter 24 is a great landing spot for you.

If *all* these topics sound interesting (and of course they do), first enjoy Part 1 and then see where it leads. Not sure where to start? Look at the table of contents or the index and follow whatever topic grabs your attention.

Give yourself a pat on the back for doing your part to make the world a better place. Even small steps to reduce waste and improve materials can quickly translate into big rewards for you, your company, your family, and everyone else.

1

Linear Is Out, Circular Is In: An Economic Revolution

IN THIS PART . . .

Recognize the need to switch from a linear economy to a circular one

Evaluate how the linear economy is actually working against you

Identify the key challenges in implementing a circular economy

Chapter **1**

Rejecting Waste, Rethinking Materials, and Redesigning the World

We humans are all now finding ourselves in a troubling-yet-exciting time of human existence. We're more capable and smarter than ever, yet we still maintain and perpetuate an issue unique to the human race: waste. Waste doesn't exist within the natural world; there, every output of a system acts as an input for another. Leaf litter isn't litter at all, but a source of food for insects and eventually a food source for the tree to grow leaves again next year. The carbon dioxide emitted through animal respiration is harvested by vegetation and replaced with the oxygen required to future support animal respiration. Material lifecycles within nature are circular, not linear. Every output of one systems serves as an input for another.

Though waste doesn't exist within the natural world, it most certainly — at an extremely accelerated rate — exists within the human world. Though populations and demand for resources continue to surge and the rate at which materials and products are purchased and disposed of increases, so will the creation of waste. To avoid this situation, the modern management of material lifecycles must transition from a linear model (one based on the take-make-waste philosophy) to a circular model (one based on designing out waste, keeping materials in use for as long as possible, and regenerating natural ecosystems). To make this transition, those in charge of the global economy will need to reject waste as a necessary component of that economy, rethink how material lifecycles can be managed to maximize product resiliency and recyclability, and redesign how the human race manages its resources in the future.

In this chapter, we outline the main areas of focus that this book covers and provide some resources for you to immediately get acquainted with the thoughts and concepts behind the circular economy.

Rejecting the Idea of Waste

The current, global economy is based on a take-make-waste platform. Within this management of materials, resources are extracted from the earth (take), processed to form a product (make), and immediately discarded when the product no longer serves a purpose (waste). This management of materials — one where waste plays a critical role — is referred to as *linear*.

Waste became an accepted component of human life as scarcity of resources diminished. Once abundance was introduced into a large portion of the global economy, there was no need to bother with keeping materials in use. Instead, for some reason, it made sense to the people of that day to simply throw these materials away and start a new lifecycle from scratch. Waste was considered a necessary component of a fruitful and active economy and was often incorporated into the design of products — via planned obsolescence and cheap materials — to ensure a never-ending demand for new products. In addition, by excluding the eventual cost associated with environmental pollution and the impact on human health from material lifecycles, the use of cheap materials has inaccurately been deemed an economically beneficial strategy to make goods and resources affordable.

REMEMBER

To create a sustainable management of natural resources, we need to reject immediately the idea that waste is a necessary component of the global economy. In addition, we need to fully design out waste from our material and product lifecycles, by increasing their durability and resilience and by fully recycling materials.

Extracting raw materials from the earth and then shipping them around the world to be processed and manufactured into products that require further shipment before ultimately being used is an extremely wasteful process. The waste associated with the linear economy can be greatly reduced by rethinking waste altogether. Waste isn't necessary and is instead a resource that has not reached the next step in its lifecycle.

Waste as a driver of the economy

Waste has historically been seen as a necessary driver of the economy. Sales are tied to the amount of a product supplied, which is directly dependent on the demand for that product. Therefore, if you design the product to eventually be wasted, you can ensure that the demand for more products will be sustained.

Many strategies have been incorporated into product design and use to ensure that waste is inevitable, such as planned obsolescence, limited access to tools for repairs, and use of cheap materials. All these strategies ensure that the consumer will have limited access to the product in use and will eventually require a replacement.

Those who supported the idea that waste is necessary to drive demand failed to realize that prioritizing the elimination of waste via repair and remanufacturing creates a different kind of demand: products as a service. Through this setup, companies simply lease out products that were once sold directly to the customer. By way of this transition of ownership, companies maintain revenue by offering maintenance and repair services and are encouraged to develop resilient products rather than cheap, single-use products. The customers, then, receive access to products at a fraction of the cost and don't need to worry about the time and expense associated with maintaining, insuring, and replacing the product.

Waste is a human concept; it cannot be found in nature. Only when waste is rejected as a concept will the true value of materials be fully understood.

Waste as a resource

Although the scales of the global economy have been tipped to incentivize waste, a major opportunity is missed by failing to acknowledge waste as a valuable resource. You aren't planning to throw away all your clothes because they're piled up in a laundry basket. You can wash them and use them over again. So why are all the other materials we utilize seen differently? A resource becomes waste when it no longer has a next step in its life.

LEADERS FOR CHANGE

The Ellen MacArthur Foundation (www.ellenmacarthurfoundation.org) is the leading voice in promoting (and advocating for) the circular economy. Their mission is to accelerate the transition to a circular economy, and you'll see their amazing efforts woven throughout this book. Here's how they present the work they do:

The Circular Economy

The circular economy is a systems solution framework for building a resilient economy that delivers both long term prosperity and a means to address global challenges like climate change, biodiversity loss, waste, and pollution. It is based on three principles, all driven by design: eliminate waste and pollution; keep products and materials in use; and regenerate natural systems. Restorative and regenerative by design, it is a resilient, distributed, diverse, and inclusive economic model that presents opportunities to create better growth; going well beyond merely addressing the symptoms of today's wasteful and polluting linear economy. Crucially, it is at the design stage that we need to rethink everything, eliminating waste and pollution from the outset and designing instead for circulation of materials and regeneration of ecosystems.

Tackling global challenges

The climate crisis, the effects of which are being felt around the world, is a product of the take-make-waste linear economy that fails to manage resources for the long term. This fossil fuel reliant, extractive system puts enormous, untenable strain on natural resources and ecosystems. A step-change is needed if we are to have any hope of putting the world on track to meet the 1.5°Celsius target set out in the Paris Agreement and to achieve zero emissions by 2050.

Waste and pollution are yet another symptom of the current, linear economy. Every second, the equivalent of a rubbish truck of clothes is burnt or buried in landfill. Year on year, millions of tons of plastic, worth billions of dollars, ends up in landfills, is burned, or leaks into the environment and we only collect 14 percent for recycling. A staggering 8 million tons leaks into the world's oceans every year and, if we don't rethink its use, there will be more plastic in the ocean than fish by 2050. Currently, a third of all food produced globally — worth USD 1 trillion — is thrown away each year. This represents a huge loss of nutrients and is a major cause of environmental issues such as soil degradation. A circular economy, by contrast, eliminates waste and pollution, designing from the outset for the continuous circulation of materials — through means such as reuse, refurbishing, and remanufacturing — and regeneration of natural ecosystems by returning nutrients to the soil. In terms of climate change, circular economy strategies could help to address the 45 percent of greenhouse gas emissions associated with making products that can't be tackled by shifting to renewable energy.

The case for changing the operating model of the global economy has never been more compelling and megatrends such as shifting demographics, digitalization and increasing resource scarcity are further reinforcing our need and ability to transition to a new model. Reassuringly, the shift towards a circular economy is already taking place and continues to gain momentum year by year.

Delivering solutions at scale

A growing number of businesses across sectors are already turning to circular economy approaches. By adopting circular economy designs and business models these businesses are capturing new opportunities, meeting the changing preferences of their customers, and mitigating their exposure to market risks such as commodity price fluctuations and extended linear supply-chain risks. It also provides a means to achieving their sustainable development goals.

Projections by sector indicate just some of the multitude of transformation opportunities. In fashion, for example, clothing resale — one of many circular economy strategies for the industry — is expected to be bigger than fast fashion by 2029. Meanwhile over 1,000 organizations have united behind the New Plastics Economy Global Commitment, a common vision and set of targets for a circular economy for plastic in which we eliminate the plastics we don't need; innovate to ensure that those we do need are reusable, recyclable, or compostable; and circulate all of the plastic items we use to keep them in the economy and out of the environment. These organizations, including businesses from across the plastic packaging value chain representing more than 20 percent of all plastic packaging used globally, are reporting annually on progress towards their agreed 2025 Global Commitment targets.

There has been an equally noticeable increase in the development of circular economy policy strategies and initiatives across all tiers of government — examples include the European Commission's Circular Economy Action Plan, the African Circular Economy Alliance, and the Latin America and the Caribbean Circular Economy Coalition. This activity is sending positive signals to entrepreneurs and innovators, and is laying the foundation from which to develop appropriate, coordinated, enabling conditions. In cities and municipalities, states and national governments, and international institutions, the circular economy is gaining attention for the role it can play in meeting public policy objectives.

Support for circular economy initiatives is also emerging in the financial sector. The number of public equity funds dedicated to the circular economy has grown steeply from two in 2018 to 13 at the end of 2020, totaling USD 4.6 billion in assets under management (a 14-fold increase in 2020 alone). Venture capital, private equity, and private debt also saw a rapid acceleration of circular economy activity, with the number of

(continued)

(continued)

private market funds increasing tenfold since 2016. A similar trend of steep growth is visible in the bond market, bank lending, project finance, and insurance. This rapid uptake marks a significant shift that can enable circular economy opportunities to scale and catalyze the efforts of businesses and governments to change the way they operate.

Accelerating the transition

It is abundantly clear that there is an urgent need to shift away from our current linear economy toward a circular economy that is restorative and regenerative. The first steps of this shift are already being taken by pioneering businesses and governments, but the time has now come to accelerate and scale the transition rapidly across all corners of the global economy. Enabled by digital technologies, business models, products and services, policies, and infrastructure all need to be redesigned in line with circular economy principles if we are to create an entirely new system that benefits the economy, society, and the environment.

Rethinking Material Lifecycles

Once you identify zero waste as a real possibility for the future, you need to make a number of adjustments to all areas of a material's *lifecycle* — the various steps that take place during its sourcing, use, and recovery. To understand what opportunities are available to create a waste-free future, you first need to analyze where current lifecycles stand and where waste is generated. From there, you can incorporate conservation methods, efficient use, and proper regeneration of materials as part of your product lifecycle.

Current lifecycles rely on a linear processing of materials. Here, materials are extracted from the environment, made into products, and later sent to landfills or incinerated when the product no longer serves a function. This lack of proper management causes valuable resources to be lost forever and further drives the need to extract new and raw materials from the environment. It's so unnecessary to throw things away, because every material — if properly managed — can be recaptured and applied to serve another purpose.

REMEMBER

Though different materials require different management strategies, the opportunities are not only available but also clear. Whether it's developing a community sharing network, localized repair centers, or a dedicated community workspace to upcycle or downcycle faulty products, the opportunities to eliminate waste are available if members of the global economy take the time to rethink how to manage material lifecycles.

Take, make, and waste

The linear way of managing resources is built on the notion that waste is inevitable and acceptable. In this style of resource management, raw materials are taken from the earth and made into products and eventually wind up as waste. These three major milestones of a lifecycle don't stand isolated from the others, either, but fuel one another.

If waste is an assumed part of a lifecycle, there's motivation to ensure that the materials that are sourced to make the product are as cheap as possible and the product itself is designed to last only a short amount of time. Keeping costs low also incentivizes the user of those products to dispose of them at the end of their useful life rather than repair them. You wouldn't try to repair a plastic fork when it breaks. You'd throw it away and go find another one. Using cheap materials and making cheap products fuels the purchase of new products and maintains a consistent supply/demand relationship between manufacturers and customers.

Rethinking material lifecycles can transform the conventional take-make-waste approach toward a new management focused on eliminating waste as a necessity; making long-lasting, resilient products; and regenerating the natural systems on which the human race is dependent.

TIP

Rethinking (and improving on) a material lifecycle requires that you identify every element of the cycle. The more details you can identify, the more opportunities you'll find to improve the lifecycle. First analyze the entire lifecycle, and then find opportunities to conserve resources, increase the efficiency of how those materials are used, and, finally, explore how those materials can be recaptured at the end of their useful life.

Making technical materials circular

Technical materials are those that cannot be grown. Metals, plastics, and other finite materials are in limited supply and must be managed accordingly. To keep technical materials in use for longer periods, we humans need to harness new strategies. Although recycling technical materials is better than disposing of them, recycling should be seen as a last resort when considering circular materials management. Sharing, reusing, repairing, and remanufacturing products are all resource management strategies that should be employed before recycling.

One major issue in making technical materials circular is that the current products we use aren't often designed to allow for sharing, reuse, repair, or remanufacturing. The innate capability of products to do all those things will need to be designed into the product itself. Unless this happens, it's quite challenging to support a circular lifecycle, and recycling becomes the only option. For circular lifecycles to become a reality when it comes to technical materials, a proper support infrastructure needs to be in place to allow for sharing, reuse, repair, and remanufacturing to take place. Look around the room and find something made of technical materials. If the item stopped working right now, would you easily be able to have it repaired? Or would it be easier to simply throw it away and buy a new one? This reality also supports the notion that consumers must have an incentive to support a circular economy, because they have the incentive now to support a linear economy by way of low prices and convenience.

Making biological materials circular

The main difference between technical materials and biological materials is that biological materials can be regenerated or grown from the earth. Metals, plastics, and other technical materials are finite and cannot be regenerated. Cotton, timber, and other biological materials can be regenerated, which greatly affects how their lifecycles must be managed within a circular economy. Biological materials can be kept in use for longer periods by allowing the materials themselves to *cascade* — repurposing from a high-value product to a low-value product. Once the material can no longer serve a function, the biochemical feedstock of that material can be extracted as heat or energy, and the remaining organic material can be utilized as nutrients to fuel the growth of more biological materials.

Cascading keeps biological materials in use for longer periods. Doing so increases the value of that material. For example, rather than cut down a tree and process the fiber to become a piece of paper (low-value product), the tree should be made into something of high-value first, such as a building structure. From there, after it no longer can serve as a building structure, it can cascade into a lower-value product, such as a table or plywood. From there, it can cascade *even further* to the lowest-value product possible, like a piece of paper. Because a product becomes more valuable the longer it maintains its use, cascading materials acts as a strategy to maximize the value of the biological materials extracted from the earth.

Once that piece of paper has been used, it may seem like waste at this point. It can't be used as paper again, and it certainly can't act as a building structure. However, the material itself has an innate value that can be biochemically extracted. Paper can be incinerated to create heat, or the fibers of the paper can be recycled into new paper. Whatever the future of that piece of paper may be, it's critical to never see it as waste. There is always the embodied value of a material.

Once the material has been fully utilized, the remaining biological content can be directed toward the regeneration of natural systems and the creation of new biological materials. The magical property of biological materials is that they can help grow other materials as a component of compost. Paper pulp can be processed into a nutrient-dense compost to grow more trees, and food waste can be processed to grow more food. When waste is eliminated as a construct, you can start processing materials in a circular manner and waste can be fully eliminated.

REMEMBER

Technical materials are materials that cannot be regenerated. They are finite. *Biological* materials are materials that can be regenerated over and over again. The adjustments made to any material's lifecycle should reflect this critical difference.

WARNING

Beware of *greenwashing,* or false claims about a product to convince you that it's beneficial to the environment.

Upcycling versus downcycling

Technical materials as well as biological ones can be made into new products that are either more or less valuable than their original use. Glass bottles can be upcycled into more valuable pieces of artwork and shattered to form mosaic art, or they can be downcycled instead to act as an aggregate in a kitchen counter. In either instance, value is created by maintaining the use of the product rather than disposing of it.

Upcycling is a strategy that reuses a product in a way that holds more value than the original product, whereas *downcycling* reuses a product in a way that holds less value than the original product. Though at first the idea of downcycling a product may seem valueless, downcycling is still advantageous because it's a better alternative to recycling or disposal. The idea of upcycling or downcycling materials into new products, as a concept, is a critical component of supporting a circular economy. However, if you don't provide the right infrastructure, individuals and institutions won't have the means to support this strategy of extended use.

Large subcultures of *makers* — that range of designers, builders, and crafters — are booming around the world, and the spaces they use provide the very infrastructure and tools necessary to promote upcycling and downcycling. By providing access to computer numerical control (CNC) machines, 3D printers, and other technologies, makers now have more power than ever to maximize the value of their products by repurposing them.

Redesigning the Future to Be Circular

Before we can create a circular future, waste must first be rejected as an acceptable component of material lifecycles, and those who manage those material lifecycles need to rethink how materials are managed. Only when we achieve these two critical milestones can the world begin to redesign how our food is grown; how our infrastructure, products, and clothing are managed; and how a circular economy could work for everyone.

Food production

Redesigning the food production system to be circular will require shifting away from commercial strategies that are dependent on fossil fuels, pesticides, and artificial fertilizers to a more localized approach that relies instead on permaculture design strategies, developing polycultures rather than monocultures, and utilizing circular production strategies, like aquaponics. (For more detail on the circular economy and food production, see Chapter 15!)

The industrialized method of growing food is extremely wasteful in many ways. It requires the use of equipment that's dependent on fossil fuels, high levels of harmful chemicals through the use of pesticides and fertilizers, and global shipping networks to deliver all these goods — not to mention the packaging required to preserve the produce. In addition, these methods create large amounts of food waste during the process because this system doesn't support the recapture and reuse of unused or spoiled produce. Absolutely nothing about linear, industrialized food production supports the idea that waste is an unnecessary component of the food cycle.

By relying on a more localized approach to food production, many sources of industrialized wastes can be eliminated, such as transportation waste and food waste. Utilizing new methods of growing produce can also support the transition from a linear production to a circular one. Technologies such as indoor aquaponics allows for multiple ecosystems to flourish by utilizing the waste of one system to act as a resource for another. In such systems, fish waste acts as nutrients for the plants, and the plants then filter the water for the fish. Mimicking natural ecosystems is the only way we can redesign the food system to be circular.

TIP

The more a food production system mimics the natural world, the more efficient and effective it will be. You don't see entire fields of single, row crops anywhere in nature. This fact alone is a major red flag.

Circular businesses, products, and clothing

Creating a circular economy will require a massive shift in the way we manage and exchange materials and products. Businesses will need to collaborate with their partners to eliminate the need for raw-material extraction. Products will need to be designed to stay in use for longer periods, and the clothing industry — one of the most wasteful industries in operation — will need to make massive adjustments to eliminate waste. To top it all off, adjusting all these variables will require high levels of coordination and partnerships between all stakeholders involved.

Businesses are realizing that the way they operate and the impact they have on the environment greatly impacts their ability to maintain customers. Transitioning from a linear way of producing products to a circular one won't be necessary only from an environmental perspective, but from a social and economic perspective as well. To minimize the negative impact on the environment, businesses will need to adjust the relationship they have with customers to maximize the value of the products they create. Rather than businesses viewing success as the number of products made per year, they will instead base their bottom line on the number of products *kept in use* per year. Though waste certainly creates a demand for companies to continue selling new products, eliminating waste doesn't have to eliminate demand. By maintaining the ownership of a product rather than selling it, new business opportunities emerge in the world of maintenance and repair. Though eliminating waste minimizes the need for new products, it certainly increases the need to service existing products. The circular economy will demand that new business models focus on *maintaining* products rather than on making new products.

In addition to the relationship that businesses and customers have, the way products are made will also require a major shift. Accepting waste as a component of a product's lifecycle encourages production processes where the sourcing of the required materials and durability of those materials remain as cheap as possible. Products are designed with planned obsolescence and minimal opportunities for repair for a reason: to encourage the purchasing of new products. However, by eliminating waste as a necessary step in a material lifecycle and shifting business services from product production to product maintenance, products can be designed to last for longer periods.

One major industry that will need a major overhaul is the fashion industry. Poor material usage, fast-fashion, and poor sharing-and-reuse networks act as only a handful of reasons that the fashion industry leads the way in terms of waste and pollution. The fashion industry's transition from a linear production of clothes to a circular one will require these four major steps:

1. The industry will need to phase out fabrics and materials that aren't fully recyclable — fabrics and materials that act as a major source of pollution.

2. Manufacturers and businesses will need to redesign how clothing is made and how it's used. No longer will customers be required to purchase clothing, but opportunities for sharing will emerge under membership programs.

3. Clothing that is made will need to stay in use for longer periods. This translates to using more durable materials and offering sharing and buyback programs so that clothing that's no longer being used has the potential for continued use.

4. The resources required to support the fashion industry — like cotton and hemp — will need to be regenerated to ensure that the demand for clothing can be met.

A circular economy for all

Whether you're interested in making a career of the circular economy or in learning how neighborhoods, universities, and the food service industry will look different after they've shifted to a circular management of their materials and products, you need to know about the major shifts that are coming our way. This book can help. Whatever the future focus might be, a common thread is already clear: We humans need to eliminate waste, keep materials and products in use, and regenerate the environmental systems on which we are dependent. A circular economy will be part of all those efforts.

Chapter **2**

What's Wrong with Being Linear, Anyway?

The earth has been around for 4½ billion years. We know that living systems have been around for most of that time (3½ billion years) and will probably be around for a few billion more. We humans, on the other hand, have only been part of these living systems for around 200,000 years — a fraction of that time. Yet even in that small period, humans have managed to disrupt every living system on the planet.

In nature, there is no landfill, no concept of waste. Everything in nature becomes a material flow (a natural resource) for something else — either food, nutrients, or energy. Everything we have is right here on the planet. The only incoming resource we have is sunlight (and maybe the occasional asteroid or two).

All living systems on Earth (except humans) are able to live in harmony with that balance. Species are born, they live, they die, and they feed their nutrients back into the soil safely. The sun provides warmth and energy, and it all just works well, in an elegant, closed loop — a circular approach to resources.

We humans follow quite a different approach, one where we take, make, use, and, eventually, waste — or take-make-waste. We extract natural resources until they're exhausted; we package products in containers that cannot be reused; and we design products that can't be repaired so that people are forced to throw them away and buy new ones. We ignore the free energy from the sun and instead burn the last bits of energy in the ground left by the death of the dinosaurs. It doesn't work — all the linear approach does is slowly convert our human resources into waste.

Every time we humans follow this linear approach, we're slowly chipping away at our limited and finite supply of natural resources and leaving toxic waste in its place. We simply can't keep going like this forever, and the worst consequences of our irresponsible actions haven't even caught up with us yet.

Take, for example, the fashion industry. Each year, millions of tons of raw materials are harvested from the earth. We use massive amounts of fossil fuels to power machines to manufacture those materials into clothing and then to ship them around to stores across the planet, which fills the atmosphere with greenhouse gas emissions. As if that weren't bad enough, after wearing these clothes, we decide at some point (one year, three years, ten years), to throw them away and three-quarters then end up in a landfill. (See Figure 2-1.)

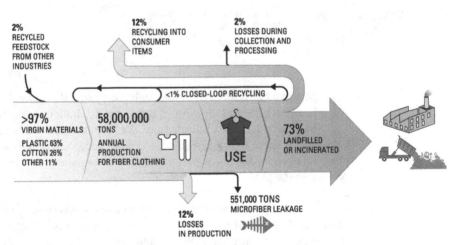

FIGURE 2-1:
The typical approach to making clothing is the linear model.

Because we've been doing it this way for so long, we fail to see the opportunities to improve this linear process. Imagine, instead, that we took the approach outlined in Table 2-1.

Seen in this light, the linear approach isn't that great, is it? A circular-economy approach seeks to take those linear approaches to materials, energy, and reuse and bend them into a more circular approach — an approach that mimics what happens regularly in nature.

TABLE 2-1 **Prescription for the Future**

Replace This	With This
Extracting natural resources	Using recycled or bio-based materials
Packaging in single-use plastic	Packaging in reusable packaging or none at all
Burning fossil fuels for energy	Using clean, renewable energy
Shipping products around the planet	Creating local networks of manufacturing
Making products that become outdated	Designing durable products that can be adapted or updated
Tossing products into a landfill	Designing products to be repairable, biodegradable, or recyclable

In this chapter, we explore how this linear approach isn't exactly working for the planet and why we humans need to drastically change how we produce our food, products, packaging, and everything else in order to be more circular — like all the other living things in nature.

We're Taking the Wrong Stuff

The linear take-make-waste approach to work depends on the use of a lot of materials. Companies harvest and extract raw materials and use them to produce a product, which they then sell to consumers. Eventually, the consumer discards the product when it's no longer of use to them. In 2020, more than 90 billion tons of raw materials were put into the linear system of production. The sheer scale of all this wasteful manufacturing activity is overwhelming.

Unfortunately, humans are harvesting materials that are limited in supply and difficult and expensive to extract — and the materials aren't designed to be replenished. When those products end up in the landfill, they don't magically restore the original raw materials. As a result, materials are getting increasingly more difficult (where we can even find a sufficient supply) to extract safely and affordably, harvest a useful supply, and ensure quality.

For example, as the supplies of easily accessible oil and natural gas have run out, it's become harder and harder to find plentiful sources of those resources. Energy companies have had to drill deeper and go further offshore, and employ riskier techniques, such as fracking, to scrape up the last bits. As a result, the oil and gas they now extract is less pure, of lower quality, and more expensive to find.

Because nearly all linear systems either are powered by fossil fuels or use them to manufacture their products, products grow more expensive and difficult to produce. Costs rise, prices follow and rise, and consumer spending is affected. It's difficult to keep running a linear economy when your key materials are volatile in price and availability.

The linear economy depends on the wrong assumptions: an endless supply of cheap, abundant energy and materials. Now that those things are no longer true, companies are starting to question their original assumptions and to transform from a linear economy to a circular one.

PLASTIC: BY THE NUMBERS

No other material is as troublesome as plastic. A whopping 8.3 billion metric tons of plastic was produced in the past century, and half of that was designed to be used only once. Let's look at the impact of all that plastic:

- Ninety-one percent of plastic isn't recycled, and 79 percent is sitting in landfills.

- Most of the products discarded in curbside recycling bins end up not being recycled because of food contamination.

- The rapid increase in plastics manufacturing has doubled roughly every 15 years.

- Plastics production has outpaced nearly every other human-made material.

- Plastic takes more than 400 years to degrade, so most of it still exists.

- By 2050, if trends continue, landfills will hold 12 billion metric tons of plastic. That amount is 35,000 times as heavy as the Empire State Building.

- Half of all plastic becomes trash in less than a year, whereas half of all steel remains in use for decades.

- One million plastic drinking bottles are purchased every minute.

- Humans produce about 330 million tons of plastic waste every year.

- The amount of plastic produced annually is nearly equivalent to the weight of the entire human population.

- By 2050, the plastics industry could account for 20 percent of the world's total oil consumption.

- Nine million tons of plastic end up in the world's oceans every year.

- If current trends continue, the oceans could contain more plastic than fish by 2050.

We're not importing this stuff from space

Everything you've ever bought, everything you've ever owned, everything you've ever touched, is still here. It's right here sitting on Planet Earth. If you don't know where it is, that's probably because you threw it away. But where is "away"?

"Away" is an imaginary place — or so we humans tell ourselves in order to feel better about all the waste we've created. In reality, "away" is probably a landfill somewhere in the world, where your stuff is sitting and waiting while it slowly breaks down over hundreds of years and drips toxic chemicals into the soils and waterways. "Away" doesn't exist anywhere else.

The only resource we humans get from outside the bounds of Earth is an abundance of free sunlight, coming in from 93 million miles away. No one is making a killer line of shoes made from asteroids. Not a single company is designing handbags made from the soils of Mars. Everything we humans make is made right here from stuff found on Earth, and we're simply using up everything.

Recently, scientists from the Weizmann Institute of Science in Israel reported that the weight of all the human-made stuff (things we've produced) outweighs the weight of all living things on Earth. Apparently, all the buildings, cars, toys, avocado slicers, and every other item we've made now weighs more than the remaining life on the planet.

Many of the resources typically extracted are materials that have a finite amount, such as coal, natural gas, oil, sand, iron ore, stone and minerals. As supplies of these resources begin to dwindle, humans have been forced into recycling them, to make new products.

Other natural resources we harvest can be replenished but often aren't, such as trees, plants, fish, and animals. The demand for these items has increased so much that the source is often destroyed in order to reach them — forests are clear-cut, animals go extinct, or the entire ecosystem is damaged. Humans are just starting to look at sustainable management practices for forests, waterways, fisheries, and habitats.

All this fishing, hunting, gathering, drilling, mining, farming, chopping, excavating, digging, and harvesting has finally brought us to one inescapable conclusion: Earth is the only planet we have, and we have to better manage how we use it.

Scientists estimate that it would take five Planet Earths to support humans if everyone consumed the same as a typical American. Let's look at two simple examples of US consumption — the typical soda can and the typical plastic bag:

>> **Soda can:** That soft drink you're holding in your hand seems like the perfect container. It's cool to the touch, easy to open, easily stackable, and easy to hold. But that can is made from aluminum, which is made from mining clay-ore bauxite out of the ground — a nonrenewable resource. Bauxite is typically mined in Australia and Brazil and ships all over the world, where it's manufactured into aluminum. That process is toxic and produces a significant amount of waste — about five tons for every ton produced. The can has only a 1-in-3 chance of getting recycled. Plus, it's lined with plastic, which makes it harder to recycle, and that plastic leaches toxic chemicals into the soda you drink. The saddest part: That soda can you're holding had a useful life of only six months from the time it was packaged to the time you drank it.

>> **Plastic bag:** That plastic bag the cashier just handed you is made from oil, which means it's a nonrenewable material and difficult to recycle. It's one of 500 plastic bags you'll use this year, and it has a useful life of about ten minutes from the time you leave the store to when you get home and throw it away. Fewer than 10 percent of these bags get recycled, and most end up polluting our waterways instead.

Everyone keeps having kids

Though the resources on the planet are finite and limited, the population keeps increasing, which is driving demand for more and more stuff. As a result, there's a direct link between population growth and the size of our human impact on the environment.

REMEMBER

As you have more children, you increase your environmental footprint (your impact) in terms of the waste produced, food consumed, energy required, and carbon emissions released. It makes sense: more people, more stuff needed.

In a study from Oregon State University, they found that not having an extra child in your family is the most effective thing you can do to reduce your environmental footprint. This choice was 20 times more impactful than any other green action you take in your life, including becoming a vegan or driving an electric car or using solar power in your home. (See Figure 2-2.)

Tons of CO2-equivalent per year for one person undertaking each action

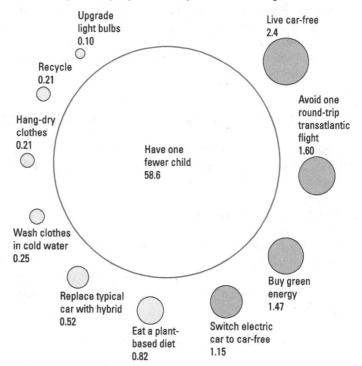

Upgrade
light bulbs
0.10

Recycle
0.21

Hang-dry
clothes
0.21

Live car-free
2.4

Avoid one
round-trip
transatlantic
flight
1.60

Have one
fewer child
58.6

Wash clothes
in cold water
0.25

Replace typical
car with hybrid
0.52

Eat a plant-
based diet
0.82

Switch electric
car to car-free
1.15

Buy green
energy
1.47

FIGURE 2-2:
Having one fewer
child, which saves
65 tons of carbon
emissions per
year, is the
greenest thing
you can do,
compared with
other lifestyle
choices.

Now, don't start telling your neighbors that "those mean authors" are telling you to not have kids — that's not it at all. Kids are wonderful. In fact, we were kids once, too. If you want to have kids, please do. The point is that as long as humans continue to rely on the linear economic system of take-make-waste, every additional person brought into the world will increase the amount of waste and carbon emissions generated. (See Figure 2-3.) A linear economy cannot scale with population.

Population and CO_2 Emissions, 1750-2015

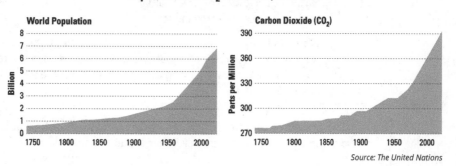

FIGURE 2-3:
If you compare
population
growth to carbon
emissions, you
see a direct
correlation.

Source: The United Nations

Despite all that bad news, another 225,000 new people joined us on Earth today. (That's more than 150 people per minute!) Each of our new neighbors will only increase demand and strain on our linear economic system. Simply not having any more children isn't really an option here, so we have to change the economic system from linear to circular.

We don't have as much as we thought

In addition to having a finite number of planetary resources and a growing demand from an ever-increasing population, it turns out that what we thought was an endless supply isn't endless at all.

Our global natural resources are depleting by 45 percent every year. The United Nations reports that soil degradation was proceeding so quickly that only 60 harvests might remain until food supplies severely decline. Our water supplies are constrained; most of the water is in the oceans or undrinkable, and another 2 percent is frozen in the polar ice caps, leaving only 1 percent left for people to drink as a freshwater supply. Unfortunately, 70 percent of that supply is polluted.

Look at the planet's dwindling resources:

>> **Water:** By 2025, 1.8 billion people won't have access to clean drinking water.

>> **Coal:** Though the planet has a large enough supply of coal reserves to last until the year 2200, if we burn that supply, it will release so much in carbon emissions that it will radically transform the climate. In the next decade, scientists expect that the earth will hit *peak coal* — or the point at which coal production reaches its maximum rate and drops every year afterward.

>> **Oil:** The earth hit peak oil back around 2003 or so, and scientists estimate that we have only enough oil in the ground to last another 45 years (at the current level of demand).

>> **Natural gas:** Known reserves will last only until 2075 or so, and supplies of new gas sources are growing scarce.

>> **Wood:** Deforestation causes around 8.2 million acres to be lost every year, contributing 15 percent of global greenhouse gas emissions. (Trees absorb carbon dioxide, in case you forgot.) An area of forest the size of Italy disappeared in 2020.

The pressures on our natural resources, combined with population growth, are driving the need to change our linear economic models.

It all revolves around oil

The linear economy has always depended on cheap energy to power it. It has lasted this long only because energy was, until recently, still relatively inexpensive and abundant.

REMEMBER

The postwar boom in the United States in the 1940s stemmed from US dominance over the world's energy supply. Cheap energy powered the country's growth, its economy, and its innovations.

This cheap energy also drove the mindset that our stuff needs to be made cheaper and cheaper. We made everything so cheap, in fact, that it was easier to just throw something away and buy a new one. Cheap energy devalued everything else, bringing in cheap materials, cheap labor, and cheap credit to buy it all with.

Unfortunately, the extraction and use of fossil fuels is the largest contributor to greenhouse gas emissions and the climate crisis facing humans today.

The oil age is over. Because it's no longer cheap or abundant, the cracks are starting to appear in the façade. The famous English economist John Maynard Keynes famously said, "If the facts change, I change my mind; what do you do, sir?"

The fact is that fossil-fuel-based energy is expensive and destructive to the climate. As our dependence on fossil fuels must change, so too must our linear economic model change.

We're Making the Wrong Stuff

The linear economic model of take-make-waste isn't flawed only in the resources we're taking; what we're *making* is also out of step with reality.

Every year, humans produce 300 tons of new plastic, most of which ends up in landfills or oceans. If you look around your home, you quickly discover how many items are made of plastic. If you take a peek into your trash and recycling bins, you might also notice how much of that is plastic as well.

Companies use plastic because it's durable, flexible, colorful, and washable, but more importantly, because it's cheap. The raw materials for plastic are easily available, and you can mold it into any shape you want. That's why we humans use so much of it.

Relying on plastic for so much of what's produced isn't the only issue with the stuff we make. There are several common problems with all the stuff we produce:

>> **Poor materials:** The product uses cheap materials that pollute during the production process.

>> **Lack of durability:** The products are designed to break, forcing customers to buy new ones after a short time.

>> **Energy intensive:** The products require massive amounts of energy to produce, which results in the release of carbon emissions.

>> **Produces waste:** Every ton that's produced creates many times that amount of waste.

>> **Doesn't reflect the product's true cost:** The cost to operate or maintain the product is paid later on by the consumer.

>> **Doesn't reflect the product's true impact:** The damage to the environment isn't paid for or cleaned up by anyone.

>> **Not upgradable:** The product can't be upgraded after parts are outdated.

>> **Not repairable:** The product isn't designed to be repaired.

>> **Not recyclable:** The product mixes materials that makes recycling them difficult or impossible.

>> **Doesn't disassemble:** The product cannot be taken apart to make recycling or repair easier.

>> **Not as useful as possible:** The product has a single, limited, or short-term use that isn't as useful as it could be.

>> **Not local:** The product is produced from materials sourced from faraway or that must be shipped long distances to reach the hands of customers.

REMEMBER

Most of the products people buy feature some (or even all) of these shortcomings. These issues only perpetuate the linear economic model. What's needed is a rethinking and redesign of all our materials and products to fix these problems and allow us to bend those linear pathways to become circular.

You're buying trash

Because the linear economy depends on the excessive consumption of take-make-waste, it means that everything people buy is expected to end up in the landfill at some point. If everything is designed to end up in the landfill, then everything we buy is really just trash in an earlier form.

TIP

Finding ways to extend the useful life of a product delays this outcome. Finding ways to ensure that a material will get recycled or reused at the end of its life is even better.

Even kids can build with blocks

Your smartphone is a technological marvel, but will that always be the case? Next year, the latest smartphone model will be released, with a new camera, better screen, and faster chip. You want that new phone, but your current phone still works perfectly fine, and it seems a waste to discard it. If only you had another option between keep-the-old and buy-new-and-discard?

Imagine instead that your smartphone is smart enough to be modular. That way, you could pop out your old camera module and pop in the newest version. You could pop out the old screen and pop in the new one with a higher resolution. You could even pop out the processor chip and replace it with a newer, faster model.

This approach allows for each component of a product to be upgraded, and extends the useful life of that product by years or even decades.

Trying to recycle the unrecyclable

If you're one of those green-minded folks who recycles everything in your house, that's great! You're doing your part to minimize your impact and to keep valuable resources from ending up in the landfill.

Unfortunately, most of the materials that humans recycle weren't designed to be recycled. Even materials such as glass, aluminum, plastic, and paper still require complex machinery and large inputs of energy in order to make them recyclable.

This statement isn't intended to discourage you from recycling, but rather to highlight the need to use materials that are easily recyclable in the first place. In addition, some people might assume that it's okay to continue buying single-use plastic, because they know they will recycle it, but this strategy just perpetuates the linear economic cycle. Instead, we need to engineer innovative new materials that are designed to be recycled.

AirCarbon is a new, alternative plastic, made by capturing carbon dioxide from the atmosphere. This alternative is *carbon-negative:* It uses no fossil fuels and can be made into virtually any product that would normally use plastic. At the end of its life, the AirCarbon can be collected and remade into new products again and again. For more on AirCarbon, check out its manufacturer's website at www. newlight.com.

We're using materials that are bad for us

Perhaps the most tragic part of this entire story is that most of the products we use every day contain known cancer-causing (*carcinogenic*) chemicals that are harmful to human health.

That cute new baby blanket you just bought? It contains brominated flame retardants that are known to be linked to a host of neurological and cognitive problems in children.

That handy, reusable plastic water bottle you take with you every time you go for a run? It probably contains a hardening agent known as BPA (Bisphenol A) that has been linked to an increased likelihood of Alzheimer's, childhood asthma, metabolic disease, diabetes, and cardiovascular disease.

REMEMBER

Though our foods are highly regulated for health risks, consumer products are not. In the 50-year history of the Toxic Substances Control Act (TSCA) in the United States, only 9 chemicals have been banned (of the 80,000 chemicals commonly used). Most of the common cleaning products you use every day in your home contain some risk to human health.

We're Wasting the Wrong Stuff

Although the linear economic model of take-make-waste depends on resources that are scarce in order to produce products that are poorly designed, it also creates a pile of potentially valuable resources that instead go to waste.

It all comes at a big cost

Americans generate an average of 4.6 pounds of trash daily per person. Modern landfills have evolved into elaborate material-recovery facilities, where they sort through the waste stream and pull out valuable resources that were thrown away by mistake. Despite these advancements, the environmental and economic impact of landfills is immense.

REMEMBER

Municipal landfills are the third-largest source of human-caused methane emissions in the United States, accounting for approximately 16 percent of total emissions and 91 percent of all methane emissions. (Methane is an even worse greenhouse gas than carbon dioxide, with 84 times the potency.)

We're running out of room

According to a report by the Solid Waste Environmental Excellence Protocol (SWEEP), most of the more than 2,000 active landfills in the United States are nearing their capacity. The earth is expected to run out of landfill space by 2040. This looming environmental disaster will require people to start looking to landfills as a source of new materials.

Flip to Chapter 9 to read about some amazing ways people have been converting trash to treasure.

It's expensive to throw things away

Waste is a luxury we can't afford. It's expensive to simply throw things away and replace them with new items all the time. Whether it's a simple plastic water bottle or a complex new laptop, all waste comes with a hidden cost.

REMEMBER

In the US healthcare system, medical waste annually costs between $760 billion and $935 billion. Cutting this waste could save a total of $191 billion to $286 billion every year.

In the US construction industry, demolition and construction waste accounts for nearly 65 million tons a year, making up almost a quarter of all landfills. Contractors must pay to dump all that waste, but could instead make money by recycling it into new building materials.

In the US restaurant industry, about a third of the food is wasted. The US Department of Agriculture estimates the total annual cost of the wasted food at $1,866 per household. Those food scraps could feed the hungry, of course, but could also be made into a form of energy called *biogas* — a mixture of gases released when food decomposes.

The debt collector is knocking at the door

The total costs of producing this never-ending stream of waste are finally becoming clear. The climate crisis is causing stronger hurricanes, more intense heat waves, and faster wildfires, costing the federal government around $250 billion every year.

REMEMBER

From 2015 to 2020, the US has experienced more than $500 billion in losses directly from climate-fueled weather disasters. According to the National Resources Defense Council (NRDC — www.nrdc.org/), by 2100 the four big climate impacts — hurricanes, real estate losses, energy costs, and flooding — will cost 1.8 percent of US GDP, or almost $1.9 trillion annually.

Change Is Really Hard, We Know

Despite all these logical arguments around the need to rethink the linear economy, transforming your industry is still a scary proposition. Change is hard even when you know you have to change. So how do you begin to have a conversation about radically rethinking and changing the design of everything?

The answer is simple: Confirm that the results these changes will bring will be so attractive that you'll want to do it immediately.

If it ain't broke, don't fix it

One of the most common arguments against changing is that "it's working perfectly fine now, so there's no need to change it." But in reality, the linear system doesn't work perfectly, given all the diminished resources, overflowing waste, and soaring environmental impacts resulting from it.

A great way to start the conversation around making change is to start to map out some of the assumptions of the linear economy and highlight how they're not working.

Table 2-2 contrasts the linear economy with the circular one.

TABLE 2-2: **Comparing Circular and Linear Economies**

Linear	Circular
Runs on fossil fuels	Runs on sunlight
Produces waste	Creates surplus resources
Pollutes the soil	Feeds the soil
Is efficient	Is effective
Make	Remake

By recognizing that the linear economy is flawed at its core, you open up the possibility of embracing a circular alternative approach. By playing with these contrasting models, you start to see how the circular economic approach just makes so much more sense.

Taking risks

For most companies, the desire to switch from a linear economy to a circular one isn't so much about saving the planet. Ultimately, every company is a business, and a business must be economically successful and profitable. So, in order to entice companies to take a risk and transform how they do business, they need to know that, by going circular, they increase their profits.

To quote architect and futurist Buckminster Fuller (1895–1983):

> You never change things by fighting the existing reality. To change something, build a new model that makes the existing model obsolete.

Companies generally see four types of value in switching from linear to circular. These benefits will encourage them to change their business models:

>> **Sourcing:** These are the direct financial gains that come from switching to a *closed-loop system* — where materials are looped back to be recovered or reused — including savings from reducing risk, reducing waste, and using less commoditized materials.

>> **Environmental:** These are the gains to your brand from sharing your sustainable approach with your customers.

>> **Customer:** These gains come from the product improvements to your customers in terms of repairability or reuse.

>> **Informational:** Once you start taking an active interest in how your products are being used and disposed of, you find a wealth of customer data and insights that drive future product decisions.

The best part of these drivers is that they start to encourage and feed more circular thinking. For example, as you look for ways to reduce waste, you redesign your products to be repairable. As customers bring in products to be repaired, you improve your relationship with them and gain valuable insight into their needs.

NADINE GUDZ SPEAKS

Nadine Gudz is an award-winning sustainability leader and the former global director of Sustainability Strategy at Interface, one of the world's leading modular flooring companies. They also happen to produce some of the most sustainable carpeting available. Its initial founder and chairman, Ray C. Anderson, transformed his company in 1994 after reading *The Ecology of Commerce* by Paul Hawken and committed his company to eliminating "any negative impact the company may have on the environment by the year 2020."

This daunting challenge was referred to as "Mission Zero" inside of the company, and they called their efforts "climbing Mount Sustainability." The authors sat down with Nadine to discuss the challenges of taking a resource-intensive product like carpet and transform it into a circular product.

Carpet is a massive, material intensive resource. Raw materials are inserted into one end of a machine and carpet comes out the other. Despite its popularity, carpet also has a huge environmental cost, where after only 5 or 7 years it gets thrown into the landfill and replaced. So it makes sense that a carpet company like Interface would pioneer how to improve on this.

Nadine Gudz: There are so many learning opportunities to think differently throughout a carpet's supply chain — purchasing, installation, maintenance, how you interact in that relationship. Context is really important.

It was very exciting to be a part of a manufacturer that was open to trying different things. For example, the launch of Interface's Embodied Beauty, the first carpet tile to absorb the carbon it takes to produce it.

What's become clear to you as you've tried to implement the idea of "carpeting as a service?" On the one hand, it seems like a simple thing to tell customers that you'll provide the benefits that carpet provides, but without having to own it. But on the other, I know it's much more complicated than that.

Nadine Gudz: It really is. When Ray [Anderson, CEO of Interface] first talked about the idea of the evergreen carpet leasing program, it generated so much interest. The program was piloted with one friendly customer who was willing to try it out. It didn't go anywhere. It was impossible to sell this idea of leasing or renting carpet. It just didn't fit with our customer's traditional mindsets around budgets.

There continues to be a lot of interest in this from customers and passion for it at Interface. And now with the momentum around circular economy, I think the conditions might be right to bring it back.

Interface pioneered how to green their sourcing and supply chain. Why were you so successful with that? In what Interface refers to as "climbing Mount Sustainability," how did you take on the challenge of changing your supply chain, knowing that it would be hard?

Nadine Gudz: It was so hard, but the timeframe really matters here. The company's sustainability awakening occurred in 1994. It didn't take long to get a team on board to help advise Interface and create this roadmap to Mt. Sustainability, setting a bold, audacious goal we call "Mission Zero" — to eliminate any negative environmental impact by the year 2020.

The big shift, which was a very difficult decision-making process, had to do with letting go of suppliers who were not willing to invest in the technologies to recycle nylon [the chief ingredient in carpeting]. The key fibers used in Interface products were more sustainable, and in order to get to zero carbon, Interface could not be using virgin nylon in its products.

The company quickly realized that using recycled nylon would dramatically reduce the company's carbon footprint. It took 13 years for Interface to actually procure recycled nylon from suppliers who were both willing and technologically able to make these recycled yarns.

Today Interface uses hundreds of color palettes with a majority of recycled nylon (a huge jump from 1994 to 2007!) It took 13 years to address the main culprit in the supply chain, and its thanks to two primary suppliers who were willing to step up, invest, and see the potential and the opportunity. See how the market has shifted?

How did they source the recycled nylon?

Nadine Gudz: It's an amazing global partnership, starting with fishing communities in the Philippines and a very progressive supplier, Aquafil.

Their CEO, Giulio Bonazzi, was inspired by Ray and Interface's story. Their team found a way to make nylon fibers from discarded fishing nets. That inspired our innovation team to ask the question: "Where would fishing net recycling do the most good in the world?" In conversations with biologists at the Zoological Society of London, the answer was: the Philippines.

That's what started our Networks program, and it has now expanded to Indonesia and Cameroon. It's a self-sufficient, stand-alone program supporting local economic stability along with sustainability efforts.

(continued)

(continued)

Residents are paid fair market value for the nets that are being collected from the ocean and the shorelines. They run community banking associations where they get access to micro-finance solutions that didn't exist before.

It links so beautifully with some of these themes around circular economy and social well-being, in addition to the obvious environmental benefits of these kinds of partnerships.

In hindsight, it seems as if Interface knew this would be a challenge. You didn't call it "downhill sustainability." You called it "Mt. Sustainability," implying that it would be a labor of love, and it was going to take time.

Nadine Gudz: You're totally right. You need to wrap your head around the fact that these sorts of changes don't happen overnight. It requires big commitment. It requires conviction. It requires a flexibility and adaptability.

From an organizational cultural perspective, Interface gave its employees permission to pursue these ideas and these partners. It wasn't Interface who was recycling the fishing nets; it was this very inspired, innovative supplier. That's what creates this life-changing innovation and ripple effect.

IN THIS CHAPTER

» Evaluating the surging need for
circular economy solutions

» Understanding the various drivers for
this rapid change

» Getting to know the environmental
precedents for the circular economy

Chapter **3**

A Growing Demand for a Circular Economy

A recent report by the business consultant group Circle Economy (www. circle-economy.com) states that the current global economy is around 9 percent circular. This figure was calculated based on the share of recycled/reused materials balanced against all of the material inputs into the global economy. Clearly, humans have a long way to go if they want to achieve a true circular economy.

The current linear economy is locked into a system that depends on the take-make-waste approach to production. The limitations of this approach are starting to be reached as we fully understand the environmental, economic, and social impacts this linear way of thinking brings. This lock that the linear economy holds over us is starting to weaken.

Circularity, and the demand for a true circular economy, is starting to gain traction. It has moved beyond being merely an attractive concept and into mainstream business planning for companies around the world. That demand is only set to increase as constraints around materials increase and the climate crisis continues to worsen.

Companies will greatly benefit by transitioning and shifting their operations over to the circular economic principles outlined in this book. We detail all the benefits of this transition in the next chapter, but we're convinced that companies embracing this approach can, in a nutshell, uncover new opportunities to increase profits, new ideas to slash operating costs, and new ways to reduce risks from a more sustainable supply chain.

These four clear and overwhelming trends demonstrate this growing demand for the circular economy:

>> **Reuse is on the rise.** Decades of pushing by environmentalists have led to a surge in popularity of reusable bags, bottles, and containers. Clothing resellers such as The Real Real (www.therealreal.com) and reusable packaging such as Loop (www.terracycle.com) have investors placing big bets on customers' interest in reusable goods.

>> **Handmade is making waves.** The maker and craft movements shown on sites like Etsy (www.etsy.com) and Uncommon Goods (www.uncommongoods.com) demonstrate the increasing popularity of handmade and salvaged materials.

>> **Piles of plastic proliferate.** Municipalities are up to their eyeballs in plastic waste and are finally taking steps to mandate its reduction. From plastic bag bans to plastic packaging elimination, they are regulating manufacturers in new ways to limit the amount of plastic waste and expand materials management.

>> **Material metrics matter.** Companies are starting to track the circular nature of their products and services using a suite of new tools and standards. The Ellen MacArthur Foundation (www.ellenmacarthurfoundation.org) launched Circulytics, a comprehensive set of measurement tools designed to give companies a clear set of circularity indicators to track and follow. The Global Reporting Initiative (GRI) released its GRI306 standard to measure waste reduction. Manufacturers are releasing publicly available versions of its lifecycle assessments (LCAs) and environmental product declarations (EPDs).

The interesting aspect of these four trends is that they all happened independently of each other, driven by people understanding the need to reduce (and eventually eliminate) waste. So just these trends show that people have an interest in reusable products, in platforms to sell and showcase reusable products, in new regulations designed to encourage reasonable products, and in metrics and indicators to quantify all of this.

Imagine that every time you order takeout food, rather than throw the containers in the trashcan, you simply hurl them into the corner of the room. Very quickly, you'd see a mound of pizza boxes; Chinese food containers and sandwich wrappers would start to overtake the room. Now, having a bigger room would buy you more time, but it wouldn't change the outcome: Eventually, you'd be overtaken by trash. This is where the world stands with landfills.

Look at these numbers:

>> Nine-tenths of all solid waste in the United States doesn't get recycled.

>> The United States throws away $11.4 billion worth of recyclable containers and packaging every year.

>> Over 11 million tons of recyclable clothing, shoes, and textiles make their way into landfills every year.

>> Of the 62 million newspapers printed daily in the United States, 44 million are thrown away (roughly 500,000 trees worth).

>> Eighteen billion pounds of plastic trash winds up in the ocean every year.

We can no longer ignore the mound of pizza boxes in the corner. The world's trash problem has become a survival problem. This problem, above all others, will likely be the biggest driver for transitioning into a circular economy.

Forces are pushing everyone in the direction of a circular economy, but it would be wrong to assume that this transition might happen all on its own. People still have a long way to go before they see a truly circular world. We have to mention two notable examples in this regard:

>> **The fashion industry (which we cover in detail in Chapter 18) is one of the worst producers of waste.** The push for fast fashion and for updating wardrobes every year produces clothing that is seen as a disposable item. In the past two decades, the average consumer has increased by 60 percent the number of garments they purchase — and they're keeping them for only half as long as they did previously.

>> **As economic growth improves the quality of life for people all over the world, it leads, ironically, to an increase in the amount of consumption per person.** As global population grows, so too will our dependence on the linear economy and the need to transition faster to a circular one. A wealthier world is generally less inclined to reuse products, and more inclined to do the easy and convenient thing — toss them when they're no longer needed.

In this chapter, we help you explore some of the drivers — financial, health, compliance, and sustainability — that will carry us humans to this bright future of the circular economy.

The Drive to Make Money

The primary motive of any business is to make money. There's nothing wrong with that; without the drive to make money, why would businesses open at all?

Because of this basic fact, one of the first drivers we discuss is how the circular economy increases profits. It turns out that eliminating waste from your supply chain by reusing materials or sourcing better materials can translate into significant cost savings.

According to a report by the Ellen MacArthur Foundation, a transition to the circular economy represents a potential net savings in material costs between $340 and $380 billion. The report goes on to state that a fully advanced transition could net a savings of up to $630 billion. And that's just savings from materials.

There are also considerable savings in energy and operations to be had, which indirectly translates into carbon emission reductions as well. Some of the savings will be recouped by the company directly, but some of the savings will benefit the city.

Let's explore some of these cost-and-operational savings:

>> Just one recycled plastic bottle saves enough energy to power a 100-watt bulb for 4 hours (while also creating 20 percent less air pollution when compared to manufacturing a new bottle).

>> If the United States were able to boost its recycling rate to 75 percent (from the current 34 percent), it would be the equivalent (in emissions) of removing 50 million passenger cars from the roads.

>> The energy needed to make 1½ million tons of plastic could power 250,000 homes. Every year, humans produce 300 tons of plastic.

>> Materials such as glass and aluminum are infinitely recyclable.

>> A single ton (2,000 pounds) of recycled paper saves over 350 gallons of oil, 17 trees, and a large area of landfill.

Redefining risk and liability

When it comes to business, *risk* is defined as any exposure the company might have that would affect its ability to make profits or cause it to fail. Risk is anything that threatens a company's ability to meet its financial goals. Large companies often have entire departments dedicated to identifying, reducing, and mitigating the various risks that threaten the company's bottom line.

The linear take-make-waste economy represents a significant amount of business risk that often goes unaccounted for. Here are some common risks found in the linear economy (which the circular economy can reduce or eliminate):

>> Single-source supply chains are risky if your company is dependent on just that one supplier. A disruption threatens the entire product line.

>> The price volatility and supply chain disruptions of resource-intensive materials risks your company's ability to deliver your products.

>> The unpredictable and fluctuating costs of fossil fuels threatens your company's ability to set pricing, which affects profitability.

>> The growing threat of climate change is driving adoption of a carbon tax on emissions, which would force your company to address its carbon footprint.

>> The unpredictable and more severe weather patterns caused by climate change are threatening to disrupt your operations, driving the need for redundant systems and resiliency planning.

>> The ever-increasing frequency of hurricanes, wildfires, and floods threatens to leave some of your company assets stranded, further driving the need for change.

REMEMBER

As more and more companies begin to address their liability in terms of waste, carbon, and material sourcing, many of these risks will become more apparent and better managed. All this will only drive further adoption of a circular approach.

In addition, the circular economy offers certain risk reduction advantages over the linear economy, including these:

>> Having a more robust and sustainable supply chain reduces the risky side effects of your business (pollution, waste, damage) that normally would be ignored in a linear economy model.

>> By reusing, reselling, and recovering your products, your company can significantly reduce its material costs; using longer lasting materials also reduces customer returns while still under warranty.

>> Having your customers return your products to you at the end of the product's useful life also improves the quality of your customer interaction and boosts customer loyalty.

>> A product that's designed to be repaired or upgraded easily also reduces product complexity and the chance of things going wrong. With the right design, a broken item can be cheaply repaired or replaced with fewer product losses.

Innovating to attract new customers

Creativity, ingenuity, and innovation have always been a great way to attract new customers. The circular economy is a chance to rethink and redesign your entire approach to the value you bring to your customers.

Consumer behavior is continually evolving, driving the need for new ways to stand out from your competition and attract new customers.

The Drive to Be Healthier

More than ever before, consumers have the ability to research and understand what impact your products may be having on their health and wellness. This drive to be healthier can be seen in the growing trends of a still-expanding $84 billion per year yoga industry, a $100 billion fitness industry, and a $200 billion dietary supplements industry.

Lifestyles that foster health and sustainability

The official marketing demographic describing people seeking to take better care and control of their health and their environmental impact is referred to as the lifestyle of health and sustainability — or LOHAS, for short.

The LOHAS community consists of customers who are environmentally aware and socially attuned and who hold a global worldview that takes into consideration the ethical, moral, and political outcomes of their decisions. This market demographic, which is considerably influential, feels that no product or service is incapable of being "greened."

Central to the LOHAS worldview is the conviction that, by insisting that companies give them a selection of healthier and more environmental choices, customers can contribute to making a positive contribution to the environment in a way that suits their lifestyle. They overwhelmingly care about the environment and regularly boycott a brand or company that has unacceptable business practices.

This group is typically the early adopter of green and sustainable businesses.

Wellness as a priority

Beyond the hard-core LOHAS crowd, you'll find a larger group of regular consumers who prioritize their own health and wellness when it comes to their purchasing decisions.

This wellness industry is now worth $3.4 trillion, making it nearly three times larger than the worldwide pharmaceutical industry. People in this group (which probably includes everyone reading this book) often seek to

>> Eat healthy, with a focus on nutrition

>> Balance their weight, with a focus on exercise and movement

>> Explore preventive health, with a forward-looking approach to disease prevention

>> Foster beauty and antiaging regimens, with an interest in looking and feeling good

>> Seek out trusted brands, with less blind allegiance to old brands and a willingness to try new ones

>> Reduce their environmental impact, with a focus on consuming, owning, and spending less for the benefits that an environmentally conscious effort brings

>> Share instead of own, with a growing dependence on sharing services for items such as cars, bikes, tools, and more

REMEMBER

Given the increasing numbers of consumers who are taking wellness issues seriously, it's clear that your company is facing a smarter and more informed customer than ever before. This is the start of the behavioral and mental shift that is needed to transition to a full circular economy. There's clearly an audience waiting for circular solutions.

The Drive to Be in Compliance

Business *compliance* refers to how a company complies with the laws, regulations, and policies that govern its business. These compliance requirements vary from industry to industry and from location to location. Some industries, such as the chemical industry, are highly regulated because of their potential health risks. Other industries, such as the automotive industry, are highly regulated because of their potential safety risks. Lastly, still other industries, such as the financial industry, are highly regulated because of their potential fraud risks.

Companies with high regulatory requirements tend to have entire teams and departments focused on staying within compliance. Such regulations are enforced to protect the safety of the general public.

Compliance represents an important but expensive aspect of business operations. It sometimes takes a lot of money to stay within compliance, but companies pay up because they don't want to run afoul of the law. The thing is, companies often assume that the cost of compliance is tied to the cost of doing business, but they rarely step back and question whether there was a better way to avoid the need for this compliance entirely.

For example, a company working with petroleum-based chemicals is highly regulated and needs to remain in compliance. If its leaders were to embrace circular economy principles, they could explore the use of plant-based chemicals that are not regulated.

Note: After every crisis, companies often face a flood of new regulatory compliances to deal with. After the great financial crash of 1929, new regulations and compliance requirements were instituted. After the great financial crisis of 2008, even more financial regulations and compliance requirements were put in place.

REMEMBER

In a warming and more crowded world, expect that more regulations will come around, targeting waste and carbon emissions. Transitioning to a circular model can put your company ahead of the game, where you're in compliance before any regulation of policies requires you to make a sudden change. It's much better to make the changes now, at your own pace, than to be forced to make them quickly because of some pending legislation that's about to go into effect. Five hundred major organizations have seen the writing on the wall and have publicly signed on to the New Plastics Economy Global Commitment (www.newplasticseconomy. org), pledging to eliminate unnecessary plastic by using design and innovation.

Environmental, social, and corporate governance

Environmental, social, and corporate governance (ESG) refers to a group of standards used by companies to monitor, track, and evaluate their performance in relation to their impact on the environment, society, and equity. They're also used by socially conscious investors to evaluate and track their investments.

The simple idea behind ESG standards is that a business should be measured by more than just its financial performance. Basic business decisions made for financial reasons alone ignore how that company performs in relation to society as a whole.

Investors have taken notice. Companies embracing ESG standards often outperform their traditional competitors. In fact, those companies using a circular model typically deliver even better returns — and with lower risk.

According to Deutsche Bank, 95 percent of assets under its management (around $130 trillion) will be governed by ESG compliance standards by 2030. These compliance standards are a form of corporate transparency, where companies publicly disclose their progress toward meeting these environmental targets.

REMEMBER

The benefit of ESG standards is that they provide a standardized approach to metrics and terms so that everyone can compare companies equally and hold them accountable for their progress toward their ESG commitments.

This list describes some ESG standards (and investment funds) related to the circular economy:

- >> **BlackRock** (www.blackrock.com): BlackRock has launched the BGF Circular Economy Fund, which aims to drive investment in businesses already benefiting from, or contributing to, the transition to a circular economy.

- >> **European Commission** (https://ec.europa.eu): The commission has created the EU Taxonomy for Sustainable Activities to create the first green list of sustainable economic indicators.

- >> **Circulytics Indicators:** Developed by the Ellen MacArthur Foundation (www.ellenmacarthurfoundation.org) in coordination with dozens of partners, these indicators are part of a comprehensive circularity measurement tool for companies.

- >> **Material Circularity Indicators (MCIs):** Developed by the Ellen MacArthur Foundation and Granta Design (now Ansys Granta, www.ansys.com/products/materials), this tool lets companies identify additional circular value from their products and materials as well as mitigate risks from material price volatility.

- >> **Circular Transition Indicators:** Developed by the World Business Council for Sustainable Development (www.wbcsd.org), this framework can be applied to all industries and companies to help them transition to a circular economy.

Corporate social responsibility (CSR)

ESG is often lumped together with another movement, called corporate social responsibility (CSR). Though they're related, CSR should be credited as the true trailblazer here, by coming up with the idea that a company should be a good environmental steward of the environment. Without CSR, there would be no ESG, but the two are often confused as being interchangeable.

In reality, ESG consists of a series of clear guidelines and standards for companies to follow to track their CSR goals and targets and ensure that they're in regulatory compliance.

CSR began as more consumers started showing their awareness of a company's social responsibility and wanting to support that company.

Climate and shareholders

Eventually, every company will be held responsible for the climate impacts they produce. Many countries have been debating the use of a carbon tax to encourage companies to curb their emissions.

A *carbon tax* is a fee ($ per ton emitted) on the carbon content of fossil fuels, and those taxes are used to pay for carbon capturing activities (such as planting forests). More than ten carbon pricing bills are in the congressional pipeline in the United States alone, with more expected.

For companies engaging in any heavily polluting industries, such as energy intensive mining or fossil fuel extraction, a carbon tax is a huge potential liability. This is why a large coal company like Koch Industries reportedly spent $11 million in 2019 lobbying Congress to block any legislation that would put a price on carbon emissions.

Implementing a price on emissions, such as a carbon tax, will further drive companies to transition to a circular approach.

A Larger Drive Toward Deep Sustainability

The circular economy movement is part of a longer narrative around sustainability that began in the early 1960s with Rachel Carson's book, *Silent Spring*, a story of the detrimental effects of pesticides on the environment. She is credited with launching the modern environmental movement as we know it today.

This has been brewing for a while

Though the larger, general sustainable movement has been around for more than half a century, dealing with the specific issues of waste and resource depletion has been building up for a while.

Global population is growing so quickly that it has quadrupled in the past century, and the planet is projected to exceed 9 billion people by 2050. This will further strain its limited resources and produce even more waste that it doesn't have the space to handle. All this population growth will rapidly increase the demand for redesigned and sustainably harvested materials that produce little to no waste.

REMEMBER

Here in the United States, the federal government has been incapable of passing national standards or regulations around sustainability, leaving most of the policymaking up to the individual states and cities. High-population states like California have taken the lead in addressing environmental regulation around climate change, committing to being carbon neutral by 2045.

Precedents

The whole idea of taking a linear approach (take-make-waste) and reducing its environmental impact is nothing new. The entire notion of a circular economy has deep historical roots in sustainability. In fact, the whole idea of cycles, nutrient loops, and waste reduction has been around since the start of the industrial revolution.

The circular economy owes a debt of gratitude to some philosophical pillars of sustainability. Let's look at some of these schools of thought.

Regenerative design

Conceived by California landscape architect and professor, *regenerative design* is an approach that grew out of an assignment that John T. Lyle gave his landscape architecture graduate design class in 1976. Lyle challenged his students to design a community where daily activities were based on the value of living within the limits of the available renewable resources. Today, the Lyle Center for Regenerative Studies, part of the College of Environmental Design at California State Polytechnic University, Pomona (https://env.cpp.edu/rs/rs) offers courses on how to design without degrading the natural environment.

Industrial ecology

Industrial ecology, popularized in 1989 by the article "Strategies for manufacturing," which was written by Robert Frosch and Nicholas E. Gallopoulos and appeared in *Scientific American*, is the study of the material and energy that flow through an industrial system. It brings science to manufacturing by focusing on the connections between the manufacturers and their supply chains. Industrial ecology seeks to create closed loop processes where any waste is recaptured and returned to the system.

The goal of industrial ecology is to design all the manufacturing and production processes so that they mimic and perform as close to living systems as possible. The framework is often referred to as the *science of sustainability* because of the way it connects various disciplines.

Biomimicry

Biomimicry exploded on the environmental scene with the 1997 book *Biomimicry: Innovation Inspired by Nature*, by biologist Janine Benyus. She advocated for designing the way nature designs and not seeing nature for what we can extract or harvest from it but rather for what we can learn from it. She described nature as the ultimate designer that has already solved most of the problems humans are now grappling with.

REMEMBER

The science of biomimicry stresses that humans can find solutions to all their self-made challenges by simply looking and understanding the solutions provided in nature. For more on this idea, check out `https://biomimicry.net`.

Natural capitalism

Natural capitalism was popularized in a 1999 book by Paul Hawken, Amory Lovins, and Hunter Lovins. The book, *Natural Capitalism: The Next Industrial Revolution*, describes how the next industrial revolution will be one that relies not on natural resources in order to succeed but rather living in harmony with nature. It promoted the idea that the economy is linked to the environment and that the two aren't adversaries but rather go hand-in-hand. The book encourages readers to recognize the importance and the value that the natural ecosystem provides as a service (such as fresh air, clean water, and healthy food).

REMEMBER

Natural capitalism is presented as an alternative to traditional capitalism by showing how a company's success depends on its relationship to the environment.

Someone looking to ensure a sustainable and secure economy for the future could start by following these natural capitalism guidelines:

>> Increase the productivity and ecologically sound use of the world's natural resources.

>> Keep waste out of the system through reuse and remanufacture.

>> Follow a service-based business model.

For more on the natural capitalism model, see www.natcap.org.

Cradle to cradle

If most products follow a simple linear process where they're born, they're used, and then they die (they're discarded), then that's what you would call a cradle-to-grave approach to manufacturing. Cradle-to-cradle advocates for a truly closed loop system where a product is born, is used, and then gets reborn as the same or better product. It's a process of birth and rebirth, or cradle to cradle.

This concept was put forth in *Cradle to Cradle: Remaking the Way We Make Things*, a 2002 book by William McDonough (an architect) and Michael Braungart (a chemist). McDonough and Braungart radically questioned (with great success) how we view waste— in fact, Chapter 4 of the book, "Waste Equals Food," is one of the core pillars of the circular economy. It shows how nature has no concept of waste because everything in nature eventually becomes food or nutrients for something else.

If you view the earth as a closed system (which it is) and waste as missed allocations of valuable resources that need to be redesigned, then the vision of cradle-to-cradle consists of healthy products that can be infinitely recycled.

To achieve this goal, cradle-to-cradle follows these three core principles:

>> **Eliminate the concept of waste.** Collect and recover value for any materials put into the system.

>> **Use renewable energy.** The sun provides more than we need.

>> **Celebrate diversity.** Both social and technological diversity is the key to innovation, and it supports the biodiversity and health of ecosystems.

TIP

The Cradle to Cradle Products Innovation Institute (https://www.c2ccertified.org) has produced a certification for products that meet its rigorous standards.

The performance economy

The *performance economy* model calls for a shift from offering products to offering Products as a Service (PaaS). The idea is that, rather than buy a product you'll eventually throw away, you buy the service that the product provides. Rather than buy disposable lightbulbs, for example, you would buy the service of lighting.

The result is a push toward reuse and remanufacturing, which is less labor-, resource-, and capital-intensive than producing new products all the time. It shifts the paradigm from "products have value" to "products provide a service that's valuable."

Walter Stahel, who wrote the book *The Performance Economy* in 2006, offers a new business model that's driven by values, gains knowledge and insight into its customers, and relies on circular systems based on biology.

The blue economy systems approach

Proposed in 2009 by the former CEO of Belgian cleaning product company Ecover, Gunter Pauli, the blue economy approach takes advantage of the rise of the open-source movement. Based on a set of 21 principles, the *blue economy* stresses business solutions determined by their local environment that could potentially create "100 innovations that can create 100 million jobs within the next 10 years."

For more on the blue economy approach, see www.gunterpauli.com.

Looking to the future

The concept of a circular economy offers a way to overcome the wasteful, energy-and-resource-intensive approach of the last 200 years. The strain of keeping up with the take-make-waste system is starting to be felt, driving companies to start measuring, tracking, and reducing their impacts in meaningful ways.

As the trends, economic indicators, and investments are showing, interest in the circular economy is on the upswing, and companies can capture some valuable benefits by choosing this approach.

The financial, health, compliance, and sustainability drivers will carry the world to a bright circular future.

SHAR OLIVIER SPEAKS

Shar Olivier, senior sustainability consultant at Vessel, an environmental services and clean energy consultancy group based in New York, has the following to say about developing a circular economy strategy:

Strategy in the circular economy creates closed loops. Currently, our economy and industry use a take-and-make linear model. Raw materials are mined and used as products and then thrown away. Waste, pollution, and resource scarcity are hallmarks of this linear model. In the circular economy, most materials enter back into either the biological or technical streams. In our work, we strive to create design thinking for the circular economy model. We use data, lifecycle assessment, and design thinking to create solutions through products and services that foster a closed loop, zero-waste strategy.

Over a decade ago, we started a disposable paper product company called Full Circle. We used post-industrial waste (sugar cane husk fibers) that were headed for the landfill or incinerator as our material. We took the ground-up fibers (also known as *bagasse)* and shaped them into plates and cups that could then be composted after use. We saved the material from ending up in a landfill or, worse, being burned and releasing greenhouse gases, furthering climate change. That material then became our product. By creating a zero-waste production plan, we prevented pollution and created a viable product that could then be returned to the biological stream through composting. We created an everyday product like paper plates, but instead of using virgin forest trees as fibers, we took the stalks from sugar cane, used to make sugar, and reused the spent fibers to make useful products that would then be composted. We closed the loop!

Petroleum-based plastic is an enemy of the circular economy. Only 2 percent of plastic sent to be recycled actually gets recycled. Single-use petroleum plastics clog our waterways and, by 2030, it is estimated that there will be more plastic than fish in our oceans! As part of the solution strategy for plastic, we designed disposable, compostable, plant-based plastic cutlery from vegetable starch. Potatoes and other plants that contain high levels of starch provide excellent binders needed to create sturdy, plant-based plastic cutlery. After use, instead of ending up in a landfill, our forks and spoons can be safely composted. These bionutrients go back into the stream and we closed the loop.

Another terrific example of transition strategy to the circular economy model is when a large. US-based household company that produces detergents and other solvents brands has thousands of tons of waste detergent annually, due to specs not being met for human use. The make-and-take-then-dispose linear model dictates that this soap (hundreds of thousands of tons of it!) be sent to a landfill each year. This company's sustainable strategy team decided to cull it from the waste stream and sell it to car washes.

(continued)

(continued)

This created millions of dollars in a new revenue stream while saving hundreds of tons of waste from the landfill. They closed the loop!

Recycling, reuse, and zero-waste streams are at the core of the circular economy model. In our consulting with large companies, universities, and government agencies, we strive to create strategies, policies, and production processes that realize our natural resources are finite. We cannot afford to use up and throw away petroleum, forests, precious metals and other resources that then create pollution, contaminate water and air, and become hazardous to wildlife and biodiversity. When we understand and embrace the circular economy strategy, scarcity, deforestation, pollution, and waste become problems of the past.

Chapter 4

From Linear To Circular: What You Need To Know

When scientists drop the scary-sounding term *entropy* into a conversation, all they're doing is describing the amount of waste or disorder in a system. Even within the most efficient circular systems — like the ones this book is focused on — waste and disorder will exist. And it *has* to exist, because waste is a vital component of the second law of thermodynamics. If you paid attention in physics class, you'll remember that this second law addresses the irreversibility of natural processes and the limitation of efficiency. Does it ring a bell? No? Okay, well, for those of you who passed notes during physics class, the idea here is that there's a limit to how efficiently energy can be transferred between systems — waste will always exist, most commonly as heat loss. This is why neither a fully circular economy nor a perpetual motion device will ever exist. Wait — you might believe that this statement massively contradicts the intentions of this book, but we promise you, you would be wrong.

Most people grow up believing that waste is just something that goes "away," right? You put your white, plastic trash bag in the garbage can and some big, diesel-powered truck magically removes it from your life to a faraway land. But that's the wrong way to look at waste, and, honestly, that perspective is responsible for why the world is in the pickle it's in today. Waste — or the energy that will inevitably leave a system — doesn't need to be piled a mile high in a landfill.

It doesn't even need to go away. We're wasting precious resources every time it does go away. If we humans redefine what waste means to us, acknowledge that it doesn't need to exist, and redirect it based on how energy flows occur in nature — as food for another system— we can eliminate pollution and the natural tendencies of entropy.

REMEMBER

This idea that waste equals food is clearly identifiable within the natural world. A leaf, for example, acts as an energy collection source for the tree, eventually falls gently to the ground, and then becomes a habitat and/or food source for a wide variety of little critters. Insects in the soil then consume the leaf matter and convert its material back to nutrients that provide the tree with what it needs in order to grow new leaves. Waste = Food. It's as simple as that. Imagine if insects decided to instead collect all the leaves and pile them up far away. Would the trees suffer or flourish? What if insects had landfills?

So Much Chaos: Understanding Entropy

Knowing all about entropy is great if you want to win at Scientific Trivial Pursuit, but what does entropy have to do with the circular economy? The second law of thermodynamics suggests that, throughout the various conversions of energy in nature — like the sun's rays melting snow or energy from a coal-fired power plant being converted into electricity — waste will always exist. Entropy is a measure of the energy unavailable to people in a closed thermodynamic system. In other words, *entropy* is the loss of energy that cannot be transferred from one matter to another.

So, how does this concept apply to the circular economy? It's relevant because, as the second law of thermodynamics tells us, even in a closed, circular system, waste will exist — regardless of how efficient we make those systems. So, for a circular economy to exist, waste and the need for new, raw material inputs must be accepted and built into the process. The goal isn't to eliminate waste completely — because that's impossible — but rather to eliminate *controllable* waste, also known as *externalized costs*. Then, by comparing the way a linear economy functions (where waste is an accepted part of a material's lifecycle) to a circular economy (where controllable waste is eliminated), we can discover how to eliminate manageable waste by learning from the natural world and applying what we learn to our own system.

Externalized costs

The first goal of the circular economy is to design out waste. To achieve this task, you will need to address and minimize externalized costs — costs in the form of waste that are imposed on a third party as a result of an interaction between a producer and a consumer. This third party that's impacted by this interaction may be a person or an institution or natural resources, like air, water, or soil. External costs typically occur in situations where resources aren't owned by one entity or individual or when the ownership is uncertain. In this context, think of oceans. Despite how much area is covered by oceans, they aren't owned by any person or institution, so any pollution that's imposed on these bodies of water cannot be tied to anyone, nor can anyone be held responsible for the remediation of that resource.

The existence of externalized costs is the result of a failing system — a market failure, in other words. A *market failure* exists when the market doesn't distribute its flow of resources in an efficient enough manner to balance the costs and benefits of a transaction; the waste of that market failure is imposed on a third party. (See Figure 4-1.) The economy that our global society relies on holds a lot of benefits, such as providing the opportunity for businesses and consumers to interact and determine the demand for various products. But what should be done when this way of doing business results in external costs being imposed on a third-party entity who isn't acting as either the business or the consumer?

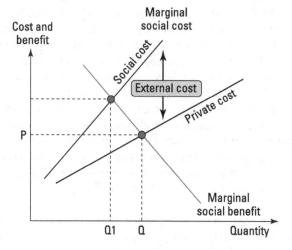

FIGURE 4-1:
Determining external costs.

Imagine, for example, that your city government wants to turn an underutilized building façade into a movie screen with hopes to generate revenue for the city on the weekends. This building happens to be positioned directly across from your apartment, so you will have access to an array of movies throughout the year at no cost. In this situation, the sellers and purchasers of movie tickets may both be happy with their exchange — a small fee for a movie — but you have no power to influence their transaction. Although the individuals who pay to watch these films have the option to expose themselves to the noise and array of people who show up to watch the films, you have no choice but to listen to movies being projected outside your home every weekend.

REMEMBER

By minimizing the range of external costs imposed on the natural environment, we allow these natural systems to regenerate and bounce back from the endless pressure we've applied to them with our society's waste and pollution. Externalized costs are attributed to the take-make-waste philosophy and are a key defining factor of the linear economy. Within a circular economy, externalized costs aren't costs at all, but instead are resources that can be used as fuel for another system. (If you're keeping count, note that externalized costs are one major difference between the linear and circular economies.)

Linear versus circular: A hilarious-yet-depressing comparison

You may have picked up this book never having heard of the term *circular economy,* and that's perfectly fine. Although the concept itself dates back to the 1960s and has had many names along the way — circularity and cradle-to-cradle, to name just two — the circular economy is finally gaining global traction as a new approach to organizing our lives as consumers. As it should. We've been stacking our dirty diapers and cheap, plastic crap in the landfill long enough, haven't we? Compared to the linear economy, the circular economy offers so much to us, and it makes no logical sense to not begin the transition to this framework. The circular economy can't promise less baby poop — the quantity of that stuff will keep growing with our population, unfortunately — but the circular economy can offer us less garbage overall, lower costs for products, the freedom to choose between buying new or fixing it yourself, and higher levels of overall health as we allow the natural world to regenerate the systems on which we depend. We can finally stop being such a burden to the environment — which, if you didn't know, is responsible for providing us with everything we need. Doesn't that seem much better than sitting on a mountain of baby poop?

So, if the circular economy is inherently great and fantastic and the linear economy is the equivalent of baby poop, why hasn't the circular economy taken over yet? What's stopping it? Well, think back to when you were 5 years old. If your mother had held up an apple versus a brownie to you back then, which one would you have chosen? Just because we know something is better doesn't mean we're going to pick it. We know cigarettes cause cancer — yet over 200 billion of them are sold in the US every year. We know sugar can increase the risk of heart disease, diabetes, cancer, and depression, but over 170 metric tons of the stuff is still consumed worldwide annually. We know that the linear economy produces waste, is fueled by the destruction of the environment, and results in cheap, fragile products, but we're still hanging on for dear life to that economy as if doctors will soon discover that a diet of sugar and cigarettes really is the secret to a happy and healthy life. Just because we know something is better doesn't mean we're going to pick it.

The same goes for the circular economy. We can know that it's better for us in the long run, but that doesn't mean we're going to pick it. To motivate the businesses, manufacturers, and governments responsible for shaping the economy, the financial benefits will need to be stronger than those offered by the linear economy. Don't misunderstand us: There are advantages and disadvantage to both the circular and linear economic structures, but only one pathway leads to a healthier future for not only you but the rest of the world as well.

If you're not familiar with the circular economy, you may have a lot of questions running through your head right now: What exactly are the advantages of the circular economy? What are its weaknesses? Are there opportunities tied to it worth sharing? Are there potential threats we should be aware of? The following sections aim to answer all those questions for you.

Examining the strengths of the circular economy

The circular economy offers a lot for businesses and consumers. By incorporating the circular economy framework within a business structure — eliminating waste, keeping products in use for longer periods, and renewing natural resources, in other words — the company will have a competitive edge over businesses that are sticking with the aging take-make-waste model. Now, more than ever, consumers are interested in supporting businesses whose leaders care about their impact on people, the economy, and the environment. Additionally, by incorporating a circular process into a business model, the amount of raw material required to facilitate the production of products will drop to nearly zero.

REMEMBER

Within a circular economy framework, products aren't disposed of at the end of their useful life. Instead, they're returned to the beginning of the lifecycle to be reclaimed, repaired, refurbished, or reintroduced. Eliminating the need for raw materials means that the cost of that raw material no longer needs to be represented in the sales price. In addition, by maintaining the material within the lifecycle for many generations of products, any cost fluctuations that may occur from the sourcing of raw materials are no longer relevant. So, what if the price of oil spiked overnight? Plastics are recyclable, and the business structure no longer depends on raw materials. Lastly, by instituting a product manufacturing process that prioritizes the development of durable materials, the focus of your research-and-development will follow suit and aid in the generation of new materials that last longer and can easily be reintroduced into the material lifecycle when they reach the end of their life.

Looking at the weaknesses of the circular economy

The complexity of production processes is rarely acknowledged. To get you your products, hundreds — if not thousands — of variables are in play when it comes to sourcing base materials, processing those materials, manufacturing the product, packaging the product, shipping the product, storing the product, and selling the product. The point here is that making a system circular is extremely difficult because of the complexity of those systems. Making a product lifecycle isn't just about collecting a broken product and delivering it back to the processing center. It requires massive changes at every juncture. This is one of the biggest hurdles that allows the linear economy to keep going strong. Even if a business was committed to implementing circular processes, where would they begin? There isn't a lot of guidance available to businesses on how to properly shift the lifecycle for their products from linear to circular. This lack of proper education, combined with a lack of resources, is a significant barrier when it comes to the growth of the circular economy. Lastly, no formal standards have been developed by governing bodies to regulate the processes required for manufacturers, distributors, or retailers to properly implement a circular economy.

Evaluating the opportunities of the circular economy

To truly get the circular economy implemented on a global scale, the opportunities involved need to be well established and communicated. Though endless opportunities are available, the key opportunities that deserve highlighting are described in this list:

» **Leveraging the closed loop:** Allowing product materials to stay within a closed-loop material flow would greatly reduce the amount of raw material extraction required. This act alone would eliminate billions of dollars in annual costs tied not only to the extraction of these raw materials but the processing, storage, and delivery of them as well. This large saving would then, in a perfect world, adjust the sales prices of products.

» **Fostering optimization:** After developing a system that values durability, implementing the circular economy framework would encourage the development of optimized products — products that last longer and can be easily repaired or refurbished, customized to suit your preferences, and, ultimately, easily recycled and made into a new product.

» **New jobs:** One of the best opportunities to implement the circular economy involves the creation of new businesses and jobs. With the education required, the optimization necessary for material manufacturing and shipping processes, and the inevitable growth in material science studies, many new businesses and job opportunities will have to be created in order to support this transition from a linear economy to a circular one.

Recognizing the threats accompanying the circular economy

Where there are opportunities, there will always be threats. The circular economy isn't unique in the sense that there aren't things to be concerned about — there most certainly are. However, with proper planning, these potential threats can be addressed and eliminated.

One major threat is cost control. If a company were able to manage every step involved in the processing, manufacturing, distribution, and sale of a product or material, it would have total control over the pricing at every step. This isn't good news for the consumer, especially if this item is a need and not a want. Even if it's not just one company controlling every step of the lifecycle, a similar concern can be justified whenever multiple companies are involved — companies that could develop an anticompetitive business structure that would function as a *cartel* (a group of manufacturers and suppliers that collude with each other to dominate a specific market).

Another threat worth identifying is tied to the costs required to make the actual transition from linear to circular. It won't be a cheap transition, by any means, and a major concern is that implementing policies that require businesses to adjust their operations to a circular format will be too much of a burden for small companies to accept. Requiring this transition would have a major negative impact on small businesses, which is certainly not a preferable outcome.

If you completed a business course in college, this emphasis on strengths, weaknesses, opportunities, and threats might ring a bell. Put them together and you have the pieces for a SWOT analysis, a common decision-making tool in the business world: *s*trengths, *w*eaknesses, *o*pportunities, and *t*hreats. Figure 4-2 summarizes the SWOT analysis for moving to a circular economy.

The SWOT Analysis for a Circular Economy

Strengths:	Weaknesses
• Circular business models offer a competitive edge to business • Eliminating waste reduces material costs and resource dependency • Circular material flows reduces price fluctuations • Incorporating circular R&D efforts aids in the advancement of material science and durable products	• Coordinating every element of a product's lifecycle to make it circular is extremely challenging • Businesses have no implementation or guide on how to properly build or adjust existing business models to become circular • No internationally recognized standard has been developed to help with the regulation of circular economy practices
Opportunities	**Threats**
• Reducing the amount of material input required by circulating existing materials would save the global economy billions of dollars annually • Implementing circular design and manufacturing practices will result in optimized products. • Introducing a need for circular economy management expertise opens up business opportunities in the market	• If a single company owns every component of a product's lifecycle, they have the power to control costs and inflate prices • Holding the ability to manage every step of a product's lifecycle creates an opportunity for anti-competitive business behaviors • The financial requirements of transitioning from a linear economy business structure to a circular economy business structure will be detrimental for small businesses and will challenge their ability to maintain a competitive edge

FIGURE 4-2: Strengths, weaknesses, opportunities, and threats.

Borrow from nature, not from the future

It's a big question: How do we humans maintain abundance and a high standard of living while also eliminating the waste and pollution associated with that effort? The first step in successfully answering this question lies in not assuming that being smart about how we manage our resources means that we will suffer and end up with less. The whole intent of the circular economy is to be smart in ways that help us obtain more and pollute less. To do this will require us to discover how to pair innovative manufacturing with minimal externalized costs. But at the end of the day, the way we transition to a circular economy is to borrow from nature, not from our future.

REMEMBER

It's critical to always use nature as a perfect example of how a circular economy could work and not forget that we are a part of nature, not separate from it. In nature, waste will always become food for another system. By mimicking this via a circular economy, we can continue to meet all of our wants and needs without being fearful of the negative impacts of acquiring those wants and needs. Transforming a linear economy to a circular economy is a completely different approach to consumption. Within a circular economy, the slogan Reduce, Reuse, Recycle is misleading. We've all heard this ecofriendly mantra, but it only applies within a linear economy because it was developed under the premise that waste and pollution will always exist in civilizations. This notion was derived from the Industrial Revolution, where waste and pollution act as a defining variable. We need to realize, however, that the take-make-waste model will be the end of modern civilization if we don't evolve to align with the natural systems we depend on. To transition the linear systems we've developed into circular systems, the natural world *must* act as our primary model.

Consider a tree, for example. A single tree can produce thousands of pieces of fruit in a single season. Even though not every single piece of fruit will be harvested to eat, there's an abundance of produce. The tree doesn't dictate how much fruit it produces based on the demand of the systems around it, because it doesn't have to. There's no downside to abundance in the natural world. The extra fruit isn't wasted, however — it's consumed by birds and other creatures who then spread the seeds to produce more trees. Whatever the future of the fruit may be, wherever it falls, it cycles back into the system to encourage the production of more fruit the following year. It doesn't do it alone, either; a wide array of insects, fungi, chemicals, and minerals is involved in this process. The tree itself isn't controlling everything, but instead relies on a diverse network of partnerships with the surrounding environment.

We can take this model of resource management and begin to translate it to whatever lifecycle we're trying to transition from linear to circular. Our product is the fruit, our distribution agents are the birds, our process partners are the insects and fungi, and so on. With this framework established, it's quite easy to figure out where the gaps are. When the product isn't purchased, do we have necessary partners involved who can take that unused material and produce something from it that will further strengthen our operations? Can our seeds be shared to create opportunities for greater levels of production? Whatever waste is developed within the business needs to be seen as potential nourishment for another system rather than simply discarded to the landfill.

The industrial revolution took a small amount of time to develop its waste management functionality, when compared to the natural environment. Mother Nature has had much more time to fine-tune the process and reach a waste-free status. So rather than spend billions of dollars a year on research-and-development efforts, why are businesses not instead spending that same amount of money by studying how the natural world functions? Imagine if there were a way to design our world like Mother Nature has designed her own.

It turns out that there *is* a way to design our world so that it functions more like our natural world. It's called *biomimicry*, a scientific approach to extracting the ideas and design concepts from the natural world to adapt and apply them to human systems. (We mention biomimicry here, but there's more on the subject in Chapter 3.)

REMEMBER

The intent of this section is not to convince you to toss aside the Reduce, Reuse, Recycle mantra and begin ignoring altogether the impact you have. By all means, reducing, reusing, and recycling are all critical components of the circular economy. But you also need to focus on the other actions that will be required in order to shift the linear ways of the world to a circular method. Check out Chapter 12 for more details on how this would work.

TIP

Not sure how to fix a problem? That's okay — you probably don't need to come up with the solution all on your own. There's a good chance something else in nature has dealt with the same issue and has come up with a solution. So, the next time you're trying to figure out how best to capture water in the desert, look up the darkling beetle. If you need to design a building that utilizes natural ventilation, check out how termites build their mounds. If you need an answer to a problem, see how others in nature have solved the same problem. This is biomimicry at its best.

Waste = Food: Redefining Disposal

We have only one planet to work with. Despite its being a relatively big planet compared to the size of human beings, we still have only one planet — and just one set of resources. In this world of limited resources, it's becoming more and more apparent that the way we manage these resources needs to change in order for us to continue to support the demands of the global population. As populations continue to rise, so does the negative impact we humans have on the world around us. Although we have gotten better at increasing our efficiency in many sectors — energy, for example — the reality is that the global economy is still extremely inefficient and has an end date if a transformation doesn't occur soon. For us to continue to sustain our lives, our waste needs to be seen as a valuable resource rather than a discarded item.

The global economy has done a decent job of developing more efficient methods, but within specific areas, not *across* different areas. Take a production of a bottle of Coke and the shipping materials required to deliver that bottle of Coke to retailers. The manufacturers of Coca-Cola have surely scaled their production processes efficiently to maximize their returns while minimizing their losses. As for shipping these products, they have surely determined the optimal level of packaging required to deliver these bottles unscathed to their retailers. However, the right questions haven't been asked about the connection between these two elements of the lifecycle. Is there a kill-two-birds-with-one-stone opportunity here? Of course there is! A large percentage of Coca-Cola is composed of water. Water is readily available in every household, in private buildings as well as public ones. So why not eliminate water from the recipe initially and simply have the consumer add it themselves? Doing so would reduce the costs of producing Coca-Cola and would greatly reduce the amount of packaging required to deliver the product to the customer.

Once waste is eliminated by transitioning from a linear economy to a circular economy, the demand for raw materials will drop dramatically and the value of materials existing within the circular lifecycle will increase because of the lack of replacement costs required. For example, Desso, a company that produces an array of carpets and artificial turfs, is already discovering the waste reduction and value associated with alternative business strategies. Through a combination of designing materials to be fully recyclable and managing to lease out certain products, it has invested in generating longer-lasting products and harvesting the resulting value.

REMEMBER

It's critical for the concept of waste to be reconsidered within our global operations. Waste as an idea is flawed from the beginning, by assuming that it needs to exist. Every piece of packaging can be reused. Every amount of water can be utilized for another purpose. Every piece of organic waste that stems from agriculture can be returned to the fields to act as a fuel source for next year's harvest. Ultimately, harnessing the power of the circular economy isn't about using as little of a resource as possible. Instead, it's about developing efficient systems that don't care how much of something you use, because, at the end of the day, it won't go to waste. Creating this reality will require that we humans change the way we view and manage what we consider waste and adjust our processes to identify and utilize its potential value.

Accepting this idea that waste doesn't exist isn't just a concept that should be limited to business operations. To account for the complexity of the global economy, this type of circular thinking should be addressed in every sector of a product's lifecycle. Customers, governments, suppliers, and communities should all be included. If customers demand that a product be made with 100 percent recycled materials, then the suppliers, manufacturers, and business entities involved will be forced to address their demand within their operations. This future idea of all companies operating within a circular fashion (by the way, check out Chapter 18 — our chapter on the fashion industry) isn't so far off into the future. Companies that are tackling this task early on will be better positioned to compete against other companies that take on this initiative when the circular economy is no longer optional, but mandatory.

All materials have another use

The take-make-waste philosophy suggests that once a material or product is used, it no longer serves a purpose. That is so unbelievably far from the truth, and it's one of the main misunderstandings that has caused the global economy to produce so much waste and pollution to begin with. The recycling and reuse (or repurposing) of materials, which is one key principle of the circular economy framework, is a prevalent standard of the natural world.

Within the circular economy framework, materials are kept in flow by the continued repurposing or reuse of materials. In addition, these materials have the potential to transfer between organic and inorganic states via a particular biogeochemical cycle.

TECHNICAL STUFF

The biogeochemical cycle may sound complex, but it is essentially the range of vehicles used to circulate the nutrients of our planet! Organic matter can then be transferred between their various human uses and these natural storage compartments. But, for this management of materials to work properly, the way our global products are engineered and designed must be built to facilitate this material recycling to eliminate waste and provide a quality service to mankind.

Two standard practices of engineering can help design the world: traditional (or human) engineering and ecological engineering. *Traditional* engineering often results in the production and collection of various waste materials that not only offer no value to other systems but also hold the potential to damage the value of adjacent systems. The design's priority is to provide humans with a service, and it doesn't acknowledge the externalized costs associated with its implementation. *Ecological* engineering — or the design of sustainable ecosystems that integrate human society with its natural environment for the benefit of both — does just the opposite. Ecological engineering aims to minimize the externalized costs associated with the design and to discover creative ways to redirect its waste as an input for another system. An example of this concept may be the utilization of riparian acreage — the vegetation barrier between land and a body of water, in other words — to filter inorganic fertilizers out of stormwater runoff before it enters rivers and streams.

By reviewing the Ellen MacArthur Foundation's butterfly diagram — see Chapter 10 for a deeper dive — you'll see that organic and inorganic materials must flow through their individual systems differently. The process of harnessing and maximizing the value of inorganic materials requires different processes than organic materials. Within both systems, however, waste can become a non-issue as the output of one system can feed into another system.

Looking at reuse programs

Many of the items tossed into the garbage could be utilized by other people. This isn't a new concept — people have been having lawn sales and garage sales for decades now. With the evolution of Craigslist and Facebook Marketplace, for example, the ability to sell items you no longer have a need for is becoming easier. You no longer have to set up a dozen folding tables out on your front lawn and then paste little round, neon stickers on that creepy porcelain baby doll that your grandmother gave you. You can post your sale online instead, where someone who didn't have a weird grandma might find it. Aside from online marketplaces, thrift stores provide an excellent setting for gently used items to find new owners, instead of being tossed into the landfill.

REMEMBER

Keeping items in use longer is one of the main principles of the circular economy. Finding a new destination for what you might consider a bunch of junk is the right move, no matter how trashy it might be. Aside from household items, one of the next booming industries will be the salvaging and resale of building materials. Entire building certification systems support this diversion of construction and demolition waste already —the United States Green Building Council, for example — but not on a whole-building scale. Check out Chapter 17 for more about building-reuse strategies.

Exploring community cooperatives and exchanges

Sometimes, it makes little sense for a single person to purchase a tool or item that they'll use for only a short time. This is why you'll find that hardware stores like Lowe's and Home Depot provide their customers with a variety of rental opportunities for tools, carpet cleaners, and even trucks. Imagine if you had to buy a moving van every time you wanted to move into a new home — it just doesn't make sense. With this understanding, many cities now offer exchange programs or co-ops to provide their community members with access to a wide array of items — but without the cost of owning them. The Station North Tool Library in Baltimore, Maryland (www.stationnorthtoollibrary.org) is a great example of this successful platform. It offers not only a range of tools but also educational programs, at very little cost, to teach homeowners how to fix a wide range of items in their homes. The main goal of community cooperatives is to primarily keep usable items out of the local landfill and at the same time provide access to those items to a wide range of people at minimal cost (typically, via a membership fee).

Product stewardship

Policies alone won't facilitate the transformation of the global economy from a linear state to a circular one. Companies and institutions will need to voluntarily restructure their designs, sourcing, manufacturing, and entire business structure to facilitate this transition. This voluntary initiative, referred to as *product stewardship,* can take many forms, but generally speaking, businesses that participate would adjust their products to facilitate ease of recycling, include appropriately sized packaging, and adjust the physical design of their products to allow for reuse, repair, and recycling — rather than force their products to end up in the landfill by utilizing the take-make-waste lifecycle approach. The ultimate goal of product stewardship is to adjust operations to allow for a cradle-to-cradle product lifecycle rather than a cradle-to-grave product lifecycle. (For more on the cradle-to-cradle idea, see Chapter 3.)

Imagine that an institution has accepted this product stewardship opportunity but has no idea where to begin. Fortunately, organizations are available today that can assist all types of institutions — from state and local governments to federal agencies and from retailers to manufacturers — to solve waste management issues and optimize product lifecycles. For example, the Product Stewardship Institute (www.productstewardship) — a nonprofit organization — does just that. With its office located in Boston, the institute works to encourage the adjustment of product designs by hosting stakeholder collaboration meetings. Aside from institutions that voluntarily accept the product stewardship challenge, some others may not have an option for much longer because of state-driven initiatives and laws that would require manufacturers to make significant improvements to their product lifecycles.

As population numbers continue to rise, so does the waste associated with those populations. Given this fact, it's becoming increasingly more important for governments on all levels to provide — or support programs that provide — increased levels of material collection, reuse, and recycling. With that being said, the whole intent behind the product stewardship concept is to relieve the implementation burden from government entities and empower the companies themselves to make the change. Under this organization, the role of government then is to deliver the appropriate resources and incentives necessary to encourage the growth of companies that support product stewardship.

The point here is that a full commitment by either just business or just government won't work; it will take a collective effort and partnership between the two to make any progress. Successful implementation of product stewardship acts as a product-centered initiative with a shared responsibility distributed between the public and private sectors. The following list details the main players and stakeholders who need to be involved to help maximize the value of product stewardship:

>> **Manufacturers:** Manufacturers will be responsible for eventually eliminating the use of toxic chemicals within their processes, for increasing the durability, reuse potential, and recyclability of their products by utilizing appropriate

materials, and for taking ownership of the product after the product has been discarded by the customer.

>> **Retailers:** Retailers will be responsible for selecting only product providers that can offer the customer products with innate value to both the consumer and the environment, for providing appropriate sources of media to educate customers on their options, and for providing the necessary infrastructure and incentives for customers to return products at the end of their useful life.

>> **Consumers:** The reality of the situation is that the consumer should not be expected to make the right decision out of a sense of civic duty. As unpopular as that opinion might be, for the value of the circular economy and product stewardship to be relevant, the benefits tied to making the right decision should be extreme and motivational. For example, if everyone were handed a dollar bill for every plastic bottle returned to a recycling center, do you think we'd have so many plastic bottles floating in the ocean? Of course not.

>> **Government:** The role of the government is to provide the proper playground for businesses to play. Governments will need to facilitate cooperation between community stakeholders, leverage purchasing programs to incentivize the purchase of environmentally preferable products, and produce legislation that encourages businesses to incorporate the circular economy framework into their operations.

Building Resilience Through Diversity: Redefining Strength

In the modern business economy, a strong business is seen as one that brings in a lot of money. Having that money on hand provides the company with the power to essentially buy its way out of trouble. Although having money in the bank is indeed a strength of a business, it's limited in its value when responding to change. Having a lot of resources isn't always the answer, but having the capacity to respond to change is. Having a bunch of cash is useful, but not if you're stranded on a desert island.

REMEMBER

When addressing the resilience of the circular economy, it's critical to understand that diversity plays a major role — diversity of products, of manufacturing processes, of sources, of customers, and of partners. If you have a retirement account set up through your employer or you voluntarily walked down to an independent investor and opened a Roth IRA, you'll see that a similar safeguarding practice is taking place. Pull up your 401K account right now and you'll see that your investments are distributed among different investment categories rather than just one.

Brokers do that to ensure that a collapse in one area doesn't destroy your entire retirement fund. Do you remember that old saying, "Don't put all your eggs in one basket"?

Within the circular economy, diversity is achieved by creating products that are modular, versatile, and adaptable to different applications. It's important to understand, however, that in order to develop an effective, well-functioning system, diversity and efficiency need to find a balance. The most efficient product lifecycles will have very few nodes or areas of connections, but will be much more vulnerable to any severe changes that may occur. If, for example, a restaurant has only one available produce supplier and that farmer's supply gets destroyed, so does the restaurant owner's business. On the other hand, product lifecycles with low levels of efficiency and a diverse level of connections have multiple nodes and will be well prepared to respond to severe changes. If the same restaurant owner had multiple produce suppliers, one farmer's misfortune wouldn't destroy the restaurant owner's business.

If you look toward the natural world as the prime example of the circular economy in practice, you see that diversity is one of the natural world's key design principles. In permaculture — a design framework that guides the design of ecosystems intended to be sustainable and self-sufficient — you can see that use-and-value-diversity is one of the design principles extracted from the natural world. (For more details on the permaculture concept, see Chapter 15.) The innate goal of the natural world is to preserve the opportunity for tomorrow. "Only the strong survive" and "survival of the fittest" —both sayings suggest that the individual elements of a system that survive over time are strong and durable, and fit in with their surroundings. Why can't the global economy act in a similar fashion? In the future, when we move away from monocultures (planting one type of crop throughout an entire field) and move toward polycultures (planting many plants throughout an entire field), we'll see that the resilience of these fields will be stronger and they'll have the ability to bounce back from any natural or human-caused disruptions.

Responding to disruption

Considering the proposed methods of a circular economy business model, it's difficult to comprehend the reasons behind their delayed implementation on a global scale. It really does seem like common sense. Developing more durable products that last longer, increasing the repairability and customization potential of products, developing smarter material lifecycles and collection methods, recycling waste, and creating community sharing platforms are all methods that prepare businesses to respond to disruptions. On top of all this, implementing circular economy practices saves customers money, reduces waste, keep products in use longer, and allows the natural world to regenerate itself.

A whole range of companies is already implementing circular economy principles within their business processes — like Airbnb, General Motors, and Patagonia — which proves that the future of the global economy is circular. This is bad news for the business-as-usual approach to systems design. This linear approach will seem like anything *but* usual in the coming years. It makes sense that these industrial giants are adopting the essential principles of the circular economy now rather than later as the best approach to minimizing disruption down the road (even if, for some, it's a somewhat bitter pill to swallow). Most of these industrial giants have had their moment of realization and acknowledge the opportunity behind turning waste into wealth.

Takes a lickin' and keeps on tickin'

"They don't make 'em like they used to." Raise your hand if a grandparent shouted out that phrase every time a car or an appliance (or even you, when you somehow managed to strike out during T-ball) didn't perform as expected. Although it's a phrase we commonly use to mock older generations, unfortunately it's incredibly accurate. Products are no longer designed and manufactured to last, and durability is rarely a performance priority for common products like plasticware. If you had a dollar for every plastic fork you have broken, you'd have enough to buy an actual silverware set. Though some products — like the plastic fork — are designed to be extremely cheap to make in order to maximize revenue, for other products, the lack of durability is deliberately a leading design influence. When you design products that can't last, they won't last and you'll find yourself in a position where buying another one is the only option you have available. If products were built to last, what reason would the consumer have for acting as a repeat customer? They wouldn't have one.

Designing a product that's built to last — like Ford claims its vehicles are — will lead to happy clients, but designing a product with planned obsolescence built right into the product will lead to repeat clients if they lack better options to choose from. *Planned obsolescence* is the act of intentionally designing a product to have a limited lifespan and/or manufacturing a product that will eventually fail. There are many reasons a company would decide to minimize the durability of a product and instead focus on limiting its lifespan; here are a few examples:

>> The materials used to make the product are extremely cheap and allow the company to make a larger profit.

>> Tech support and spare parts may be made available for only a limited time and are eventually withdrawn for last year's model.

>> The product might be updated with new features and technology that leave the customer with no choice but to purchase an upgraded product. One example is

Apple and its infamous iPhone "Batterygate." Apple found itself on the receiving end of public outrage when it revealed that the phone's batteries had been designed to slow down as they aged. Apple claimed that this strategy was implemented as a means to preserve battery life, but customers weren't satisfied with that answer. Because of this setting, Apple customers were indirectly forced to upgrade their phones to newer versions in order to maintain a high level of performance. Now, if users had been in a position to replace the battery themselves, this wouldn't have been an issue. Unfortunately for the user, iPhone batteries can be changed only by Apple. This isn't the only situation where the company has utilized planned obsolescence as a business strategy: The company's sudden switch to the lightning charger made older-style chargers obsolete, which meant that if you bought a new phone, you also had to buy a new charger.

There's no question why businesses choose to leverage the money-making abilities of planned obsolescence. Repeat business drives in the big bucks, and as long as you give the customer an enjoyable experience with a product, when that product fails, the customer will more than likely buy from the same company again because it's familiar to them. But, unfortunately, the world is at the point where change needs to happen and the global economy needs to support products designed to be durable and to produce no waste, that can be repaired and used over and over again, and that can be controlled by their owners. The global economy needs to support products that can be rented rather than owned, remanufactured to be made new again, made available for those with low incomes, and constructed with materials that can be easily reintroduced into materials flows and made into new products. The circular economy can facilitate the development of this reality, but are companies and consumers aware of the value attached? Well, not all, but some do.

Durability and reparability policies

Improved durability and the incorporation of policies that empower the product owner to repair the products they own are two key principles missing from the modern economy. A product's ability to be durable, reusable, repairable, upgradeable, and "remanufacturable," for lack of a better term, begins at the design phase. This is where the greatest potential for material and cost savings can be embedded into the design of the product itself. By incorporating circular methods into the design of the product, manufacturers can greatly reduce the cost of raw materials required while also benefiting the end user by eliminating replacement costs. Although replacement costs may be substituted with repair costs, the cost of maintaining a product is much more affordable than buying a new product every time a single element fails. But what does durable really mean in this context? How do you define what's durable? Because durability is relative to the product itself, its rate of use, and thousands of other variables, determining what makes a product durable is nearly impossible. You can see how this makes the development of durability policies difficult to produce and enforce.

Aside from that difficulty, one key strategy is associated with durability: repairability. The innate ability of a product to be maintained, repaired, customized, reused, and upgraded inherently makes it durable. Therefore, addressing durability will always require addressing repairability as well. But what's the value of buying a repairable product if fixing it is nearly impossible? That's a great question, my friend. On top of ensuring that the product has been designed to be repaired (and is therefore durable), manufacturers must make sure that spare parts, and the tools necessary to swap out those parts, are easy to acquire (both physically and financially). They must also ensure that the information or step-by-step guide required to make the repair correctly is readily available.

Although these two enabling conditions for repairability are critical, many manufacturers intentionally try to limit the number of sources who have access to the variety of parts and pieces required to properly repair their products. Building this customer dependability into products ensures that the range of competition is limited from the start and that the additional revenue associated with repair and replacement is directed back to the business rather than to its competitors. This is why, historically, the screws used in the Apple iPhone require a specialty drill bit to remove — not one typically sold in stores. Other strategies for limiting the repairability of products is to make the spare parts in older models incompatible with new models so that customers are required to purchase tertiary items to support their purchase of the primary product.

To fight against this built-in, planned obsolescence, standards will be required in order to accommodate minimum requirements for product variables such as lifespan, repairability, and recyclability at the end of its useful life — assuming that there is an end of life. There are few examples where these standards now exist, because it's difficult to determine the anticipated performance of products while accounting for user error, rate and duration of use, and so on.

Although it will be difficult to create innovative policies that affect the repairability, durability, and recyclability of products of the future, two approaches look promising: legal requirements and customer education. By developing legal requirements that make products more repairable, durable, and recyclable, products will need to be designed correctly at the start of the lifecycle process — rather than be adapted later. Other legal requirements may include making spare parts available for a certain number of years after production. As mentioned earlier, repairability of a product is irrelevant if the proper information on how to repair products properly is unavailable. Manufacturers should be required to provide adequate information to not only their customers but also repair companies that want to repair an array of popular products. Assuming that it costs less to repair a product than to purchase it new, implementing these legal requirements and education materials are the key to increasing the repairability, durability, and recyclability of products within a circular economy.

2

Rethinking Business for a Circular Economy

Chapter **5**

Identifying Your Business Opportunities

Chapter 2 talks about all the things wrong with the traditional linear economic model of take-make-waste. In this chapter, we help you explore the benefits for businesses whose leaders take up the challenge of rethinking, redesigning, and reimagining how their business operates as well as how it provides value to its customers.

Exploring the Benefits of Going Circular

The circular economy is not only an important step in protecting the environment and the world's natural resources, but it also turns out that there are numerous benefits for businesses that take a circular approach to their products, processes, and customers. Such benefits include increasing profits and lowering costs, reducing pricing volatility and ensuring greater security of the supply chain, generating new demand for products or services, and improving the quality of the interactions with customers as well as boosting customer loyalty.

Exploiting the profit opportunities

Any business is driven by profit. Without profits, there is no business. (By definition, *profit* is all the income remaining after you've covered your expenses.) Because the circular economy seeks to improve your supply chain, it provides the following opportunities to increase profits by simply lowering costs:

>> **Waste disposal costs a lot of money.** Less waste means less expense.

>> **New virgin materials cost a lot of money.** More reuse means less expense.

>> **Inefficiencies in your supply chain cost money.** More efficiency means less expense.

REMEMBER

Every year in the United States, about $200 billion is spent on solid waste management alone. This amount doesn't even include the expense of the other streams generated from other processes.

According to the Ellen MacArthur Foundation (www.ellenmacarthurfoundation. org), all the waste that humans produce creates massive economic losses. Waste costs the fashion industry around $500 billion per year, and costs the food industry around $1.3 trillion per year. Eliminating that waste also eliminates the financial burden of dealing with it.

New *(virgin)* materials are expensive. It takes about 95 percent more energy to produce virgin aluminum than it does to reuse recycled aluminum. It takes about 30 percent more energy to produce virgin glass than it does to create glass using recycled glass. It takes about two-thirds of the energy to produce plastic from recycled materials than it does to produce new plastic from raw materials.

In addition, the circular economy opens up new avenues for your products as well as new ways to connect with your customers:

>> New revenue streams can be generated by switching from a product-based model to a service-based model.

>> Customer satisfaction increases when you offer more durable products with longer life spans and improved performance.

>> New customers can be attracted to your commitment to sustainability.

REMEMBER

Investors who track investments in companies committed to a circular economy approach see higher performance gains (around 5 percent) over industry benchmarks. The consultancy firm McKinsey & Company (www.mckinsey.com) studied 28 different industries and found that all were benefiting from their circular economy activities, by improving their performance and cutting costs.

Reducing volatility and ensuring greater supply chain security

Any company that must purchase materials from suppliers knows that the greatest risk to its profits is the variability and volatility of the pricing of their supplies. A circular economy approach provides three key ways to stabilize volatile supplier costs:

>> By rethinking the design and assembly of your products

>> By reworking how to better connect your customers to your suppliers

>> By restructuring how you collaborate and partner with others in your industry

The circular economy separates resource *consumption* from the resources we all *use*. Normally, the more products you want to sell, the more resources you need to use. In a circular approach, materials are reused over and over again, separating how much you sell from how much raw material you need.

In a circular economy approach, products are redesigned to be returned into your manufacturing process, where they can be remade into the same product or repurposed into a different product. This reduces your need for virgin materials and your dependency on suppliers. Instead, you're sourcing materials for your products from things that are already in your own supply chain. This reduces volatility in both price and supply.

REMEMBER

By increasing and reusing your input of recycled materials, you know where your future materials are coming from, which gives you a more consistent and controlled material stream. Finally, less new material also means less money spent on shipping (and the carbon emissions related to moving stuff from here to there). All of this gives you a more secure supply.

Managing the new demand for business services

McKinsey & Company (www.mckinsey.com) created a framework called ReSOLVE, which is composed of these six key actions: regenerate, share, optimize, loop, virtualize, and exchange. (See Figure 5-1.) Each action represents a major business opportunity in the circular economy.

REGENERATE	• Shift to renewable energy and materials • Reclaim, retain, and restore health of ecosystems • Return recovered biological resources to the biosphere
SHARE	• Share assets (eg cars, rooms, appliances) • Reuse/secondhand • Prolong life through maintenance, design for durability, upgradability etc.
OPTIMIZE	• Increase performance/efficiency of product • Remove waste in production and supply chain • Leverage big data, automation, remote sensing and steering
LOOP	• Remanufacture products or components • Digest anaerobically • Recycle materials • Extract biochemicals from organic waste
VIRTUALIZE	• Dematerialize directly (eg. books, CDs, DVDs, travel) • Dematerialize indirectly (eg. online shopping)
EXCHANGE	• Replace old with advanced non-renewable materials • Apply new technologies (eg. 3D printing) • Choose new product/service (eg. multimodel transport)

FIGURE 5-1: The ReSOLVE circular framework, highlighting the circular economy's business opportunities.

The ReSOLVE framework offers organizations a methodology to incorporate circular strategies and growth initiatives into their business. The six elements of ReSOLVE can be applied to products, buildings, neighborhoods, cities, states, or even national economies, as described in this list:

>> **Regenerate:** Shift to renewable energy and materials; reclaim, retain, regenerate.

>> **Share:** Keep production speed low, and maximize the use of products by sharing among users.

>> **Optimize:** Develop ways to increase performance and efficiency.

>> **Loop:** Keep components and materials in closed loops and prioritize inner loops.

>> **Virtualize:** Deliver utility virtually from online shopping, self-driving cars, virtual offices, and more.

>> **Exchange:** Replace old materials with advanced nonrenewable material.

The circular economy also seeks to change from a product-based approach to a Product-as-a-Service (PaaS) model, which allows the company to focus more on its customers' needs and less on the physicality of selling them the material that will end up in the landfill. The circular approach gives companies the opportunity to personalize and customize a service based on the current customers' usage or needs.

PaaS also generates ongoing recurring revenue instead of a one-time sale. As a result, companies maintain a longer and deeper relationship with their customers. Because the focus is on the long-term relationship, the quality of the product/service improves. According to Deloitte (www2.deloitte.com), a leading professional services provider, the service profitability of services was 75 percent higher than other business units.

Here's a simple way to think about PaaS:

>> Nobody wants a fragile glass bulb; they want light.

>> Nobody wants a drill; they want a hole.

>> Nobody wants a washing machine; they want clean clothes.

>> Nobody wants solar panels; they want renewable energy.

Nobody wants compact discs; they want music.

The circular economy offers the chance to give your customers the solution to their specific problem.

Improving customer interaction and loyalty

For most product-based companies, their interaction with their customers is fairly limited. It usually only occurs at the time of sale, and they typically hear back from the customer only if they have a problem.

REMEMBER

Businesses depend on understanding their customers and fulfilling the needs of those customers. The circular economy increases the number and quality of the interactions with their customers.

Here are some ways your circular company might interact with a customer:

>> By educating your customer on your commitment to sustainability

>> By transparently sharing your sourcing and supply chain

>> By encouraging customers to return old products for resale

>> By encouraging customers to return old products for repairs

>> By encouraging customers to return old products for upgrades

>> By taking back old products to recycle

>> By reporting back to the customer how their returned product was used

- » By conducting interviews targeting client needs in order to determine the level and line of service the company can provide

- » By visiting the customer to check on and implement those services

- » By encouraging customers to share these experiences with their peer group via influencer marketing

- » By conducting surveys and collecting data from customers in order to improve this process

According to a report by Accenture (www.accenture.com), another global professional services company, the shift from a linear economy to a circular one could unlock an estimated $4.5 trillion in additional economic growth by 2030, by way of these types of additional pathways. The estimate could be as much as $25 trillion by 2050. Companies with a long-term strategy and build-sustainability targets are recognizing the opportunities that a circular business model provides.

THE FIVE BIGGEST MISCONCEPTIONS ABOUT THE CIRCULAR ECONOMY

The circular economy isn't a radical idea, but it's quite different from what most people are used to seeing. As a result, they have some common misconceptions about how businesses can employ, and transition to, a circular economy model:

- **Misconception 1: It's only about waste.**

  In a circular economy, waste is designed out so that it gets eliminated, instead of having to come up with novel ways to reuse the waste that was already created. A circular economy approach focuses on innovation, not on waste management. There's a big difference between designing out waste and designing to use waste.

- **Misconception 2: It's only about recycling.**

  The focus of a circular economy is on maintaining products and materials so that they can be used for their highest possible value for the longest possible time. We humans extend the life of materials through reuse, repair, refurbishment, and remanufacturing. Recycling is part of the process, of course, but it's seen as the last resort, to employ when all other options are no longer available.

- **Misconception 3: It's only about efficiency.**

   Traditional approaches to sustainability normally focus on efficiency: reducing the energy or materials used as a means to lower environmental impact. But efficiency can take you only so far. We humans also need to make our systems effective. Nature isn't efficient — it's *effective*. No one looks at a field of flowers and thinks, "Enough already!" The most effective systems often aren't the most efficient ones.

- **Misconception 4: It's a new buzzword for sustainability.**

   The circular economy represents a paradigm shift from the industrial economy and directly challenges the take-make-waste economic model. It pushes the industry to transform itself via redesign and a holistic, system-wide rethinking of how it all works. Rather than focus on making people feel guilty about their actions, it seeks to redesign the entire system so that it can be disconnected from consumption. It's not about being less bad — it's about doing more good.

- **Misconception 5: Waste is now a good thing in the circular economy.**

   One criticism of the linear economy is how it depends on greater consumption of resources and energy. The circular economy isn't looking to replace one bad habit for another. It isn't recommending that humans burn trash as a replacement for burning coal. It isn't trying to recycle our way out of this mess. The circular economy wants a well-designed system that keeps materials at their highest and best value. Creating a system that depends on burning trash or recycled plastic misses the entire point of the circular economy: to design something better.

Rethin*king* the Business Model

Sometimes it's easier to completely start over than it is to try to fix things. This is certainly true when it comes to designing an effective business model. In this section, we explore new approaches to the traditional business model to uncover new types of capital, new types of currency, and new ways to understand the true cost of your supply chain.

A report by Accenture (www.accenture.com) identifies five interesting ways to change your business model to support the circular economy:

>> **Relying on circular supplies:** Use only natural, reusable, recyclable, or biodegradable materials in your manufacturing process to create a reliable and sustainably sourced supply chain.

>> **Promoting resource recovery:** Treat materials as valuable, and recover them at the end of their life so that they can be fed back into another product line, transforming waste into a new product stream.

>> **Insisting on longer lifespans**: Redesign your products so that they can be upgraded, repaired, resold, and remanufactured. They should also be durable and long-lasting.

>> **Adopting the sharing-is-caring model:** Promote sharing products to increase how much they're used and how easily they're accessed.

>> **Selling services:** Rather than sell your products, keep ownership of the product and sell the service it provides.

Each of these can also help companies increase productivity and reduce risk.

Building new types of capital

Any business typically has five types of capital, each of which affects sustainability:

>> **Human capital:** The value of the health, knowledge, and skills of your employees and customers

>> **Social capital:** The value of the partners, unions, and communities you serve

>> **Natural capital:** The value of the flow of energy, waste, and materials through all your processes

>> **Manufactured capital:** The value of the material goods or fixed assets that contribute to your production processes

>> **Financial capital:** The value of the economic power that allows your goods to be sold and traded

All businesses and organizations rely on these five types of capital in order to be successful. Typically, companies only focus on the financial capital and ignore the others. The idea is that in order to be successful and maximize profits, all other forms of capital are unimportant.

REMEMBER

The circular economy attempts to redefine the business model to consider all five types of capital and incorporate them into the solution. Companies increasingly must demonstrate that their profits don't come at the expense of people or the planet.

Rethinking money as the only medium of exchange

After you switch to no longer focusing solely on financial capital but instead include human, social, natural, and manufactured capital, you can no longer regard money as the sole way that people trade goods and services. Here are some other ways to derive value, beyond merely using financial capital:

>> Generating carbon offsets from your reductions in fossil fuel energy use

>> Producing goodwill and free publicity with your customers by announcing the environmental programs you support

>> Offering a pay-as-you-grow service model to lower the barriers to entry for your customers

>> Bartering education for the insight it provides

>> Trading the excess waste you create to another company for any of its waste that you can put to use

In a circular economy business model, other types of capital beyond the financial can be used. Admittedly, it requires more interaction between you and your customers and greater cooperation between your suppliers. Rather than rely on the free market or trickle-down economics to stimulate economic activity, you're relying on resources to stimulate interest.

Surprisingly, this creates a more stable and durable financial relationship between you and your customers. Think of it this way: Focusing solely on money only perpetuates the idea of scarcity and competition. Focusing on all types of capital, however, encourages more interaction, more contact, and more interconnection.

REMEMBER

We aren't advocating to eliminate money entirely — that's unreasonable. But we are suggesting that focusing on various types of capital beyond financial provides certain opportunities and benefits.

Reflecting the true cost of products

The cost of a product isn't fully represented by the price you pay. The production of that product created some form of environmental impact that hasn't been included in the price. These hidden costs are *externalities*.

TECHNICAL STUFF

An externality is a cost that's imposed by one party onto a third party who didn't agree to incur the cost.

Understanding these externalities reveals the true cost of a product. It includes the damage done while extracting that material, the pollution released in the air and water, and the carbon emissions unaccounted for. If most products were priced at their true cost, people probably wouldn't buy them.

The biggest and most impactful externalities come from activities such as coal power generation, iron and steel milling, and cattle ranching. These types of industries have higher-than-normal environmental costs.

Normally, these externalities are ignored because no one is being charged for them. The coal plant isn't being sent a bill for the air pollution it creates. That's why they're externalities — because they're outside the normal pricing system.

The impacts of externalities typically include these elements:

>> Air pollution from burning fossil fuels

>> Wastewater runoff from fertilizers and pesticides

>> Tailings (leftover materials) from mining

>> Destruction of forest, wetlands, or waterways

Externalities can also have social costs, such as these:

>> Persistent health risks for people living near the affected areas

>> Unrelenting poverty for people working in those industries who receive less than a living wage

>> Species and biodiversity loss for decades

From 1952 to 1966, Pacific Gas and Electric Company (PG&E, the largest utility in California) dumped about 370 million gallons of chromium-tainted wastewater into leaking ponds around the town of Hinkley, California. Local residents started reporting persistent health issues, and PG&E failed to inform the local water board of the contamination until after the fact.

In 1993, a young legal clerk named Erin Brockovich led an investigation into PG&E's actions and helped secure a $333 million settlement for the ailing residents, at the time the largest amount for a class action lawsuit in US history. (Julia Roberts played Brockovich in the 2000 film of the same name.)

That groundwater pollution was an externality, and it wasn't until the company was sued that it started taking responsibility for its externalities.

If you factor in the true cost and include these externalities, you can see that we humans really can't afford to continue using a linear economy.

Embracing diversity

Nature has an interesting principle: The more diverse an ecosystem is, the stronger it is. Nature thrives on diversity and uses it to build interconnections and support systems between living things. If something is a monoculture — all one thing, in other words — it is weak and not resilient.

The circular economy embraces diversity, equity, and inclusion and looks to build it into every aspect of the product cycle.

There are many types of diversity, such as diversity of

>> **People:** To include different races, sexes, backgrounds, and creeds

>> **Regions:** To lessen dependence on transport

>> **Materials:** To lessen dependence on resources

>> **Modularity:** To aid in repairability

>> **Adaptability:** To extend useful life

>> **Uses:** To extend utility

REMEMBER

Incorporating diversity into your design builds strength and resilience (just like in nature!).

Rethinking your supply chain

With a focus on rethinking your approach to materials and waste, the circular economy highlights the need to rethink your supply chain. This means taking stock of all your suppliers, partners, distributors, and retailers and then looking for ways to eliminate the production of waste throughout that entire system.

Though that task might sound daunting, it cuts costs, reduces waste, and extracts the maximum benefit from the materials you buy.

REMEMBER

Often, the initial upfront investment cost of evaluating and implementing a new supply chain is the biggest barrier to get companies to take this on. It's what companies often call the scariest part of going circular. Once the circular supply chain is in place, however the long-term economic benefits outweigh all these initial costs. Because the company will spend less money on raw materials, it will capture ongoing savings.

Taking charge of your supply chain includes controlling your suppliers, distributors, and retailers. This also gives companies the ability to have greater control over their product from start to finish. The best example of this approach to a supply chain is Apple.

Apple is famous for its innovation and design. As one of the world's largest public companies, it manufactures millions of devices each quarter. Its secret lies not only in creating beautiful experiences but also in controlling the supply chain.

Apple purchases components and materials from suppliers around the world and gets them shipped to its assembly plants in China. Because electronics go out-of-date quickly, Apple is able to tightly control its inventory so that it doesn't have to let last year's iPhone sit in a warehouse somewhere. Apple can manufacture on-demand to produce the number of products it needs. At the end of a product's life, the customer can return the products to the nearest Apple Store, where it's disassembled for parts.

With $260 billion in revenues in 2019, Apple can also control and dictate the requirements from its suppliers. For this reason, company leaders set a goal to become carbon neutral by 2030 across the entire supply chain, and all its facilities are already powered with 100 percent renewable energy. Apple also committed to sourcing 100 percent recycled and renewable materials across all its products and packaging. Apple is the epitome of rethinking the supply chain to get the performance it requires.

Designing for the future

Design is the key to how you approach the circular economy. The idea is to redesign your products, processes, supply chain, and infrastructure to accommodate how to design out waste and make the production process more effective.

We talk more about the circular economy and design in Chapter 16, but in terms of the business opportunities involved, you should follow some key circular design guidelines:

>> Design durable and longer-lasting products.

>> Design using waste or waste byproducts.

>> Design out items that produce waste in the first place.

>> Design products so that they can be more easily repaired, upgraded, or remade rather than replaced.

>> Reduce downcycling materials into a lesser value.

>> Encourage upcycling materials into higher and better uses.

>> Eliminate unnecessary packaging, or replace packaging with biodegradable or reusable alternatives.

>> Increase the recycled content of your products as well as your packaging.

>> Experiment with packaging that serves more than one function.

>> Avoid mixing materials in a way that makes them unrecyclable.

>> Explore changing sizes or quantities to eliminate waste during production.

Assume that once the material ends up in the landfill, it's probably lost forever as a potential resource. (Yes, there's such a thing as mining landfills for material resources, but it involves only a small fraction of landfills globally.)

One example of a company that designed its products to eliminate out waste is Lush Cosmetics (www.lushusa.com). The rest of the cosmetics industry is a notorious contributor when it comes to dumping single-use plastics into landfills, but Lush reduces waste by selling dry pellet versions of its shampoo, gels, and even mouthwash — wrapping them in recycled paper and cardboard or in reusable plastic tubes.

Examining Business from a Global Perspective

The nature of business has changed over the past few decades. Every large company now competes on the world stage and must disclose in some form its global company footprint. In addition to measuring and tracking their greenhouse gas emissions, companies must consistently communicate their impacts.

To support this undertaking, a series of reporting standards and indicators have emerged, including these:

>> Carbon Disclosure Project (CDP): www.cdp.net/en

>> Climate Disclosure Standards Board (CDSB): www.cdsb.net

>> International Integrated Reporting Council (IIRC): https://integratedreporting.org

>> Global Real Estate Sustainability Benchmark (GRESB): https://gresb.com

>> Global Reporting Initiative (GRI): www.globalreporting.org

- >> International Organization for Standardization (ISO): www.iso.org

- >> Sustainability Accounting Standards Board (SASB): www.sasb.org

- >> Task Force on Climate-related Financial Disclosures (TCFD): www.fsb-tcfd.org

- >> United Nations Sustainable Development Goals (SDGs): https://sdgs.un.org

- >> United Nations System of Environmental Economic Accounting (UNSEEA): https://seea.un.org

We realize that all those acronyms can be confusing! The interesting part is how industry has moved quickly to standardize the way sustainability efforts are reported.

REMEMBER

If you were to take away just one concept from this chapter, let it be this: The current linear economic system simply isn't sustainable. It doesn't effectively provide for the economic needs of most people. In addition, it depends on, exploits, and destroys the ecological resources and social assets we humans, and the economy, depend on. The circular economy offers a model full of new opportunities to increase profits, lower costs, reduce pricing volatility, secure supply chains, generate new demand, and improve the customer experience.

RON SHERGA SPEAKS

Ron Sherga has acted as an advisor on capital raising for startups as well as mergers and acquisitions in the cleantech and green business sectors.

Eric Corey Freed: What interests me about you and the reason why I wanted to talk to you is because a lot of people in circular economy are working in recycled materials or they're working in alternative energy or they're working in energy storage. And you're working in all of those. Tell us about who you are, what you're up to, and what your focus is?

Ron Sherga: I owned and managed numerous large scale projects and strategies related to recycling, energy recovery and sustainable solutions.

I always remind people that plastics don't go off into the ocean by themselves. People put them there, but nobody wants to talk about consumer responsibility. And so, for me, it begins with that. And, as a consumer, I said, 'well, how can I be part of the solution? What can I do?' And just like everything in life, don't point to the other person and expect them to do it, take a leadership role, be inventive, be curious.

So, I started some companies in my garage, literally just tinkering away. Heck, I've never taken a business course in my life. I started tinkering away, starting with waste and scrap. I'm not going to wait. I'm going to tinker. I think simple is better. All these complicated things seem to me to be a little wacko. And, I thought, why are we trying to make this thing so complicated? I mean, granted, in some cases it might have to be, but the Keep It Simple, Stupid principle should usually apply.

You don't just need to get to the decision maker. You've got to get to the people supporting that and network to help create success and get people invested. I just tried to create stories of success. How can we get those successes?

Eric Corey Freed: On the, on the one hand, it's easy to look at this market and see, well, there's a lot of various waste streams that are going unused or ending up in landfills that you could tap into that could potentially be recycled. It looks like an abundance of it. But in my experience, as you start to get into these things, you're recycling stuff that really was not designed to be recycled. And then that means that you have to essentially invent technologies or equipment in order to process them the way that you want. Can you talk a little bit about that and maybe some of the big lessons learned from recycling an abundance of material that wasn't really designed to be recycled in the first place?

Ron Sherga: People want to do the responsible thing. There are technologies for repurposing materials, figuring out new ways, but consumers have to support that. When is the last time you walked into a store and said, 'Hey, where's your recycled content section? Where's your circular economy product section?' Right? If we're not asking for those markets and driving demand, then what do we expect?

Eric Corey Freed: Where should industry focus its efforts? Should they be dealing with the current waste problem and generating new circular loops for those waste streams, dealing with the existing polypropylene polyethylene? Where do you think the industry itself should focus its efforts?

Ron Sherga: A great question. This is polygamy, not monogamy. You can't marry yourself to one solution or one idea; you have to be open. I think we all have to work together and recognize certain solutions call for different applications.

That's been our problem. We keep fighting each other and the problem keeps growing. The waste problem derives from over-consumerism. And, sure, Big Industry is a factor. However, customers all play a role in these industries and not some robots from outer space. Big Industry — they're all people. So, when you criticize an industry, I think people need to take a deep breath and realize it's easier to attack this nebulous thing than be part of the solution. Right? For example, how good am I at home? Do I walk my talk? Do I really play my part properly? And most people, if they're honest, admit they just don't.

Eric Corey Freed: In your own mind, do you see plastics recovery as an energy solution as well? Or a waste solution or do you see it as a carbon or climate solution?

(continued)

(continued)

Ron Sherga: I think these all play a role. Let's not walk away from the energy and the stuff we're doing, but let's just see it for what it is — an intermediate step. It's diverting it out of water and running it out of air, running it out of the marine environment where it's causing all sorts of problems. I think it's multiple. It's all encompassing for plastics. If you're going to ship fuel to some country in Africa, what are you doing with those ships? You're not bringing anything back. Secondly, why don't we back haul that class of waste and then make fuel out of it and then ship that back to those countries? We've solved our waste problem. We add cost feedstock that we seem to be wanting, right? And then we're also improving our transportation footprint.

Eric Corey Freed: Can you tell me a little bit about the kind of work that you're able to do for someone like British Petroleum as an energy company or NEO, which I know is a global chemical company? Can you talk about that at all?

Ron Sherga: Absolutely. NEO just acquired all the petrochemical assets from British Petroleum. So I've of moved over to NEO with that transition to Chevron Nigerian Limited. When I came aboard British Petroleum, one of my roles was to focus on this chemical recycling initiative they had which focused on PVC plastic.

During that time, I was lucky enough to have some great leaders. And I even got an audience with Bernard Moony, the new CEO. Some of them had a little bit of the picture, but they just didn't have a maverick to help connect the dots and just beat the drum. So that's what I did. I love to tell companies when they hire me, I say, "The same reason you hire me is the same reason you're going to fire me because I'm going to be a bit of a pain in the butt. I'm going to be shaking things up and sometimes I may shake the wrong tree or the wrong person."

But the reality is I just want to get people to look at things through a different lens, not design for failure. I think petrochemical companies are all under fire. They're all struggling. But I like the fact that they're saying we're trying to direct the assets we have into these solutions.

And all I was trying to do is saying, look, these solutions can be economically viable, guys, but that's not about feeling good. It's about making the bottom line feel good too. Sustainability is about having sustainable business models that last for generations. And if you're against that, if you're looking for the quick buck, then you're just as guilty as any kind of hedge fund or any speculator. If you're not there to support long-term sustainable solutions, you're not an environmentalist.

Eric Corey Freed: That's great. Well, on that note, I think it's the perfect, um, a perfect spot to end on because I have to, I still have to edit this thing down. So, I'll keep you posted on the book.

Chapter **6**

Rethinking the Conventional Business Model

Okay, time for a basic business lesson. A *business model* describes how a company creates value for, and delivers value to, its customers. A good business model is one that generates profits for the company (of course) but also provides a product or service that's beneficial to the customer. Happy customers tell their friends about your company and that leads to more sales and more profits. That's how it's supposed to work.

The features of any business model define the value proposition to the customer, the pricing of the products and services, and the organization of the company; and it lists its partners and supply chain. This is essentially how every business works and makes money.

The *value proposition* describes how the goods or services a company provides are desirable or needed by its customers. Ideally, this value proposition is stated in a way that shows how the product or service stands out from its competitors. So, basically, a business model determines the company's success.

There are several types of conventional business models, and each can also be converted into a circular business model. Here's a list of the more traditional models:

>> **Conventional manufacturers turn resources into products.** In this business model, raw materials are extracted to create a product to sell. Components might also be purchased from others and assembled into a new product — a company that buys wire from a supplier and makes them into wire clothes hangers, for example.

   A manufacturing business can sell directly to customers [the *business-to-consumer (B2C)* model], or it can sell to other businesses [the *business-to-business (B2B)* model]. Regardless of the specifics, the conventional manufacturer business model converts materials into products that people want or need.

>> **Distributors store and resell products.** Distributors buy products directly from a manufacturer, often in bulk to qualify for better prices. They then resell these products to consumers or smaller stores. Some distributors focus on a specific category of products — a carpet distributor might sell hundreds of types of carpet, for example. Other distributors focus on a specific type of customer. (Costco is a good example of a distributor focused on families.) Because they have such buying power, distributors can often influence what the manufacturers produce.

>> **Retailers sell products to customers.** A business in the retailing business model doesn't make anything, but instead purchases products from a wholesaler or distributor and then sells what it has purchased directly to the public. Retailers can use a brick-and-mortar store location and/or online stores to showcase and sell their products. Because of the close-and-personal interactions they have with their customers, retailers often develop a certain brand awareness and are known for their service. (For decades, Sears was a known and trusted store for finding home goods, for example.)

>> **Franchises license retail stores.** In this model, a company with a popular and established approach to selling a product or service grants permission for other people to use its name and trademarks. The franchise business model, which might include any of the other business models, is an extension of a popular brand. (McDonald's is a well-known example of a franchise.)

   In the example of McDonald's, someone can license *(franchise)* any number of store locations. In return, the person agrees to purchase their supplies from McDonald's (the *franchisor),* who maintains the advertising and the quality of the brand. The person (the *franchisee)* also pays McDonald's a royalty and a share of their profits for the right to do business under its name and system.

   Purchasing a franchise has benefits because it allows you to buy into an already established and successful business.

In all these business models just outlined, something is created and sold to someone else for a profit. Each one provides some type of feedback from customers about the success of the product or service. Has its appearance gone out of style? Does it have a new-and-cheaper competitor? Is there a disruptor in the marketplace, like how Netflix disrupted Blockbuster by making it easier to rent videos?

RECOGNIZING THAT BUSINESSES HAVE LIFECYCLES

All products and services have what's called a lifecycle. (For more on this topic, see Chapter 10.) That is to say, they have a birth (production), a life (their use), and a death (disposal). Businesses that understand the lifecycle of their products can find new ways to lower costs, increase profits, and better delight their customers.

Businesses also have lifecycles. This progression of the business over time usually comes in five stages: launch, growth, shakeout, maturity, and decline. (See the sidebar figure.) Cultural changes and technological advances often disrupt a business lifecycle along these stages. (Consider all the businesses disrupted by the advent of the Internet!) Though the circular business model isn't driven by technology, it has the same potential to disrupt conventional business models by changing how we look at the basics of business.

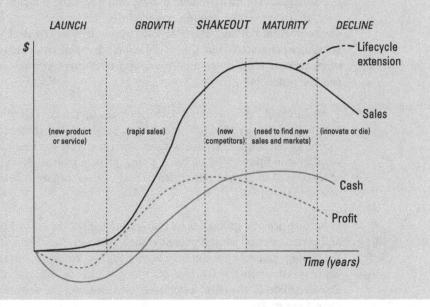

Whatever your business model, the basic principle is the same: Provide a clear value proposition to your customers to generate profits. But in a world with growing challenges around resources, waste, energy, and equity, customers are demanding more from that value proposition and driving companies to look at sustainability and circular economy issues more than ever before.

Rethinking How We Look at Cost

In the past, the cost of raw materials (also called *commodities*) tended to decrease over time as technology improved our ability to mine, extract, and harvest it. Factory farming innovations allowed farmers to grow more per acre. Global production allowed clothing manufacturers to make clothing for less cost. Making stuff got cheaper and cheaper! For a while, it all was going great!

All that mining, extraction, and resource use came with a huge environmental cost in terms of water and air pollution, waste, biodiversity loss, species extinction, and more. These damages are referred to as *externalities* because they often fall out of view from the company creating the damage. You really can't see air pollution, so unless someone complained, a company never really dealt with it.

Even for the direct waste a company produces, company reps typically would just pay a disposal company to take it away and never see it again. It turns out, however, that if you take enough commodities out of the earth, eventually all that environmental damage starts to catch up with you. To deal with these issues, governments started enacting regulations, disposal companies started charging more to deal with these new laws, and customers started demanding better-sourced products.

These kinds of environmental damages make up part of the true cost of a product that is paid not by the consumer or the producer but instead by taxpayers and future generations. Taxpayers fund the repair of damage caused by extreme weather conditions and polluted living environments. Everything we buy has some type of social or environmental cost — even organic jeans, local vegetables, or electric cars.

REMEMBER

The true price of a product is its market price, plus the cost of repairing the social and environmental damage it creates along the way. (See Figure 6-1.) This includes the damage caused by pollution, climate change, resource extraction, and harm to workers. For example, the true price might include the cost of planting trees to absorb carbon or the costs associated with cleaning the water used in the manufacturing process.

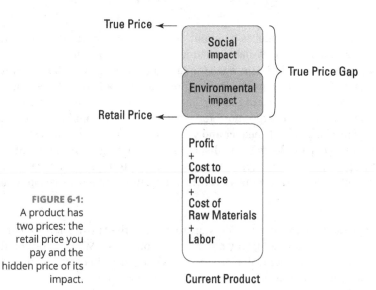

True Price

Social
impact

Environmental
impact

True Price Gap

Retail Price

Profit
+
Cost to
Produce
+
Cost of
Raw Materials
+
Labor

Current Product

FIGURE 6-1:
A product has
two prices: the
retail price you
pay and the
hidden price of its
impact.

Today, much of the low-hanging fruit in terms of our natural resources has already been harvested. All the easily accessible resources have already been extracted, making it more difficult and more expensive to obtain these raw materials. Oil companies have to drill deeper and farther out in order to collect the remaining reserves of crude oil, often using offshore rigs, fracking, or tar sands production processes — which increase the environmental damages even more. Factory farmlands around the world are seeing declines in crop yields as severe weather and soil declines affect their ability to harvest food. All these increasing challenges are causing companies to rethink their business models by looking at more sustainable, circular models.

REMEMBER

Circular business models focus on doing more with less, extending the useful life of a product, repurposing used parts, and allowing people to repair and reuse materials. These innovative strategies break that cycle of depending on dwindling raw materials and the rising costs that go with them. In short, circular business models convert the traditional business model of take-make-waste into one based on make-use-reuse on a loop. This huge paradigm shift in how a company can make profits encourages them to completely rethink their business model, their strategies, and their production processes. The issue isn't only environmental, it's also economic.

Say you own a factory that produces ballpoint pens. The pen barrel, the cap, and even the ink are all made from oil-based chemicals. In the early years of the company, sourcing the oil-based plastic was simple and cheap. Oil was abundant, it seemed, and tons of companies provided cheap plastics and ink. Over time, however, as oil grew scarcer, the cost of making your pens increased and your profits went down. You wanted to charge more for your pens, but competitors are out there making pens cheaper and cheaper and you're stuck. Plus, customers started complaining about your products being disposable and ending up in the landfill. They were being pressured by their employees and customers to reduce their waste bills as well. You're starting to worry that you can't find any other options to reduce costs.

One day you opt for something new. You start to rethink the entire supply chain. If oil-based plastic is the problem, why not use something else? What if you could produce a recyclable or biodegradable or even refillable pen? This strategy would break that cycle and shift your business model into a more circular one.

REMEMBER

The circular economy isn't just about preserving the environment. It also gives companies an opportunity to reduce the costs (normally assumed to be the cost of doing business) and rethink their business model.

The hidden cost of procurement

It turns out that sourcing the raw materials and resources that comprise a product requires careful planning, research, and processing. These costs are normally hidden to you as the customer, so when you buy a $20 shirt at the store, you have no idea how much went into sourcing the fabric, the inks, or the stitching or even the cost to the company to track all that inventory.

Some of these are *soft* costs, like the administrative costs it takes to research materials, design the product, process the orders, track the inventory, and find new distributors and stores. Other costs are *hard* costs, such as shipping, packaging, insurance, labor costs, or taxes. Normally, such soft and hard costs are just folded into the final cost of the product and assumed to be the cost of doing business. In truth, understanding how to reduce these costs is the key to going circular.

The first step in understanding the hidden costs of procurement is awareness: How much is the total cost of the goods or services being purchased? Buyers need to understand all the costs associated with sourcing their materials in order to make better decisions around sustainability and reducing its impact.

RETHINKING WASTE DISPOSAL

Located in Portland, Oregon, the waste management company City of Roses Disposal and Recycling is rethinking the entire business model and turning the city's trash into treasure by creating new materials. We authors spoke with Alando Simpson, the CEO of the company, so that we could explore his innovative approach:

How would you describe what you're doing? Describing it as waste disposal just doesn't cut it.

Alando Simpson: We are the only privately owned, permitted waste-transfer station in the city of Portland. Right now, we're on a 12-acre site in a 100,000-square-foot facility. We also have an acre-and-a-half of wetland on our property. It's a campus: fully supported by circular economy, zero waste, closed loop systems.

We have this novel idea to take wood waste from construction projects and turn it into new finished sheet goods. These are the first-ever 100 percent post-consumer FSC-certified OSB panels.

The potential for wall cladding, casework flooring, decorative tabletops, and furniture is huge. We also have 50 percent post-consumer products with a plywood backing, which is a virgin plywood piece. It's really just sorting it, doing quality control, transporting it, and then plopping it into this pretty cool technology. Our partner strips it into pieces and glues it all back together.

Our local partner, Sustainable Northwest, worked with us on creating this new supply chain model. We've partnered with Oregon State University for testing in their mass timber testing facility.

We're trying to keep up with our own demand right now and get our processes to maximize efficiency. Right now, we're just focusing on dry construction waste — for example, drywall, concrete, wood, metal, cardboard, plastics, and fiber.

Half the building is a waste transfer station; the other half is a material recovery facility (MRF). We're working with a couple of partners to gain more value out of that, as opposed to landfilling it.

How does this differ from a traditional waste management business model?

Alando Simpson: Companies make too much money on our garbage. People think, "Oh, we just pay 30 bucks a month and it's "out of sight, out of mind," but that adds up to a lot of money and that's just for collection.

(continued)

(continued)

Then there are the transportation and transfer costs to get the waste into the landfill. What people don't realize is that we import so much raw material in the form of finished products with a huge carbon footprint as part of our massive consumption addiction. The trash getting hauled away ends up in some hole in eastern Oregon.

About 70 percent of the profits come out of that supply chain from the time you throw it away to the time it ends up in the landfill. It makes no logical sense when we could be investing those dollars and public resources to close the loop, create new materials, and create more innovative outcomes.

Our innovations are keeping resources out of landfills by diverting and controlling where the waste stream goes. This creates jobs, minimizes greenhouse gas emissions, and prevents resources and capital from going to other marketplaces. Plus, the city can offer discounts to developers on development fees to recycle and use these closed loop products, which is price competitive with something they get off the shelf at Home Depot.

It's a win-win across the board.

Alando Simpson: Yeah, plus you start focusing on your new green workforce economy; and you build facilities powered by renewable energy; and you start building in blighted communities and making infrastructure investments that support a new clean, modern, innovative, technologically driven grid.

When you make capital investments in communities that need them, you're decarbonizing the economy and creating local jobs and a sustainable business model that can be replicated anywhere because garbage is everywhere.

Do you have a roadmap or vision in your head for where to take this innovative business model? It seems you have an abundance of incoming raw materials and are looking to close the loop into bringing those new life.

Alando Simpson: Everything's on the table. It's all science — going back to its original scientific origin of what created that finished product to begin with. For me, it's not just about solid waste. What I learned a long time ago about recycling is that it's not just keeping things out of landfill — it's about manufacturing. We're creating finished products.

Imagine having a production facility right next-door that's facilitating anaerobic digestion to create a renewable energy source. Perhaps we take out all the organic waste and turn it into some nutrient-rich compost. Maybe the city requires developers to have a community garden using this compost so that the tenants have access to fresh, healthy, economical produce.

It's really all about how to take human capital and put them first; take the most vulnerable populations and put them first. City of Roses Disposal and Recycling is an aspiring model for other places.

You can go in any direction. Does that mean that your biggest problem is knowing where to focus your efforts next?

Alando Simpson: No. The trick here is that everybody looks at it through an individual lens. What I've learned in this process is collaboration. We're not the expert in all areas. We're going to bring in the experts to create the campus model of collaboration.

A waste facility has very sophisticated processing equipment and human capital that's measuring, assessing, and controlling quality to ensure that we get a finished feedstock. That's our primary focus. Our second priority is making sure that we sort things into what is valuable and not valuable. Third priority goes to materials production, by partnering with a plethora of co-located organizations and partners. Partnering with academia provides important research, development, and testing.

Let's recalibrate our focus on how we see value in one another and to help other people.

What's keeping your operation from scaling? You've invented a new business model that could be done across the state.

Alando Simpson: I want to! Creating something here that is a model for the future. That's my biggest challenge.

To be totally honest, what we're proposing and doing is totally disruptive to the garbage industry. They would have to see some value in terms of investing in it and getting a return on that investment. Otherwise, they are essentially investing in the destruction of their own vertical integration model because they make so much money the old way.

Do you see yourself as, "I'm not in the graveyard business. I'm a circular economy industrialist taking your raw material and doing good with it."? How did you get onto this way of thinking?

Alando Simpson: It's been a pretty slow evolution. I've always questioned everything. I think, once you're in a hierarchal position, you have to have the humility to say, "I was wrong." That's half the battle. If you can't do that, you're shutting off your opportunity to learn and grow.

That's why I'm aligning myself with people that I can learn from. I'm aligning myself with people that are smarter than me. That's the secret because I'm addicted to learning from people.

That's how the shared infrastructure of knowledge should work. That's why I see human capital as so important. We have concentrated areas of blight as underserved communities of color. These people possess significant layers of genius and wisdom. This is human capital.

The hidden impact of transportation

Complex products often source their raw materials from all over the world. Take the lifecycle of a typical solar panel. The raw materials for the solar wafers were probably extracted from mining operations in Bolivia. Those raw materials were then likely shipped by freighter to China, where they were then assembled into one of 30 component parts of a solar panel. Those finished parts were then shipped to Texas for assembly. Finally, the panels were shipped to a warehouse in Nevada, where they sat for months until being shipped again to Los Angeles, where they will be installed. What a crazy trip!

The greenhouse gases emitted in all that transporting could take as long as five years until the solar panels "pay back" those emissions in the form of energy savings. If we start considering these transportation costs in our business model, it might cause us to source more local materials and save on those costs.

The hidden burden of inventory

For any company that produces any type of product, maintaining inventory is a necessary part of operations. Without enough inventory on hand, you won't be able to fill orders quickly. On the other hand, if you have too much inventory, you run the risk of paying to store your products, paying to maintain your products, or having the products expire or pass their expiration date. Having the right amount of inventory is a balance.

Inventory can also be a block to introducing new and innovative circular products. If you have 10,000 units of your product sitting on shelves, you might be less likely to redesign and reinvent that product with circular strategies.

Inventory can also expire, become outdated, or obsolete — which can really be a drag on profits. Products become obsolete for a number of reasons, as the following list makes clear:

>> **Discontinuation:** A product is discontinued and cannot be remanufactured into new products. Mixed materials cannot be separated.

>> **Shelf life:** A material exceeds its shelf life. Food expires, chemicals lose potency, or pigments fade, for example.

>> **Market saturation:** Popular products saturate the market and are no longer in demand. A circular business model would reuse or remake those products.

>> **Updated technology:** A new faster, cheaper, better technology comes along, making the product outdated. Computers, cell phones, and storage are continually updated, for example.

>> **Safety regulations:** New regulations or safety requirements are more stringent and the product is obsolete: Examples are car recalls, baby product safety, and fire regulations.

The hidden secrets of quality

The conventional wisdom in manufacturing states that every product must be nearly identical to one another. Imperfect products are discarded and rarely recycled back into the manufacturing process. This includes products differing in appearance, color, performance, taste, or finish.

Now, if you're buying plates, you'll probably want them to be identical. But if you're buying 300 tables for a hotel, no one will ever notice any slight differences between them. Yet the push for perfection continues and comes at a great cost.

In a circular approach, such imperfections could be turned into an opportunity. They could be:

>> Sold as a reclaimed line at a discount

>> Designed to be disassembled and remade

>> Reimagined to encourage these unique imperfections so that every product is a bespoke original

Maximizing Your Value Proposition to Customers

When you start to let go of the traditional business model, new possibilities and considerations start to open up that you might have previously ignored. At the beginning of this chapter, we authors talked about how you can design a business model around the customer value proposition — that is to say, the benefit that your product brings to your customer. A circular business model transforms the way you look at doing business and the value that you can bring to your customers.

Here are some specific strategies you might want to use to boost the value proposition to your customers:

>> Redesigning your product for durability, repairability, or reduced toxicity

>> Discovering ways to reduce your environmental footprint across your entire manufacturing process

>> Encouraging and pushing suppliers to reduce their environmental footprint as well

>> Providing customers with recommendations on how to extend the useful life of your product

>> Uncovering opportunities to source more local materials to lessen their transportation impact

>> Highlighting all the ways you're incorporating sustainability into your company and your products

>> Offering your circular products as the default (and making your traditional products the alternative)

>> Designing your product so that it's cheaper to repair than replace

>> Creating pathways for disadvantaged and low-income households to participate with your products

>> Communicating all of the positive things your product does for the environment (which could include restoring a natural habitat or providing workers with a living wage)

Becoming a mission-driven company

A circular economy business model is about more than just materials — it's also all about emphasizing equity for your workers and addressing the balance of power between your company's highest-paid and lowest-paid workers. Here are some strategies you can use to address this issue:

>> Shifting your business model rationale from a profit-maximizing model to a mission-driven business

>> Partnering and collaborating with other mission-driven companies, including minority-owned and small businesses

>> Developing a comprehensive company policy on diversity equity and inclusion

>> Applying for a company-wide certification, like B-Corp (https://bcorporation.net) or Just (justorganizations.com), that testifies to the fact that your company balances purpose and profit

>> Considering cooperative or employee-owned business structures that offer employees partial business and stock ownership

>> Changing your business model mindset from offering a product ("we sell carpet that you buy") to offering a service ("we provide and maintain your flooring needs")

Safeguarding your workers

The staff and employees in a company are often more than just the people in the office. The employees also includes the workers in your factories and in the factories of your suppliers. To protect all the workers across your entire value chain (all of the activities a company does to produce their product), follow these guidelines:

>> Ensure that workers are paid a living wage.

>> Support their rights to bargain collectively or unionize.

>> Establish meaningful social dialogue between management and the worker representatives.

>> Engage in fair trade and circular procurement policies.

Companies that embrace these equity- and mission-driven business models often see greater brand loyalty, greater worker retention, and higher sales and profits.

Greenwashing

When a company embellishes or exaggerates some of its environmental claims, it's called *greenwashing*. Though it's easy to understand why a company wants to tout its environmental and sustainability efforts, they can easily cross the line from honest transparency to misleading and glorified marketing.

To avoid any type of greenwashing or an attempt to deceive your customers, we suggest these strategies:

>> Communicating honestly and openly about how circularity is central to your business

>> Continually monitoring your suppliers and supply chain to track their environmental and material footprints

>> Transparently reporting and disclosing those footprints to your customers

>> Being open about your business practices and embracing transparency as a larger strategy to build brand loyalty

>> Acknowledging where you're meeting your circular goals and admitting where you're falling short (rather than misrepresenting that everything is perfect)

Here are five simple signs that a company is greenwashing:

>> **Jargon:** An environmental statement should be clear and concise. If a company is using a lot of confusing jargon or technical terms, things may not be as simple and green as you may hope.

>> **Fake friends:** If a company cannot obtain a legitimate and respected certification, someone will create their own version. Beware of labels, seals, or awards that are fake or made up.

>> **Tiny amounts:** Just containing a smidgeon of recycled content isn't enough. Beware of products claiming to be green but containing only 4 percent recycled content, especially if the raw material isn't green to begin with. (Even 100 percent recycled vinyl is toxic at every stage of its life, for example.)

>> **Running alone:** Offering one green product line out of dozens of nongreen ones is greenwashing. If this single line of products is the company's "green" line, what would you call its other products? The toxic line? Beware of companies trying to appease people with little effort.

>> **Suggestive ads:** Avoid companies painting a picture of perfection. Beware of companies showing images of flowers flowing out of a tailpipe or rainbows that end with a pot of their product as gold. Simply painting on a green happy face doesn't make a product green.

Turning Obstacles into Opportunities

Circular business models offer many opportunities to circumvent the shortcomings of conventional business models, as outlined earlier in this chapter. Consumer attitudes around sustainability have reached a tipping point, leading them to avoid brands that don't prioritize sustainability and environmental issues.

Increased honesty and transparency into a company's supply chain and production processes means that consumers get to pick and choose brands that are better for the environment. A circular approach seeks to reduce waste, encourage reuse, and provide better products — an amazing way to attract a customer's attention!

Listening to customers

Customers want a circular economy, even though they might not realize they want it. People want brands and retailers to offer responsible, sustainable ways to stay in business. People want easy and simple ways to reuse or share your products.

In a circular business model, customers are no longer responsible for dealing with the product at the end of its life because a circular product's life doesn't end. The company either takes back the product, repairs and renews the product, or replaces the product (usually, as part of a maintenance service plan). Manufacturers, distributors, and retailers are responsible for reintroducing the product into a production lifecycle.

UK-based cosmetics company Lush (lushusa.com) embodies this approach. Though the rest of the $500 billion cosmetics industry is a significant contributor to putting single-use plastics into landfills, Lush reduces waste by selling solid versions of its shampoo, shower gels, body lotions, and toothpaste, saving over 20 million plastic bottles from being thrown away. Additionally, Lush packages its products in recycled paper and cardboard without labels. Its Black Pot take-back program allows customers to return five product containers in exchange for a free face mask. These containers are then cleaned and reused. The result are fiercely loyal customers.

In a recent study by ING Group, a multinational banking and financial services corporation, the majority of consumers surveyed believe that they have a role to play in tackling environmental issues — for example, 83 percent of consumers believe that their behavior and product choices have a positive impact on addressing global environmental issues. The study shows that some consumer groups are more driven by sustainability and are prepared to abandon their regular brands over these issues. You can check out the ING Group report at www.ingwb.com/media/3076131/ing-circular-economy-survey-2020-learning-from-consumers.pdf.

Customers are also putting more pressure on companies to deliver durable and reusable products that are designed to last. Circular business models address the issue of *planned obsolescence* — the practice of designing products to deliberately wear out to force you to buy more.

The benefits of circular economy models are legion: They have widespread appeal, in addition to the fact that they address the environmental imperative we humans face as a society. Consumers want to be better armed with brand information and will continue to increase the pressure for full disclosure over the next few years.

Creating unspoken demand

According to a recent survey by McKinsey & Company, a global management consulting firm, you can expect consumers in the COVID-19 era to be more cautious and focus on getting more value. For decades, brand loyalty has decreased as consumers have learned to be more discerning in their purchases. Quality and mission are more important to customers when choosing which brands to buy. You can see the survey results at:

```
www.mckinsey.com/business-functions/marketing-and-sales/our-insights/
    a-global-view-of-how-consumer-behavior-is-changing-amid-covid-19
```

For younger generations, the push for circular business models is even stronger. Faced with economic insecurity, millennials are open to buying used products, repairing instead of replacing, and participating in the sharing economy rather than making a purchase at all.

All these customer trends play into the strengths of circular business models and offer opportunities for circular start-ups and conventional businesses that are willing to reconfigure to a circular business model.

Rethinking old assumptions

In a world of increasing competition, businesses are having to rethink their old assumptions. In shifting toward more circular models, how can we address the unintended consequences of conventional business models?

Manufacturers who assumed that they would always work with raw materials might rethink that assumption and explore ways of converting waste into new products. To take just one example, buying disposed electronic parts and extracting the valuable rare metals they contain could create a new revenue stream or an inexpensive source of these metals. Plus, it offers the value-adding services of reuse and waste reduction and keeping toxins out of the waste stream.

Bending linear into loops

Traditional business models using the linear approach of take-make-waste assume a never-ending supply of cheap, natural resources. After two centuries of their abuse of our planet's natural resources, though, this assumption no longer applies. Nonrenewable resources — such as plastics, minerals, and metals — are increasingly becoming harder to source, which is creating massive demand for recycled and alternative sources of these materials.

Closed-loop systems keep products, including their parts and materials, at their highest utility and value — reducing the need to extract more resources and, as a result, reducing their impact on the environment. Rethinking your linear loops into closed loops is a way for businesses to tap into cheaper and more stable sources of materials for their products.

These related business models are working to close the loop:

>> **Circular supplies:** This model involves using renewable, bio-based, or fully recyclable materials to replace single-lifecycle inputs. Interface (www. interface.com), a flooring manufacturer committed to combatting global warming, is continuously improving its carpet tiles to avoid using petroleum-based fibers and increasing the use of alternative raw materials. As of this writing, Interface offers a zero-carbon, zero-vinyl carpet tile.

>> **Resource recovery:** Here, the idea is to recover useful resources/energy from disposed products or byproducts. Net-Works, one of Interface's global partners, collects discarded fishing nets and facilitates their repurposing into carpet tiles. (For more on Net-Works, check it out at https:// net-works.com.)

>> **Product life extension:** The goal here is to extend the working lifecycle of products and components by repairing, upgrading, and reselling. Smartphone manufacturer Fairphone (www.fairphone.com) is one example, offering modular components as a way to extend the usable life of its mobile handsets.

>> **Sharing platforms:** This model enables increased utilization rate of products by enabling shared access. (For more on this topic, see Chapter 7.)

>> **Product as a Service (PaaS):** This model offers access or outcomes while retaining product ownership. (For more on this topic, see Chapter 7.)

Thinking of businesses as a system

The term *systems thinking* describes an approach to looking at how all of the various parts fit together and how their relationships work. It involves looking at your business model as a whole system and it's quite different from the traditional approach of adding on greater and greater complexity.

A systems thinking approach seeks to connect all the various parts, focusing on relationships and how the parts benefit one another.

While the traditional business model has worked for decades, it overlooked some important realities about the environment and the impact it creates. This creates an opportunity to question everything about a business, including: the value you bring to customers, how waste costs money, and how the products are even designed. Once you are willing to let go of a traditional business model, it really presents an opportunity.

A circular business approach is an opportunity to be innovative. By rethinking how you source raw materials, reuse your waste, discover new materials, or extend the useful life of your product — you can boost your connection to your customers and even potentially save money. So what are you waiting for? Start exploring how to upend your business model to a circular one today!

IN THIS CHAPTER

» Identifying the value of the Six Rs:
Refuse, Reduce, Reuse, Repurpose,
Recycle, and Rot

» Exploring the steps involved in
creating a circular business practice

» Investigating how some businesses
are thriving by embracing the circular
economy

Chapter **7**

Exploring the Essentials of a Circular Business Model

Wherever there's a problem, there's also a solution. And wherever there's a need, there's a product available to meet that need. That's what drives all business. Within the circular economy framework, the solutions are already available, but they need the support of companies, nonprofits, and other institutions to be properly facilitated at a global level. Look around and you'll see an abundance of problems needing resolution: depletion of resources, lack of materials, and the nonstop need for recovering, extending, and sharing products and resources. On top of the growing demand of a rising population on a planet with finite resources, the problems at hand need smart, adaptable solutions.

You might be thinking your particular business interest area has nothing to do with the circular economy, so this chapter will be of no benefit to you. Our response to that? You couldn't be more wrong, so read on! The best part about developing a business with the circular economy as a motivation is that it doesn't matter what your business is — you can follow essential best practices to make any business model circular. If you find yourself drawn to developing a new business that functions on a circular economy platform, this chapter is for you.

In this chapter, we explore not only the best practices for creating a new business under a circular economy framework but also which business opportunities are available within that framework. We also outline how other businesses are thriving by implementing circular economy concepts.

The Six Rs: Your New Circularity Mantra

Are you familiar with that spiffy-looking triangle made up of three green arrows — the one that can commonly be found on recycling bins and posters referencing the Reduce, Reuse, Recycle slogan? Well, as helpful as the strategy of reducing, reusing, and recycling might be, it doesn't fully cover the steps necessary to build a circular business model. In fact, it gets you only halfway there. Aside from these three well-known steps, you need to adopt three additional steps if you want to fully incorporate the circular economy as a strategy for designing out waste and pollution, keeping products and materials in use, and regenerating natural systems. Add the three additional steps to the original trio and you end up with six total steps to account for, in this order: Refuse, Reduce, Reuse, Repurpose, Recycle, and Rot.

The rest of this section breaks down these six terms, explains why they act as critical steps to implementing a circular business model, and offers an array of examples of how these six Rs can make an impact in your business venture.

Refuse: Say no to what you don't need

A single person has some power to influence the world, but a collection of people have a much greater power to influence the world and create the change they want to see. That's why the first R — Refuse — is all about the overarching power of decision-making: Does the consumer want to support your product or service? Or will they want to refuse it?

As a potential business owner, you probably know how massive the research-and-development (R&D) sector has become. Global business networks invest large amounts of money to determine what exactly the consumer wants to see in their products. In total, the top 1,000 most profitable companies in the world — including big names like Alphabet, Amazon, Microsoft, Samsung, and Volkswagen — spent a combined $858 billion dollars on R&D in 2018. (See Figure 7-1.) This initial phase of product development helps to determine what the consumer wants to buy.

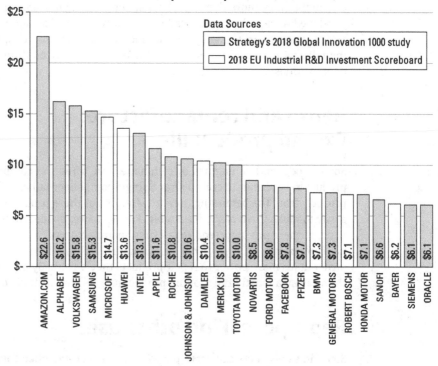

World Top 25 R&D Spend 2018 (US$ billions)

Data Sources
- Strategy's 2018 Global Innovation 1000 study
- 2018 EU Industrial R&D Investment Scoreboard

AMAZON.COM $22.6 | ALPHABET $16.2 | VOLKSWAGEN $15.8 | SAMSUNG $15.3 | MICROSOFT $14.7 | HUAWEI $13.6 | INTEL $13.1 | APPLE $11.6 | ROCHE $10.8 | JOHNSON & JOHNSON $10.6 | DAIMLER $10.4 | MERCK US $10.2 | TOYOTA MOTOR $10.0 | NOVARTIS $8.5 | FORD MOTOR $8.0 | FACEBOOK $7.8 | PFIZER $7.7 | BMW $7.3 | GENERAL MOTORS $7.3 | ROBERT BOSCH $7.1 | HONDA MOTOR $7.1 | SANOFI $6.6 | BAYER $6.2 | SIEMENS $6.1 | ORACLE $6.1

FIGURE 7-1:
Companies spend a lot of money on R&D.

Recognizing that industry sees the benefit of satisfying consumer demand means that the consumer has the ability to motivate a positive change and encourage the move to a circular economy. When the needs and requests of the consumer change, so should the product itself — if your company wants to survive, that is. By refusing to purchase products that aren't sourced, manufactured, and sold within a circular economy framework, consumers encourage your company to adjust your business operations accordingly.

Reduce: Use less for longer

Whether we're talking about reducing costs, reducing the quantity of a material, or reducing the negative environmental impact a material lifecycle has on the environment, the second R is focused on conservation. As the thought-leader of the business, you must develop simple strategies that reap a maximum reward. Using Lyft as an example, the ride-share program reduces not only the number of vehicles on the road but also the cost for an individual to get around by eliminating the need to purchase their own car. In addition, by setting the goal of utilizing 100 percent electric vehicles by 2030, Lyft has the potential to avoid tens of millions of metric tons of greenhouse emissions and to reduce gasoline consumption by more than a billion gallons over the next decade. Lastly, Lyft has developed a special program called LyftUp which utilizes an array of initiatives and products to drive change within underserved communities, such as connecting folks with the resources and health services they need through discounted or donated rides.

Reuse and remanufacture: Extend product life

Some products, like engines or cellphones, are often too complex for the entire product to be remanufactured after a single component fails; however, if designed properly from the beginning, new generations of these products can be crafted in a way to make them easily repairable. Furthermore, by identifying which components of these products tend to fail first, manufacturers can isolate those individual components in a way that makes them easily replaceable. By doing so, the owner holds more power to repair products they've already purchased rather than throw away a mostly functioning product just because a single component fails.

Repurpose: Find other uses

Sometimes products can serve purposes you never imagined they could. The idea of repurposing a waste source into a useful one takes creativity and can often result in a revolutionary outcome. Take Toasted Ale Brewery, for example. To help with the food waste crisis in the United States, the brewery partners with bakeries to repurpose excess bread to become an ingredient in its beer products. Surplus bread makes up a large percentage of food waste, so the creative thinkers at Toasted Ale found a way to repurpose what would have been wasted material to create a new product. Since its inception, Toasted Ale Brewery has repurposed hundreds of thousands of pieces of bread and helped reduce food waste during the process.

Recycle: Return materials for rebirth

Recycling acts as the end of the line — the last resort — of the technical material lifecycle. After technical products can no longer be utilized, their individual components are disassembled and the raw materials recycled to create new products. Timberland Shoes has harnessed the value of recycled products by incorporating recycled rubber sourced from tires into the soles of their shoes and boots. By doing so, Timberland has helped to extend the life of this raw material and has diverted massive amounts of waste from landfills at the same time.

Rot: Return it to the soil

Just as recycling acts as the end of the line for technical materials, rotting (or, to put it more delicately, "returning materials to the soil") is the end of the line for biological materials. If you consider the two concepts — recycling and rotting — one and the same for two different types of materials, you can see that the process and benefits are similar. The purpose of recycling is to break down a technical material into a form that can be reintroduced to the global economy so that a new material lifecycle can start. The same is true for biological materials when they're allowed to rot. By returning biological materials to the soil, you're breaking down a material into a form that can be reintroduced to the global economy, thus starting a new material lifecycle. The value of any product made of biological materials — such as wood, cotton, or vegetables — can be harnessed and reinvested in the natural landscape to produce further resources. A good example of this concept in action is the common, mutually beneficial relationship that has sprung up between brewers and farmers. Quite often, spent grain from the brewery process — in addition to the food waste from the restaurant portion of breweries — is sold (or often given away) to farmers. Farmers then utilize this spent grain as feed for their livestock. After the livestock is able to extract any remaining nutrients from this pulp, the remains are returned to the soil. Rather than simply send the spent grain to the landfill, this partnership between brewers and farmers allows tons of waste to be diverted from landfills while also feeding livestock and regenerating soils. (For more details on the differences between the technical and biological material lifecycles, see Chapter 10.)

Developing a Circular Business Structure: The Bones of the Operation

The way a business is structured can determine whether it will be successful, which is why you must take the time to explore the essential elements of crafting a circular business model. From identifying material lifecycles and alternative business models to engaging employees in the process, developing your business's message, and continuously improving on your process, these five steps (shown in Figure 7-2) can assist you in not only generating your business structure but also adapting your existing one. Read on to get started!

1.	2.	3.	4.	5.
Identify potential material loops	Consider innovative business models	Involve employees and other stakeholders	Develop a message	Test, learn, and improve
Inventory the material flows in your organization and identify how they can be optimized.	Understand the user's need and consider developing a new business model to satisfy these needs, while creating added value and saving resources.	Brainstorm with your employees, establish partnership with the local community, commit clients, etc.	Create a narrative for your circular economy strategy to engage more stakeholders.	Research, benchmark, and design, the measure impacts and collect feedback to improve.

FIGURE 7-2:
The five steps to crafting a circular business model.

Identifying potential material loops

Everyone has heard the popular phrase "What gets measured gets managed," and there's a darned good reason for it: It's absolutely, positively, 100 percent true. Before you can improve your material or product resource efficiency, you must first identify which resources your institution uses and then determine how they are used and how their use can be reduced in a cost-effective manner. Doing so can often be easier said than done, which is why an array of tools is available to help. Lifecycle assessment (LCA) tools, for example, help to organize data to understand the lifecycle of a product or material and then pinpoint specific areas that have excess waste and could benefit from material loops. Exploring your material flows through LCA analysis software can help with these tasks:

>> Diagramming your company's flow of materials

>> Incorporating up-to-date material metrics and data from source to recovery

>> Identifying optimal flows of material that harness the value of conservation and efficiency

Considering innovative business models

We talk about traditional business models in Chapter 6, but it pays to revisit the topic, to look at ways to repurpose them for a circular economy:

>> **Circular supplies:** These products have the potential to produce no waste and no harm to the environment. Clearly, circular supplies lend themselves to a business model that uses circular methodologies. The business of circular supplies is especially important for those companies that deal with scarce resources, such as water, energy, or food. Although these markets make up some of the largest markets in the economy, the circular supply industry is certainly not limited to those specific markets. Scarcity is a sign of value in the business world — it's what makes diamonds and other jewels valuable. When supply is low, the cost is high. To achieve a future built upon circular supplies, the global economy must replace traditional material inputs with bio-based, renewable and/or recovered materials, reducing the demand for virgin resources extraction in the long run.

>> **Resource recovery:** Companies interested in utilizing the circular economy to practice resource recovery are focused on harnessing the value of materials that would otherwise be wasted. These companies can leverage a wide range of software and technology to eliminate material waste and maximize the value derived from these materials. As a real-world example of recovering a lost resource, Walt Disney World Resorts recognized the opportunity that was missed by sending their food waste to the landfill instead of recovering the innate value of that material. Understanding the opportunity at hand, the organization diverted its food waste to an anaerobic digestion system, which utilizes anaerobic bacteria to digest the food waste and produce natural gas to generate electricity.

>> **Product life extension:** Companies driven toward product life-extension services focus exclusively on extending the life of products for their customers. Doing so minimizes replacement costs and ensures that expensive products remain financially beneficial. If this business opportunity didn't exist, these products and materials would be sent to the landfill. Instead, thanks to companies that offer product life extension as a service, the lifecycle of these products and materials is extended by way of remanufacturing and repairing efforts. As an example, Caterpillar — the company that provides an array of construction-related, heavy machinery — has developed their own program aimed at minimizing waste and overall costs to the user. The Cat Reman program incorporates remanufacturing and repair as a strategy to provide "same as new" machinery to their customers at a fraction of the price.

>> **Sharing platforms:** This business model relies on the idea that not everyone needs to own their <insert product here>, especially if that product typically has an extremely low or inconsistent rate of use. By maximizing the time of use these low-use products have, companies that leverage the sharing-platform business model are able to create additional value by maximizing usage. Some of the most widely known businesses that have applied the sharing-platform business model are Uber, Lyft, and Airbnb. Each of these companies identified products that hold an opportunity to be shared by a collective rather than by an individual.

>> **Products as a Service (PaaS):** Companies that choose to follow the Product as a Service business model provide what is typically a costly product via a leasing program or a pay-to-use program rather than a purchase-to-own arrangement. Doing so places the responsibility of the total lifecycle costs of these products — including installation, maintenance, and replacement — on the company rather than on the owner. A good example is a power purchase agreement, or PPA. When agreeing to participate in a PPA, a utility company installs renewable energy systems — typically, solar panels — on private property and maintains those panels as long as the owner of that property agrees to purchase from the utility the energy that's sourced from these systems. Because an entire solar panel array is often too expensive for individual companies or families to want to invest in, it makes more sense for the utility companies to offer businesses and individuals this Product as a Service opportunity instead.

Who's at the table? Engaging your stakeholders

Whether you're starting a circular business from scratch or adjusting an existing business structure, successfully implementing a circular business model requires participation at all levels. Simply stated, change can't happen with a single individual — it requires input from all stakeholders. With this premise, it's important to ensure not only that proper avenues are available for employees and other stakeholders to express their ideas on opportunities for improvement but also that systems are in place to incorporate those strategies in ways that allow them to function in a circular manner.

Getting stakeholders involved unlocks the creative spirit of those involved in <insert your business activities here>, but it also makes people want to work with and for you. Although it's quite simple to persuade people to share their ideas — via face-to-face discussions or surveys, for example — it's much more difficult to identify how these suggestions fit into your overall company structure and how they will be properly implemented. Potential solutions may come from other stakeholders, which is why it's critical to allow opportunities for stakeholder engagement. This can take place as part of a regular discussion forum or a project kickoff meeting.

REMEMBER

Aside from internal influences — from staff and other members of your organization — successfully implementing a circular business structure also calls for the participation of those from outside your organization. These outside stakeholders may consist of the general public, government officials, city managers, nonprofit organizations, or other business owners. Regardless of who they are, get them involved and provide the opportunity for collaboration.

Developing a message

According to the Ellen MacArthur Foundation, in order to attract interest in your company's circular products or services from potential partners and customers, you simply must establish a story around your business and explain how it connects with larger circular economy initiatives. (See Figure 7-3.) Although theoretical stories about the value of your business's products or services is a good start, you should highlight real-world benefits and examples of your circular economy platform in practice. This strategy allows the stakeholder audience to connect with your mission, and, because it's a real-life example, it can be supported by an array of support data, making it easy for potential partners to imagine the potential value you could provide to their organization.

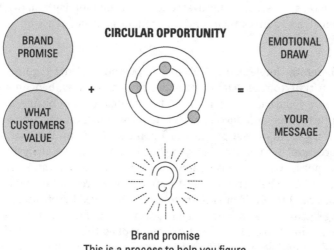

FIGURE 7-3:
Telling your
brand's story.

Brand promise
This is a process to help you figure
out how your circular opportunity reinforces
your brand value.

Although a story paired with graphics can attract the interest of individuals in your circular economy business venture, it isn't enough to capture a wide audience. To reflect the true nature of the circular economy — a strategy built on the platform of collaboration — your message to the stakeholder group should work on multiple levels and reference the array of partnerships incorporated into your business model. To further support your overall message to your potential customer, be sure to also incorporate opportunities for education about the circular economy into your stories or business performance.

TIP

To support your company's narrative development, the Ellen MacArthur Foundation provides a free Brand Promise tool on its website. Check it out:

`www.ellenmacarthurfoundation.org/assets/design/Brand_promise_Final.pdf`

This exercise is useful for businesses that want to identify their brand promise, their customers' values, and the opportunities provided within a circular economy framework to generate the needed emotional response from your customers. Once these items have been addressed, the business can discover the message for your company.

Benchmarking and improvement

Here's a trippy thought for you: Translating a linear business model to a circular one is in fact not a linear process. (*Inception*, anyone?) Instead, this transition and growth into a circular way of business is inextricably tied to ongoing research, failure, success, and improvement. This transition isn't an overnight process, but is instead an investment of days or months, if not years, to get the wheels spinning smoothly.

Therefore, implementing a circular business model requires an investment of your time to research potential business structures, benchmarks, and strategies before you decide to press Play. This testing phase of business development reaps both failures and successes; the failures, however, also prove valuable to your development of best practices, so don't avoid them! Whether your strategies are successful or fail miserably, you should allow time for analysis following the testing phase. Why did this strategy work, or why did this strategy fail? How can this information help craft my next initiative as a circular business owner? What feedback can I receive from the stakeholders involved in this process to aid in improving business operations? This process is circular in nature: It takes the lessons learned at the end of a venture and applies them to new ones. This continuous loop of operations and improvement — which is the secret weapon to circular business model success — is never fully complete: There are always lessons to be learned and new ideas to be tested.

Figure 7-4 shows a helpful checklist you can use to walk through some key questions within all five categories described in this chapter: identifying potential material loops, considering innovative business models, engaging stakeholders, developing a message, and benchmarking and improvement.

Identify potential material loops	YES	NO
Do I know exactly which resources my organization is using?	☐	☐
Can I reduce my resource consumption?	☐	☐
Can I find ways to make better use of them, through recovery, reuse, refurbishment or recycling? In other words, can I create more material loops in my organization and beyond?	☐	☐
Have I considered the entire lifecycle of my products or services, to optimise resource and eliminate waste through the whole value chain?	☐	☐
Can I optimize my resource consumption with other partners?	☐	☐
Can I make use of other organizations by-products or waste or trade the ones I have?	☐	☐

Consider innovative business models		
Have I identified which service my product or service is providing for its users?	☐	☐
Could I provide the same service while increasing my resource efficiency, for example through a new business model such as leasing?	☐	☐
Could I partner with other organizations to test a new business model?	☐	☐
Is there any support available in my region?	☐	☐

Involve employees and other stakeholders		
Have I put in place processes to involve my employees?	☐	☐
Does my organization provide the right environment for idea generation?	☐	☐
Can I involve other stakeholders in my circular economy strategy?	☐	☐

Davelop a message		
Have I defined my value proposition?	☐	☐
Can I effectively communicate to my stakeholders how it fits into a circular economy?	☐	☐
Have I identified innovative ways to share my story with them?	☐	☐

Test, learn and improve		
Have I identified new ways to improve my resource efficiency?	☐	☐
Can I test my ideas in real conditions and with my partners?	☐	☐
Have I implemented processes to collect feedback?	☐	☐

FIGURE 7-4: Making a list and checking it twice.

CAROLYN BUTLER SPEAKS

As chief executive officer of Borobabi, a company committed to selling sustainable, ethically made children's clothing, Carolyn Butler has some definite ideas regarding the circular economy. Here are a few:

In theory, a circular business model mimics nature's genius: a whole system model that creates prosperity while still maintaining the delicate balance between using earth's resources, and regenerating more of those resources. The idea is a drastic shift from the take-make-waste linear system that humans have become so

(continued)

(continued)

accustomed to since the industrial era. As we reach the limits of our natural resources and the pollutive load our planet can handle, many people are realizing that something must change — but what, and how?

Circular-ish

To be circular means to design with the entire ecosystem in mind. Today, very few companies control the entire value chain of their product or service. Mostly, they look to optimize their piece of the puzzle and often fall woefully short of achieving true circularity. The Ellen MacArthur Foundation has done much to define the pillars of the circular economy. Simply put, circular economies regenerate natural systems, utilize products to their fullest potential, and eliminate waste.

The sustainable commerce trend today is to pick one pillar and to optimize it in a company silo, without much regard to its effects upstream or downstream of the value chain. One example of this model would be a company that recycles single use plastics into products that cannot be further reused or recycled again. Additionally, there are large investments into recycling technologies without investigating materials that don't generate waste in the first place. These companies are circular-ish, at best. Although not truly circular, perhaps these companies are a required stepping-stone in the transition from linear to circular business models.

Many established industries cannot easily pivot their entrenched linear business model to a circular one for a multitude of reasons. Existing capital infrastructure, long term supply contracts, and shareholder expectations of profitability are major barriers to corporate circularity.

Circular Business Model By Design

New companies have a unique opportunity to optimize all pillars of the circular economy and create more profitable, sustainable business models. Circularity needs a holistic approach — it starts with design, and it often means going back to the drawing board to rethink the entire system.

Let's use the practical example of the fashion industry — an almost $2 billion global industry fraught with pollution, waste, overconsumption, and exploitation.

Borobabi, an American circular retailer, looks to reimagine fashion from the ground up. Laser focused on maternity and young children's wear due to the short periods of hyper-growth during childhood and massive underuse of clothing, Borobabi optimizes all parts of the value chain to benefit people, planet and business.

Regenerating Natural Systems

Borobabi only partners with ethical and sustainable brands that pay their workers a living wage. They meticulously source clothing made from natural fibers because — unlike synthetics — they are renewable. The goal is fiber sourced exclusively from organic and regenerative farms, where no pesticides are used, animals are treated fairly, carbon capture techniques are utilized, and farmland is preserved. Certifications like GOTS and OEKO-Tex ensure customers zero use of non-hazardous chemicals during growing and processing. This guarantee is safer for workers and the environment, and also safer for young, developing bodies.

Upcycling to Utilize Products Fully

Borobabi offers two ways to get the most out of garments. Customers rent or purchase clothing, but what's innovative about the e-commerce platform is their incentive for customers to return these garments forever called "lifetime return." The company promises to manage the cleaning and repair of all of their garments, extending their useful life as much as possible. These customer incentives create the opportunity no other retailer offers: the management of products when they've been fully used by their first owner. Borobabi believes that companies should take more responsibility for the items they introduce into the market, and through their platform they are able shift the responsibility of dealing with outgrown clothing from the consumer back to Borobabi.

Eliminating Waste

It's imperative Borobabi collects all of their used clothing so that they can manage to responsibly recycle them. The loop is closed at this stage, and the sourcing of the materials comes back into play. Borobabi's original choice to source natural and organic mono materials means they can be easily disassembled and recycled back into fiber for new materials. The original focus on non-toxic chemicals made composting an additional option as well, thus diverting the harms of landfilling, where most post-consumer clothing ends up.

IN THIS CHAPTER

» Investigating material lifecycle
performance

» Exploring how to make material
lifecycles smarter

» Identifying the basics of creating
circular products

Chapter **8**

'Round and 'Round: Making Your Products Circular

M anaging industry's material lifecycle performance is the pathway on which the global economy can transition from a linear way of operation to a circular one. Assessing and improving the sourcing, manufacturing, distribution, usage, and end-of-life management of the products that people rely on is the only way to make the circular economy a reality. For the longest time, initial cost optimization has been the driving force behind the global markets that people depend on today. Unfortunately, this linear way of managing resources isn't sustainable and must be drastically changed to support later generations.

How can material lifecycles be improved? Generating products that are designed for reuse, remanufacturing, and recycling eliminates much of the waste and pollution that stems from raw material extraction and the disposal of waste after a product has been used. The materials and products people rely on can become circular by creating effective and serviceable products rather than cheap, ineffective products that are designed to fail. On top of it all, incorporating flexibility into operations by accepting change as an inevitable component of the future allows material lifecycles to evolve as technology and material science do.

Responding to change and ushering in a circular economy is made much easier by collaboration and partnerships. For everything to come together, the transition from linear to circular needs to start accepting the very costs that have forever been delayed for future generations to deal with. The improvements required to create a circular economy can be more easily implemented by increasing lifecycle transparency and harnessing the power of collective impact.

Managing Material Lifecycle Performance

Sustainable materials management focuses on the activities tied to optimizing a product's lifecycle. It also represents a shift in how lifecycles are managed and how to account for *all* costs tied to a product's lifecycle — not just first costs. By analyzing all components of a material's lifecycle, those involved in creating the global networks that support human demand can discover opportunities to not only utilize natural resources in a way that encourages minimal raw material extraction but also provides opportunities to regenerate *natural capital* and ensure that meeting the needs of the current generation can be done in a way to make it easier for future generations to fulfill those same needs. Natural capital is the collection of natural resources that the human race depends on and are quite often free to the public, such as soils, air, water and living organisms.

The demand for resources and the negative impacts of our industrialized society on the environment will continue to grow with the global population. The tension between countries with and without global influence — both politically and economically —will also grow as resources become less available and economies begin to adjust in response. The efficient use of existing materials paired with a reduced negative impact on the environment can help ensure that conflicts tied to resource availability don't escalate and provide people with a future full of abundance and resourcefulness. Materials are tied to costs at every stage of their life, whether that stage is tied to material extraction, manufacturing processes, distribution, use, and/or end-of-life management. However, by understanding that a material's lifecycle doesn't need to end at the end-of-life management stage and can instead be circulated back to the usage stage, the costs tied to material extraction, manufacturing, and distribution can be mostly avoided.

How can companies, institutions, and governments be certain that any adjustment to the material lifecycle will prove to be beneficial? It's true that creating a product that can be reused will eliminate costs associated with the development of replacement materials, but who is to say that the costs of maintenance and repair of a reusable material or product won't result in even more costs? To explore the resulting costs of different lifecycle designs, lifecycle assessments act as a useful tool. These assessments take into account many costs that have historically been ignored in the business world. Now the costs of energy use, material processing, research-and-development, and air, water, and soil pollution can all be incorporated into lifecycle assessments to determine the ultimate route moving forward.

Designing products for reuse

Designing products for human use will always require a sourcing of raw materials. In addition, it has always been accepted that waste was a necessary element of product lifecycles and was required in order to fuel demand within the global economy. By accepting this (false) assumption, businesses and manufacturers have focused only on the first costs of material lifecycles. "How much will it cost us right now?" is always asked, though the question "How much will it cost us ten years from now?" is never posed.

With the understanding that waste is a natural part of business, many plastic products have been designed to be single-use and disposable because the raw material input costs are so incredibly low. This has resulted in low-quality products made from low-quality materials that lack the built-in potential for reuse. Through a business lens, having the potential for reuse means that a product isn't designed to be single-use or disposable and therefore isn't made of materials that facilitate the false assumption that waste is inevitable and products should not hold the potential to be reused. Incorporating durability and resiliency into products facilitates their potential to be reusable, but may come at a higher first cost.

Though designing reusable products may be contradictory to common business practices — how can companies continue obtaining revenue if they're selling fewer products? — there is an opportunity for business within a reuse culture. The idea here is not to sell more and more products every year, but rather to offer maintenance and repair services to customers who have purchased your products. For many global enterprises, their annual success depends on the answers to these two questions:

>> Were more products made and sold than the year before?

>> Was more money made than the year before?

Within a linear economy, making and selling more is the only way to make more money. However, within a global, circular economy, more money could actually be made by making and selling fewer products and by selling maintenance and repair services instead.

Designing products to be remanufactured

Remanufacturing is truly amazing — we want to start this section by stressing that fact. Remanufacturing includes the recapture, disassembly, assessment, repair, and reassembly of products to create a new product out of reused — yet still functional — components. The fact is, many components of a broken product are still functional and therefore can still be used after a product stops working. (This is, in fact, the main reason that remanufacturing is such a valuable strategy behind the circular economy.) Take a simple item, like a bicycle. The premise behind remanufacturing is that even if the tire of your bicycle pops and is no longer functional, there's no reason the value that remains in the rest of the bicycle should be neglected. Nor does it make sense to throw away an entire bicycle because the tire went flat. Remanufacturing understands that the handlebars, the gears, the seat, and even the other tire that didn't pop still hold value and can be remanufactured by simply replacing the faulty tire with a functional one.

The assumption that the time and effort involved in the remanufacturing of products is less valuable than the disposal of a broken product and the creation of a new one from raw materials could not be more mistaken. As absurd as it seems, that's the only explanation for remanufacturing not holding more weight within the global market. Everyone can agree that it would take less time to disassemble a bicycle, assess the pieces, repair or replace whatever item is faulty, and then reassemble the bicycle than it would be to extract all the necessary raw materials to build a new bike from scratch.

Remanufacturing products removes the faulty components and keeps the functioning components in use for longer periods. Doing so eliminates the demand for raw material extraction and removes the need for the environmental destruction associated with raw material extraction. In addition, it increases the value of the components left in use by increasing their total lifecycle and rate of use. Lastly, remanufacturing reduces the creation of waste and pollution and allows for natural systems to regenerate themselves.

Designing products for recycling

Making products that are fully recyclable isn't possible. There is always waste of some sort in the form of energy, water, or materials. However, we can still attain a circular economy even if some waste exists, by allowing the rate of environmental regeneration to surpass the rate of waste generation. This is why delaying waste as long as possible by facilitating products that can be reused and remanufactured is critical.

Only when products have been reused to maximum capacity and have been remanufactured as many times as possible should the components and materials of a product be directed toward recycling. Recycling, within the flow of technical materials, should be seen as the last resort. When Apple iPhones can no longer be reused or remanufactured, Daisy, Apple's newest disassembly robot, is responsible for disassembling the products and extracting the various elements that make up an iPhone. Daisy is able to disassemble roughly 200 iPhones per hour and recapture a number of valuable materials that were commonly disposed of — cobalt, for example.

REMEMBER

Some products can be recycled, and others cannot, which is why material selection is also an extremely critical decision in determining the future fate of a material or product. If you're using materials that cannot be recycled, you're building the potential for waste into the product design itself.

Even plastics can be recycled, but only a certain number of times before the quality of the plastic reaches a point where virgin material will need to replace the plastic that can no longer be recycled. Though plastic is recyclable, the use of plastic only further delays the creation of waste — it doesn't eliminate it. To fully realize a circular economy, plastics will need to be replaced with material science innovations. Until then, the global economy needs to prioritize the use of materials that can be fully recycled over millions of lifecycle generations, such as glass and metal, and the use of materials that can be fully composed to fuel the growth of new materials, like hemp and other biomaterials.

Making Your Product Lifecycle Smarter

Product lifecycle management is the process of making your product lifecycle smarter. Unlike the way lifecycle management has historically been tackled — by relying first on cost minimization as a priority — the circular economy relies on total lifecycle improvement. The management of the product's lifecycle should be driven by optimization, not by first costs. The global economy wouldn't be as wasteful as it is today if total lifecycle costs were considered.

Historically, prioritizing first costs meant designing for *manufacturability* — in other words, designing products at the lowest possible initial cost, optimizing the process to eliminate excess, and selling the product to obtain the highest possible revenue. Designing in planned obsolescence was also commonly built-in so that customers would be forced to eventually circle back to buy another product from the manufacturers. This process not only encouraged environment degeneration via raw material extraction but also relied on waste as a means to fuel demand. This isn't how you make your product lifecycle smarter.

Within a circular approach to product lifecycle management, you consider the total cost within a product's lifecycle, not just the costs associated with the manufacturing. To make your product lifecycle smarter, you must make your product designs and process smarter by creating effective and serviceable products, adopting flexibility, and seeking collaborators who are willing to shape the future with you.

Creating effective and serviceable products

The best way to make your product lifecycle smarter is to ensure that the product does the job it says it will do. Ensuring that the products you develop are effective reduces the need to replace that product with other products that claim to serve the same purpose. You probably have someone in your life who has the "trusty" version of some tool — a hammer, a car, a spatula — whatever it might be. That's because it does the job well, and therefore the owner of that product has kept it around because of its effectiveness.

Another way to make your product lifecycle smarter is to design the product to be serviceable. Many products in use today cannot be repaired if even a single component breaks. If that trusty hammer wasn't designed to be serviceable, it needs to be thrown away after the handle breaks, even if the head of the hammer is still in working order.

Maintaining the durability and resiliency of a product by making it effective isn't a blow to business — rather, it's an opportunity for new types of business centered around servicing. Products that are designed to be repaired create an entirely new market focused on serviceability, repair, and customization.

Being flexible

Change is inevitable, and it should be embraced as a reality of the future. With that, customer demands will change, material science will innovate, the properties of materials will change, governing bodies will create stricter standards, and your business operation requirements will change. Accepting change as a part of growth, rather than as a roadblock to success, will make the transition toward a circular economy much easier.

As new forms of technology and innovation continue to emerge around the globe, the way products are made, used, and managed will also change. Historically, bridges would be built by hand by a number of masons over the period of weeks, months, or years. Now, as digital fabrication capabilities are emerging, businesses such as Autodesk are remaining flexible and adjusting their business practices to embrace these emerging capabilities. A Dutch company, MX3D (https://mx3d.com), is partnering with Autodesk (www.autodesk.com), a major developer of engineering and construction software, to print metal bridges in 3D. This technology and the application of 3D printing technology are growing around the world and will surely become the new way of constructing structures. If companies like Autodesk didn't remain flexible to the changing world around them, they would be left in the dust and replaced with emerging companies that are flexible. This new style of bridge-building has been made possible by flexibility, but also by finding the right partners.

Seeking collaborators and partners

Transitioning from a linear economy to a circular economy will require higher levels of collaboration and partnership than what is typically seen within a business market. Typically, a company offers a product or service as is — the product is the same regardless of who the customer is. This strategy works well within a linear economy, but needs to change within a circular economy.

No longer will products be designed within a closed box, with one designer in charge. Instead, cross-collaboration between different stakeholders will need to become the new business-as-usual. Business development managers will need to collaborate with material reclamation teams to minimize the amount of raw material required. Maintenance professionals will need to coordinate with material science engineers and product assembly strategy teams to ensure that the repairability of products is maximized. The future of the global economy is reliant on integrative processes and cross-collaboration.

REMEMBER

Within a circular economy, businesses can still offer products and services as is, but they also need to collaborate and partner with other businesses and customers to ensure that their products are capable of being reused, repaired, and refurbished. They need to collaborate and partner with customers to find appropriate ways to replace products that have broken, that no longer provide the service the customer required, or that are no longer satisfying the customer's needs. As the market transitions from a linear economy to a circular economy, marketing teams, sales teams, distribution networks, business managers, customers, resale agents, maintenance managers, and every other member of the lifecycle chain will need to continuously collaborate and partner with each other to ensure that they're able to make a successful transition to a circular economy.

How It All Comes Together

Everything is circular first, and this is represented in all forms of a product's lifecycle — design, material sourcing, manufacturing delivery, use and reuse, and recycling. Materials that can't be fully recycled at the end of their useful life must be immediately removed from the global economy, regardless of the environmental impact that stems from the alternative. Perpetually relying on nonrecyclable items as a means to minimize negative economic, social, and environmental impact is a similar strategy to covering a stab wound with a Band-Aid: In the short term, it's helpful to stop the bleeding, but in the long term, the stab wound still needs fixing.

In a circular economy, everything is transparent as a means of providing more opportunities for improvement. A prime example of how transparency can fuel innovation is the open source network. Everything is made public and available within an open source network, which allows for more innovators to spend more hours on improving whatever process is being addressed. These results are then also made open to the public so that more innovation can take place. Transparency is the leading strategy behind advanced innovation.

Everything is circular first

To properly transition from a linear economy to a circular economy, rule 1, Everything Is Circular First, needs to take effect immediately. What does this mean? Well, it means that humans can no longer ignore the future costs associated with the poor material selections happening today. These days, the rationale behind many material selections focuses on minimizing first costs while also ignoring the secondary and tertiary costs associated with pollution, human health impacts, and environmental degeneration. We must no longer accept nonrecyclable or noncompostable materials and products within the global market, despite the impacts they have on first costs.

When selecting materials based on first costs alone, plastic can be framed as a better alternative to glass or metal. Although it's cheaper to make and transport products made from plastic than from glass, the fact that plastic can be recycled only half a dozen times before it erodes to the point that it can no longer be reused should deem it unusable. Coca-Cola switched from glass bottles to plastic bottles because glass bottles weighed more than plastic to ship. This additional weight meant extra fuel and distribution costs, and therefore more pollution emitted to the environment. This study was valuable in the sense of comparing the environmental impacts of two materials, but it failed to acknowledge the limited capacity for plastic to function as a material in the future. It ignored the fact that glass can be recycled millions of times and plastic cannot. The study results ignored the immense costs tied to regenerating the ecosystems that are destroyed by plastic pollution and the fact that oil isn't a renewable resource.

REMEMBER

When nonrecyclable materials and noncompostable materials are removed from the market, the demand for replacement materials will fuel the necessary innovation required to obtain them. The more pressure that is placed on a community to obtain a solution, the more likely they are to obtain that solution quickly. If there's no demand for an alternative solution, communities will continue to function under business-as-usual principles. Only when rule 1 (Everything Is Circular First) is adopted by the global economy will the world see a substantial and effective transition from linear to circular.

Everything is transparent

Today, consumers rarely insist on owning the products they use. Instead, customers are more interested in obtaining access to one product or another. With ownership comes the additional fees and efforts of repair, replacement, and troubleshooting, as indicated by the increased use of shared vehicles, machinery, and other daily-use items. In addition to this increased desire of access comes an increased desire for transparency of the products to which customers are requesting access — transparency of the business processes that produce the product, transparency of what materials were used, how they were sourced and processed, and what efforts are being made to improve upon the product's overall material lifecycle.

Since implementing the circular economy will require more collaborative environments between product lifecycle stakeholders — including customers — than was the case with the linear economy, product transparency at all levels is sure to become a critical component of a successful transition from the historical, degenerative, linear way of managing product lifecycles. Transparency of process alone builds credibility between all members involved in developing a product. Providing details tied to the environmental, social, and economic impact of product development, manufacturing, and use will allow for companies to successfully compete with their competitors to gain and retain a customer base.

Internally, transparency of process allows for opportunities for innovation and improvements to the process. Without seeing how the business works behind the curtains, employees who are closest to the process are unable to offer insight into potential improvements. By increasing transparency, innovations and improvements can stem from internal resources rather than from external consultants. Making the inner workings visible to all allows for adjustments to be made to materials sourcing, manufacturing processes management, shipment strategies, and much more.

Patagonia (www.patagonia.com) is leading the way in supply chain transparency. Though most companies would see supply chain transparency as a barrier, Patagonia sees it as an opportunity to acknowledge the downfalls of its supply chain management strategy and to improve on it by reducing the negative environmental or social impacts of its business activities. To reinforce this effort to make its supply chains transparent to staff and customers, the company launched its Footprint Chronicles initiative, a series of online videos that reveal details about Patagonia's supply chains.

A customer who is viewing an article of clothing on the Patagonia website can also access the associated Footprint Chronicles video. By reviewing these videos, the customer gains a better sense of each step in the product's supply chain — where the materials come from, how they're processed, and how they're created, for example. Patagonia doesn't show only the good side of its process, either. If an element of the supply chain is unfavorable, Patagonia shows that too, and encourages customers to collaborate to come up with a better solution. By embracing transparency, Patagonia is empowering not only its own employees to take ownership of the process but also its customers to take ownership as well and help the company improve its process to provide better products to the market. This is a prime example of how everything — transparency, collaboration, and circular processes — comes together.

JULIA FARBER SPEAKS

Julia Farber, noted sustainability expert, wants to share some words of wisdom with you:

Dear Intrepid Circular Economist,

As you embark on your journey to embed circular economy principles into your organization, you'll absolutely need to present your case and gain supporters. To do so, might I make a few suggestions: present the circular economy in a way that makes it adaptable to your industry and your organization's culture, make a plan that reflects your needs, and establish your progress markers to reflect the goals achieved overtime.

Typically, new ideas have to arrive in familiar packages for lasting adoption. This is standard practice; other organizations do the same. How do I know? Throughout my career, I've worked in collaboration with or directly for many Fortune 500 companies that are committed to embedding various concepts of sustainability, including the circular economy, into their design and manufacturing approach. From tech to consumer goods to building products, each manufacturer puts its own stamp on new ideas that come through the door.

The circular economy approach is no different. For example, at the organization where I currently work, our circular economy program has a name that mimics other well-known programs that have been adopted internally. This rebranding helps ensure endorsement of the program. Our program name is focused on eco-design, which is one of a handful of core concepts within the circular economy. Not all names will use the words circular economy when starting out. Some organizations do. Some use eco-design or may focus on regenerative approaches, or extended producer responsibility, or perhaps it will be a concept used by the design team as part of your broader sustainability efforts. There are many acceptable names for these programs, so long as they are focused on improving efficiencies, eliminating waste and hazardous materials, and extending the original life of the product, they fall under the circular economy.

What else do they have in common? Generally, all well-run organizations have some form of stage-gating intended to assist with sifting through new products and services. Business ideas with the strongest muster are then piloted before it is determined if or when to roll them out more broadly. Several manufacturers have embedded circular economy or eco-design methodology into the product design workflow. At my current employer, this program is designed to scale up through our engineering teams, while our product designers, purchasing teams, sales and marketing teams, and others are trained on our new approach. Our product engineers have already redesigned over a dozen core products, and are on track to complete dozens more redesigns in the years to come. We also have targets at the corporate level that we must meet as part of our commitments to our stakeholders more broadly. By aligning our program into our broader global strategy, the leadership makes clear what success looks like and provides accountability. Many leading organizations are excellent at defining goals, major milestones, and reporting on outcomes of their programs. These tried-and-trusted methods can be repurposed for this type of program too. Once you've defined the goals, and get buy-in from your champions, it's time to experiment.

Fortunately, a concept like the circular economy is extremely malleable to the organization itself. The circular economy principles provide the fodder to create all kinds of new ideas. By breaking down a products' purpose to its core, you can uncover the true needs of your users. Then, as you proceed, consider all the ways you can make the product and its elements last. What aspects of modularity can be built in? What can you recover? What other services can be offered? What new sales channels can you tap into? What core materials and elements have to stay before you compromise your product's safety or durability? At what point will this product not meet the standard required to sell it to the market? At what point have you invented a new category that requires new standards and certifications? The possibilities and linkages between one supply chain and another have yet to be tapped. If your design team is feeling stuck, introduce them to this concept. Once the design teams have some good ideas flowing, set some targets and goals, and see what they can do. Position it as a challenge at first internally. Incentivize those who can think up the best ideas. Align the goals with your broader mission, and assuming you have one, your corporate social responsibility or sustainability plans.

(continued)

(continued)

As you explore what works for your organization, develop external partnerships. Right now many organizations are seeking to learn from one another. You could join a pre-competitive initiative, or follow the conversations that are now ongoing about what it really means to be circular and how can we measure progress? There are standards in development right now, and there will always be pathways to get engaged in those conversations at the industry, national, and international level. Visit the UL, ANSI, or ISO websites for more. The Ellen MacArthur Foundation and the Cradle to Cradle Institute are also excellent sources for more information.

To recap: The circular economy concept is a big call to action to redesign the products and services we use every day. Organizations of all sizes will benefit from understanding the idea, and how it can help tap into or invent new markets. But bringing it into an organization requires familiarity. Pitch it the same way you would pitch other process or design changes. Ask for funds to start a pilot. Get a champion on your side. Create a catchy name that reflects your organization and your needs. Design your goals to match your mission, track your progress and report out. The circular economy might be complicated, but your roll out can be simple. Good luck! We can do this.

Chapter **9**

From Trash to Treasure: Converting Waste into Products

As the old saying goes, "One man's trash is another man's treasure." This isn't true just for antiques — it also refers to sustainability and the circular economy.

In a circular economy, materials that would normally be thrown away and end up in a landfill can instead be reinvented and remade into new, useful products.

Not all waste is truly garbage. A lot of stuff is treated that way because it doesn't fit specific standards or is part of the process of making something else, such as fruit peels and seeds discarded during the process of making fruit juice. Just because something is the unintended consequence of another process doesn't mean that it needs to end up in a landfill. You can find a new path for waste (other than the landfill route you may already be familiar with) in one of these three main ways:

>> *Reducing* the amount of waste produced at the source and across supply chains is the key to diverting waste from landfills. Regulatory policies that put a price on waste or ban single-use items, as well as increased efficiency and optimizing recovery during the manufacturing process, help reduce the production of waste.

>> *Reusing* waste, whether it's reincorporating old product components and unused materials back into the manufacturing process or finding a new way to repurpose and sell it, also keeps waste in the loop.

>> *Recycling*, which is a topic that everyone is likely familiar with, allows people to convert specific materials — like plastics, glass, metals, and papers — into reusable materials.

We intentionally placed the three Rs — reduce, reuse, and recycle — in order of importance in this list because reducing consumption is the most important approach to reducing your overall environmental and societal impact. Reusing an item requires significantly less energy than recycling and retains more value than when a product is broken down into its components. In this chapter, we discuss ways that you can make money from reducing and reusing waste.

Seeing Why the Circular Economy Is All About Retaining Value

Throughout this book, we discuss many of the benefits of making a business more circular. One clear way you can obtain more value from a circular business strategy is by reducing and repurposing waste. By assessing where the most waste is produced in the creation of a product, businesses can understand how to restructure processes that produce the most waste, or they can make use of the waste in other ways. Identifying major waste streams or byproducts allows companies to find new ways to close their production loop and use materials that would normally be discarded.

REMEMBER

Byproducts are unintended materials, made during the manufacturing process, that can be sold as new-and-different products. Straw, for example, is a byproduct of grain production that can then be used for various products, such as livestock bedding, animal feed, or basket-making.

You can retain value from managing waste in one of two major ways:

>> **Simply reduce the amount of waste generated during manufacture.** This strategy offers several clear cost savings, including conserving energy, reducing reliance on virgin material procurement, increasing supply chain efficiency, and reducing waste management costs. In other words, better management of waste allows businesses to save resources and cut costs, all while maintaining their routine levels of production. This can be done by conducting waste assessments and audits, improving storage and inventory management, reducing packaging material, and updating old, inefficient infrastructure. Enhanced resource recovery by using more advanced processes also enables manufacturers to capture more materials throughout the production cycle.

>> **Come up with creative ways to use (or reuse) waste and byproducts.** If reducing waste isn't an option, byproducts and other outputs can also be reincorporated into the manufacturing process, designed into new and similar products, or sold as entirely different materials to external vendors. Because natural resources fluctuate in price and have to be shipped long distances, buying raw materials is a huge liability for companies. Finding ways to reduce reliance on such materials by reincorporating processed materials or byproducts into manufactured goods can greatly improve a company's success.

In this chapter, we focus on the second way of retaining worth, and give you some useful examples of companies that are transforming waste into profit. Keep reading to see more about how you as an individual or a profit-making business can retain value from waste.

COMPANIES THAT CONVERT TRASH INTO TREASURE

We humans produce so much waste that it makes sense that companies would see it as an opportunity to use a cheap, abundant resource to make new products. Here's a partial list of our favorite amazing companies doing incredible things with waste to turn them into new products:

- **Adidas + Parley** created a line of running shoes made entirely of recycled ocean plastic. (www.parley.tv)

- **AeroAggregates** produces aggregates (used in concrete mixes) made from 100 percent post-consumer recycled glass. (https://aeroaggregates.com). (In this context, "post-consumer is just another way of saying "already used.")

(continued)

(continued)

- **Algalife** produces fabric fibers from algae. (www.alga-life.com)

- **Algramo** provides a reusable packaging system that customers refill with cleaning products to avoid single-use bottles. (https://algramo.us)

- **Aquazone** upcycles sewer wastewater and converts it into a nutrient-rich fertilizer for farming. (https://aquazone.fi) (Here, "upcycle" means "reusing to create a product of higher quality or value than the original.")

  Bionic produces yarn for clothing and bags by breaking down recycled ocean plastics and turning them into a weaveable clothing fiber called Bionic Yarn. (https://bionicyarn.com)

- **Borobabi** collects discarded maternity and children's wear and then repurposes and resells it. (www.borobabi.com)

- **Bureo** collects discarded fishing nets, from coastal communities in South America, that are then shredded, melted into recycled pellets, and made into new products. (https://bureo.co)

- **CleanFiber** manufactures building insulation made from natural cellulose without chemicals (instead of the typical coated fiberglass). (www.cleanfiber.com)

- **Eastman** turns waste plastics of all kinds back into new plastics, continuously, with no loss of quality. (www.eastman.com/pages/home.aspx)

- **Evrnu** is a fiber technology company that converts garment waste into new, high-quality fiber for the creation of new clothing, in partnership with brands and retailers. (https://evrnu.com)

- **Full Cycle** transforms organic waste into a compostable alternative to oil-based plastics. (https://fullcyclebioplastics.com)

- **Glavel** produces an alternative to gravel (used in slabs and foundations) that's thermally insulating and made from 100 percent post-consumer (already used) recycled glass. (www.glavel.com)

- **GreenMantra** converts post-consumer and post-industrial plastics such as bottles, plastic films and bags, yogurt cups, and other waste items into specialty polymer additives. (https://greenmantra.com) (In this context, "post-industrial" means "leftover from manufacturing.")

- **HomeBiogas** develops household- and community-size anaerobic digesters that convert food and biological waste into clean energy. (www.homebiogas.com)

- **IntegriCo** manufactures composite railroad ties made from recycled plastics. To date, it has diverted over 80 million pounds of plastics normally headed to the landfill. (www.integrico.com)

- **Levi's** collects old pairs of its popular jeans and, after repairing and cleaning them, produces them into a new line called Second Hand. (www.secondhand.levi.com)

- **Loliware** produces a seaweed-based, plastic-like material that biodegrades and can be used to replace single-use plastics. (www.loliware.com)

- **Looptworks** repurposes and upcycles abandoned, pre-consumer and post-consumer materials (such as discarded airplane seats and seat belts) and remakes them into beautiful new bags and accessories. (www.looptworks.com)

- **MethodHome** produces a line of its popular household-soaps packages in bottles made from recovered ocean plastic and post-consumer recycled plastic. (https://methodhome.com)

- **Newlight Technologies** produces a new type of plastic, called AirCarbon, that captures carbon dioxide from the atmosphere to make plastic — a carbon-negative alternative to plastics made from fossil fuels, in other words. (www.newlight.com)

- **Patagonia** takes back its outdoor wear and patches it up to resell and extend its useful life. (https://wornwear.patagonia.com)

- **Pentland Brands** produces new fabrics from recycled bottles and fishing nets recovered from the oceans. (https://pentlandbrands.com)

- **Preserve** recycles used yogurt containers and remakes them into new products, such as toothbrushes and containers. (www.preserve.eco)

- **G-STAR RAW for the Oceans** (by singer Pharrell Williams) is a clothing line that recovers plastic found on the shoreline and turns it into wearable fashion. (www.g-star.com/en_us)

- **The Renewal Workshop** partners with retailers and manufacturers to collect discarded clothing, which they clean, repair, and certify to be resold as preowned. (https://renewalworkshop.com)

- **Re-Nuble** is an agricultural technology company that converts food waste into industrial grade, water soluble, organic hydroponic nutrients for soilless farming. (www.re-nuble.com)

- **Salubata** produces modular shoes made from recycled goods. (https://salubataofficial.com) ("Modular" here means the shoes are put together from distinct parts.)

- **Steelcase** creates furniture using a closed-loop system of recycled textile waste that is turned into new materials. (www.steelcase.com)

- **Tarkett**'s Desso line of flooring is made from recyclable yarn and takes back discarded tiles for reuse. (www.desso-hospitality.com)

- **Timberland** partnered with a tire manufacturer to produce footwear soles made from recycled tires. (www.timberland.com/blog/archive/timberland-tires.html)

- **TOUS** has been in the jewelry business since 1920, giving pieces of jewelry a second life by restoring them to their former glory. (www.tous.com)

Stop Being Linear: It's a Waste of Time

We humans don't have the resources or the capacity to continue with our linear economy. The planet now has 7.8 billion people on it, with that number projected to reach 9.7 billion by 2050. In 2020 alone, we extracted almost 78 billion tons of resources from our planet's surface. If every human consumed as much as citizens of the United States do, we would need upward of four Planet Earths to sustain the population and absorb our waste. Every day that we continue with the business-as-usual approach to manufacturing and consumption, we waste more and more invaluable natural resources and make it harder for the earth to rebound from our extractive practices. The thing is, we're running out of time to transform the way we make goods and products before we cause the irreversible collapse of entire ecosystems.

If global food systems aren't transformed soon, we have only a little more than a quarter-century until we run out of the food we'll need to feed the world population. The Food and Agriculture Organization of the United Nations predicts that more than 1.8 billion people will lack access to drinking water by 2025. The oil, natural gas, and coal supplies that generate our electricity and fuel our cars are expected to run out in the next 50 to 100 years if current demand continues. Because these resources are nonrenewable, once they're used up, they're gone for good. These projections might sound alarming, and they should. The linear economy functions as though a limited planet has unlimited resources and space, which puts the health of the entire planet and its many ecosystems at risk. Overall, human consumption of products has led to a huge waste problem. As of 2020, the Great Pacific Garbage Patch is almost 2.1 million square kilometers (the combined size of India, Europe, and Mexico). That's right — we have a name for the huge pile of trash floating in the Pacific Ocean. And it's only getting bigger.

Luckily, there are solutions to these problems that both individuals and business can work to implement. Taking a circular economy approach to waste reduction and reuse can transform how people think about trash. By designing waste out of our system, we humans are designing for the future. Rather than reach the point where natural resources are depleted and there's nowhere left to put our waste, we can start adhering to a system that requires neither the extraction of resources nor the disposal of materials. By reducing waste and increasing product utilization, we greatly benefit the environment and our society. Reducing waste helps us

>> **Greatly reduce related waste management costs:** It costs a lot of money to throw things away. In disposing of a product, you're not only throwing away the value of the raw material used to make the product but also contributing to the large costs involved with waste management. In the US alone, more than $200 billion is spent on solid waste management. That's a lot of money that could be spent elsewhere if the waste were diverted for other uses.

>> **Combat climate change:** The extraction of natural resources is responsible for a significant amount of carbon dioxide, or CO_2, in the atmosphere. Cutting-and-burning forests for resources releases massive amounts of CO_2 into the atmosphere and reduces the number of trees available to sequester carbon. It's estimated that 1.5 billion tons of CO_2 are released annually as a result of deforestation alone. All manufactured goods also use resources like water, metal, wood, and fuel that emit carbon dioxide in the production process. When these products are sent to landfills, the emissions used to produce them are wasted. Further, waste that accrues in landfills generates immense amounts of methane, a potent greenhouse gas with the warming potential 84 times greater than that of CO_2 within the first two decades of its release. Eliminating human demand for raw materials and limiting our production of waste greatly reduces the amount of carbon entering the atmosphere and in turn can help slow the pace of human-induced climate change.

>> **Reduce pollution and protect ecosystems and waterways:** All the resources that people take from the earth must end up somewhere, whether it's in your house, your car, commercial buildings, or a landfill. It also holds true that all waste that's generated from our everyday life must also go somewhere. It's no secret that excess waste pollutes the environment and leaks into waterways. Some 14 billion tons of garbage end up in the ocean each and every year. Entire habitats and ecosystems are altered by runoff and trash leaching into waterways. Chemicals that are harmful to wildlife seep from landfills and can cause declines of entire populations of species. Trash accumulates in waterways and marine habitats, threatening both aquatic and mammalian wildlife.

>> **Create cleaner communities and healthier people:** Reducing the amount of waste entering the environment means cleaner water, cleaner air, and cleaner surroundings for all. Healthy environments provide a multitude of ecosystem services, ranging from providing people with goods and resources, regulating climate and water, providing recreational and educational outlets, and supporting the maintenance of natural global water cycles and nutrients for food production. Limiting the amount of waste we create means that less will enter and pollute the environment.

Why Buy Waste When You Can Sell It?

The current linear, take-make-waste model doesn't do a good job of retaining value from old products. In fact, the linear economy encourages manufacturers and companies to make products that break easily and require frequent replacement.

Sometimes called *planned obsolescence,* manufacturers specifically design products to fail or become out-of-date soon after purchase, as well as restricting consumers from repairing their purchased goods. As a result, consumers are perpetually forced to spend more money on replacing faulty products and obtaining unnecessary upgrades. This cycle promotes shortened product lifetime and poor material use, which results in more products being trashed at a greater rate.

Another huge problem the human population faces is the production of single-use products. These products, designed to be used just once and then disposed of, drive the current linear economy and accelerate the sheer mass of waste heading off to landfills. Single-use plastics are extremely potent and take thousands of years to decompose. As a result, they're accumulating in the environment and starting to do some damage. Of the 86 million tons of plastic produced annually, only about 14 percent are recycled and only 2 percent are recycled into a plastic of similar or better quality. Annually, $80 to $120 billion in plastic packaging is lost to the economy. At the same time, almost 9 million tons of plastic are leaked into the ocean every year, largely because of human consumption and the immediate disposal of single-use plastics. In fact, the Ellen MacArthur Foundation projects that there may be more plastic in the ocean than fish by 2050. And that's only plastic waste we're talking about. Single-use products and poorly made items, which are one of the leading drivers of the take-make-waste society, have no place in a circular economy.

We humans also pay a lot of money for our trash. Currently, cities use tax revenue to pay hourly fees to pick up residential and public trash. Further, businesses pay private waste hauling firms to manage waste. New York City, for example, pays $1.5 billion annually for solid waste management. Another $730 million is spent by private entities, like restaurants and commercial buildings, to take care of their trash. In total, about $2.3 billion is spent on local waste management in NYC. That is no small fee to manage something unwanted.

Developing more advanced recycling programs is one alternative to ensure that only the bare minimum is headed to landfills. Recycling essentially turns waste into a resource that can be repurposed and resold. Cities with more advanced recycling systems can minimize waste disposal costs and instead reuse and sell recycling and composting material. Finding ways to break down the materials naturally (composting) can also help companies and institutions cut back on landfill fees as well as increase their environmental credential.

What if companies designed long-lasting, durable products instead? Products that can be repaired easily or at least be resold at a reasonable price? What if fewer resources could be used to make better products, allowing the planet to rebound from our consumptive patterns of the past? This is exactly what the circular economy represents at its core: significantly increasing the utilization of products and reducing the amount of virgin materials used in the manufacturing process. For companies, optimizing the use of waste and byproducts means more profit using fewer resources. For individuals, it means having some extra cash in your pocket at the end of the day, from refurbishing, repairing, and reselling old items. For consumers, it means buying products with a longer lifetime that have to be replaced less frequently, thus saving you time and money.

Selling your old stuff

You as an individual can contribute to the circular economy and make some extra money doing so in a bunch of different ways — from repurposing or repairing old goods to selling usable parts to inventing new ways to use old stuff. In the next few sections, we outline a few ideas for transforming waste into value.

Selling junk cars for scrap

Even though your car may not be functioning properly or is way past its manufactured due date, you can likely sell it for its parts. Most cars can be remanufactured or have parts that are still in solid condition. These cars and parts can thus be sold for profit, whether it's to local cash-for-car businesses, to friends, or to strangers online. Trading in your car when you buy a new car is another option for people who are looking for an upgrade. And, even if your car is complete trash, the average payout for a junk car ranges from $100 to $400, depending on which parts can be resold or reused. Recycling your car by selling it to an auto shop can prevent it from sitting unused in a scrap yard for years. Tools like the Green Vehicle Disposal (`https://greenvehicledisposal.com/about`) ensure that end-of-life vehicles are recycled in an efficient manner, depending on the condition of the car.

Resell your clothes and household goods to consignment shops and online outlets

Chances are, you have clothes in your closet that you haven't touched in years, or brand-new jewelry that isn't your style. Rather than contribute to the 92 million tons of waste that fashion produces every year, you have several ways to make money from your old garments and jewels. Secondhand stores are a great way to get rid of old products or clothing that still has some life in them. You can choose from four main types of secondhand shops:

>> Consignment stores

>> Thrift shops

>> Pawn shops

>> Classified ads

The difference between these retail stores depends on when the seller hands over ownership of an item and is paid for doing so. In a consignment shop, the owner maintains ownership of an item until it's sold. (Think The RealReal, an online and brick-and-mortar marketplace for authenticated luxury consignment.) In a pawn shop, you sell your product there, giving up ownership on the spot before the pawn shop resells it. (Think Plato's Closet and Buffalo Exchange.) Classified ads get rid of the middleman and allow you to sell your clothes on a platform and interact with the buyer directly. (Think eBay, Amazon, or Craigslist.) If you're feeling generous, thrift stores allow you to donate clothes and other items for free and can get you a deduction on your tax return for doing so. (Think the Salvation Army.) Depending on what you are trying to get rid of and the shape that it's in, any of these options are a great alternative to throwing old clothing in the trash.

Reuse and remake what you can with you have

There are many everyday objects that you might normally throw out without thinking twice. You can find a do-it-yourself (DIY) tutorial online for almost any product or item you have, whether it's used cans, old furniture, or broken plates. Check out DIY websites like Pinterest and Etsy for creative ideas on repurposing broken household items and other scrap materials so that you can transform them into new useful, artistic creations.

Sell old technology and computer components to computer factories

We have an ever-growing demand for highly efficient and updated technology. Computers and other electronic devices are always in need of upgrades, and people are constantly awaiting the release of the next best smartphone or laptop. Because folks are quick to buy up the latest product on the market, a lot of electronics are easily forgotten about. Rather than allow old gadgets to collect dust, there are many ways to turn your components into cash. Computers are made of thousands of parts consisting of many different materials. Find a local electronics store or turn to online buyers like eBay or Facebook Marketplace, where buyers can search for specific parts they need. Someone will likely find a use for your old electronic parts, depending on the parts' condition and age.

Spruce up old appliances and resell them

Repair or replace? It's a big question for billions of consumers globally. Though replacing an item that's old or that isn't functioning properly may seem like the easier option, repairing old items can have many environmental and economic benefits. For one, repairing items diverts waste from landfills and prevents further pollution of the environment. It also saves resources by reducing the number of products being replaced with new stuff and increasing the circulation of repaired products. As circular economy principles grow in popularity and breadth, so too are the platforms that give you the opportunity as a consumer to learn how to repair your own products instead of replacing them. The IFixit website (www.ifixit.com) provides consumers with free solutions for repairing items ranging from laundry machines to computers to cars and trucks. Similarly, the Restart Project (https://therestartproject.org) teaches people how to repair electronics and reevaluate their consumption patterns. Whether you're repairing an item for yourself or to sell somewhere else, it's a great way to save money and resources.

Buyback programs are a good last option

Keep an eye out for *buyback programs* — strategies put forth by companies to repurchase old products from customers for recycling and reuse. Companies like Ikea and Apple have specific programs that will buy back old, used products and refurbish them. For example, Ikea will buy back your old furniture for an agreed-on price and give you store credit in return. Apple has a trade-in program that enables you to trade in an old device for credit toward a new device. Though these programs may not get you the most bang for your buck, they're a much better alternative to simply trashing old furniture or devices.

Get creative and innovative

A lot of the start-ups that find innovative ways to reuse old products and waste were initiated by average people, like you and me, who happened to stumble across a cool idea. Take the founders of Ugly Pickle Co., for example. (www.eatuglypickle.com) The company, which upcycles wasted produce into pickles and condiments, was founded by two individuals who met at a farmer's market and happened to share a passion for food justice and reducing food waste. Now, they're tackling food waste through their products and promoting sustainable consumption in the process. Whether it's finding ways to create snacks from old food waste, repurpose scrap fabrics, or create entirely new markets from wasted manufactured goods, the possibilities are seemingly endless for converting trash to treasure. We discuss more of the business side of the circular economy space in the next section.

Starting your own business

Starting a circular economy business may be easier than you think. All it takes is a little creativity, business smarts, and a good waste stream to capitalize on. Ultimately, inventing a new way to incorporate scraps or waste into a new product or design can be a moneymaker and help save the planet at the same time.

Upcycle, or "creatively reuse," all materials in the supply chain

If you're already running a company that's creating products at scale, upcycling may be a useful way to increase profits and reduce waste. *Upcycling* is the process of transforming byproducts, waste, or any other unwanted or unused material made during production into valuable products that can be used and sold. At its root, upcycling represents the process of transforming trash into treasure.

Upcycling has many environmental benefits, including the conservation of limited natural resources, the protection of ecological habitats, and the reduction of pollution. Further, upcycling products makes great economic sense. Why not use up every last bit of a resource created along your production line, or try to sell materials that you would otherwise discard? The economic and societal benefits of upcycling include reduced production costs, support of local industries and businesses, and increased creativity and innovation along the life of that product. Other businesses will actually buy manufacturing byproducts at a reduced cost and transform them into brand-new products to sell and market, which puts more money in the pocket of the manufacturer. Take the lumber industry, for example, which sells shredded wood, chips, and sawdust for use elsewhere, all of which are byproducts of the industry.

Many markets exist for upcycled products. The upcycled food industry is now worth more than $46.7 billion, with an expected annual growth rate of 5 percent. Finding inventive ways to transform food scraps into marketable products is helping make a dent in the 40 million tons of food waste the US produces annually. Upcycling is also popular in the fashion industry. Reusing existing fabrics and repurposing vintage clothing are examples of the upcycling that's happening in the retail space. Annually, over 15 million tons of clothing end up in landfills, a lot of which can be repurposed and either repaired for further use or upcycled into new items. By finding ways to incorporate old or scrap fabrics into new products, people can reinvent the way that the fashion industry generates clothing. Today, companies such as Planetarians are transforming animal feed (a byproduct of the ethanol-and-beer industry) into alternative meats (www.planetarians.com). Mi Terro (www.miterro.com) is transforming spoiled milk into clothing fibers. Renewal Workshop (https://renewalworkshop.com) is transforming discarded apparel into renewed products or recycled feedstock. The list of companies finding innovative ways to transform food and fashion waste into sustainable products goes on and on.

Develop new markets and customers

Upcycling and byproduct opportunities are everywhere, in every sector and industry. When you make one product, you inevitably create something else in the process. As we humans transform how and where we source our materials, there exists great opportunity to use what is already at hand. As discussed earlier in this chapter, creatively reinventing how byproducts are used creates a new market for sustainable shopping. Consumer awareness and education are the keys to persuading the sustainable shopper to choose one product over another. Customers need to know how and why one product is better for the planet than another, which can be done with labeling, certification, and industry standards. Developing new markets and products that make it easy for sustainable shoppers to discern whether products are actually equitable and sustainably sourced will help sustainable shopping become something that's easier to commit to and more competitive with traditional products.

Write a business plan

You should have a few key things in mind when starting a business. These are the main considerations to take into account when drafting a business plan:

>> Understanding the scope of your business

>> Researching customers and competitors

>> Recruiting investors and others who are interested in your mission

>> Understanding how to market and sell your idea to others (partners or consumers, for example)

By outlining these factors to meet the specific needs of your business idea, you will already be off to a good start.

Join a business networking support group with similar values

If you have applied for a job recently, you may have come to realize that networking is everything. Finding business support groups with similar values enables you to share research and strategize with like-minded individuals who have a whole range of experiences.

One example of a group that connects similar businesses is the Upcycled Food Association (UFA, at www.upcycledfood.org), a nonprofit focused on growing the upcycled food economy by bringing together upcycled food companies under a common classification. The Upcycled Food Association defines *upcycled* food as products made from food materials that "would not have gone to human consumption, are procured and produced using verifiable supply chains, and have a positive impact on the environment." This highly specific definition ensures that upcycled foods are actually diverting food from landfills and reducing food waste. The association helps individuals and businesses collaborate on innovative ways to reduce food waste as well as provides a platform for publicizing their new product. It also offers networking, research, and strategies for companies interested in entering the upcycled food space. Additionally, the UFA is working on an upcycled food certification standard that will help develop an upcycled food market with clear labeling and criteria.

Set up your own electronic storefront

Let's face it: Online shopping has begun to dominate the retail space. As physical storefronts begin to disappear, even more shops are popping up online. The e-commerce industry is booming, having grown about 313 percentage points in the past decade.

From 2019 to 2020, e-commerce grew from accounting for 16 percent of total retail sales to a whopping 33 percent of total sales, representing a 10-year increase in e-commerce penetration in just one year. Companies are finding ways to rapidly expand their online presence to keep up with the growing demand for online shopping. After you figure out your million-dollar idea, which of course involves finding an innovative way to use waste, finding a way to sell and market it online may be the key to success. You may choose to develop your own website, use existing platforms, or partake in a combination of both.

Troubleshooting a Wasteful Product Lifecycle

We humans must face the fact that we live in a globalized world. Food, natural resources, and commodities are shipped thousands of miles to reach consumers. Labor is outsourced to various countries where it's much cheaper, but the quality of working conditions is much lower. Supply chains are long and complex and involve a multitude of players across a range of countries and geographies. As a result, we are distanced from the people who build our stuff and natural resources that go into making our goods, making it more difficult to understand our direct impact on both the environment and workers in these other places. Overall, 80 percent of total greenhouse gas emissions and 90 percent of the environmental damage from consumer goods companies come from the supply chain. Understanding where these impacts occur and finding ways to localize production and reduce reliance on raw materials can help cut down the societal and environmental impacts.

Where the wild things are

Natural resource extraction and its associated activities result in unintended consequences to the landscape and ecology of entire regions. Since 2016, 28 million hectares of forest have been cut down or burned annually, an area larger than the size of the state of Colorado. Major causes of deforestation globally include beef, soy, palm oil, and timber production. The US toilet paper industry alone is one of the leading causes of destruction of the most important boreal forest in the world, located in Canada. Boreal forests store vast amounts of carbon dioxide (CO_2); logging in Canada's boreal forest emits at least 26 million metric tons of carbon dioxide annually. Further, when harvested, wood products retain only a fraction of the carbon content that trees do. Wood products continue to release carbon dioxide over their lifetime until they're eventually discarded, emitting both methane and CO_2 as the wood decays in landfills. The high demand for toilet paper is not only resulting in the destruction of entire forests but also releasing immense amounts of CO_2 into an atmosphere that's already suffocating.

Resource extraction doesn't just hurt trees. According to a report published by the United Nations, around a million animal and plant species are now threatened with extinction. The main drivers are deforestation and habitat loss, overexploitation of resources, and climate change. Land use and deforestation cause habitat fragmentation, which can isolate populations of animal and plant species, reducing their genetic variation and subsequent chance of survival. The Holocene extinction, also known as the *sixth mass extinction,* is occurring right now — as a direct result of human activity. We humans are changing the face of our planet and are, in the process, putting the survival of many species at risk.

Signed, sealed, delivered

Although globalization has led to immense economic growth, it has also resulted in the increased exploitation of natural resources far away from home. As a result, the sustainable management of supply chains has become increasingly complex. Globalization has made it difficult for us to perceive the direct impacts of our consumption patterns because we are distanced from the resource extraction and natural habitat destruction that goes into making consumer goods.

In reality, products and their many components travel long and far to reach consumers. In the US, the average food product travels 1,500 miles from farm to fork. Called *food miles,* the transportation of food accounts for about 11 percent of total lifecycle greenhouse gas emissions from the food-and-agriculture industry. That avocado you have in your salad most likely traveled thousands of miles to reach your plate. That hamburger you had for lunch is likely made from beef imported from Australia or Latin America. Transporting food is no easy task because it requires refrigeration and high levels of efficiency and energy to make it to the supermarket before spoiling. Food refrigeration significantly increases the amount of energy and CO^2 emissions produced during the transportation process. Transporting food far distances also requires the use of increased packaging and preservatives, such as single-use plastics and chemical compounds that persist in the environment after being thrown away.

Further, more and more products are being purchased online, requiring shipping from all corners of the globe. In the US, the postal service processes and delivers 472.1 million mail pieces each and every day. UPS and FEDEX deliver upward of 34 million packages a day, combined. That's a lot of products being sent from one place to another. The shipping industry itself has a huge waste problem. Packaging involves many resources and materials to ensure that your product makes it safely from fulfillment center to your door. From boxes to single-use plastics, and from packing tape to polystyrene for cushioning fragile products, a lot of additional resources go into any product that's sent in the mail.

Waste not, want not

If everyone uses our resources wisely and sparingly, we won't need or want more in the future. By designing out negative externalities, like waste and air pollution, companies can improve product sustainability and profitability while increasing customer satisfaction. Restorative and regenerative business models can help tackle issues of using resources sparingly. We can find ways to use materials efficiently and conservatively that enable resources to rebound at a faster rate than they're used up. For example, regenerative agriculture focuses on generating healthy soils and increasing biodiversity while combating climate change and creating a thriving crop lifecycle. This process not only leads to enhanced crop recovery but also supports a healthy agricultural ecosystem that removes carbon from the atmosphere. Another key step in reducing our reliance on limited resources is increasing the number of renewable and recyclable materials used to make products and produce energy. In this way, we become less reliant on the natural resources that, when extracted and exploited, negatively impact the planet, and utilize the resources that are always available, like sun and wind.

Being a sustainable shopper

The consumer can do a lot to be more sustainable. Buying locally is a helpful way to reduce your individual impact. Supporting businesses within your community and buying locally grown food not only reduce packaging waste and transportation-related greenhouse gas emissions but also support a thriving local economy. Another way to buy more sustainably is to diversify consumption. Diversification is an important element of the circular economy. Diversifying what you eat and consume means that you can source more items locally, eat fruits and veggies that are in season, and buy what's readily available without having to ship it thousands of miles. Lastly, educating yourself and supporting companies that make sustainably sourced goods is a powerful way to use your purchasing power to make a difference. We are already off to a good start. It's predicted that the US sustainability market will reach $150 billion by 2021. More than 64 percent of households purchase sustainable products, with that number likely to increase as sustainable products become more readily available. As consumers put an increased emphasis on sustainable products, companies and manufacturers will come under increased pressure to be transparent about how their goods are made and where their commodities come from.

Finding value in the ugly

There are many ways to transform trash into treasure. Take Fresh Kills landfill, for example, which was recently transformed into a thriving city park. Fresh Kills landfill was, when still functioning as a landfill, the largest in the world. It covered 4 square miles in Staten Island, rose 100 feet high, and accumulated 2.9 billion cubic feet of trash. At its peak, Fresh Kills landfill received 26 million pounds of commercial and household waste per day.

After it closed in 2001, urban planners redesigned the once-toxic waste disposal site into a thriving public park. Freshkills Park — note the new spelling — is now a 2,200-acre recreation area three times the size of Central Park. With its specially engineered landscape, the park has become a thriving spot for wildlife — one that fosters education, recreation, and a sense of community in the area. This is just one example of the ways that humans have found to transform something toxic and harmful to the environment into a thriving ecosystem.

The ugly food movement also supports this idea of finding value in the ugly. The movement is centered around valuing and using produce that's deemed too ugly to sell, according to traditional supermarket standards. In the US, some 6 billion tons of produce are unharvested or thrown out because of aesthetic imperfections. Such unrealistic cosmetic standards dictate that produce that's perfectly edible and nutritious never makes it to market. Recently, companies like Imperfect Foods (www.imperfectfoods.com) and Misfits Market (www.misfitsmarket.com) rescue damaged produce and sell it on their platform, giving consumers access to misshaped produce at a fraction of grocery store prices. Supermarkets are also coming under pressure to start selling these ugly fruits and vegetables for a lower price. The ugly food movement not only helps reduce some of the world's immense amount of food waste but also provides cheaper options for buying fresh produce.

Other companies are finding ways to transform scraps and wasted materials into new-and-unique products. For example, the acoustic and acrylic panels company 3Form (www.3-form.com) started a reclamation program that reuses and recycles materials taken from installations or damaged panels. The result is unique, intricate panels that are trimmed to the size and fit that customers need. A step further is its reformation program, which sells oddly sized or blemished panels that are made from upcycled materials. The reclamation and reformation programs provide a perfect example of an architectural products company finding ways to transform scraps into elaborate, profitable panels.

REMEMBER

Our entire concept of waste is flawed. In nature, nothing is waste, but instead becomes nutrients (food) for something else. As you can see, discarded materials are actually valuable resources that can be remade, reimagined, and reinvigorated into thousands of possible uses and functions. By questioning our perception of what's what, perhaps people can start to embrace a true circular economy.

DAVE BENNINK SPEAKS

Dave Bennink is the director of the Building Deconstruction Institute as well as owner of Re-Use Consulting, an international consulting firm helping with all issues related to building material reuse and building deconstruction.

Eric Corey Freed: Tell us about reuse consulting and what you do and what you see as your role in this crazy world?

Dave Bennink: I've been in the reuse industry for 28 years. I've worked in 44 states, 4 provinces, 1 U S territory, and 7 different countries helping people, teaching people, and consulting with people about all aspects of re-usable building materials in all forms.

Our projects include helping people start reuse warehouse stores-like used Home Depots. On the flip side we help lower income homeowners find affordable building materials. I teach groups how to disassemble buildings — the official term is deconstruction. I consult with architects and manufacturers in designing for more efficient disassembly and waste reduction/elimination. Historic preservation is another service we offer along with sustainable alternatives to demolition. We do a lot of job creation within inner city neighborhoods, jobs for disadvantaged workers, low-income folks, and previously incarcerated individuals. You name it! There's so much good to be done!

Eric Corey Freed: How much do you think of yourself as a circular economy practitioner or circular economy pioneer, as opposed to an educator pointing out a problem that needs addressing?

Dave Bennink: Pioneer is an interesting word. "Circular economy" is a term that's relatively new, yet practices of reuse have been around forever. For example, we have photos and signs of people doing what we do for hundreds, even thousands of years. It's not a new concept to save and to be responsible with materials. We've just forgotten the scale and importance of it. Now we're beginning to remember. Now we're seeing buildings taken down where the lumber has been used twice before. That's at least a 100-year old building. The materials could be more like 200 years old. So, we don't really call ourselves "pioneers" we are more "revivalists," bringing back a crucially important practices.

A good portion of my time is dedicated to educating. Reclaimed materials are sustainable, carbon free with no new trees cut down. Everyone's looking for answers on how to save the world, fight climate change. Yet they're overlooking the most sustainable materials they're surrounded by everywhere. We're desperately trying to educate people that the most sustainable material they can find is in the already existing buildings.

Eric Corey Freed: I'm struck by the metrics your company uses. Clearly, it's important to you because you're tracking and updating them. On your last update two and a half million pounds were diverted from landfill, 16 jobs were created and 6 new reuse companies were established. I love those metrics of success! How much did you have to learn about metrics of success and how to measure that? Did it come naturally and is what and how you're measuring still evolving?

Dave Bennink: I love numbers. They have a real power if used properly. People often manipulate numbers for their own gain and to confuse the issue. For us, there are so many different benefits we can measure honestly from the work we do. The numbers you just quoted are from one year of our operation. Our total contribution is one hundred million pounds diverted from landfills, creating over 500 jobs, and working on over 5,000 projects to date.

We tried to quantify every day, you know-slugging it out, but it just didn't seem like that big of a deal. My thought was it might be better for morale if I quantified how much we've saved and reused over the 28 years. In that time, we've saved the equivalent of 10,000 acres of standing forest. Somewhere out there, there's 10,000 acres of trees still standing because of our projects. Even with that, as an individual company, I realized we would never make a dent in the waste stream. That's when I started my consulting company. If I could help people start their own reuse businesses, maybe a hundred, maybe a thousand businesses, across the nation or globally — now that's impact.

We were talking with the EPA and they said the average American wastes about 4.4 pounds of material every day. So, over a lifetime, 75 years, at 4.4 pounds per day, it comes out to 120,450 pounds. The average home that we're deconstructing weighs about 125,000 pounds. That means the average building we're deconstructing is equivalent to a lifetime's worth of waste. If you choose to demolish your home, you're wasting double the average amount per lifetime. I'm hoping you'll put this kind of information in your book, help me get the word out. Let people know if they're making the choice to

(continued)

(continued)

demolish their home, throw it away, there's no walking that back, no matter how many plastic bags they recycle. We're trying to encourage and educate people without guilt tripping them. A lot of the negative impacts made on our climate, our society, are made a little bit at a time, even individual demolished homes can seem like a small thing. But they're not. They represent huge sustainable opportunities.

Eric Corey Freed: For anyone working in sustainability or social entrepreneurship, the issue that comes up time and time again is how to scale impact, and specifically how to scale my own efforts and my own impact that I make. It's something I've struggled with my entire career. Would you speak a little bit more about your drive to scale impact.

Dave Bennink: I'm addicted to the win-win scenario. Say I was only trying to help the environment — maybe that would be enough. However, the fact that we help so many people start their own reuse businesses and low-income homeowners find less expensive materials, that we create jobs and support historic preservation — we're helping in so many ways with climate, education, economy, social justice. That's a full-on win-win.

We look for projects that have more meaning. Our next project is taking a barn down, we're actually disassembling the barn and labeling the parts so that it can be reassembled on another property. If we wanted to just take barns down, we could just do that every week and end up with a bunch of barn wood. But what we're doing is saving that barn's history and aesthetics. That's so cool!

We run a financially sustainable business helping the environment and helping people. That's pretty addicting. We're planning an innovation center as a way to optimize services and increase income. Profit margins are low in this business. We'll have 10 or 12 reuse businesses at the same facility. That way, we're creating synergy and sharing expenses.

Eric Corey Freed: The other side of that social entrepreneurship and scaling impact is learning how and when to say no. Is that something that you're constantly evaluating?

Dave Bennink: I was saying to a person the other day, if there was one reuse business that needs to survive, it would be exactly what I'm doing. It sounds selfish, but really, if my reuse business is starting other reuse businesses — starting hundreds of those — then from a very practical standpoint it's invaluable. Yes, I do say no. Even within a given project I might say no to lower value materials. For example, say I'm an idealist and I want to save every single item from a building and see it repurposed. And I'm going to take the time to make that happen. In fact, I take three and a half weeks saving materials. Well, while I was saying yes to everything and spending time that way, ninety nine other structures went directly to landfill. So, when you're saying yes to one thing, you're really saying no to many others. So, you need to be paying attention. We did a study of what we say yes and no to. We were often saving three times more from the landfill than some others who were more idealistic about it. I have a prospective flooring project right now. It's got glue all over it. It's got carpet glued to it. It's likely, we're going to say no to that. You simply can't say yes to everything and expect to do a hundred structures a year.

Eric Corey Freed: You're based in one of my favorite places on the West coast, which is Bellingham, Washington. In listening to you talk and your vision and enthusiasm for it, it doesn't surprise me at all, because it seems like such a Bellingham thing to do.

Dave Bennink: Bellingham is surrounded by natural environment, so it's on our mind — you know, preserving it. Of course we have all kinds here, like everywhere else, but we also have people who are more environmentally conscious and we have an environmental college too. That helps.

I've been working in Portland on and off, helping the city for the last five or so years. We also have a reuse operation starting just across the border in Vancouver. I'm working with five women- and minority-owned contractor firms.

Eric Corey Freed: There's something about the Pacific Northwest, it has a frontier spirit to it. Listening to you talk about it feels familiar. Your way of communicating your vision and purpose isn't a hippy dippy, kumbaya, everybody hug and heal the earth approach. When you speak about it, you do the same thing I do, a rational approach. It's illogical to handle materials and resources wastefully. You're offering a practical, sustainable alternative.

Dave Bennink: I agree with that. I'm very, business-based and we happen to heal the environment. We don't apologize for that. We're definitely trying to create economically viable business models and practices. We essentially get paid twice to take buildings down. We get paid by the building owner, and then we get paid when we sell the materials. It's a way of saying "this is worthy."

We're hoping to create products out of reuse materials that are not just from homes. We would be taking waste from a larger variety of sources. My focus is building materials, whatever products would be leftover — Industrial processes, manufacturing, and so on.

Eric Corey Freed: There are things that really lend themselves to deconstruction and reuse —fireplace mantels, wall studs, and so on. However, if we use wood studs, but use spray foam insulation, which seemed like a good idea at the time, it makes those things more difficult to recycle. Are there general lessons that come to mind, given all you've seen around designing for disassembly. What's your advice to architects and designers?

(continued)

(continued)

Dave Bennink: Well, it's complicated. Yeah. I have put a lot of thought into that. Take older buildings. Many don't even have insulation and are only nailed together. If we just put in the work, we can save these materials, but it's a lot of work. Then we started getting newer buildings and adhesives, spray foam insulation, absolutely terrible. Everything that spray foam was sprayed on becomes instant trash. A lot of these decisions were made a long time ago, relatively speaking. I've had to adapt. There's a deck and it's nailed down and then there's a deck that's screwed down. And then there's a deck that's using the hidden fasteners. I just mentioned the nails are more predictable because they pry up the board and you pound out the nails. Then screws came along and they seemed like a better idea because all you have to do is unscrew them except that the inferior quality screws, they tend to strip. And now the screw is stuck in the board, too hard to pry up without damaging things. Then you go, well, shoot, that didn't work. Unless we use quality screws those materials are less re-useable.

Those hidden fasteners you see in today's decking, we've gotten really excited about those. When we do take them apart the material is preserved nearly 100 percent. The fasteners may not all survive, but the material almost always survives. If you're asking me, I like those because we've had the best success.

When it comes to spray foam — that's an interesting lesson. Let's just say it was in the walls. We pretty much had to throw the entire wall away. Then it occurred to me — why am I taking this wall apart? I realized I could just sell the walls intact to people. Now I sell walls, I sell floors, I sell staircases, I sell trusses, and roof panels. That sounds insane. They're very heavy, but we do sell them. We've created over a hundred building kits. If you need an 8 x 12 shed, we will sell you an 8 x 12 section of floor structure with two eight-foot walls and two 12 foot walls. We call them post fab panels. The panels have siding on them, they have windows and It's amazing. You instantly have your shed. And it looks like a little mini house because it is. It was a house and now it's a shed. We sell these affordably because we don't have to take them apart. And you didn't have to put them back together, so there's no waste. So now we've taken this spray foam issue and turned it around because we had to. We've completely solved it. I'm excited about that as a concept.

So now we're not trying to save materials as much as we're trying to save assemblies. We're not going to take a set of stairs apart, so you can build a set of stairs. We're going to preserve the set of stairs. We're not worried about the fact that the walls are two by four framing because we're not using them to build homes. We're using them to build unheated storage sheds etc. We're also starting to build emergency housing and housing for people that don't have homes. Imagine that! We just have all these panels and they get cut to size and they get stood back up and fastened together. We save the spray foam floor panels and wall panels. They're more rigid and pre-insulated.

Eric Corey Freed: How much focus needs to be put on creative solutions in deconstructing, reuse or repurposing? On the flip side, how much focus needs to go into redesigning in new ways that support disassembly and reuse?

Dave Bennink: It depends on your reader. Let's say your reader is an architect and they're saying, what if I can make my structure with pre-fab panels, modular construction, right? An entire room gets delivered. If they crane an entire room in place, you build up a bunch of boxes and you've got a senior center. Well, if they stacked up those boxes, what's keeping me from unstacking them? You know, it's really about how they're fastened together then. Some day in the future, I'm going to work with these modular builders and say "just think about this when you're building these independent modules, how they get put on a truck, how they get craned to the job site, how they get stacked in place and how they get fastened together. Make sure that I can someday unstack them." That's all I'm asking.

If I was reading your book and interested in helping with the circular economy today — the thing is, today's buildings won't be taken apart for 50 years. That won't help us in the next 50 years. Hopefully those buildings will at least last 100 years before they're taken apart. However, as long as they last, they're not going to help us with today's environmental problems. It's almost like it's too late. In 50 years, our climate is going to be a disaster. People say, if you change your behavior today, it won't help. But it still needs to happen. We need to start designing buildings now that are more easily disassembled, just in case.

3

Rethinking Material Lifecycles: The Circular Perspective

Chapter **10**

Understanding the Circular Material Lifecycle

B
oth authors of this book would like to kindly inform you that 99.9 percent of the sustainable items you're exposed to aren't sustainable at all. Sorry to be the bearer of bad news. Denial is the first of five stages of grief, though, so please be aware that anger is coming shortly. Maybe you should take a deep breath before continuing with this chapter.

In today's world, you can make the claim that any product you come up with will have a net-neutral or net-positive environmental impact if you present it the right way. However, the whole lifecycle of a product is rarely considered when a company claims to you that its product is good for the environment. Typically, only the product itself is addressed, not the lifecycle of that product. Paper straws, for example, are made from organic materials. Yes, they're compostable and eliminate the need for plastic straws — but that doesn't necessarily mean they have a net-neutral or net-positive impact on the environment. You need to ask more questions before you can know whether the lifecycle of this paper straw is indeed circular.

So let's start asking some questions. This paper straw originally came from fibers taken from a tree. How was that tree grown? How much energy, irrigation, maintenance, soil, labor, and time was required to grow and harvest that tree? How far did the tree have to travel to be processed and formed into a straw, shipped to a distributor, packaged and sent to the restaurant? What happened to that straw during the post-iced-coffee stage of its life? More than likely, that straw was shoved into a plastic garbage bag, thrown on a diesel-powered truck and sent away to a landfill after only 30 minutes of use. That raw material will never be used again, despite the large amount of effort and energy it required to be produced and shipped to the final, end user.

What about that particular lifecycle seems sustainable to you?

In this chapter, you'll find out what *sustainable* actually means, by comparing it to its alternatives using the sustainability spectrum. You'll also learn how biological and technical product cycles should function and you'll see that waste is a direct biproduct of poor design. Lastly, you'll also discover how renewable energy can not only act as a continuous resource to fuel everyone's way of life but also be invested to develop more sources of renewable energy.

Viewing the Entire Spectrum of Environmental Impact

For a few hundred years now, everyone has known that energy cannot be created or destroyed, so it's mind-boggling to think that people still accept waste as a reality. *Waste* is simply energy in an unusable form — it's a fact that cannot be denied. If the global machine built by the developing world to power its economy continues to extract natural resources, produce products, and then waste them, we'll eventually run out of the very materials our society needs in order to survive!

Many areas of the developed world claim to be sustainable when, in reality, they have a net-negative impact on the environment. A *net-negative* lifecycle has a 1-to-2 (or worse) energy trade-off. No product can stand on its own as sustainable unless the whole lifecycle of that product is net-zero. *Net-zero* equals a 1-to-1 trade-off, meaning the lifecycle of any material or product resulted in no negative impact on the environment. Net-zero also means, however, that there was no positive impact on the environment, either. For real progress to occur, the energy flow must be *net-positive* — a 2-to-1 (or greater) trade-off, in other words. The lifecycle process of any material or product resulted in a positive impact on the environment. Consider wind turbines as an example: The quantity of energy generated by a turbine outweighs the energy required to extract, manufacture, transport, and assemble that turbine.

It's *really* difficult to know what sustainable means in today's world, especially with the global marketing efforts that have been developed in an effort to sell you goods and services. But there's hope! Once you understand what makes something truly sustainable, grasp how natural and technical lifecycles should function, and see how energy can be best used or invested, determining what is sustainable — and what isn't — becomes second nature. Keep reading to find out more about degenerative, sustainable, and regenerative lifecycles.

Defining degenerative lifecycles

The way humans have designed many of our global systems — the systems we depend on to maintain our current ways of life — has always followed the linear take-make-waste model. In industries such as fashion and plastics, packaging, products, and systems have been designed in such a way that more than 80 percent of material flows resulting from the production process are destined for landfill or incineration or even leaked into our natural environment. By definition, this linear model is degenerative in nature.

A *degenerative* lifecycle is a system that produces less value, energy, and materials at the end of its cycle than what they had originally. Imagine placing a mere $100 in a retirement fund early in your career, in the hope that when you reach retirement, you'll have thousands of dollars available to fruitfully live out the rest of your days in a retirement community in Palm Beach. However, when retirement comes, you're sad to see that, because of inflation over the course of 50 years, you're able to retrieve only $50 from the account and you have to kiss your Florida dreams goodbye. The retirement fund, in this example, is degenerative — if you were to keep the remaining $50 in your retirement fund longer, you would not only lose the remaining value completely but, if the stock market tanked on you, you could also eventually find yourself in debt.

Defining sustainable lifecycles

Improving on a degenerative lifecycle and finding yourself with a sustainable lifecycle means that all waste is eliminated. Whatever it is you're dealing with — business, finances, manufacturing, buildings, or packaging — it can functionally continue forever if you insist on a sustainable lifecycle. If a degenerative lifecycle is a system that produces less value, energy, and materials at the end of its cycle than they had originally, then you can assume that a *sustainable* lifecycle is a system that produces no less (and no more) value, energy, or materials at the end of its cycle than it had originally. From the same example earlier, imagine placing $100 in a retirement fund early in your career. However, when retirement comes, you see that your investment return matched inflation, so your original $100 is still available — no less and no more than your original $100. The retirement fund, in this example, is sustainable, meaning if you were to keep the original $100 in your retirement fund forever and all other factors remained the same, you would neither lose any money nor make any money. Although this is better than a degenerative lifecycle, why settle for sustainable when a better future is available?

Defining regenerative lifecycles

Improving on a degenerative lifecycle and finding yourself with a sustainable life-cycle is one thing, but going beyond sustainable and functioning within a circular economy framework is a whole new ballgame. When starting at a neutral ground, maintaining a sustainable, net-neutral way of life is acceptable. However, because our society has functioned heavily within a degenerative state for longer than the past 100 years, we must not only transition to a sustainable state of living but also offset the negative impacts of our past way of doing things. To do that, we need to design our future to be in a regenerative state, not merely a sustainable one.

Progressing from a sustainable lifecycle to a regenerative one requires a net-positive flow of energy and materials through our globalized society. Again, using the retirement fund as an example to illustrate this, imagine entering your career with $10,000 of debt. Despite that, you decide to place $100 in your retirement fund early in your career. In a regenerative state, the fund can take that $100 and generate enough value for you to not only pay off your $10,000 of debt but also allow you to save $10,000 more. The retirement fund, in this example, is regener-ative by definition because it not only offsets your debt but also provides you with more than what you invested. (By the way, if a stockbroker promises you a rate of return that turns $100 into $20,000, run — don't walk — away from that deal, because you're going to lose money.)

REMEMBER

The circular economy is focused on developing a regenerative way of life. By understanding what's degenerative (takes more than it gives), sustainable (takes what it gives), and regenerative (gives more than it takes), you can now look at any system, understand where it falls on the spectrum of environmental impact, and begin to identify areas of improvement. Improving a materials lifecycle from a degenerative state to a regenerative state requires you to first identify how materials typically flow. Luckily, the Ellen MacArthur Foundation's Butterfly Diagram does just that. Keep reading to learn more about it.

WARNING

The goal of any company is to persuade you to purchase its product rather than its competitor's. Many industries spend millions, if not billions, of dollars annually on marketing efforts to persuade you to give them your money. In an attempt to sell you on their product, companies provide misleading information by way of text, imagery, colors, and labeling to make their products something they really aren't — a strategy known as *greenwashing*. So the next time you find yourself purchasing a product because of its practices labeled green or sustainable, we recommend that you take an extra minute to explore what it is exactly about their product that is supposed to be green and/or sustainable, after all.

Understanding the Ellen MacArthur Foundation's Butterfly Diagram

The Ellen MacArthur Foundation (www.ellenmacarthurfoundation.org) was launched in 2010 to accelerate the global transition from a linear economy to a circular economy. Since its creation, it has emerged as a global thought leader, establishing the circular economy on the agenda of decision-makers across business, government, and academia. Its vision is a new economic system that delivers better outcomes for people and the environment.

Within this circular economy structure, business models, products, and materials are designed to increase use and reuse, replicating the balance of the natural world, where nothing becomes waste and everything has value. A circular economy, increasingly built on renewable energy and materials, is interdependent, diverse, and inclusive.

Examining the circular economy's structure: The bones of the operation

A circular economy seeks to rebuild capital, whether it's financial, social, or natural. (For more on the different kinds of capital you can make use of, see Chapter 5.) This aim ensures enhanced flows of goods and services. Figure 10-1 illustrates the perpetual circulation of materials through the value circle.

The circular economy system diagram, shown in Figure 10-1, was developed by the Ellen MacArthur Foundation. Meant to be read from top to bottom, it can assist you in optimizing your products-and-materials lifecycles. To fully use this graphic to optimize material flows, each stakeholder of that lifecycle needs to be involved. From sourcing raw materials to shipping, manufacturing, end use, and material collection, all stages of a material lifecycle must be addressed to properly transition from a linear status to a circular one.

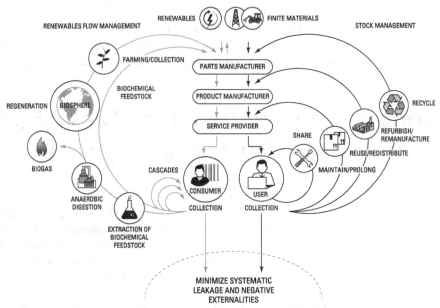

RENEWABLES FLOW MANAGEMENT · RENEWABLES · FINITE MATERIALS · STOCK MANAGEMENT

FARMING/COLLECTION

PARTS MANUFACTURER

REGENERATION · BIOSPHERE

BIOCHEMICAL FEEDSTOCK

PRODUCT MANUFACTURER

RECYCLE

SERVICE PROVIDER

SHARE

REFURBISH/ REMANUFACTURE

BIOGAS

REUSE/REDISTRIBUTE

CASCADES

MAINTAIN/PROLONG

ANAEROBIC DIGESTION

CONSUMER

USER

COLLECTION

COLLECTION

EXTRACTION OF BIOCHEMICAL FEEDSTOCK

MINIMIZE SYSTEMATIC LEAKAGE AND NEGATIVE EXTERNALITIES

FIGURE 10-1:
The Ellen MacArthur Foundation's Butterfly Diagram.

Source: Ellen MacArthur Foundation (www.ellenmacarthurfoundation.org
[Drawing based on Braungart & McDonough, Cradle to Cradle (C2C)]

Two types of materials are represented within the circular economy structure, shown in Figure 10-1: biological and technical:

>> **Biological** materials are biodegradable or can break down into their basic chemical elements naturally over time — food, wood, and cotton are examples. The defining factor of biological materials is that they can eventually be returned to the soil and support the growth of new materials.

>> **Technical** materials aren't biodegradable, such as metals, most plastics and polymers, and other materials that need to be recovered and fed back into the system at the end of their lives by way of physical and chemical recycling.

REMEMBER

It's critical to differentiate between biological and technical materials, because the optimal lifecycle required to maintain a circular economy for these various materials types looks completely different. Unfortunately, most products are designed to use both biological and technical materials, making the necessary lifecycle of these products much more difficult to manage. This hurdle is a common one for the fashion industry because clothing is often made with a blend of materials. Polycottons, for example, are materials developed by mixing a plastic (a technical material) and cotton (a biological material) to form a piece of clothing. Recovering these two materials from that final product is almost impossible. Remember: You can't unscramble your eggs!

The circular economy systems diagram (refer to Figure 10-1) has been developed on three key principles, which act on the platform for all circular economy initiatives:

>> Preserve and enhance natural capital by controlling finite stocks and balancing renewable resource flows.

>> Optimize resource yields by circulating products, components, and materials in use at the highest utility at all times in both the technical and biological cycles.

>> Foster system effectiveness by revealing and designing out *negative externalities* — the costs imposed on a 3rd party, such as people or the environment.

Renewables flow management: Harnessing biological cycles

When looking at managing biological materials, the following two approaches show promise:

>> **Cascading:** Natural materials, such as wood, cotton, and others, can hold a range of uses. By allowing the product to *cascade,* or drop from one use to another before ultimately being returned to the planet, these natural materials can stay in use for much longer. Using wood as an example, once a tree is cut down, that stock of timber can be processed into boards and assembled to make a sturdy table for your family to use. Once that table has reached the end of its life, it can be burned and returned to the soil, or it can cascade to another function, like particle board. That particle board can then be sent to a construction site and used in a building for 50 or 60 years before it too is deconstructed. That particle board can then either be burned and returned to the soil or cascaded into another use. By extending the life of a natural material, the value of that material increases, because it removes the need to purchase replacement material. Once that piece of timber can no longer cascade into a new use, it can be returned to the soil to feed a new tree and begin the cycle again.

>> **Regeneration:** Regeneration is, first and foremost, an opportunity just waiting to be realized. The industrial course that the Earth is on has been extremely degenerative and extractive in nature, and regeneration is an opportunity to offset the damage that has occurred. In some parts of the world, the top soil conditions in the agricultural fields are estimated to be able to support only 16 harvests before they can no longer support crops. Regeneration is an opportunity for humans to begin collecting the biological

waste that stems from the global food system — such as human and food waste — and feed it back into the biological system to ensure food security and quality for years to come. (For more details on the detrimental effects of the agricultural industry, see Chapter 15.)

TIP

Renewable flows of materials can be stunted by incorporating toxic or artificial materials into that flow. Take toxic ink, for example: To allow cotton to cascade from a T-shirt to padding to paper and then back into the natural biological cycle, you *must* make use of only natural pigments for your products.

Stock management: Optimizing technical cycles

Although the end goal for technical materials is similar to the end goal for biological materials — keeping them in use as long as possible before returning the individual components to the source of origin — there are some key differences between how these two material types are managed throughout their lifecycle and eventually reintroduced to the system. With the understanding that the circular economy's three main goals are to design out waste and pollution, keep products and materials in use, and regenerate natural systems, humans clearly will have to employ an array of strategies to achieve these goals. Because it's best to allow biological materials to cascade first, before eventually returning to natural systems, a similar set of preferable strategies can be identified for the technical cycles, with sharing the preferred circular economy strategy and recycling the strategy of last resort. The following list presents these strategies, in order of effectiveness:

>> **Sharing:** Sharing a product is the best way to keep products and materials in use for longer while minimizing the investment required to do so. What did your first grade teacher always tell you during recess? "Sharing is caring." Regardless of whether you were the nice kid who always played well with others or the bully who wanted all the toys for yourself, the circular economy can convince everyone that sharing is an extremely valuable solution to many of our society's issues around waste. For example, we'd like to ask you to go into your garage, shed, or basement and pick out a tool you'd commonly find in a home. How about that screwdriver in the corner, covered in dust? That tool — like the dozens of others you'll find stored in a toolbox — has the potential to be shared by a community rather than sit unused for 99 percent of its life. Sharing also reduces the quantity of tools needed to be made in the first place, reducing the material, carbon, and logistics associated with new tool production.

>> **Repair and maintenance:** Repair and maintenance keeps products in use at their highest level instead of letting them go to waste. Considering that some of the most complex devices — like cell phones, laptops, kitchen appliances, vehicles, and farming equipment — do break, once one component fails and the product no longer functions, it's not just that single component that gets thrown away — but rather the entire product. In time-sensitive situations, having to wait for a repairperson rather than already having the capability to fix products yourself can cost businesses a small fortune. This inability to self-complete repairs on everyday products, which is an extremely short-sighted approach to material lifecycle management, results in an absurd amount of technical material waste. Unfortunately, the reason most products aren't repaired by the user is that most products aren't often designed to be repaired. They are, instead, designed to offer a competitive, first-cost price — rather than maintenance costs — to the potential buyer to undersell those competing companies trying to sell you the same product. Long-term costs, or the costs required to replace that product after it breaks, aren't considered.

Sometimes, products are even produced to require tools that the average Joe won't have. The typical automobile, for example, consists of complex elements that are held together by a special fasteners, five that are unique to that specific vehicle. Building vehicles in this way is valuable for the manufacturers of these products. When the consumer's ability to repair their own products is eliminated, they're forced to rely on the manufacturer for maintenance services or a new product. Products are often designed to have a short lifespan so that the consumer will need to buy the manufacturer's latest-and-greatest model.

Let's consider an alternative approach that maintains the innate value of a product, extends that product's lifecycle, and results in no waste. Rather than throw away a malfunctioning product, consider the possibilities if a product's lifecycle can be extended by repairing and maintaining that product. Imagine if products were designed to be repaired easily by everyone. By doing so, the cost and energy required to remanufacture, recycle, or replace that product is ultimately eliminated and the power to extend the lifecycle of a purchased product now falls into the hands of the owner, not the manufacturer. Although it isn't a common practice for all technology, the trends do seem to be shifting, because the global market is now full of DIY repair kits for cell phones, cars, household items, and other items. This framework allows the users of a product to claim ownership of it and avoid replacement costs with a small investment of time and resources.

>> **Remanufacturing:** Making a new product from raw materials takes more time and money than remanufacturing an existing product that needs repaired. Let's use the car engine as an example.

When that engine fails, it's important to understand that those individual elements of the engine still hold a lot of value. Like the elements of a cell phone, these elements of a faulty engine can be stripped down, cleaned, and assessed for damages before ultimately being used to reconstruct a remanufactured engine. A lot of time and energy can be conserved if a remanufactured engine is used instead of a new engine. Roughly 80 percent of a faulty engine can be harvested and used to create a remanufactured engine, whereas the remaining 20 percent can be maintained and used as replacement parts. That's 80 percent less energy, 80 percent less material, and 80 percent less research-and-development required when compared to the construction of a new engine developed from raw materials.

>> **Recycling:** Just as waste is the last resort of a linear economy, recycling should be seen as the economy's last resort. Although it's absolutely critical to reclaim technical materials and provide a means for them to be circulated back into the system, recycling is still a lucrative process, and products (the combination of material) hold more value than the materials themselves.

Let's take another look at your cell phone. Pull it out and examine it closely. How many pieces can you identify? At first glance, you'll be able to call out half a dozen components that make up the shell of the device. Inside that shell, you'll find *dozens* more components of different sizes, shapes, and materials. Yes, those individual materials have value, but the value of a functioning cell phone comes from those materials working together. In reality, the functionality of the cell phone is much greater than the sum of its parts. This is the key reason that keeping a product in use for as long as possible will always outweigh recycling.

By recycling materials, you're losing value by removing the innate use of that product.

Technical materials can't be safely burned, composted, or returned to the soil, like biological materials can be. Doing so produces waste and pollutes the natural environment. These negative implications should be reason enough for supporting the idea that the circular economy's approach to technical materials — sharing, repairing, remanufacturing, and recycling — is critical for a healthy future.

If a product is designed with remanufacturing in mind, further savings can be obtained by proactively assessing and identifying the components that typically fail first. By designing this component on the assumption that it will need to be replaced at the end of its lifecycle, the cost and maintenance required for high-value products can drop severely.

Promoting environmental restoration: Investing now to obtain even more later

The most important differences between the technical material cycle and biological material cycle is the level of dependency on natural systems to provide a service and the potential for generating new resources. When reviewing the circular economy framework for technical materials, it soon becomes clear that ecological services aren't utilized to process these materials, nor are humans able to produce additional technical materials because they are *finite* — a category of material, like metals and fossil fuels, that can't be regenerated. In other words, in the technical material lifecycle, raw materials aren't accepted and broken down by natural systems to provide a new resource for extraction, nor can natural ecosystems be utilized to create new resources. Instead, humans are solely responsible for circulating and processing these finite, technical materials.

When reviewing the circular economy of biological materials, however, you can see that ecological services are utilized to process these materials, and the opportunity to generate new materials is possible because they're *renewable* — a category of material, like wood and cotton, that can be regenerated. In other words, in the biological material lifecycle, raw materials can be accepted and broken down by natural systems to provide a new resource for extraction, and natural ecosystems — powered by the sun — can be utilized to create new resources. This dependency on ecological services results in a serious takeaway: The only way to maximize the quality of these key, environmental systems that support our global economies is to incorporate their regeneration into the lifecycle of the products they provide.

Biological materials can take two different routes after they have had their chance to cascade through various uses. The first available pathway is the direct return to the manufacturing process as a raw material, and the second pathway involves its deconstruction into its basic elements to regenerate natural ecosystems. Here's a further explanation of both processes:

>> **Direct return:** After a material has cascaded through multiple uses, such as a timber building structure to building rafters to a wood pallet and then wood chips, materials still hold properties that can be incorporated into other products. The wood chips might, for example, be sent back to a manufacturer facility and combined with a glue to make oriented strand board (OSB) for a new building. The benefit of this pathway is that it takes little effort and energy to repurpose existing material into a new product.

>> **Deconstruction and regeneration:** In this pathway, the innate energy of the material is extracted and the remaining bioproduct is returned to the earth to regenerate the systems from which the material was originally sourced. Unlike direct return, materials that take the deconstruction and regeneration

pathway go through a much longer process before being used again. Let's say that, instead of being sent to the manufacturer facility to make OSB, the wood chips were sent back to the soil. From here, microorganisms — including bacteria and fungi — do what they do best and break down these materials into the basic elements of biological structures. These elements are then made available for new generations of plants, which will then be harvested to begin the material lifecycle all over again.

The major difference between pathways 1 and 2 is the regeneration of ecosystems. By reintroducing used materials to the soil through deconstruction and regeneration, the spent materials are directly regenerating the very ecological systems that produced those materials to begin with. With this understanding, the ability for us to continue to extract valuable, biological resources from these various ecosystems is directly dependent on our ability to deliver valuable, biological resources to those same ecosystems. The only way we can recover these key platforms that support our global economies is to incorporate their regeneration into the lifecycle of the products they provide.

MARISA GRUBER SPEAKS

Marisa Gruber, Partnerships Manager at the Cradle to Cradle Products Innovation Institute, likes to talk about where she works:

Making the circular economy into a practical reality ultimately depends on one thing: the global availability of products that have been designed and made to move easily from one cycle of use to the next.

To achieve this, future-focused product designers, manufacturers and brands must use safe materials that can be reclaimed, recycled or re-purposed once a product reaches the end of its useful life — over and over again. The Cradle to Cradle Certified Product Standard provides a framework for doing just that.

Widely recognized as the world's most advanced science-based standard for safe and circular materials and products, Cradle to Cradle Certified is based upon a set of design principles introduced by architect William McDonough and chemist Dr. Michael Braungart in their 2002 book *Cradle to Cradle: Remaking the Way We Make Things*:

Eliminate the concept of waste

Use renewable energy

Celebrate diversity

Cradle to Cradle Certified enables companies to put these principles into practice by providing the holistic guidance and technical requirements that ensure products made for the circular economy have a positive impact on people and on our planet.

Cradle to Cradle certification is awarded by the Cradle to Cradle Products Innovation institute to products that have been verified for rigorous performance across five critical areas of sustainability:

Material Health (ensuring a product's ingredient materials are as safe as possible for humans and the environment)

Product Circularity (designing a product so that its materials can be reclaimed, reused and re-channeled through multiple cycles of use)

Clean Air & Climate Protection (using renewable energy and best-in-class manufacturing practices that support a positive impact on air quality and the balance of climate-changing greenhouse gases)

(continued)

(continued)

Water & Soil Stewardship (implementing practices that safeguard watersheds and soil ecosystems, and ensure clean water and healthy soils are available for all people and organisms)

Social Fairness (upholding human rights and applying fair and equitable business practices)

Certification is awarded at ascending achievement levels from Bronze to Platinum, giving companies a clear pathway for continuously improving their existing products, and for innovating new safe and circular materials and products over time.

Showcasing the Cradle to Cradle Certified logo on their certified products also gives companies a valuable method of demonstrating to their customers that their products meet the world-class standard for product circularity and sustainability.

Cradle to Cradle Certified is widely used by brands and manufacturers across all major industries around the world, from the built environment to fashion, household goods to cleaning products, personal care to packaging. Tens of thousands of certified products are available at every stage in the global supply chain.

To learn more, visit www.c2ccertified.org/.

Chapter **11**

Analyzing Material Lifecycle Processes

Material choices play a fundamental role in designing for a circular economy. By choosing only materials that flow through a circular lifecycle, not only can you ensure safety for both humans and the environment, but you also make sure that the materials used to make your products can be reused without causing waste or toxicity. The good news is that a wide palette of such materials exists.

An important consideration when it comes to selecting circular materials is determining where they come from — how they're sourced, in other words. (The technical term for this process is *feedstock selection*.) Because of the possible negative impact on the environment and local communities from raw material extraction, the preferred feedstock selection method should be to recycle and reuse materials while also relying on renewable resources.

If your material is part of a technical cycle — material that cannot be broken down and returned to the earth as a result of biological processes — you have a number of areas to explore to ensure that the material flows within a circular lifecycle. These considerations include determining whether the material can be derived from waste from another industrial process or whether it's possible to derive it from waste sourced from the consumer. For both these options, you have to determine whether the waste stream has been properly defined so that you avoid the risk of future harm.

If your material can in fact be broken down and returned to the earth as a result of biological processes, there are also a number of different areas to explore to ensure that the material can be sourced in an ecologically responsible and renewable manner. These considerations include determining whether the material can also be derived from waste, such as agricultural byproducts or food waste, and whether resource extraction can occur while maintaining biodiversity and supporting critical ecosystems. In addition, it's important to determine whether the consumption of the material occurs at a slower or faster rate than the resource can regenerate. Within a circular economy system, the resource should always regenerate quicker than the resource is harvested, to ensure sustainable resource management and environmental regeneration.

REMEMBER

Claims are one thing — facts are another. With all these considerations, you *must* ensure that there's proof that these materials are responsibly managed for environmental, social, and economic benefits. A number of certification programs out there verify industry claims about the ecological impact of their products. Examples here are the Forest Stewardship Council (https://fsc.org), the Program for the Endorsement of Forest Certification, (www.pefc.org) and the Sustainable Agriculture Standard (www.sustainableagriculture.eco).

When you have selected a safe material and considered its lifecycle impacts, it's important to explore how the product containing the material would fit in a circular design. These considerations apply to both biological and technical materials. Start by asking these questions:

>> Will this material be combined with other materials or chemicals in the product? Can these materials be easily separated?

>> How durable is the material for the expected uses of the product?

>> What is the expected lifetime of use of the product containing the material? Will it require repair or maintenance?

>> How can the value of the material be recovered after the use phase of the product?

When you have selected a safe material and considered its circular design, you can then reflect on what will happen to the product after its use phase.

Beyond the questions listed here, you have to consider some additional variables. These areas in question differ depending on which type of material you're focused on:

>> **Technical:** With technical materials, recovery at the end of a lifecycle is a key element to ensuring that a lifecycle holds the opportunity to be circular. Here,

it's important to determine what is needed to recover the product, component, and/or material. Exploring this area of a product's lifecycle may include communicating with the customer and coordinating and collaborating with partners involved in the process. Once the product is recovered, you still need to incorporate further steps in order to make the process fully circular. You need to ask yourself how you could better design the product so that it's easier to recycle its constituent elements. One example is designing the product for ease of disassembly.

» **Biological materials:** In this regard, biological materials are the same as technical materials: Recovery at the end of a lifecycle is the key to ensuring that a lifecycle can be made circular. Beyond its capture, however, biological materials lack the option to be recycled, so you need to determine whether the material has been designed in such a way that it can biodegrade safely. Does the material need some special process (such as composting fermentation or wastewater treatment), technology, or infrastructure before it can return to the biological cycle?

Looking at Material Processes

The ecological impact of material processes used in the production of goods — cars, clothes, computers, whatever — poses a serious issue around the world. Many of the common materials used in the production of these goods are eventually thrown away and wasted during the production process. These materials are lost from the economy, and it would be extremely costly to reintroduce them to the global market after they arrive at the landfill. It has been calculated and estimated that roughly one-fifth of the materials extracted from the planet around the world are eventually discarded as waste. This, in terms of weight, is roughly 12 billion tons of waste material per year.

The level of economic progress and the astronomical rise in human population worldwide over the past 100 years has run parallel to extreme environment degeneration of the very resources that life itself depends on — not only the life of animals in the wild but human life as well. That means you. Around the world, humans are continuing to use more and more natural resources to fuel what Wall Street movers and shakers like to call "economic growth." In the grand scheme of things, not much has truly changed in the way humans produce materials. We have the potential to be smart, but it turns out that we can be pretty dumb as well. (Maybe it's that whole yin and yang balance at play?) As smart as we humans are, we continue to waste much of the raw materials we extract. One pound of every three pounds of food produced for human use is either allowed to rot before it's consumed or is wasted altogether. To no surprise, this situation is most common in the developed nations, where wasted food doesn't equal starvation. This continuous demand for raw materials — due to a lack of circular processes — is causing overextraction and environmental degeneration.

Over the years, the amount of material used in order to supply human needs has increased at an alarming rate. In the United States alone, in 2018, 292 million tons of waste was generated. That's just under five pounds of waste generated per person. Although roughly a third of it was properly recycled or composted, the United State is still miles away from managing its waste in a circular fashion.

The amount of material actually used by high-income countries is greater than their own domestic material generation, indicating that consumption in those countries relies on materials from other countries through international supply chains. On a per capita basis, high-income countries rely on 9.8 metric tons of primary materials extracted elsewhere in the world.

As higher-grade reserves are depleted, the quality of the remaining raw materials is degraded, leading to increases in energy and chemicals required to fill the gap. These additional requirements lead to larger releases of greenhouse gases, which then contribute to climate change. The kinds of chemicals and materials humans choose to use throughout the product lifecycle matter because they can pose risks to humans and the environment. Developing an awareness of the risks that stem from these material choices is the first step toward designing in a different way.

REMEMBER

When optimizing material processes for a circular system, it's critical that the implications of material choices are assessed within each phase of its lifecycle. From production and the use phase to the after-use phase and from the recapturing of materials to when materials are reintroduced into the system again, understanding how material choices impact the lifecycle is essential.

TIP

You can take a number of different approaches to ensure safer material choices. Mapping the product lifecycle can help you spot where the product's hazards may pose a clear risk to humans or the environment. Start by drawing a circle and listing every step along the materials progression around it. Sourcing, manufacturing, delivery, and recapture may be a few elements of the lifecycle you'll want to include.

After drawing a circle, identify where in the circle you foresee the potential for risks at each stage of the lifecycle. Here are some questions that may help you identify some areas of concern and potential improvement:

>> Where are your materials sourced from? And how?

>> Which chemicals may be used in the processes of sourcing, manufacturing, production, use, and after-use?

>> Which chemicals may be released as waste into our air and water during manufacturing? What happens to manufacturing wastewater?

>> Who will interact with the material at each lifecycle stage? Consider workers, communities, wildlife, users, and maintenance workers, for example.

>> What are the pathways to exposure? Are they through air, water, soil, ingestion, inhalation, or skin contact?

>> Are there aspects of the product design that may reduce hazards in the product to humans or the environment?

You have now identified where material and chemical risks can occur within your lifecycle. From here, take a look at where the potential risks fall. Cam any patterns be identified? Maybe the major risks occur during the production of the material rather than during the recycling, for example. Taking a deep dive to identify these patterns helps in adjusting the lifecycle at a systems level rather than at a surface level. Once the key areas of concern have been identified, fixing these areas of concern is a different ballgame. Mitigating these risks begins with three different approaches: transparency, chemical management, and innovation.

Fostering transparency

Material transparency, historically, has been a lot like a game show, if you think about it. You know, the old series where a helpless contestant would tremble aimlessly in front of three different doors and be directed to "pick one." Material transparency can often feel the same way. How can the consumer be expected to make the right decision when they can see the doors, but not what's behind them? Material transparency aims to open the door for customers and allow them to make an informed decision about the materials they want to interact with, build with, and even sell.

In the context of material health, exploring the lifecycle process allows the user to create an inventory of the materials and chemicals used in a product's manufacturing process. Compiling accurate and transparent information on the chemicals and materials used in a product is the first step toward ensuring that they comply with your standards. Activities related to the inventory approach include engaging with raw materials suppliers and creating a materials inventory or bill of materials (BOM).

Instituting chemical management

The screening and eventual denial or acceptance of chemicals takes place in a number of ways. If a chemical has been identified by a governing body as safe, it's

free to circulate through an open market. If a chemical is found to be hazardous —
to various degrees — that material is either removed from the market completely
or its use is limited. From regulatory compliance and restricted substances lists to
proactive toxicological assessments, data is used to eliminate known or suspected
hazardous substances and move toward safer chemistry.

Rewarding innovation

As the demand for various materials continues to evolve as new problems arise,
innovation steps in to offer a solution. When suitable substitutes don't currently
exist from a chemistry perspective, design innovation can help eliminate the need
for chemicals of concern while also ensuring that a product continues to meet its
function, quality, performance, value, and aesthetic requirements. These innovations rarely stem from inside the system itself. The United States post office didn't
invent email, and a candle maker didn't invent the light bulb. So, when innovation
is required to solve a problem, look outside the current system for influence
elsewhere.

The Lifecycle Principles: Identifying Where Change Can Happen

Knowing when and where change should be implemented in a material lifecycle is
difficult. That's why things aren't as peachy as they should be. When considering
alternative lifecycle processes — for any material — it helps to know where
change can actually occur. Within a circular economy framework, these three key
principles break up a material lifecycle:

>> **Focus on material sourcing:** The goal here is to preserve and enhance
natural capital — both renewable and finite materials — by controlling finite
stocks and balancing renewable resource flows. This principle, which applies
to both biological and technical material flows, is considered the first opportunity for change to occur within a material lifecycle.

>> **Optimize resource yields:** Here, you want to optimize yields by keeping
resources in circulation and increasing the rate of usage. Although addressed
differently, this principle also applies to both biological and technical materials. For biological materials, the material's end of life is delayed through
cascading and the extraction of biochemical feedstock before eventually being
returned to the earth. For technical materials, the material's end of life is
delayed by way of sharing, maintenance, reuse, and remanufacturing before
eventually being recycled. See Chapter 12 for more detail on this principle.

>> **Focus on minimizing systematic leakage and negative externalities (cost):** Essentially, the goal of this principle is to eliminate waste of all types — monetary waste, physical waste, labor waste, and so on. By optimizing the first two principles first, the amount of waste seen in a system should gradually diminish.

REMEMBER

By knowing how to address alternative lifecycle processes by referencing the circular economy framework principles just listed, process managers can more easily identify where change can actually occur.

Preserving natural capital

Let's take another look at the Ellen MacArthur Foundation Butterfly Diagram of the circular economy system — this time, in light of the three principles for creating alternative materials processes. (See Figure 11-1. For more on the foundation's Butterfly Diagram, see Chapter 10.) At the top of the diagram, you'll find Principle 1. In this area of the Butterfly Diagram — Renewable Flows Management and Stock Management — we are addressing the source of materials. Here, there's a separation between renewable feedstocks (called biological nutrients) and finite materials (technical nutrients, in other words). Clear features distinguish these two cycles: biological nutrients (wood, paper, cork, or cotton, for example) have the ability to decompose when returned to nature; whereas the technical nutrients (aluminum, iron, or plastic, for example) do not decompose, which is why their useful life must be prolonged by design.

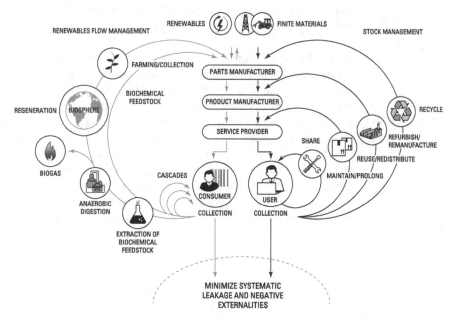

FIGURE 11-1:
The Ellen MacArthur Foundation Butterfly Diagram of the circular economy system.

Products must be redesigned to facilitate the separation of each product's components so that at end of life it can be easily disassembled and the parts reused. Designing highly intricate products with an array of materials to perform amazing services is great and all, but if it can't be used for very long or it can't be recycled to create another product with a similar level of performance, is it truly valuable?

Enhancing the usefulness of products, components, and raw materials

Slotted in the middle of the Butterfly Diagram, you'll find Principle 2. Within this area of the diagram, you see the meat of the lifecycle and the processes involved. When analyzing the process steps between the extraction of resources and the use of the final product, you see a number of steps. Each uses energy to accomplish its task. And each step produces waste.

On the technical side of the Butterfly Diagram (refer to Figure 11-1), note that the component parts of any product are designed and manufactured to be uniform so that they can be reused after they've been safely and easily disassembled. Allowing this to take place facilitates their continuous reintroduction into the production system. Doing so eliminates unnecessary waste and keeps down the demand for raw materials. Looking at this through a business lens, rather than have product sellers, we have service providers that optimize the use of resources through a wide range of strategies, such as modular design, durability, and repairability. Decreasing the amount of raw materials required eliminates the cost of extraction, resulting in a competitive advantage. By reducing the need to produce new components, we also reduce our dependence on virgin resources.

On the biological nutrients side, the first opportunity for the user to eliminate waste and maximize the value of a resource is called *cascading.* This creates a platform for products to be cyclically reused for several purposes. For example, clothes made of organic cotton can be reused to produce new articles of clothing, which in turn can be reused to produce insulation material for construction or for filling pillows or beanbags. The same statement applies to materials such as cork or wood. Once a material has reached the end of its life, value remains in the material, in the form of energy. Through various biochemical extraction techniques, the same energy that was required to grow the original product can be extracted once more for further use. Finally, the remaining biological nutrients can be safely returned to the biosphere in the form of compost, thus regenerating the soil and its fertility and closing the nutrient cycle.

Developing effective systems that minimize negative externalities

At the bottom of the Butterfly Diagram (refer to Figure 11-1), you find Principle 3. Within this area of the diagram, the goal is to eliminate *negative externalities* — waste from the system, in other words. It's possible to not only minimize the volume of resources that end up in a landfill but also recapture the waste generated within lifecycle processes.

REMEMBER

For a long time, organizations have been attempting to do less harm by focusing on the efficiency of processes rather than on the process itself. It's like trying to sharpen the corners of a square tire to make it run more smoothly. The problem is that "less harm" is still doing harm. Efficiency doesn't eliminate the opportunity for waste; it only reduces the amount produced. If you have the outlook that "the glass is half-full," I'm sure you're eager to explain why efficiency is still important, and it is. Please don't get the wrong idea. But the focus of Principle 3 isn't efficiency. The focus should be on doing well via effectiveness and building resilient systems. Doing well involves creating value for all parties involved, including organizations, communities, living beings, and the environment.

Looking at Opportunities for Optimization

The first opportunity for optimization is through potential sharing services. By sharing certain materials and products, the use rate of whatever it is that's being shared is optimized, at no additional cost. Those willing to share gain more freedom to live their lives unencumbered — and some extra cash as well. Share what you own and what others own. Share almost anything, including cars, extra rooms, tools, books, kitchen utensils — anything that's used only occasionally. It's probably best to shy away from sharing underwear, spouses, and other intimate items, though. But other than that, go for it!

REMEMBER

The circular economy depends on you sharing with others and on others sharing with you. More often than not, it makes a great deal of sense to share. Imagine an alternative history where Henry Ford developed the Model T under a community sharing program instead of selling them outright to individual owners. Even during the initial explosion of the automobile, the car wasn't something that was used nonstop. Today, the average American uses their car 4 percent of the time. During the other 96 percent of the time, that car — which suits your personality perfectly, by the way — is just sitting there, losing value. You're sitting on your rear in an office so that you can pay to not sit in that car you bought.

Aside from cars, others have discovered opportunities for optimization by sharing. By utilizing accommodations that would otherwise be sitting empty, Airbnb and the other accommodation services reduce the need for new construction of hotels and motels. With companies like Uber and Lyft, you can hail a ride from drivers in their personal vehicles. With services like Turo and Zipcar, you can rent a vehicle, owned by a for-profit or nonprofit organization, and pay only for the time you drive it. And with newer companies like GetAround, you can rent privately owned cars by the hour or day when their owners don't need them.

We can see the confusing look on some of your faces. Where's the opportunity for optimization in Uber and Lyft? Anyone who has been to New York City in the past decade has seen the wave of yellow taxicabs crash down Broadway to provide rides to the ever-expanding population of the Big Apple. Though taxis and rentals aren't new concepts and have made successful business models for quite some time, sharing these personal vehicles offers a lot of additional incentives and can cost close to half as much as a traditional taxi ride. Knowing that some people won't want to rent a car for an entire day — maybe they just need a car for a quick grocery run — companies like Zipcar instead charge only for the time and the distance driven. This allows companies like these to increase their competitive edge by charging their customers much less than a conventional rental car company. I'm sure it hurts some business's bottom line, but sharing is the future. Got to catch up or get left behind.

Because sharing greatly increases the hours of use for any product, the total number of products needed to meet the needs of a community are greatly reduced. The total time of usage is unaffected, but there's a decreased demand for new products, and therefore the amount of mineral extraction and emissions from the manufacturing process are also reduced.

Look back at that product lifecycle map you developed earlier and see where there may be opportunities for sharing. What else can be shared? Where are there other opportunities for optimization?

Refusing the new: Reusing the old

Say goodbye to the endless and repetitive purchase of things. Now that companies are providing a product as a service, you pay for the performance of a product rather than for the privilege of owning it. Rather than be responsible for the purchase, maintenance, repair, and replacement of a product, companies are now providing the full use of an item but without the costs and hassle of owning them — and at a much lower cost and at higher rates of efficiency.

For example, HP realized that selling ink cartridges created a high product-to-waste ratio and ended up costing both the company and end user a lot of money in the end by constantly requiring the input of new, raw materials. HP realized the opportunity for optimization via reuse and changed their operations in response. Now, HP's new printers are able to notify the company when its user's ink cartridge is running low and automatically order them a new one. Once the user receives their new cartridge, they can send back their old cartridge via a prepaid envelope. This process allows HP to reuse its plastic cartridges multiple times, which reduces its supply costs and optimizes its profits through reuse.

HP is not the only company that has realized the opportunity for optimization via reuse. eBay and Craigslist are built for reuse! They allow you to buy, sell, and trade new and used goods with little or no face-to-face interaction. You can pretty much find anything you're looking for on these websites, which has led to their continued use and popularity. Though you can find almost anything you want on these platforms, others — like Kidizen (www.kidizen.com), an online marketplace exclusively for children's toys and clothing — successfully focus on specific niches.

Buying anything new is rough because you will, without a doubt, be paying more than what the product is actually worth. Online and in-person retail centers will always charge extra to keep their services up and running. When you buy a previously used item on eBay, Craigslist, or other reuse sites, however, those costs are avoided.

Employing the remaining factor: Remanufacturing

Machines of all types are spread out across the globe. Before they were constructed, thousands of man-hours, as well as large sums of money and time, were invested to create these extremely detailed machines. The advantage of machines is that tedious work can be eliminated to focus instead on creative and organizational activities. The disadvantage of machines is that they have a limited lifespan and can often be difficult and/or expensive to repair and maintain.

When a machine stops working, traditionally it has often been more economical to replace the machine completely rather than hire someone to troubleshoot and repair it, with little to no certainty that something else won't go wrong with the machine the following day! Having one machine down can cost a company thousands, if not millions, of dollars, as its rate of production drops. This understanding results in a high level of technical waste.

This doesn't have to be the case, however. There's an opportunity for optimization via the remanufacturing of these machines. If machinery is remanufactured rather than built from scratch with virgin materials, components could be cheaper to make — at the same time saving large amounts of money in material inputs and reducing emissions. Guangzhou Huadu Worldwide Transmission, a Chinese auto parts supplier, acts as a useful case study to illustrate the value of remanufacturing as a service. This company not only creates effective channels for the collection and distribution of used and remanufactured transmissions but has also been authorized by more than 30 major auto companies to provide maintenance services.

REMEMBER

Machines are heavy and pricey, and the potential for remanufacturing machines makes this opportunity for optimization a hopeful opportunity for businesses. Not only will customers be able to obtain remanufactured — yet still high-quality — products at a better price, but the producers of those remanufactured items are also able to receive a higher profit margin. Remanufacturing is a no-brainer when you consider how you can improve your material lifecycle. Remanufacturing requires next to no virgin materials, keeps products and materials in use for longer periods, and eliminates the majority of waste commonly found in machine lifecycles.

Biochemical extraction for the win

Once a natural material can no longer be used, it's often immediately considered waste and thrown out. There are, however, numerous opportunities to extract the very energy that was used to grow that material to begin with. *Bioenergy* is energy derived from any fuel that originated from biomass — timber, for example. Biomass is a renewable resource, just like wind and solar — even if it often isn't recognized as such by the general public — and therefore is an alternative (and resilient) source of sustainable energy. Historically, biomass in the form of firewood has been used to provide energy through direct combustion.

The value of biochemical extraction is that biomass residues and waste resources are able to be converted into new resources. (Keep in mind that this is waste that would otherwise have been left to decompose.) Although some biomass is specifically grown to be used as fuel, biochemical extraction allows additional energy to be extracted from residue as well as waste resulting from resources that were grown for other purposes, like food or fiber. Though this conversion of biowaste to a new energy source involves many complex processes that don't need to be addressed in this book, the main takeaway is that additional value can be extracted from waste material.

REMEMBER

Opportunity for optimization is not only available within the technical lifecycle — biological waste also often still holds value at the end of its useful life. Technology and processes are available to fully extract the value of a resource before it's returned to the earth to support the growth of further resources. For biological materials, the essence of value creation lies in the opportunity to extract additional value from products and materials by cascading them through other applications. In biological decomposition, whether it's natural or in controlled fermentation processes, material is broken down in stages by microorganisms, like bacteria and fungi, that extract energy and nutrients from the carbohydrates, fats, and proteins found in the material.

Examples of extending the value of a biological material through biochemical extraction are described in this list:

>> **Food fermentation:** This is a creative (and ancient) way to process and preserve food. The processing strategy involved here utilizes the growth and metabolic activity of microorganisms — real, living creatures — for the transportation of food in one form into a completely different form. Fermentation was originally crafted as a way to preserve perishable agriculture food items. This built-in a certain level of seasonal resilience, allowing people to survive on leftovers from last year's harvest during times of drought and low crop yield. Since its origins, though, the technology involved in the process of fermentation has evolved dramatically to serve as more than just a backup plan. Fermentation is now a tool for creating desirable organoleptic, nutritional, and functional attributes in food products.

>> **Livestock waste:** This type of waste can be an alternative energy source for livestock farmers through the use of a biodigester. An anaerobic digester partially converts livestock waste into energy, in the form of biogas. This biogas — made up of mostly methane — can be used to run farm operations or be sold to local distributors. Manure is easily collected on dairy and hog farms where cows are routinely confined. Biogas is most efficient when used directly for heating, and dairy farms have a year-round demand for hot water. You can see how a closed loop system, developed to manage livestock waste while also generating and utilizing a renewable energy source, would fit well into a circular economy model.

>> **Biodigesters:** As difficult as they are to build and develop, biodigesters are fairly simple to understand. Organic materials that are decomposed by bacteria in an airless environment release biogas, as part of the respiratory process of these microorganisms. As long as farmers continue to funnel continuous amounts of livestock waste into the digesters, the living organisms within the system that produce the natural gas will continue to feed on the organic waste and maintain a consistent flow of renewable energy. (That's a pretty good deal, if you ask us!)

The best part about the closed loop process of biodigesters is that it is truly a closed loop. After all the gas is extracted, the slurry within the digester can also be extracted and sprayed onto fields as a form of fertilizer. This fertilizer then helps to grow the same crops that will feed the cows, who then generate the livestock waste that will again be funneled into the digester and circle back to the beginning again.

JEFF FROST SPEAKS

Jeff Frost, Project Manager and Materials Specialist at Brightworks Sustainability, has a few things to say about where he works:

Brightworks Sustainability is a multi-disciplinary sustainability consulting company whose clients are frequently Fortune 500 companies with large, often global, real estate portfolios. In recent years, as the imperative to address our global climate catastrophe becomes harder to ignore, an increasing number of companies are setting pioneering sustainable goals — such as being carbon neutral by 2030 and carbon positive by 2050. With these new commitments and an increase in stakeholder and shareholder pressure to meet them, our industry is seeing new tools and resources emerge to meet these challenges.

At Brightworks, we developed a scoring framework called Brightside to help our clients interpret the complexities of the market. It allows us to take complex criteria and factors from our industry and assign numerical values across six primary impact categories: health, carbon, circularity, water, waste and social. For circularity, where metrics are lagging, we turned to a recently updated methodology by the Ellen MacArthur Foundation called the Materials Circularity Indicator, or MCI. The MCI is part of a broader Circular Indicators Project that allows companies to identify additional, circular value from their products and materials.

While the MCI presented a viable framework, we felt the need to make some qualitative adjustments based on current industry practices. For instance, the MCI values all sustainably-sourced materials equally (whether recycled, reused, or biodegradable) and values all landfill avoidance strategies equally (such as recyclable, reusable, compostable, energy recovery). Our industry has already placed preferences between these different options. Looking at the end-of-life strategies, we know that it's better to have a material be recycled versus end up in energy recovery and on the sourcing side we know that not all recycled content is the same.

At Brightworks, we found their methodology to be both rigorous and highly adaptable and, more importantly, numeric; giving us an output that would fit into our scoring model approach.

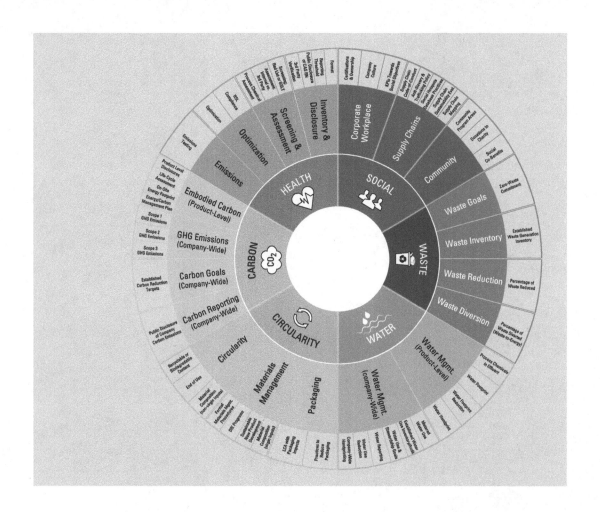

Chapter **12**

Improving the Material Lifecycle

E very material has a lifecycle: It has a birth (extraction), a process of growth (manufacturing), a life (use), and eventually a death (disposal). If you grasp that basic fact, you can then start to identify ways to improve the quality of that lifecycle and ways to minimize and mitigate its impact on the environment. Surprisingly, the best way to improve the lifecycle of anything — any product or material — is to start questioning the way we humans do things.

The way people produce products and manage materials has remained relatively unchanged for the past century. The world has seen, of course, advancements in manufacturing, robotics, and processing, but at the end of the day, we're still just pulling valuable commodities out of the ground and slowly turning them into landfill in the most expensive way possible.

Most of the manufacturing-and-design decisions behind how our current economy works have gone unquestioned. And why would it be questioned, anyway? Manufacturers were able to cheaply source, extract, produce, and ship their products to everyone all over the world. For a long time, there seemed to be no reason to even think about improving the lifecycle of their materials.

Today, we know better. We know that ignoring the impact of a product's lifecycle on the environment has dire consequences. From pollution to species extinction to the climate crisis, we humans can no longer afford to continue doing things the way we always have been doing them. That's why we need to rethink and improve the lifecycle of everything.

Improving How Material Lifecycles Function

At the end of 2020, a team of scientists from the Weizmann Institute of Science in Israel ran the numbers and determined that humans have officially crossed a dark threshold: The weight of human-made stuff (all the things we've produced and built) has surpassed the weight of all living things on Earth (biomass). In other words, all the built environment now weighs more than all the animals, plants, insects, and bacteria on the planet. Human-made stuff weighs approximately 1100 gigatons, and 9 gigatons of that amount is just plastic. Animals are only 4 gigatons, so plastic outweighs animals by more than 2-to-1. (And yes, we're including all animals, even whales and elephants, in that arithmetic!)

As Bill McKibben reported on this research in *The New Yorker* magazine, "In 1900, the weight of human-made mass was three percent of the weight of the natural world; we were a small part of the big picture. No longer. We live on Planet Stuff."

We explore how to understand the lifecycle of a material or product in Chapter 10, and we dive into how to analyze it in Chapter 11. In this chapter, we examine some ways to improve the lifecycle of your product so that its quality and experience improve as well.

Analyzing the lifecycle of your materials begins by asking some simple questions:

>> Where did this material come from?

>> What are the by-products of its manufacturer?

>> How is the material delivered and installed?

>> How is the material maintained and operated?

>> How healthy are the materials?

>> What should we do with the materials when we're done with them?

To really improve your materials lifecycle, however, you have to ask different questions that inspire innovative, circular thinking. Over in Chapter 7, we talk about the following six steps to circular systems:

>> **Refuse:** Say no to what you don't need.

>> **Reduce:** Use less for longer.

>> **Reuse:** Extend the life of a product.

>> **Repurpose:** Find other uses for a product.

>> **Recycle:** Return materials for rebirth.

>> **Rot:** Return materials to the soil.

Following these strategies raises new questions about your material or product. Remember: These questions are supposed to be challenging. (Hey, we didn't say going circular is easy!) By asking these questions, you can start to create a road-map to improve the lifecycle of your product:

>> Can we redesign the product to use less mass and material? Is every part critical to the function?

>> Which parts fail or wear out first that need to be redesigned so that they don't force our customers to throw away the product?

>> What if our product lasted forever? Could we redesign the product to be upgradable?

>> Are there additional functions or uses for our product so that it can have more utility?

>> Are there ways to use recycled or reclaimed materials in the production process instead of virgin material? What if we took back old products and provided replacements?

>> How do we redesign the product to be easily disassembled and repaired? Can we make it from recyclable or compostable materials?

Figure 12-1 summarizes how a traditional, linear approach to the economy answers these questions compared to a circular approach.

REMEMBER

No one thinks these types of questions are easy to answer. Asking them just reframes how you design your product to anticipate a circular economy. Use these questions as a design exercise for your team to explore how to rethink, reimagine, and redesign all your products.

LINEAR ECONOMY

RESOURCE EXTRACTION | PRODUCTION | DISTRIBUTION | CONSUMPTION | WASTE

CIRCULAR ECONOMY

RECYCLING SECTOR
RE-USE/REPAIR/RECYCLE
PRODUCTION
DISTRIBUTION
CONSUMPTION

FIGURE 12-1:
Comparing a linear versus a circular approach to lifecycle.

Looking at Materials in a New Way

If the traditional lifecycle of a product is linear because it's a straight line from the raw material to the product being used to the product becoming waste (take-make-waste), then the lifecycle of a circular product is (unsurprisingly) circular. So this requires "bending" some of those linear lines into loops that bend resources back into themselves.

A company called doTERRA (www.doterra.com) produces a whole host of personal care products from all over the world, including essential oils, skin care, and supplements. The branding focuses on how the products contribute to a healthy lifestyle, and the customers expect them to source responsibly.

The mission statement reads: "With responsible and sustainable sourcing, our mission is to improve the lives of your whole family and families around the globe with every doTERRA purchase."

Understanding this mission deeply, the company realized that the local plant growers in 40 countries around the world are their partners. Fully aware that the company needs to protect the long-term sustainability of its partners, it has paid them a fair and livable wage and trained them to ensure that their supplies will last for generations.

Another company, Bionic (`https://bionicyarn.com`) harvests waste plastic from the ocean and transforms it into a durable yarn that can be made into anything. This process not only reduces the need for using new materials, because it's using a recycled product, but it also helps clean up the plastic waste from the oceans, which increases the biodiversity of aquatic life.

Such innovations don't just happen — they come from inspiration. They require identifying potential problems and their impact along a material's lifecycle to spark an idea.

Getting to know your lifecycle

The process of analyzing and mapping out all the impacts of a product lifecycle is called a *lifecycle assessment*, or LCA. The LCA is usually the first step a company can take to understand the full scope of the impact that their products have on the environment. Not all the information contained in the LCA is bad news. Companies are often delightfully surprised to find that some of their suppliers may have already taken more responsibility for how they source their raw materials.

WHO NEEDS "NEW" THINGS, ANYWAY?

Somewhere in our culture, we decided to glorify new products as somehow being better than old ones. The push has always been to replace "that old thing" (which might be working fine) with a shiny new version of the same thing.

Companies, of course, want you to buy more of their product, so they have discovered ways to entice you to get rid of that old product and replace it with a new one, even if you don't need it. For example, last year Apple told everyone that its newest iPhone is the "best one they've ever made" and "so much better" than the one you already have. The temptation to upgrade your phone is strong, so you do it. But now it's a year later, and Apple again puts out a new iPhone that's the "best one they've ever made," and this one has all these new features that your new phone does not. Once again, you're tempted.

There's something to be said for maintaining and preserving products so that they last. Beyond the environmental arguments of reducing waste is a romantic and sentimental reason to keep using the same products you already own (not to mention how much cheaper it is to save your money!).

Part of the challenge of embracing a circular economy is overcoming how people have normalized constantly buying more stuff.

(continued)

(continued)

Complex products like cell phones are difficult to recycle and tend to end up in the land-fill. Worldwide, electronic waste (or *e-waste*) makes up more than 5 percent of all municipal solid waste. Only around 15 to 20 percent of e-waste gets recycled.

If your customers understand that they don't need new things all the time, perhaps this is a chance to find other ways to sell them your products without relying on total replacement, including software updates or individual component upgrades or designing the product to be fully recyclable.

Legendary furniture company Herman Miller (`www.hermanmiller.com`) first designed its Mirra chair in 2003 to be fully circular. This fully adjustable chair is made from nearly half recycled materials, and despite all its parts, can be disassembled in less than 15 minutes, allowing the company to take it back and remake those parts into brand-new Mirra chairs with a 97 percent reuse rate. That "new" chair you're sitting on might not be new at all.

Refuse before you reduce, reuse, and recycle

If complex products are difficult to recycle, you might assume that it's okay to continue buying products if they're easier to recycle. Though it's certainly better to buy products that are made from recycled content or are easily recycled, it doesn't address the prevailing mindset that we have to keep buying new stuff all the time — even if we don't need it. Part of the challenge in forming a true circular economy is learning to refuse that temptation to buy new whenever it can be avoided. Let's romanticize the idea of reuse instead of buying new!

If you have to buy new things (and, obviously, we all do, from time to time, and you shouldn't feel guilty about it), here are some purchasing issues to consider before you click that Add to Cart button:

>> Is it a single-use item?

>> Does it come in nonrecyclable packaging?

>> Can I reuse or recycle it when I'm done with it?

>> Does it have only one use or function?

>> Do I already own an item that can do the same thing?

If you answer yes to any of these questions, you might want to rethink that purchase.

Examining Operations in a New Way

Just as a product or material has a lifecycle, so too does a business. Because a circular business is one that builds and rebuilds the overall health of our environment, it also needs to follow the same basic circular economy principles we discuss throughout this book:

>> Design out waste and pollution.

>> Keep products and materials in use.

>> Regenerate natural systems.

REMEMBER

Whether your company produces physical products or not, there are certainly opportunities to do all of these: Design out waste and pollution, keep products and materials in use, and find ways to regenerate natural systems. Every business has some sort of operational impact that can be examined and improved.

Looking at human capital

People are at the heart of every business. They are your customers, partners, and employees. Your relationship to these people determines whether you have happy customers, satisfied partners, and productive employees. Their well-being is critical to the success of your business. Taken together, the resources such individuals provide represent what is known as *human capital.*

The Social & Human Capital Coalition (`https://social-human-capital.org/`) has developed guidelines on how to look at the circular and sustainable approaches to your human capital that measure them beyond financial performance, by looking at the ethical and societal benefits of the people you serve.

You can be everywhere

Typically, people have clustered together in cities, making them densely packed hubs of activity. Most jobs and services were located in urban centers, forcing most to move to cities or to surrounding areas and commute into the city daily. All this resulted in polluted and crowded urban areas.

A circular city changes this model. Rather than face more pollution and more crowding, the city is designed to be restorative and regenerative through the use of green spaces and urban forests and eliminating the models that produce waste. Once products and services are decoupled from depending on endless consumption and waste, suddenly there's an endless and abundant supply of materials and resources to be used over and over again. Your products and services can be sold to everyone, everywhere, without worrying about the impact such sales create.

A business whose operations are designed around the circular economy uses only renewable materials and renewable energy and takes responsibility for the impact from its products or services.

Connecting Sourcing, Suppliers, and Customers

Thanks to the connectivity and availability of information on the Internet, customers can easily monitor, track, and speak out against the negative environmental impact of your company's products or services. As a result, an increasing number of companies are embracing transparency.

Transparency refers to disclosing all your sources, distributors, and suppliers and the ingredients in your products. For some manufacturers, being transparent with the supply chain starts to uncover opportunities to reduce or mitigate the impact their products create. According to a 2018 report by Nielsen Company, LLC, 48 percent of consumers in the United States say they would adjust their purchasing habits to reduce their impact on the environment.

This cultural shift has led businesses to connect their customers to their supply chain in ways never seen before, in order to build trust and brand awareness and attract new customers. Truly circular organizations invite their customers in to join them along each step of the redesign-and-innovation process.

In 2019, an online petition posted by the environmental nonprofit organization Greenpeace was signed by over 91,000 people and led grocery chain Trader Joe's (www.traderjoes.com) to quickly eliminate a million pounds of plastic from its more than 500 stores. The store is achieving this goal by reducing how it packages produce — by replacing Styrofoam trays with recyclable, compostable, or renewable alternatives, for example. The store, which also stopped offering single-use plastic bags to customers, has since announced a new goal to eliminate more than a trillion pounds of plastic across its stores nationwide.

Figure 12-2 is an example of how a grocery store can share its commitment to reducing plastic waste. Such simple educational posters have been shown to have a big effect on their customer's behavior.

Popular footwear company Keen (`www.keenfootwear.com`) publicly set a design goal to eliminate a long list of "chemicals of concern" from its supply chain. Per-fluorinated chemicals (PFCs) are typically used to repel water, dirt, and oil on footwear, but are also toxic and persist in the environment. Keen is now at 95 percent PFC-free (with the push to reach 100 percent).

This situation translates into more enthusiasm and sales for Keen, as well as a clear market signal to its competition that they need to do the same to stay relevant. That's the power of transparency and sharing your goal to improve your company lifecycle. The potential benefits of shifting to a circular economy extend to the natural environment and into our overall economic health.

REMEMBER

Transition to a circular economy produces impacts that will be felt throughout our culture and economy. The potential for economic growth can be found in all these recommendations. A lower cost of production increases profitability. Material changes could result in massive material cost savings of up to $700 billion annually, according to estimates by the Ellen MacArthur Foundation.

In addition, the increased spending, lower prices, higher quality, and job creation from new recycling and remanufacturing efforts will fuel an economic boom, according to a study by the Centre for European Economic Research. More innovation also leads to more competition, which leads to more economic growth. These changes in supply-and-demand ripple throughout the entire economy. Understanding and improving your lifecycle is the key to achieving these amazing results.

ABRAHAMSSON LINDEBLAD SPEAKS

IKEA (www.ikea.com) is perhaps one of the most well-known furniture and lifestyle brands in the world. You probably have an IKEA product in your home right now. The company has set a bold goal to become 100 percent circular across its thousands of products by 2030. We asked Peter Abrahamsson Lindeblad, a circular business designer at IKEA, to share the company's efforts on this ambitious and impressive goal:

Ingka Group is the largest IKEA franchisee. Its core business is IKEA Retail, which consists of 378 IKEA stores across 30 markets. Each year, Ingka welcomes 706 million visitors to these stores, and it sees more than 3.6 billion visits to IKEA.com.

In 2016, Ingka Group started out its circular transformation journey by trying to understand how customers can be incentivized to bring back textile materials to stores. It soon dawned on company leaders, when meeting with the customer, that this was very much an inside-out way of looking at circularity. To stay true to the IKEA vision to create a better everyday life for the most people, the leaders had to turn things around and start with an understanding of people's real challenges in relation to circularity. The journey to the creation of circular business models starts by comprehending the problem from a user's point of view. Only then can solutions be created that are viable in the long term, relevant for the many, and better for the planet.

To-date, the circular team at Ingka Group has spent hundreds of hours talking to hundreds of people in places all over the world to capture their thoughts, feelings, and friction points in relation to consumption and circularity. Those meetings, planned interviews, and spontaneous interactions with all these people have helped the company identify the common challenges people face in their lives at home. We've learned that circularity as a concept is too complex and distant — people just want help in living their everyday lives and doing the right thing. Though there are many differences, we're seeing common themes around ownership, restoring value, and the desire to declutter emerging in many places.

People are increasingly living in smaller spaces, and there's a growing awareness of the impact of consumption on the planet. This means that people value possessions more and have different expectations of new products and services. For example, they want things that offer personalization, community, and a more emotional connection as well as quality, durability, and functionality. Most people also feel bad about throwing things away, and there are often no good options to part with things in a sustainable way. This can lead to excess clutter at home or feelings of guilt. People generally view the idea of giving away, selling, and fixing positively, but they need support and it needs to be convenient.

The key to circular business transformation lies in the way we as a company empathize with people and respond to the friction points in their everyday lives in a way that prevents things from falling out of the use system. Customers need to be offered alternatives — alternatives that solve people's challenges and creates new, sustainable, and viable business for us as a company while also reducing the dependency to a constant in-flow of virgin materials. In short, we need to enable people to live healthy and sustainable lives within the limits of the planet.

Chapter **13**

It All Comes Down to Selecting the Right Materials

Sometimes, identifying and selecting the best materials for a circular economy is like looking for a needle in a haystack: It's hard, but it's possible if you know what to look for and you understand the overall goals of the circular economy. But what if you don't know the difference between a needle and a stack of hay? Without knowing what makes a material the right choice, it's nearly impossible to pick one out.

The most common materials you'll find circulating through the global economy are plastics, metals, glass, and wood-based and paper products. Each of these is popular because it has some sort of material benefit that serves a need well. In a perfect world, the advantages of these materials must outweigh the disadvantages for them to stay in circulation, but unfortunately that's not the case. Many hazardous chemicals are part of the production process for materials that are still in circulation and being used regularly. Many of these chemicals can be found in your immediate space as well. Unfortunately, though companies regularly make the advantages of these common materials clear to the end user, they often keep the disadvantages — environmental degeneration, pollution, harmful chemical release, and so on — "unintentionally" hidden.

So, how is the end user to know which is the best product to choose? Fortunately, the majority of products that are actually worth considering have certain characteristics that are often highlighted as part of the product's marketing campaign in a specific document known as an environmental (or health) product declaration.

Environmental product declarations, or *EPDs,* for short, are documents that outline the findings of a product's life cycle assessment. By poring over these documents, users can discover what impact the product has on the environment. Common variables that are often reported are the quality of recycled content contained within the product, the global warming potential, and smog creation. Health product declarations, known as — you guessed it — HPDs are similar to EPDs because they address the product's impact on health. However, rather than address the product's impact on environmental health, HPDs address the product's impact on human health. Common variables often reported include the quantity of volatile organic carbons (VOCs) and formaldehyde emitted. Having resources such as EPDs and HPDs available increases product transparency and provides the user with the necessary information for them to determine which products can support a circular economy.

The Good, the Bad, and the Ugly: Exploring Materials

Thousands of material types are flowing through the global economy at any given time — plastics, metals, paper, cardboard, glass, and everything in between. Each of these material types has good characteristics (which make them of interest to begin with) and bad characteristics (which make alternatives for them of interest). The sourcing, manufacturing, use, and end-of-use of all these materials play a major role in determining which material makes the most sense for which use.

In this section, we identify the top materials used within the global economy, identify unintended consequences of their use, spell out their advantages and disadvantages, and give examples of how their use (or misuse) can be improved.

Oil or Plastics — They're Really Much the Same Thing

Not many people know that the word *plastic* is of Greek origin and that it means "able to be molded or shaped." This definition is fitting because it's one of the most valuable aspects of plastic: its ability to take so many different shapes and forms. In addition to being able to take many forms, most plastics are extremely durable and long-lasting, making it a useful material in the construction of homes and other buildings. In the world of auto manufacturing, plastics have contributed to the growth in safety, improved fuel efficiency, and the creation of the aerodynamic form that allows for smooth travel at 70 mph.

Plastic also helps to preserve food and drinks that would otherwise spoil if not protected from air. This ability reduces the amount of food waste and allows for exotic foods to be shipped around the world for everyone to enjoy. Without plastic, folks in the United States would have to kiss most of their foods goodbye.

You might think: "Why not use glass instead of plastic? It serves the same purpose, doesn't require oil, and can be fully recycled." Well, glass, for one, weighs substantially more than plastic does. Replacing plastic with glass would vastly increase the weight of the product being shipped, resulting in more use of fossil fuels. This exact reason is why Coca-Cola swapped out its glass bottles for plastic bottles. The amount of fossil fuels required to ship the glass bottles outweighs the amount of fossil fuels used to produce the plastic bottles.

Though these benefits have made plastic an absolute necessity for the global economy, it's well-known that plastic pollution causes harm to pretty much everything: humans, animals, and even plants. The fact that plastic will not fully decompose for hundreds (if not thousands) of years makes the mismanagement of plastic a critical issue worth resolving. (*Mismanaged* plastic waste is plastic that isn't properly reintroduced into various lifecycle opportunities and instead ends up in uncontrolled landfills or dumps; from there, plastic can eventually leech into oceans via waterways, wastewater outflows, and wind.)

For a look at the global scope of the mismanaged plastic-waste problem, check out Figure 13-1.

Plastic isn't going away anytime soon, either. Global plastic production continues to increase, bringing with it a rise in the negative impact on the environment. It's estimated that the global economy has generated roughly 8.3 billion pounds/375 metric tonnes of plastic since the mid-20th century. (See Figure 13-2.) Of this amount, less than 10 percent of it has been recycled, just over 10 percent has been burned, and the rest has ended up in landfills or free in the environment. This, unfortunately, doesn't account for the synthetic fibers used in clothing and other products, which accounted for roughly 61 million tons of plastic produced in 2016 alone. (For more details on the circular economy for fashion and clothing, see Chapter 18.)

Thanks to global research, we now know that roughly 90 percent of the raw material used to make plastic is lost at the end of its original use — which means that less than 10 percent of it's recycled into another use. That also means the consumer is forced to continue paying — during each purchase of a plastic product — for not only that new, raw material but the extraction and processing of that material as well. This wouldn't be the case if plastic were properly managed within a circular economy.

Mismanaged plastic waste, 2010

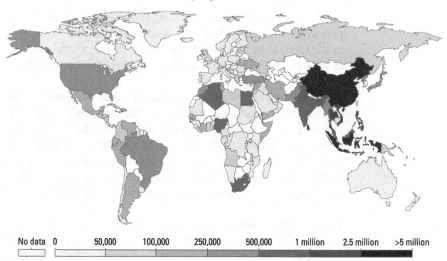

FIGURE 13-1:
Mismanaged plastic waste.

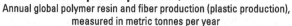

No data | 0 | 50,000 | 100,000 | 250,000 | 500,000 | 1 million | 2.5 million | >5 million

Global plastics production, 1950 to 2015
Annual global polymer resin and fiber production (plastic production), measured in metric tonnes per year

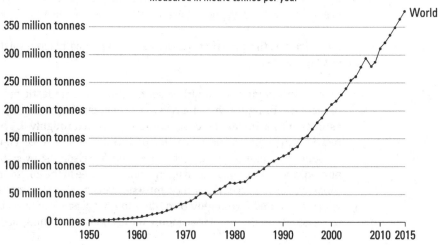

FIGURE 13-2:
Measuring global plastics production.

Not all plastics are created equal, which makes the proper management of plastic a difficult issue to solve. But plastic today is harder than ever to manage and properly source. So many types of plastic are floating around that it's difficult to know where everything goes. The only resource the end user has is the famous Recycle logo, encircling an identifying number and posted on the bottom of most plastic containers. Go ahead and find a nearby plastic item — does it have a recycling logo on the bottom? Would you know if that number is a sign that this plastic item can be recycled?

What does this number even mean? It turns out this number identifies which type of plastic makes up that product and, as we mention earlier in this chapter, not all plastics are created equal. Though most types of plastic technically can be recycled, it's most often up to the various city, state, or county authorities to determine whether that type of plastic is recyclable. There's no consistency in how plastic is managed, which aids in the confusion on the part of the consumer when it comes to identifying role in ensuring that plastic pollution is reduced and the materials are kept in use for longer periods. Some recycling facilities still throw away plastic if it hasn't been emptied or properly rinsed of any food.

Generally, there are seven common types of plastics and, luckily for you, they're *easy* to remember (just kidding): polyethylene terephthalate (PET), high-density polyethylene (HD-PD), polyvinyl chloride (PVC), low-density polyethylene (LD-PE), polypropylene (PP), polystyrene (PS), and others (O). Got it? Great. Table 13-1 shows a breakdown of the numbers associated with these types of plastic, their names, and their common application.

TABLE 13-1: ## Plastic Types and Applications

Number	Name	Common Application
1	PET	Water, soda, sports drink bottles
2	HD-PD	Detergent and shampoo bottles, grocery bags
3	PVC	Plumbing pipes, children's toys, vinyl flooring
4	LD-PE	Bread bags, produce, newspapers, and garbage
5	PP	Yogurt containers, furniture, luggage
6	PS	Cups, plates, packing peanuts
7	O	CDs, baby bottles, headlight lenses

Some plastics are safe. Other plastics are not. And without a doubt — as unpopular of an opinion as it might be — plastic is a chemical marvel that has become a necessity in the global economy. Plastic can be shaped into just about anything, it's light and durable, and it can help maintain the freshness of many critical resources, like food. Its major downfall is the amount of pollution and unsafe plastic circulating around the world right now. It's a bit out of control, to say the least.

TIP

Don't know which plastics your local recycling service will accept? Check your service provider's website for details.

What's Harder than Rock? Metals

Metals are amazing. Their very atomic structure gives them so much power to be useful. Because of this structure, metals are extremely good conductors of both electricity and heat. On top of that, metals can be extremely *malleable* — able to bend and stretch when placed under enough stress rather than simply snapping in two. This ability provides metalworkers with the opportunity to shape this magic material into different shapes and forms to make a wide array of products.

Though the advantages of metals are endless, metal materials definitely have some disadvantages to them as well. This list describes a couple of them:

>> **Corrosion:** Some metals — if not properly treated — are susceptible to corrosion. This means that metals commonly exposed to moisture — cars, pipes, and those tools you keep in the basement, for example — will eventually erode and no longer be of any use to you. Water and air both play a large role in the corrosion of metals. (People often forget that the Statue of Liberty wasn't originally green.)

>> **Expense:** On top of corrosion, some metals are extremely expensive because of their rarity and the amount of processing required to make them into something useful. The amount of energy required to extract and process metals into useful products also holds a lot of weight, not to mention the environmental degradation that stems from the extraction of metals from the earth.

REMEMBER

Different problems call for different solutions, and metals solve a lot of problems. Depending on which characteristics you're looking for — aside from superhuman strength or glow-in-the-dark capabilities (for now) — there's a metal that can provide it. Steel, iron, aluminum, magnesium, copper, brass, zinc, titanium, nickel, tin, lead — the list of available metals seems to be never-ending. And the physical and chemical differences between all these metals is absolutely astounding! The following list describes some of the most common metals and their common application:

>> **Aluminum:** Aluminum — or "uh-LOO-mini-um," for those of you across the pond — can be used in a lot of different ways. From electronics and soda containers to aircraft and power lines, there's a lot that aluminum can do. In addition to its ability to serve a lot of different functions, aluminum is infinitely recyclable. It has good conductivity and is relatively malleable — allowing it to be shaped into many different items, like ladders and doors. It's one of the most favored metals in a circular economy system because of its ability to be fully recycled without losing any of its value during the recycling process (unlike plastics).

>> **Titanium:** Titanium is not only stronger than iron but also half as dense. This combination of properties makes it one of the best metals to choose for structural elements. It's quite often used by the automotive, aerospace, and marine industries because of its strength-to-weight ratio. In addition, titanium resists corrosion and has a high heat tolerance. For this reason, it's also often used for cookware, electronics, and other appliances. As if we haven't said enough about how great titanium is, it's also biocompatible, which makes it a useful metal to pair with living tissue as part of surgical procedures. (At what point does a human become a cyborg? Asking for a friend.)

>> **Iron:** Iron is definitely the most used metal of them all. Why, you ask? Because it's naturally abundant in the natural world, it's relatively inexpensive, and it can be used for a wide array of services. It's easily recyclable and possesses no major environmental threats in its pure form. Although iron has these advantages that make it a popular option for electronics, it's extremely vulnerable to rusting when it comes in direct contact with air. So, unless it's combined with other alloys — like steel — iron may prove to be problematic in some applications.

>> **Graphene:** This material is amazing — graphene not only is harder than a diamond but also has higher elasticity than rubber. On top of that, it's more durable than steel and is lighter than aluminum. It's a metal that you'd imagine a superhero using to build the ultimate suit. It's extremely thermal and electrically conductive, which makes it extremely useful for electronic applications such as bendable screens, optimized transistors, and advanced circuitry. Given that it's made up solely of carbon — the most abundant element on earth — it's environmentally friendly. Although the make-up of the material is environmentally friendly, the production of this material certainly isn't, as many harmful solvents and chemicals are necessary to make graphene.

Paper Products and Cardboard

Although the digital era is upon us, the global economy is still dependent on paper products and cardboard. Globally, per year, the production of paper is hovering around 550 million tons. That's equivalent to 5 million blue whales, ten *Titanics,* or 84 great pyramids of Giza. That's a lot of weight! And we can't ignore the source of that weight: trees. Unsurprisingly, massive amounts of paper production will also require massive amounts of natural resource use. To put this statement in perspective, to produce just one ton of paper, you need roughly 24 trees, 17,000 gallons of water, and 32 million BTUs of energy. Not only are all these resources needed for the production of paper but additional resources are also needed upstream for the actual harvesting of these resources and downstream for the disposal or recycling of these resources.

Upstream, the biological materials required to create paper and cardboard are being extracted without properly being replenished. This isn't a sustainable setup. Though some aspects of paper production do have the potential to be renewable — the production of timber, for example — other aspects, like freshwater, are outside of human control. You can make freshwater out of wastewater or saltwater, but it's extremely energy intensive and often not worth it in the long run. If you've taken a single economics class in your lifetime, you know that, as the availability of a product begins to decrease, the cost of that product increases. How, then, will the paper industry adjust as these resources become more and more scarce?

Downstream, unfortunately, paper and cardboard are often trucked off to landfills or are released back into the environment. Although this natural product will break down and return to the soil, it's still an unused resource that could be harnessed by manufacturers to offset the amount of raw material required to serve the demand for paper products. Fortunately, the answer to our question at the end of the previous paragraph can be answered by fixing this problem downstream.

REMEMBER Within a circular economy framework, the waste of one system becomes the food for another. The paper-and-cardboard industry is no different: By properly collecting and reintroducing wastepaper products back into the manufacturing process, the amount of waste produced as well as the quantity of raw materials required can be drastically reduced. It's a win-win situation.

Four main phases need to be addressed to transition the current, linear process of paper production to a circular one. Here's what's entailed in each phase:

>> **Design:** This is where the magic happens — where the issues are identified and resolved. No matter the material, the transition from a linear lifecycle to a circular one starts in the design phase. Designing paper and cardboard products to be durable and recyclable is a prerequisite for achieving a circular

lifecycle. Regarding durability, a product holds more value the longer it's kept in use due to the lack of energy and raw materials required to replace it. Once a product can no longer be used, it must also be designed to be fully recyclable. By this, we don't mean that the product is designed to fit in the hole of a recycling bin. Instead, the product must be fully composed of recyclable materials. Just adding a single toxic dye or glue into the mix may prohibit the entire product from being recycled.

The main goal of the design phase, again, is to identify where the issues fall and how best to resolve them. If you're using this book as a resource to do just that, start by sketching out your own material flow. Identify the areas of virgin material input, how this material is circulated, and where the material is lost as waste. Figure 13-3 shows an example to get you started.

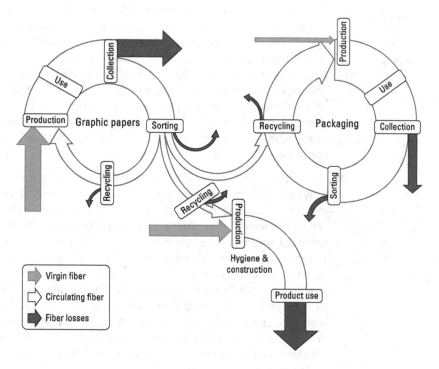

FIGURE 13-3:
Picturing materials waste.

» **Production:** When addressing the production phase, there are two primary areas of concern:

- *Material inputs,* or which materials (energy, water, and wood, for example) are required in order to produce your product and what improvements can be made to reduce the negative effects of those inputs

- *Material outputs,* or which materials (gas emissions, chemicals, or wastewater, for example) are a result of the production process and what improvements can be made to reduce these hazards

Within a circular system, virgin resources need to be replaced with secondary or tertiary resources. These are resources that have been reclaimed after their original use and are not sourced directly from the natural environment. These material inputs should stem mostly from other systems' material outputs. For example, the byproducts of the previous production of paper — something like cellulose pulp — should be redirected back into the manufacturing process to offset the amount of virgin material required. Because the current capacity of secondary materials doesn't meet the demand of the paper industry, raw materials should be sourced from forests that are continuously being replenished. When one tree is cut down, another is planted.

REMEMBER

The production of paper and cardboard products results in quite a bit of waste. From sludge and emissions to boiler ash and wastewater, many byproducts need to be managed via elimination or redirection. As we've already noted, some byproducts can be used again in the manufacturing process, but other opportunities are available as well. By getting creative and thinking outside the box, it's possible to make every waste product a resource for another system. For example, the leftover paper fibers and other filling agents are often used by brick manufacturers to increase the volume of their products. In addition, paper sludge can be utilized in fields as a source of nutrients. The possibilities are endless when waste is seen as a resource.

» **Usage:** During this phase of the paper and cardboard lifecycles, the responsibility transitions from the manufacturer to the user. The ultimate goal is for the user to maximize the use of the paper and cardboard they have and reduce the need for new material. Unfortunately, the system has for too long depended on the desire of the individual to support such a system without providing the necessary incentive. In a perfect world, every individual would do their best to ensure that they take on the necessary responsibility to maintain a circular economy. However, this isn't the case and should never be relied on as a means to facilitate circular material lifecycles. Extending material usage and minimizing the need for new material needs to be economically beneficial for the user in order for them to participate. This key variable should be considered during all other phases: design, production, and recapture.

» **Recapture:** As with every other material within the circular economy, there's no end of life — only the recapture phase. Waste material is material that hasn't yet seen its next life or purpose. With this notion in mind, you can see the value that can come from properly recapturing waste and funneling it to act as a new resource. Even after a product is no longer functional, the innate value of a product can be recaptured and redirected with the help of physical and chemical processes for further use.

Recycling is valuable for a lot of reasons, but the main reason is the amount of virgin material it substitutes. By recycling a ton of paper, you offset the need for 17 living trees to be harvested, 6,800 gallons of water to be used, and roughly 4,100 kWh to be generated. Unfortunately, the recycling of paper products cannot go on indefinitely. Because of the natural breakdown of the fibers and the material lost during production, additional raw materials will eventually be required. However, by recycling, the demand for those virgin materials can be reduced dramatically.

Once paper materials can no longer be recycled or cascaded into other uses, that material can be used to generate electricity by way of efficient incineration practices. (For more on the role that cascading plays in managing biological material lifecycles, see Chapter 10.) The byproducts from that incineration can then be used for a number of other purposes, too, such as compost or a soil stabilizer. The carbon emissions from the incineration process can also be captured and incorporated into other products of higher value, like plastics and concrete.

REMEMBER

A key goal of the circular economy is to keep materials in use for as long as possible. Despite not having a negative impact on the environment, keeping biodegradable products in use for as long as possible is still better than using them once and then throwing them away.

Through the Looking Glass

The best part about glass as a material is that it's 100 percent recyclable and holds the ability to be recycled over and over again with no loss in the quality of the material itself, so long as it has not been mixed or combined with other materials or variations of glass. This is one of the variables that separates glass from other materials, like paper and cardboard, which can be recycled only a half a dozen times before the material itself is no longer functional. Glass is also made from readily available materials, like sand, limestone, and cullet (which is a special term used to describe recycled glass).

Utilizing glass as a resource is extremely beneficial because of the reuse efficacy factor. The more recycled glass that's used, the fewer raw materials and the less energy required to source and process virgin materials. One ton of carbon dioxide is offset for every six tons of recycled glass used in the manufacturing process. That's a big offset. In addition, over a ton of natural resources — sand, water, and so on — are avoided and saved for every ton of glass recycled. As long as individual have incentives to return their glass products, the glass industry has a bright future ahead. States offering a deposit for used glass containers see a recycling rate just over 60 percent, and those who don't offer a deposit fall to just over 20 percent, according to the Container Recycling Institute (www.container-recycling.org).

Though the use of glass as a resource offers some obvious benefits, it also has some downsides. Though glass containers are 100 percent recyclable, in other applications of glass where it's combined with other materials, like metal and plastic (windows and ovenware, for example), the glass no longer becomes 100 percent recyclable, because of the manufacturing processes involved. Introducing these materials back into the glass lifecycle can cause some issues — and even defects in products. Recycled glass must be free of all contaminants (like metal, stones, and ceramics) if it's to be fully recycled. In situations where glass can't be recycled, there are some secondary uses available (such as a sandblasting agent), including incorporating it into tile, pavements, parking lots, and countertops and flooring.

And Everything In-Between

Though this chapter covers many of the most-often-used materials within the global economy, there are thousands of others we could address. Prioritizing those that hold the most impact means that we can't cover them all. In addition to plastic, metal, glass, and paper and cardboard, two other materials are worth mentioning:

>> **Concrete:** First things first — concrete isn't the same element as cement. Cement is an ingredient in concrete that acts as the binding agent to hold together the stone aggregate and the metal reinforcements. Concrete is used for a number of reasons because of its cost, strength, curing time, and ability to be formed into a variety of shapes. This material is used for bridges, buildings, and roads — some of the most critical components of global infrastructure. Concrete is a material that can easily be recycled and used repeatedly. Fortunately, the mix required to produce concrete is somewhat simple, allowing for it to be fully recycled at the end of its use. At the end of its life, concrete is crushed into smaller pieces and filtered to ensure that no impurities are passed on to its next use.

Though concrete is a useful material, the cement used to make concrete has a hidden cost: embodied carbon. The production of cement is estimated to be responsible for around 8 percent of the world's total carbon emissions. That's a large amount when compared to the other components that make up the other 92 percent. (See Figure 13-4.)

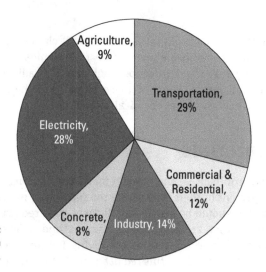

FIGURE 13-4:
Tracking carbon
emissions.

(Pie chart showing: Agriculture, 9%; Transportation, 29%; Commercial & Residential, 12%; Industry, 14%; Concrete, 8%; Electricity, 28%)

>> **Hemp:** Fortunately for us all, the industrial production of hemp — not the psychoactive plant — was legalized in 2018. This is a major step in the right direction. Hemp isn't a new material, either. Many of the US Founding Fathers owned hemp fields, and even Henry Ford made various components of his cars from hemp. Hemp fibers are some of the strongest materials on the face of the earth and can be easily recycled and reused. Though timber-based paper can be recycled only half a dozen times, because hemp is so much stronger, it can be recycled through more iterations, greatly reducing the demand for raw materials.

Hemp holds many benefits as feedstock for not only paper products but bioplastics as well. The raw materials that can be extracted from hemp are grown much quicker than timber and require less water to grow. Hemp requires no pesticides and helps to restore soil health and storage capacity, making it ideal to be incorporated into crop rotations. In addition, it's a carbon-positive plant, meaning that for every ton of hemp produced, one-and-a-half times that much carbon is taken from the air. As with all materials, the major challenge is the recapturing of the raw material after its use. Aside from that, hemp has no major downsides, and it's about time it received the acknowledgment it deserves.

Identifying Hazardous Materials

Hazardous materials are defined as any materials that have a negative impact on the health of their surrounding lifeforms. Unfortunately, many hazardous materials are in use, and it can be difficult at times to accurately identify them. These hazardous materials have been split into nine different classes by the US government: explosives, gases, flammable and combustible liquids, flammable solids, oxidizing substances, toxic and infectious substances, radioactive materials, corrosives, and miscellaneous. Some of these classes are then further divided based on their varying physical and chemical properties.

Red list materials

Within the built environment — the human-made surroundings where humans spend roughly 90 percent of their time — are ten hazardous materials, known as red list materials, that should be avoided at all costs. This red list acts as a compilation of chemicals that are harmful to humans and should ultimately be removed from the market. The International Living Future Institute (https://living-future.org) has identified this red list as part of its living-building challenge certification.

Though the ultimate goal is to remove these red list materials from the market altogether, another goal is to encourage the materials industry to be more mindful about the materials it utilizes and exposes humans to. There are certainly far more than a mere ten chemicals harmful to human health, but the current red list focuses on those that are most urgent:

» Asbestos

» Cadmium

» Chlorinated polyethylene and chlorosulfonated polyethylene

» Chlorofluorocarbons (CFCs)

» Chloroprene (neoprene)

» Formaldehyde

» Halogenated flame retardants

» Hydrochlorofluorocarbons (HCFCs)

» Lead

» Mercury

» Petrochemical fertilizers and pesticides

» Phthalates

» Polyvinyl chloride

» Wood treatments containing creosote, arsenic, or pentachlorophenol

Red list material alternatives

Though some red list materials, like PVC, have some realistic alternatives, others are harder to replace. This is why most red list materials are still commonly used today — there's just no current alternative that is competitive in terms of price and is readily available. Here are a few alternatives worth considering for some of the most commonly used red list materials:

» **PVC:** Within the built environment, PVC is commonly used for a number of products, such as electrical wire sheaths and plumbing. PVC electrical wire sheaths can be substituted for metal sheathings, but these often cost more and are harder to work with. Though PVC piping can be replaced with metal pipes — such as copper, steel, or iron — these materials are much heavier, are susceptible to corrosion, and cost a lot more. Though other alternatives, such as cross-linked polyethylene, offer the flexibility and price to make it competitive to PVC, it cannot be recycled and the health effects aren't widely understood.

» **CFCs and HCFCs:** Both of these chemicals are refrigerants that are commonly used for air conditioning and heating units as well as for refrigerators. They're also commonly found in a variety of foams and aerosol products. Hydrofluoroolefins (HFOs) are a practical replacement for CFCs and HCFCs and can act as both a refrigerant and an aerosol. In addition, carbon dioxide can act as a refrigerant alternative, but it would require a special system not commonly used. Both these alternatives are cheaper and have lower global warming potential than CFCs and HCFCs.

» **Halogenated flame retardants:** These chemicals are often found in furniture, upholstery, and insulation. Nonhalogenated flame retardants are available for use that can replace the halogenated versions with minimal change in performance. In addition, foam insulation is available that can be used to fully avoid halogenated flame retardants that are quite often found within different types of fiberglass insulation.

» **Formaldehyde:** This chemical is widely used in a range of products, like laminate flooring, glues, adhesives, and wood products. In addition, formaldehyde commonly acts as a binding agent in fiberglass insulation. Some fiberglass insulation manufacturers have identified alternative binding agents — such as acrylic — that are renewable. In addition, recycled cotton insulation can act as an alternative at no higher cost.

Volatile organic compounds (VOCs)

Volatile organic compounds — or VOCs, for short — are human-made chemicals that cannot be found in the natural world. These compounds are often used in the production and manufacturing of pharmaceuticals, refrigerants, and even paints. VOCs typically act as industrial solvents or emerge as by-products produced during the chlorination process at wastewater treatment plants and are often incorporated into petroleum fuels, paint thinners, cleaning agents, and even hydraulic fluids.

The concentration of VOCs is what should be of concern. At minimal levels, the health effects are extremely minor, but indoors, where the concentrations can be as much ten times higher than the outdoors, the health effects can be major. Look around your home or place of business and you'll surely find areas where VOCs may be present. See whether you can find any of the following items: paints and lacquers, cleaning supplies, pesticide, copiers and printers, glues and adhesives, furniture, or markers. The list goes on from there. Did you find any? (Check out Chapter 17 for more details on VOCs in the built environment.)

Sourcing, Ethics, and Standards

Part of creating a circular economy is minimizing the harm that comes from the material lifecycles themselves. Yes, the products themselves have the potential to be harmful, but the process of sourcing, manufacturing, and building with these materials and products creates massive amounts of pollution To help the builder, manufacturer, project owner, and user all make the right decisions, the appropriate information is needed to ensure that materials and products have been sourced in a strategic manner, have been ethically acquired, and have met the standards set by leaders of the industry.

Understanding strategic sourcing

Strategic sourcing is a materials approach that looks at the big picture. it's all about generating channels of exchange that take into account all activities (and partners involved in completing those activities) within the lifecycle of a product to ensure that the highest value is captured — rather than simply the lowest price. Strategic sourcing also aims to minimize the risks associated with the various elements of the supply chain, which, in case of a disruption, can cost the company a lot of dough. Don't think that strategic sourcing is just a one-time activity, either. As the market fluctuates, business goals shift and suppliers change — and so do the activities involved in strategic sourcing.

REMEMBER

The reason a circular economy isn't already a common practice within the global economy is that it takes so much coordination and money to change the structure on which the entire global economy is built. It's easy to make the small changes — for a shoe company to test out a better product in the market, for example, or for a car company to try out the functionality of metal with higher recycled content — but it's extremely difficult to change the entire system to support circularity on every level.

There's never a single entity who's in charge of managing every phase of a product's lifecycle, which is why strategically sourcing elements of a product from suppliers who share a common goal of maintaining a circular flow of materials is critical — and is a necessary first step in creating a circular flow of materials. By generating long-term relationships with these companies, you can act as an agent of change and encourage them to adjust their operations to better suit your desire to produce your product within a circular framework.

Establishing ethics

Though we're talking about the strategic sourcing of materials, we want to tackle another layer of proper material sourcing that needs to be considered: the ethics behind the sourcing of the products and materials in use. *Ethical sourcing* is the method of guaranteeing that the materials and products in circulation have been extracted, manufactured, and sold in a responsible manner, that those who are involved in the process have safe working conditions and appropriate pay, and that the environmental and socioeconomic variables have been considered.

Exploring certifications and standards

One way to ensure that a manufacturer is committed to a circular approach is to see whether its efforts have been certified by reputable independent organizations. Here's a list of certifications to look for:

>> **Cradle to Cradle Certified:** This certification (www.c2ccertified.org/get-certified/product-certification) ensures that products are composed of environmentally sound materials that aren't harmful to human health. In addition, products that receive this certification are designed for reuse, recycling, and/or composting, which is a major component of creating a circular economy framework for the future. In addition, this certification is concerned with the efficiency of manufacturing, the use of renewable energy to fuel that manufacturing, and the proper use and protection of water resources.

>> **TRUE — zero waste certification:** The goal of the TRUE certification (https://true.gbci.org/true-program-zero-waste-certification) is to divert all solid waste from landfills, incinerators, and the natural environment. Spaces that have been TRUE-certified are more efficient with their resources and help create value from waste. With the ultimate goal of closing

the loop of materials, TRUE aims to minimize the greenhouse gas emissions, risk, litter, and pollution associated with the built environment.

>> **Made Safe:** This is the first nontoxic seal in the United States for everyday products found in the home, including personal care and countless other household products (www.madesafe.org/find-products/products). The goal of Made Safe is to let the consumer know that the products they're using have been created with materials that won't cause harm to their health.

>> **Energy Star:** A program managed by the US Environmental Protection Agency (EPA), Energy Star is one of the most easily recognizable efficiency labels on the market. This program (www.energystar.gov) aims to identify which products and appliances meet certain efficiency requirements. Appliances, electronics, and lighting fixtures are all qualified to become labeled by Energy Star. Even new homes that have installed high-efficiency heating, ventilation, and air conditioning units can receive Energy Star recognition.

>> **Water Sense:** As Energy Star is focused on the energy efficiency of products and appliances, Water Sense is focused on the efficiency of — yup, you guessed it — water (www.epa.gov/watersense/watersense-products). This label is also issued by the US EPA for products that are at least 20 percent more efficient than a standard product found in the market.

>> **FSC:** This certification, awarded by the Forest Stewardship Council (FSC), accredits those forest managers and timber companies that manage their operations and consumption of timber in a responsible manner. Unlike Energy Star and Water Sense, FSC certification isn't a government-regulated certification; rather, it's a not-for-profit, independent organization, and the certification itself is 100 percent voluntary.

>> **Greenguard:** This certification (www.ul.com/services/greenguard-certification) is focused on ensuring that high levels of indoor air quality are present inside the built environment. When a product becomes Greenguard-certified, it means that it has met some of the most demanding and difficult requirements for low emissions of volatile organic compounds (VOCs) within an indoor environment. It's such a trusted certification that most of the green building codes, policies, and rating systems around the world give credit to projects that use Greenguard-certified products.

>> **LEED:** Leadership in Energy and Environmental Design (LEED) is the most widely known and accepted third-party certification system used for green buildings (http://leed.usgbc.org/leed.html). Over a million square feet of building is certified every day! Project owners decide to pursue LEED certification because of the wide range of sustainability categories the certification platform addresses. Location and transportation, sustainable sites, water efficiency, energy and atmosphere, materials and resources, and indoor environmental quality are all addressed within a LEED-certified building.

» **Living Building Challenge:** The Living Building Challenge is also a certification program — similar to LEED — but it's much more demanding (`https://living-future.org/lbc-3_1/certification`). This certification requires the most advanced sustainability performance levels within the built environment and addresses seven key performance categories: place, water, energy, health and happiness, materials, equity, and beauty.

» **Green Seal:** This certification standard (`https://greenseal.org/certification`) aims to help manufacturers, users, and businesses make the most responsible choices when it comes to fostering a net-positive impact of a business on the environment. Thousands upon thousands of products have been certified to meet the standards set by Green Seal.

Chapter **14**

Circular Materials, Products, and Packaging

W e live in a world where doing "less bad" is not only accepted — it's even seen as "doing good." You wouldn't praise a thief for stealing less than they could have ("It's okay — he only took the big bills!"), but for some reason, doing less bad has been prepped, polished, and presented as doing good. Transitioning from a linear economy, where less bad is a driving force, to a circular economy, where doing good is built in as an operational philosophy, requires planning. Waste can be eliminated (instead of reduced), products can be used much longer (rather than used once and disposed of), and environmental systems can be regenerated to provide services (instead of being harvested). But it takes planning.

Keeping products in use forever requires identifying why products are wasted to begin with and discovering alternative strategies. Who decided that waste was acceptable, anyway? Though some products are intended to fail via *planned obsolescence* — designing a product to have a limited range of use to fuel additional demand — others simply aren't designed to be reused. To successfully move away from planned obsolescence, planned permanence will need to be acknowledged as a valuable opportunity. This shift won't destroy businesses by reducing demand for products, but will rather fuel new and resilient business opportunities that promote a new demand for maintenance and repair services.

People will always require things, and on top of their maintenance and repair, the way those things are created and distributed leaves some room for improvement. The impact of distributing things can be greatly reduced by simply eliminating the need for shipment via new technologies, such as 3D printing. With the proper material and technology available, buying a replacement part from a manufacturer halfway across the world can be substituted by printing the part yourself at the maker lab down the road. Eliminating this location-dependent availability will greatly reduce the cost and emissions associated with shipping while offering new opportunities for businesses to provide a service. Not everything can be 3D-printed, however, so if a product does require shipment, improvements can be made via shipping strategies and the use of permanent packaging.

The only way for materials, products, and packaging to shift from a linear process to a circular process is by acknowledging that less bad is not good, keeping things in use for as long as possible, and being smarter about how things are sourced and shipped. In this chapter, we explore where the current management of materials, products, and shipping falls short and offer some alternative strategies that will aid in the transition from linear to circular.

Redesigning Materials and Products: The Transition from Linear to Circular

Transitioning from a linear economy to a circular economy doesn't just mean eliminating waste. This transition requires a mindset shift and a realization of what's actually possible. The linear economy has been built on the false premise that waste is a natural part of fueling the economy. If people can keep using products, businesses will go under, right? Wrong. If people can keep using products, there will be a demand for maintenance services, repair services, and remanufacturing services. The circular economy won't end business opportunities — it will create new ones.

With this shift comes the need for planning — planning for waste-free manufacturing, planning for higher product durability and an increase in demand for maintenance and repair, and planning for material reincarnation. Materials don't become value-less after their initial use. They can serve another purpose as long as the means for repurposing are available.

"Less bad" does not equal "good"

There's a major misconception that doing less bad is a good thing. Reducing demolition and construction waste by 50 percent is a start, but sending the other

50 percent to the landfill is still degenerative. Making paper out of 50 percent recycled content is better than no recycled content, but it still means that 50 percent of that paper caused the destruction of an entire ecosystem. Less bad is certainly a necessary step on the way to good, but it should not be treated equally. Rethinking how lifecycles can function, and reusing and repurposing materials and products\ are all available strategies to create a regenerative lifecycle. Simply recycling and reducing can help reduce the negative impacts of a linear economy, but they still cause harm. To properly transition from linear to circular and have a positive impact on the environment around us, eco-efficiency (reducing the negative impact on the environment) will need to gradually be replaced with eco-effectiveness (increasing positive impact). See Figure 14-1 for a graphic illustration representing this transition.

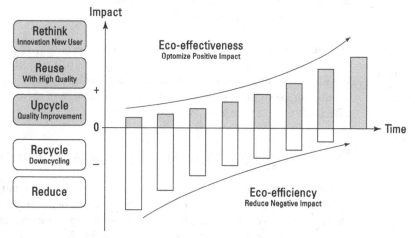

FIGURE 14-1: Transitioning from eco-efficiency to eco-effectiveness to create a positive impact.

Linear, or degenerative, lifecycles take more value out of the economy than what they give to the economy. They extract valuable resources and use them once before throwing those materials away. Overall, there's a net loss in value within a linear lifecycle. Consider the manufacturing of paper products. Trees, which provide the world with fresh oxygen, remove carbon dioxide from the environment and capture and store stormwater are harvested to produce paper products. These products are used only once before being piled up in a landfill or burned at an incinerator. An extremely valuable resource is destroyed to create a piece of paper for you to doodle on once and throw away. Within this degenerative lifecycle, more value was taken away from the global economy than what was given. (You might think your doodles are valuable, but they certainly don't create the air we breathe.) Though doing less bad is possible by managing the forests better or coming up with more efficient ways of producing paper, waste is still an expected and acceptable outcome of the material lifecycle. The linear economy has been built on this premise, whereas the circular economy is built upon the understanding that a new reality is possible.

Circular (regenerative) lifecycles deliver more value to the global economy than what is taken. Overall, there's a net gain in value within a regenerative lifecycle. Taking the same example — the manufacture of paper products — we can explore how to transition a degenerative lifecycle to a regenerative one, by using alternative sourcing and incorporating opportunities for multiple uses. As for sourcing, trees offer too many ecological services and hold too much value to be used for paper (right away). Instead, forests should be maintained for their ecological services, and proper structures should be embedded in society to recapture and reuse biomass that has already served a purpose. In a circular lifecycle, trees would be left alone, for the most part. Which trees are harvested should be used for higher-value services first, like building structures and furniture. Paper should then be sourced from those products after they reach the end of their useful life. This system allows the raw material to hold much higher value, by embedding multiple uses within its lifecycle. (If you source your paper from a rocking chair instead of from trees, feel free to doodle all you want.)

REMEMBER

Transitioning from a linear economy to a circular economy requires the rejection of the Less Bad = Good approach and the redesign of material lifecycles altogether. It will require dramatic changes in sourcing and manufacturing strategies, the elimination of single-use products from the market, and the use of products that adds more value to the global economy than they take away.

Planning for material reincarnation

Within the linear economy, achieving a zero waste lifecycle isn't realistic. Raw materials are constantly extracted from the natural world to feed the manufacturing process, and those materials are either landfilled or incinerated when they no longer serve their intended purpose. The reason that waste is inevitable within a linear economy is that products and materials aren't designed to last or to serve additional purposes. In systems where material reincarnation is supported, businesses and manufacturers design their materials and products to be *upcycled* or *downcycled* rather than simply thrown away.

Upcycling is the act of refurbishing a material or product at the end of its useful life to create something that has more value than the original material or product. An example of upcycling can be found through Adidas, which transforms plastic waste into new shoes. The company was able to take a product with little value and transform it into something of higher value. Upcycling should be considered preferable over downcycling because the resulting product holds higher value than the original.

Downcycling is the act of refurbishing a material or product at the end of its useful life to create something that has less value than the original material or product. Although downcycling isn't as useful as upcycling, given that the resulting material or product has less value than the original, downcycling is still keeping a material or product in use for a longer period, and therefore is a better alternative than recycling or disposing of that material or product. An example of down-cycling can be found on a construction site. Timber framing that has reached the end of its life can be processed to form plywood for other construction projects. Plywood isn't as valuable as timber framing, but it's value in the sense that it keeps the materials in use longer.

Upcycling and downcycling are both better alternatives than throwing something away because it no longer functions. But what happens when a product or material can no longer be upcycled or downcycled? Once a material reaches this point of its lifecycle, it should be broken down into its most basic elements and used as an alternative to raw materials. For biological materials — those that can be returned to the earth and used to grow new materials — composting and biochemical extraction should be utilized to recapture the innate value of the material. For technical materials — those that are finite and cannot be used to grow more resources — recycling should be utilized to harvest the value of the material.

Businesses are beginning to realize the value of recapturing waste and repurposing those materials to form new products. Patagonia, Apple, and Ikea all offer buy-back programs to their customers. Within these programs, companies are offering store credit or other forms of payment in exchange for old products. These companies then extract the materials from these old products and use them to create new products, ultimately reducing waste and the price of products. Although it seems like a revolutionary business idea now, the concept of reusing materials to offset operational costs has a long history. Remember the milkman? Rather than the customer having to drive to the store, buy a new carton of milk, and throw away the carton after use, milk used to be delivered in reusable bottles right to your door. After use, empty bottles would be collected, cleaned, and reused.

How To Keep Materials In Use Forever

Products used to be designed to last for a long time, back when innovation in technology and the latest-and-greatest models weren't entering the market at such a rapid pace. To encourage consumers to buy the next best thing, products are designed with planned obsolescence, or intentional failure, in mind. Products are built to work for a given period before becoming unusable or requiring upgrades to continue functioning. Keeping materials in use forever will require durable and resilient products that replace planned obsolescence with planned permanence. Many strategies can be utilized to make this transition from planned obsolescence to planned permanence, including the elimination of premature obsolescence and substituting raw materials with secondary materials.

Why things break

Things break now more than ever because of the materials involved. Historically, durability was a key buying point for the consumer. Even if it came at an additional cost, the purchaser understood that by prioritizing durability, they could offset the cost of maintenance and eliminate the need to purchase a replacement in the future. Things began to change in the early 20th century when the global economy embraced a concept known as creative waste. *Creative waste* is the intentional incorporation of waste as a necessity when it comes to maintaining customer demand. By encouraging waste, you encourage demand, and businesses would forever be allowed to thrive.

In the 1930s, a company by the name of Sears, Roebuck and Co. had the bright idea to begin introducing a new version of an appliance annually. Although the differences between models were minimal, design details made it obvious whether you had a new version or an old version of something. This strategy encouraged affluent communities to abandon their old TVs, refrigerators, and cars and upgrade to the newer versions at a phenomenal rate. Maintaining the "newest" version of a variety of goods — especially cars — allowed families to indirectly advertise their social position in the community.

This trend of upgrading from the old to the new hasn't stopped. In fact, it has sped up. Durability has been replaced as a priority with the latest-and-greatest technology and the newest trend. Companies have responded to this increase in product turnover by minimizing the durability (and therefore cost) of the materials that go into their products. In the fashion industry, this phenomenon has come to be known as *fast fashion,* or the use of cheap and inexpensive materials to rapidly produce clothing in response to the latest trends. As new fashion trends emerge, the old trends get thrown out to make room for the new trends. By increasing the rate at which trends emerge, the rate at which new clothing is purchased also increases (and so do the sales). (For more on the circular economy for fashion and clothing, see Chapter 18.)

REMEMBER

Things break because the producers of the product want them to break. If you haven't already upgraded to the newest model by the time a product breaks, you'll still have a reason to buy a new one. Planned obsolescence has become the backbone of product design and manufacturing under the premise that it's the best way to drive demand and sales; however, the opposite — planned permanence — may prove to be the better option.

From planned obsolescence to planned permanence

Take a minute to imagine a life where you don't need to buy the next version of a product because the one you currently have either stopped working or faded out of fashion. Imagine that every product you bought also had guaranteed maintenance and repair included in the purchase. Something stops working? Take it to the manufacturer to be repaired. Imagine being able to own a car for thirty years instead of only three. To make this a reality, we humans need to undergo a transition from a linear economy (where waste is built-in) to a circular economy (where waste has been designed out).

To make this transition, planned obsolescence needs to be replaced with planned permanence. Planned obsolescence involves designing a product to have a short lifespan and drive the demand for a replacement. Planned permanence focuses on the opposite by designing a product to have an extremely long lifespan and drive the demand for maintenance and repair services. Though planned obsolescence relies on the failure of a product to maintain a steady flow of demand for new products, planned permanence will rely on the durability of a product to maintain a customer base and create new service offerings to buyers, such as maintenance, customization, and repair.

Planned obsolescence has been utilized by companies for decades to ensure that they will always have buyers ready to purchase a replacement. Phones, computers, cars — all these products can be designed with a limited lifespan built-in. This can be achieved by using low-quality materials that will surely fail within a short timeframe, by requiring upgrades to system software that essentially disables old models, or by developing new products that make older versions obsolete.

Planned permanence seems counterintuitive to modern business practice. By ensuring that a product lasts, how can a company ensure that their customers continue purchasing from them? If replacements aren't needed, what will they buy? The answer to that question is utilizing a service as a product. Rather than sell a product itself over and over again, planned permanence will allow businesses to not only offer a product but services to maintain that product as well. Once a product is sold to a customer, it will last because durability has been incorporated, but it will also require repairs, cleanings, refurbishments, and other services.

Rather than sell the product outright to the customer, businesses may find that renting out the product while maintaining ownership proves to be the more valuable strategy. For example, an individual who lives in the city needs a convenient way to commute every day to and from work. Rather than spend money on a car — with the inevitable insurance and maintenance costs attached — they elect to utilize the service-as-a-product option by renting an electric scooter every day. Yes, they could buy the scooter outright rather than rent it, but by doing so, they would also be responsible for the charging and maintenance and any necessary repairs. Instead, for a small fee, the customer has a guaranteed scooter available every morning and doesn't need to worry about the up-front cost of an electric scooter, the maintenance and repair costs, or the electricity costs tied to the daily charging. Rather than sell the user a scooter, businesses can offer the rental service. On the business end of things, efficiency of scale can be harnessed by setting up the original purchase and continuous maintenance of thousands of scooters rather than simply sell them outright. Overall, it's more profitable for the company and costs less for the customer.

Shipping Global versus Producing Local

If something was manufactured on the other side of the world, you would have to wait for that product to be delivered to wherever it is you are. This way of obtaining a product requires a lot of time, energy, and resources. A large percentage of the time, energy, and resources could be offset if that same product were made available from down the street. Until Scotty is able to beam us up to anywhere at any time, shipping via trains, planes, and automobiles will be necessary. Fortunately, the global economy is shifting to look more like *Star Trek* and less like *Mad Max*, and new strategies are emerging that minimize the need to ship products around the world, by manufacturing them anywhere. Tools like 3D printing and computer numerical control (CNC) mills allow for products to be manufactured in more locations by utilizing digital designs. Increasing the availability of a product drastically minimizes or eliminates the cost of shipping globally. Most everyday items, if designed appropriately and with the right materials, can be produced locally, thanks to the capabilities of 3D printing.

Although 3D printing is emerging as an available technology to the average Joe, this increase in availability isn't the end of shipping. Some products (and/or their assembly) are so elaborate that 3D printers won't be of any help. In today's age, you can either drive yourself to the nearest store that offers that product or have it shipped by a wide range of service providers for an additional fee. In terms of emissions, which is better? Driving to the store and back in your Toyota Prius seems like a fuel-efficient option. However, is the use of millions of individual vehicles more efficient than the use of thousands of delivery vehicles? Although individual cars have higher fuel efficiency than delivery vehicles, more of them are on the roads. Delivery vehicles typically use diesel-powered engines, which emit more harmful emissions, but there will be fewer of them on the roads than personal vehicles.

When packaging is required, how can it be designed to be reusable? Most packaging is made up of paper products that find themselves in the recycling bin immediately after use, so to transition to a circular economy — where packaging is still relevant and sometimes more efficient than an individual driving to the store and back — permanent and reusable packaging will need to find its place in the shipping industry.

Building a regional economy:
A shipping substitute

The current approach to manufacturing and distribution involves a lot of waste. Raw materials are sourced and shipped from all around the world and assembled into various products at a single location. From there, that product is again shipped around the world to the consumer. Once the consumer has used it (usually once), that material is shipped "away" and either piled in a landfill or incinerated. This linear stream of materials and goods is responsible for almost half the global greenhouse gas emissions, and it degenerates the natural ecosystems that human civilization relies on and results in an instable and fluctuating global economy. This degenerative management of goods isn't sustainable and cannot go on forever.

Unlike this degenerative and linear process (the take-make-waste approach), the alternative (a regenerative and circular process) takes a different approach to managing the supply and demand of the global economy. The circular economy not only focuses on developing better products that are durable, repairable, and reusable but also focuses on developing better sourcing and distribution of those products. Products are produced not from raw materials, but from secondary and recaptured materials, and result in no waste or pollution to the natural ecosystems. Profits aren't dependent on the continuous sale of new products, but instead are achieved through the repair, recycling, and reuse of the original products.

To achieve the circular flow of materials and products, better manufacturing strategies need to be harnessed, and the wastefulness associated with centralized manufacturing and global distribution needs to be eliminated. Some products don't need to be shipped around the world if distributed manufacturing is incorporated into the manufacturing process. Distributed manufacturing, in comparison to centralized manufacturing, relies on an array of distributed microfactories to manufacture products on a more localized level. (See Figure 14-2 for more on centralized and decentralized management strategies.) Successful examples of microfactories — such as 3D Hub and Xometry — can already be found at work. These companies are able to break down the traditional, centralized manufacturing strategy into smaller, localized manufacturing locations by utilizing tools such as 3D printers, CNC mills, and other technologies. If products are designed to be compatible with this type of manufacturing, individuals and/or companies can send them to these manufacturing hubs to be produced, similar to sending an image to be printed at your local print shop.

These microfactories work well on a commercial level by offering a range of manufacturing technology to a wide range of different companies. On a personal level, microfactories aren't the best scale or solution. Makerspaces, fabrication labs, and other do-it-yourself-style, community spaces make more sense. These spaces offer the same, or similar, level of technology as microfactories, but on a more user-friendly scale. These spaces can offer members of the community design software, working spaces, tools, 3D printers, wood and metal shops, and other resources they need in order to produce products for their own use, or for local sale and distribution. Nextfab (https://nextfab.com), located in Philadelphia, as well as other makerspaces have shown that this methodology can be a successful way to empower the individual and eliminate waste by decentralizing the manufacturing process and scaling down the use of a globalized economy.

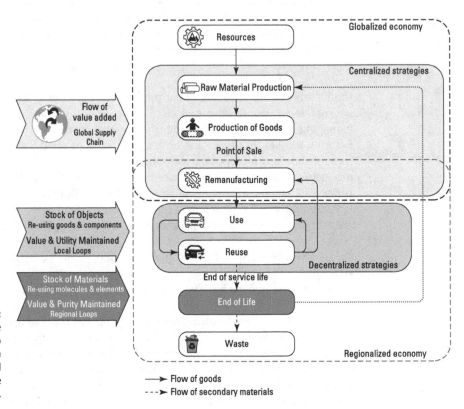

FIGURE 14-2:
Exploring the relationship between regionality and lifecycle management.

When the extraction of raw materials, their production and processing, and the production of the goods themselves are so location-based, achieving the goal of localizing these processes is somewhat unrealistic due to the geographic limitations of material sourcing and the technical machinery required for their processing. The remanufacturing of those products is an activity that will need to take place on both a global scale and a regional or local scale because of the range of services required. The key takeaway from Figure 14-2 is acknowledging that the remanufacturing, use, reuse, and management of waste can all be extracted from a globalized process and managed within a regional process. Doing so eliminates the time, energy, and resources required to transport these products around the world to be sourced and serviced. By shifting elements of a global economy to a local economy, global emissions associated with the transportation of products can be reduced by roughly 6 percent. In addition to entire products, replacement components can be printed, which helps extend the useful life of products — instead of simply throwing them away and buying replacements.

Giving value back to the localized economy will result in countless benefits. Focusing on local rather than global doesn't mean excluding the rest of the world completely. Instead, it means supporting the local sourcing, sale, use and end-of-use management of products and materials. It means supporting the employment of the local community to serve the local community. By prioritizing local operations and supporting locally owned companies instead of global corporations, more of the money you spend stays within the community. The money made by local businesses can then be spent at other local businesses. Supporting local businesses also allows for unique businesses, with unique specialties, to be sustained. By supporting local, the environmental impact associated with the globalized economy is greatly reduced, customer service becomes more of a priority, and the cost of operations drops dramatically because global distribution networks and infrastructure aren't required. (For an overview of the differences in economic impact between local and nonlocal businesses, check out Figure 14-3.)

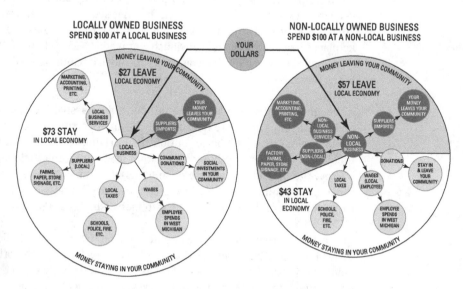

FIGURE 14-3: Comparing local and non-local businesses.

You've got to be shipping me

It's convenient — we know: You can find anything you want online and have it shipped and delivered to your door within a day or two. This convenience comes with a hidden environmental cost that isn't listed in your digital shopping cart. There's no denying it: Amazon has changed the way the world shops. With Amazon Prime now available to all, it's easier than ever to have just about anything delivered to you in record time. No more driving to the store, dealing with crowds, getting stuck in traffic, and waiting in line, only to be asked, "Did you find everything okay?"

In 2019, Amazon documented the largest case of global purchasing in history during its Prime Day sale. Within a span of a day-and-a-half, individuals and companies around the globe managed to purchase over 100 million items and flood the Amazon website with enough orders to crash it. Pairing the ease of ordering with the fast delivery, offering simple and convenient returns has motivated people to buy more and buy often. Not to mention that a global pandemic in 2020 has also further encouraged people to stay in their homes to avoid public spaces.

REMEMBER

All this convenience comes with a hidden environmental cost. By offering fast delivery rates and encouraging frequent purchasing, products don't receive the opportunity to be consolidated into one package and one delivery. This translates to not only more miles on delivery trucks and more packaging material but also more air pollution and more paper product waste — mostly cardboard. This convenient way of purchasing products has hooked nearly everyone. UPS found in 2017 that almost all shipments it delivered had been purchased on a digital marketplace, like Walmart and, obviously, Amazon. Nearly half of these purchases were made because shipping was either included or came at a reduced rate because of the purchase.

Although a lot of waste is associated with this massive increase in e-commerce and global shipping, there may actually be an opportunity for good. If optimized, buying online may be a better option than driving to the store yourself. Though millions of individuals driving to the store may not be an efficient use of time and energy, the individual delivery of millions of items can be. By consolidating the consumers' products into fewer vehicles, delivery services may have the potential to reduce a lot of waste associated with global shipping. (See Figure 14-4.)

The catch to reducing environmental impact by relying on delivery services instead of individual travel is that you have to pick one or the other. If everyone stops taking trips to the store and relies solely on delivery services to obtain their goods, there's an opportunity for reduced environmental impact; however, people are still relying on both options. Not only are individuals still making trips to the store, but they're also making these trips to the store while delivery vehicles are on the road with other products that they've purchased online.

Personal Vehicle Travel

Delivery Vehicle Travel

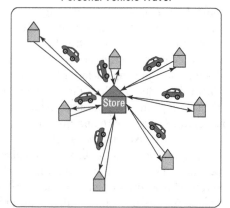
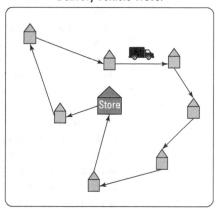

FIGURE 14-4:
Delivery services
can reduce
overall vehicle
miles.

On top of it all, by allowing for such frequent purchasing and delivery, global giants such as Amazon and Walmart aren't shipping as efficiently as they could be. Delivery drivers are driving from a warehouse to the delivery location and back to a warehouse, which is more often a further distance than the delivery location is to a local store. Offering same-day delivery, two-day shipping, and flex programs, smaller vehicles are required to deliver fewer packages at a faster rate. Walmart and Amazon's offerings have encouraged other businesses to follow suit and also offer rapid shipping. Other retailers — such as Google Express, Postmates, and FreshDirect — deliver products on demand. By reining in the time at which packages can be delivered, efficiencies can be harnessed by optimizing delivery routes to reduce the total distance traveled.

Permanent packaging

Packaging is a critical part of the global economy. It keeps products contained and protected from the elements during shipment and ensures that customers receive a functioning version of the product they purchased. It's assumed that when you buy a product, the cost of the packaging has been included in the overall cost. From the manufacturer's perspective, it's within their interest to provide packaging that comes at an extremely low overall cost to them while also maintaining the quality of the goods sold. The less packaging that can be used, the better. To achieve the lowest cost possible, manufacturers continue to find the cheapest and lightest packaging materials available in order to save themselves costs. Lighter materials are cheaper for companies to transport. Unfortunately, the materials that weigh the least amount are also those that have the lowest potential to be recycled (like plastic-based materials), whereas the materials that weigh the most are also those that have the highest potential to be recycled (like glass and metals).

Within the current setup and delivery of products in a variety of materials, it's the consumer's responsibility to recycle the packaging after their product has been delivered. However, the downside is that there's often little incentive for the consumer to follow through with the proper activities required to recycle the materials. Even recyclable packaging will end up in landfills if the customer has no incentive to recycle it. With this understanding, disposable packing needs to be replaced with permanent packaging wherever possible to incentivize the customer to not dispose of their packaging to begin with and instead, to maintain the value of the packaging in exchange for a discounted price on their next purchase. *Permanent packaging* is a packaging method that has been designed with the intention of reuse rather than waste. This concept of eliminating waste by incorporating the ability for a product to be reused is a core principle of the circular economy and a key action that must be made for the packaging industry to properly transition from linear operations to circular operations.

This transition from disposable packaging to incentive-fueled reusable packaging is a realistic strategy for many industries to adopt. For example, Blueland (www. blueland.com) designs aesthetically pleasing cleaning-solution containers that can be refilled and used over and over again. Rather than purchase a new bottle filled with cleaning fluid every time, the customer is directed to keep the bottle for reuse and instead purchase concentrated tablets. This tablet is then mixed with water from the faucet to form the cleaning solution. By changing the way its product is delivered, this manufacturer eliminates waste by removing the bottle as a part of their product and relying on permanent packaging instead. The customer, then, is encouraged to abandon the idea that their cleaning solutions must be purchased in a bottle each time, because purchasing a tablet is cheaper than buying an entire bottle filled with mostly water anyway.

To encourage the circular flow of packaging materials, waste must be designed out and opportunities for reuse must be designed in. As these package-less product trends continue to grow, large markets such as Walmart and Target will need to adjust the way their stores offer products to their customers. In the very near future, customers may find opportunities to return the packaging from their last purchase and receive a credit toward the purchase of new products. A packaging exchange counter may be your first stop before heading to the candy-and-sweets aisle. In this alternate reality, the customer would no longer be purchasing the packaging used for their products. Instead, they would be renting it, and the manufacturers would be responsible for the collection and maintenance of the packaging material. This service-as-a-product strategy will be seen in many forms as the linear economy makes its eventual transition toward a circular economy. It is, however, far from a new concept. If you're of a certain age, you'll remember when the milkman used to come to your door, grab your old, empty milk bottle, and replace it with a new, full bottle.

Until objects can be sent through the air like Mike Teevee was in *Willy Wonka & the Chocolate Factory* (in the book as well as in the movie version), shipping and packaging will be a necessity. With this understanding, it's critical that product packaging be designed for reuse. By taking this approach, both the manufacturer and customer benefit. Incorporating permanent packaging into business models will eliminate much of the waste connected to disposable packaging, keep materials in use for longer periods, and greatly reduce the amount of raw materials required to replace disposable packaging.

The current management of materials, products, and packaging is still too focused on doing less bad instead of finding creative ways to do good. The linear economy accepts waste as a necessary component of life, whereas the circular economy sees waste as a valuable resource to be harnessed. It's clear that waste was created as a means to fuel the economy. Planned obsolescence has been utilized to incentivize customer demand for long enough, when other, regenerative business strategies are available that don't prosper from waste generation but rather from waste prevention instead. Utilizing planned permanence as a strategy and relying on the demand for repair, maintenance, and remanufacturing to fuel the economy is a necessary future for the global economy if it is to continue forward. These products need to be produced locally, when possible, and shipped in permanent packaging. The future of material, product, and packaging management is quite different than the reality we all see today, but it's a future we need to realize in order to ensure our own survival.

MARK HERREMA SPEAKS

Mark Herrema is co-founder and chief executive officer of Newlight Technologies, an advanced biotechnology company using carbon capture technology to produce high-performance polymers that replace oil-based materials by out-competing on price and performance.

Eric Corey Freed: Can you tell us a little around why and how you started Newlight?

Mark Herrema: We started Newlight because we thought that if we could find a consumer-driven solution to reducing the amount of carbon in the air, that is something that could create the scale we need to help solve climate change. The mission was: using greenhouse gas as a resource, like nature does, and creating products that can improve the environment.

Eric Corey Freed: What is AirCarbon and how is it used? What could it potentially replace?

(continued)

(continued)

Mark Herrema: AirCarbon is a meltable material produced in almost all known living things, from trees to the human body. It just so happens that ocean microorganisms eat greenhouse gas and use it to make AirCarbon, and when we isolate and purify AirCarbon, we can melt it into shapes and parts as a replacement for plastic — except that whereas plastic is synthetic and non-biodegradable, AirCarbon is natural, ocean-degradable, and carbon-negative.

Eric Corey Freed: When you started, the actual process for making AirCarbon (using ocean microorganisms to convert CO2) didn't exist. Was this a search for a solution, or did you explore several technologies to produce an alternative to plastic?

Mark Herrema: Actually, the process has occurred for hundreds of millions of years in nature — what we had to do was figure out how to replicate it on land. The search began with asking how to use greenhouse gas as a resource, so we were process-agnostic when we started.

Eric Corey Freed: Did it start with a circular economy process in mind? That is, did you want a zero waste, reusable, durable, flexible raw material?

Mark Herrema: For us, the main thing was scalability, and that meant price, performance, and sustainability. We wanted something that was cost-effective, could replace a wide range of incumbent materials and products, and would generate an environmental improvement.

Eric Corey Freed: Why did you start by focusing on food ware and fashion? There are dozens of industries that need this?

Mark Herrema: With finite material, we asked where we could have the biggest immediate environmental impact. The ocean is filling up with synthetic plastic, and we can displace that plastic with AirCarbon and help end the accumulation of plastic in the oceans in this generation. With fashion, we are able to show that a material as ubiquitous as leather can be replaced with something that does environmental good — AirCarbon Leather, a carbon-negative material — and use that to help start to decarbonize the fashion industry, later moving into automotive, furniture, electronics, and others. But these segments are just the start — eventually there are many segments we intend to enter.

Eric Corey Freed: Is this scalable?

Mark Herrema: Yes. The foundation of our company is built on scalability, and that means products that work for people and the planet — both economically and environmentally.

Eric Corey Freed: What have you learned since launch that surprised you the most about developing a circular product?

Mark Herrema That we can't grow fast enough.

Eric Corey Freed: What obstacles or challenges still need to be overcome?

Mark Herrema: Speed to expansion is something that we think about a lot. Over the next few years, you'll see us working to grow in as time- and capital-efficient manner as we can.

4 Redesigning the Future to be Circular

IN THIS PART . . .

Explore a circular approach to food, design, and fashion

Apply a circular approach to these industries

Redesign everything for a circular economy

Chapter **15**

The Circular Economy of Food Production

You probably don't remember a time when agriculture wasn't a major food industry. We humans live in a world where you can't miss the endless rows of single crops — corn, soybeans, grapes — that stand out like sore thumbs compared to the natural environment around them. The pattern stands out for a reason: Those tightly controlled rows are unnatural and result in a large amount of wasted food, energy, and time. They're part of a linear economy.

The natural world is a powerful, abundant, and living system that's just begging us humans to join the circular economy club. The natural world processes *organic waste* — dead foliage, microorganisms, and other once-living elements of the ecosystem — to serve as food for newly born plants and animals. The foliage that falls from a tree is softened by the rain that falls from the sky and is later consumed by insects such as ants, beetles, and worms. The waste that those insects leave behind acts as a nutrient source to feed the tree, allowing it to produce new leaves. Each of these elements of the ecosystem uses waste as a resource. They're part of a circular economy.

Unfortunately, because agriculture focuses on a linear way of managing material and energy, every part of it has been designed to act as individual elements, not as part of a system. The way food is planted, grown, harvested, and distributed isn't a sustainable way of serving the ever-growing needs of an ever-growing, global population.

In this chapter, you find out exactly why the current way of producing food — large-scale agriculture — is such a serious problem and a detriment to natural ecosystems. You'll also find out what a circular economy looks like in food production, the basics of how to design your own food forest, which principles should guide your design, and which benefits you'll reap!

Examining the Two Ways of Producing Food

The way food is produced can be categorized in one of two ways: the industrial chain (monocultures) and the local, food forest chain (polyculture).

The *industrial chain* is unique in the sense that only one crop is grown — hence the name *monoculture*. Thousands, sometimes millions, of seeds are planted in straight rows by fossil-fueled machinery, are watered by large sprinklers, and are fed and protected via commercial-grade fertilizers and pesticides. This is an energy- and time-intensive means to grow food. Monoculture have become the go-to strategy for growing food in industrialized nations because it holds a smaller initial cost than polycultures by relying on artificial inputs rather than *ecosystem services*. Ecosystem Services are benefits provided to humans by natural systems, such as water filtration and raw material generation. Although monocultures hold lower initial costs, this industrialized food production process damages the ability for natural systems to provide those services and generates the demand for those resources to be remediated in the future. Remediating millions of acres globally will come at a colossal price.

The local *food forest chain*, unlike agriculture, produces a wide array of plants that are intermingled to minimize the external resources required to feed and protect them To eliminate waste from production, keep nutrients in circulation and allow for natural systems to regenerate, polycultures utilize ecosystem services and symbiotic relationships, also known as *companion planting* — a food growing strategy that allows certain partnering plants to provide services for other plants by sharing resources, like nutrients and water. A *polyculture*, in other words This is an energy- and time-efficient means to grow food, because human intervention is rarely required.

The distinction between industrial chain versus food forest chain allows us authors to define the key difference between the two: The industrialized model produces 30 percent of the food, but uses 70 percent of the resources, whereas the food forest produces 70 percent of the food and uses only 30 percent of the resources. As efficient as polyculture systems are, they're rarely seen in developed nations due to their higher initial cost. The rest of this chapter explains why.

TIP

To quickly identify the health of any food system, check for diversity. The quality and health of a food system is ultimately dependent on the diversity of plants incorporated into that system, the diversity of products extracted from that system, and the diversity of waste returned to the system. If the food system isn't circular, it isn't sustainable. It's as simple as that, really. Compare the lush tropical rain forests of South America to the vast, single-row, industrialized fields seen around the industrialized world. Only one of these systems will survive in the long run.

Investigating the Hidden Costs of Agriculture

The industrial way of growing food is . . . well, it's pretty dumb (and we certainly don't mean in the cool For Dummies way). As smart as the human race claims to be, we humans aren't smart when it comes to large-scale food production. We rely on agriculture to produce and distribute much of our food worldwide. This 70-year-old globalized phenomenon is not only relatively young, at least when compared to the entire spectrum of human existence, but it also fails miserably to use resources efficiently and generates unfathomable amounts of waste.

Which came first — the chicken or the egg? The extensive use of agriculture or the growth in global population? Well, they both happened in tandem. To service a growing population, the introduction of chemicals and technologies — what we know today as modern agriculture — was popularized. And once access to food was no longer an issue, people felt comfortable to have more children. This positive feedback loop is the reason we humans find ourselves where we are today. (See Figure 15-1.)

Although agriculture has greatly increased our ability to feed more people and in some respect has saved countless lives, the industrialized form of food production acts as a Band-aid to a much larger issue: long-term access to food and resources to service a growing population. With the understanding that the current, industrialized way of growing food will be unable to service us forever, an alternative, sustainable means of producing food *must* be adopted to ensure that humans have a bright future.

As the global population continues to grow, so will the negative impacts that agriculture will have on our global ecosystems. So, despite the short-term benefits of modern agriculture methods — the linear economy approach to food production — the fact that it creates enormous amounts of waste and causes environmental degeneration and severe human health concerns cannot be ignored. To guarantee food security in the future, eliminate waste, regenerate natural systems, and resolve human health concerns, the circular economy must act as the new platform for global food production.

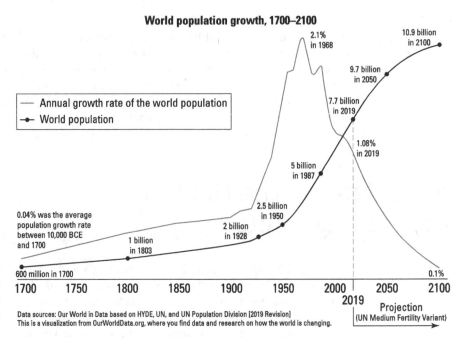

World population growth, 1700–2100

- — Annual growth rate of the world population
- —•— World population

2.1% in 1968

10.9 billion in 2100

9.7 billion in 2050

7.7 billion in 2019

1.08% in 2019

5 billion in 1987

2.5 billion in 1950

2 billion in 1928

0.04% was the average population growth rate between 10,000 BCE and 1700

1 billion in 1803

600 million in 1700

0.1%

1700   1750   1800   1850   1900   1950   2000   2050   2100

2019

Projection (UN Medium Fertility Variant)

Data sources: Our World in Data based on HYDE, UN, and UN Population Division [2019 Revision]
This is a visualization from OurWorldData.org, where you find data and research on how the world is changing.

FIGURE 15-1: World population growth since 1700.

Food waste: Expending money, time, and resources unnecessarily

Agricultural waste comes in many forms, but we focus on only these three major sources:

>> **Labor costs:** Huge and complex, the global monoculture, or conventional agriculture, system has been called by some the world's largest industry, with over a billion people involved daily — that's more than 10 percent of the global population, mind you — working each and every day to deliver food to your table. These laborers not only plant, maintain, fertilize, and harvest a range of food and agricultural products but also package, transport, market, sell, cook and/or deliver this food for you.

>> Many of these human services — maintaining and fertilizing crops, for example — are necessary because of how the food is produced. These human services can be replaced with ecological services if a circular, rather than linear, economy of food production were used. Work smarter, not harder!

>> **Energy costs:** Each and every day, gasoline and oil fuel the wide range of equipment necessary to maintain the linear way of producing food. In addition, fertilizers are required in order to supplement the soil nutrients that are no longer present in the soil while herbicides and pesticides are needed to keep weeds and pests away. All these products take large amounts of energy

to produce; they're also essential if you hope to perpetuate this linear way of producing food.

>> **Food:** Between one-third and one-half of the food produced in an industrialized setting is wasted. When food is grown in a field, it often takes days, if not weeks, until it is delivered to the consumer and eaten. This delay between harvest and consumption allows for many opportunities for food to spoil, if not properly stored, processed, or preserved.

A circular economy food production methodology would identify these elements of waste and adjust a range of lifecycle variables, such as source, means of transportation, storage opportunities, processing strategies, and other determinants to eliminate waste completely. The Maryland Food Bank's FoodWorks Program, for example, teaches its students basic cooking skills while converting perishable foods into healthy meals for distribution to those in need. This strategy educates members of the community while eliminating food waste to service those who would go hungry without their support.

WEED AND SHROOMS: EARTH'S HEALING METHODS

When human skin is injured by a cut, it forms a protective layer (a scab) first, before replacement skin is developed by the body. Weeds act the same way: When soil is damaged, weeds allow the soil to heal itself before producing vegetation (nature's skin). That's why weeds grow so quickly — they're just like scabs! Monoculture systems never allow for polyculture systems to take place by disturbing ecological succession. Ecological succession is the evolution of plant structures within an ecological climate over many years. Ecological succession is the pathway to achieving a polyculture system, which again, relies on symbiotic relationships between the living creatures of the ecosystem. Both plants and animals.

Mycelium are fungal threads that spread themselves through the soil below you and provide ecosystem services you're probably not aware of. Mushrooms — the fruiting body of mycelium — are similar to an apple on a tree. Mycelium are so small, and sometimes not visible by the human eye, that **a single cubic inch of soil** can contain roughly 8 miles of mycelium threads! Mycelium is really the hidden hero of all eco systems. This living creature is responsible for recycling some of the most essential elements of the natural world — like carbon, nitrogen and many others. In addition, the also break down both plant and animal debris to create new, fresh and nutrient-dense layers of soil. Polyculture systems harness the ecosystem services of mycelium, while monocultures do not.

TIP

Once a circular economy of food production is utilized worldwide, many of these agricultural services provided by heavy machinery, fertilizers, weed killers, and pesticides can be replaced with environmental services.

Environmental degeneration: Damaging the planet with increasing speed

The resources required to sustain this ever-growing snowball of madness that is our current food production system are vast: Fifty percent of the planet's habitable land and 70 percent of fresh water resource demand is required by agriculture. These interlinkages reach far beyond the food system itself, directly impacting many other important physical and social systems, such as climate, energy, and water, as well as land use, biodiversity, and culture. As populations continue to grow, more natural landscapes are converted into fields for agricultural use. This degenerative action pollutes local watersheds, destroys habitats, erodes soils, and eliminates indigenous ways of life as well as the historic ways of that community.

REMEMBER

Slash-and-burn farming is a common practice in the Amazon rainforest, where natural vegetation is cleared and burned as a way to prepare that land for cultivation. When that soil quickly becomes infertile because of this unnatural process, farmers then move on to new areas. The way food is produced is unnatural and causes widespread degradation to natural systems, making it harder and harder to produce food from the same area of soil.

Unfortunately, the short-term solution to this degradation of the soil was the introduction of petroleum-based fertilizers and pesticides, aimed at supplementing the natural services of ecosystems. All plants take water and nutrients from the soil, but they also leave something in return to help other plants, fungi, and animals around them grow. A food production system based on circular economy principles utilizes this collective impact to provide plants with their never-ending nutrient needs. *Legumes,* for example, (peas, clovers, beans) partner with a soil bacteria called rhizobium — Latin for "root living" — to extract nitrogen from the air and convert it into nitrates and nitrites, which can then be utilized by the plants around them. These services are extremely valuable, yet industrialized agriculture ignores them and relies on an array of unnatural chemicals instead.

Permaculture to the Rescue

Permaculture is an environmental design philosophy, developed by Bill Mollison and David Holmgren in the 1970s, that harnesses the power and functionality of natural systems to grow foods (rather than adopt the attitude of industrialized agriculture, which claims that the only way to grow food is to fight *against* natural systems). Though agriculture can be defined by monoculture crops, energy-intensive production, globalized distribution, and waste, *permaculture* can be defined by polyculture crops, energy-efficient production, local distribution, and resource recycling.

REMEMBER

The truth is, the natural world could provide everyone with fresh, nutrient-rich produce if we humans would just let it do its thing and stay out of its way. By no means should you skip the farmers market and start picking at the wild vegetation outside the back door — that will more than likely lead to a bad itch and maybe even a trip to the ER. Instead, imagine relying on a circular food system that requires minimal human input and capitalizes on natural flows of nutrients, water, and biomass.

The circular economy of food isn't a new concept, but is instead an idea that has existed for thousands of years. We humans have only just diverted from this way of life over the course of the past hundred years. Our ancestors understood that the ecosystem services around them were their source of life — by reconnecting with nature and designing our food systems to mimic the natural world, we too can once again source our food in a circular way.

Following nature's lead: Permaculture design principles

Permaculture and its associated principles act as a design philosophy that allows the designer to harness the patterns and resilient features observed in natural ecosystems to minimize waste and produce high-quality environmental resources. Using natural systems and resource management as an example, permaculture founders Bill Mollison and David Holmgren distilled nature's way of producing food into a set of 12 permaculture design principles. They argue that these principles, listed here, should be seen as a design framework and an opportunity to "think" as nature does:

>> **Observe and interact (beauty is in the eye of the beholder):**

Before you can design like nature, you need to understand how nature designs. Designers should observe the natural world, to not only appreciate how the natural world functions but also explore how we humans can duplicate its abundance.

>> **Catch and store energy (make hay while the sun shines):**

Energy should be captured and stored when it's abundant and conserved when it's rare. Value what is ample, and respect the use of what is available only occasionally.

>> **Obtain a yield (you can't work on an empty stomach):**

By investing time, energy, and resources, value is created. Enjoy the fruits of your labor.

>> **Apply self-regulation and accept feedback (the sins of the fathers are visited on the children of the seventh generation):**

The original research-and-development (R&D) system — nature — proposed that if you don't fit in with your surroundings, you don't survive. Success should be celebrated, and failure should be addressed, resolved, and prevented from happening again.

>> **Use and value renewable resources and services (let nature take its course):**

To assume that coal will last forever is foolish and extremely short-sighted. Rather than utilize finite resources, make use of resources that are fully renewable and abandon those that are not.

>> **Produce no waste (waste not, want not):**

Humans are the only living creatures on planet earth who produce waste. We need to acknowledge that waste is simply a resource that isn't being used correctly. Eliminate waste by changing how materials and products are ultimately utilized.

>> **Design from patterns to details (can't see the forest for the trees):**

Patterns like the golden ratio and the Fibonacci sequence are abundant in nature because they're efficient. We should design our human systems as nature would design them — efficiently and beautifully.

>> **Integrate rather than segregate (many hands make light work):**

Plants thrive in collective systems but perish when in isolation. Develop polycultures that rely on collaboration and cooperation to maximize resilience and value.

>> **Use small and slow solutions (the bigger they are, the harder they fall):**

Although big changes can bring with them great reward, they can also bring with them large amounts of risk. This principle identifies the value of incremental changes.

>> **Use and value diversity (don't put all your eggs in one basket):**

A diverse market is harder to crash. The tenth permaculture principle acknowledges that resilience is built on a platform of diversity. A disease can kill an entire monocrop field, but only minimally affects a polyculture.

>> **Use edges and value the marginal (a well-beaten path isn't always the right path):**

A mangrove forest, which is located where salt water and fresh water meet — on the edge of both systems — is rich with life. Highlight the value that comes from adjacencies.

>> **Creatively use and respond to change (vision is not seeing things as they are, but as they will be):**

Change is inevitable and should be planned for. Everything changes — seasons, politics, human needs — so we should design for the future, not the present.

Figure 15-2 shows the 12 permaculture principles in graphical form.

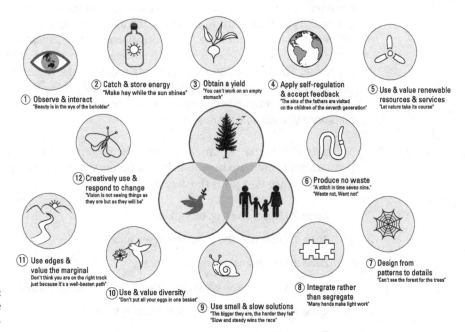

FIGURE 15-2: The permaculture design principles.

① Observe & interact
"Beauty is in the eye of the beholder"

② Catch & store energy
"Make hay while the sun shines"

③ Obtain a yield
"You can't work on an empty stomach"

④ Apply self-regulation & accept feedback
"The sins of the fathers are visited on the children of the seventh generation"

⑤ Use & value renewable resources & services
"Let nature take its course"

⑥ Produce no waste
"A stitch in time saves nine."
"Waste not, Want not"

⑦ Design from patterns to details
"Can't see the forest for the trees"

⑧ Integrate rather than segregate
"Many hands make light work"

⑨ Use small & slow solutions
"The bigger they are, the harder they fall"
"Slow and steady wins the race"

⑩ Use & value diversity
"Don't put all your eggs in one basket"

⑪ Use edges & value the marginal
Don't think you are on the right track just because it's a well-beaten path"

⑫ Creatively use & respond to change
"Vision is not seeing things as they are but as they will be"

Taking a look at permaculture management zones

Imagine you've decided to cook some pasta for yourself. As you're cooking up some sauce, you remember the potted oregano you have growing just outside your kitchen door. After a quick 10 second walk, you're dicing away and smelling the fresh oils spilling from the fresh herbs. Now imagine your herbs aren't just outside your kitchen door, but are instead planted a quarter mile away on the other edge of your land. That wouldn't be a sensible location for herbs because they're quite frequently visited and/or attended to — sometime multiple times per day. An orchard, however, isn't visited multiple times a day and is instead visited maybe two or three times per year for harvest. Therefore, it makes more sense to place your fruit trees further away from the home, rather than right outside your back door. This idea that travel time and frequency of use should dictate the location of your plants is the defining factor of Permaculture "zones."

Permaculture zones are used as a design influence and organization tool for those who wish to develop their own polyculture systems. Not only are these zones individual important, but their adjacency to other zones is also a critical component to consider. If you rely on an open grassland to feed your cattle, goats or chickens, you would certainly want to minimize the distant between these two elements to efficiently manage your time. The more attention an element of your polyculture system requires, the closer it should be located to the nexus of human activity — the home. The less attention an element requires, the father away it should be. Given both time and energy are both hard to come by these days, by spending both on simply traveling between zones, you'll certainly find that you'll have less of both once you get to your destination.

No matter the size — an apartment herb garden or a 100-acre farm — permaculture zones are here to help you decide which plants should go where — and why. Figure 15-3 gives the details.

Zone 0: House, dwelling, or settlement

Zone 1: Areas needing continual observation

Zone 2: Less intensively managed areas

Zone 3: Occasionally visited areas that still form part of the system

Zone 4: Wild food gathering, wood cutting for fuel

Zone 5: Natural, unmanaged areas

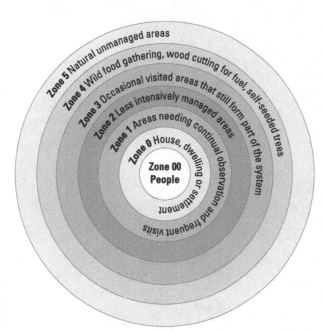

Zone 5 Natural unmanaged areas

Zone 4 Wild food gathering, wood cutting for fuel, self-seeded trees

Zone 3 Occasional visited areas that still form part of the system

Zone 2 Less intensively managed areas

Zone 1 Areas needing continual observation and frequent visits

Zone 0 House, dwelling or settlement

Zone 00
People

FIGURE 15-3:
Permaculture
management
zones.

Chapter **16**

Circularity for Design

N ow is probably the most exhilarating time in history to be a designer, but maybe not for the reasons you think.

Though recent advances in computers, fabrication, lasers, sensors, robots, and artificial intelligence seem to point to some exciting new tools coming soon for designers, this isn't why it's an exciting time. They're cool tools, for sure, but there's a much bigger design challenge ahead of us.

The reason that this is such an exciting time to be a designer is that we need to redesign everything. Yes, you read that statement correctly: Virtually everything we use, from buildings to cars to that handy little egg poacher you got from your Aunt Mildred for your birthday, needs to be redesigned. These products were designed around a set of design parameters that are simply no longer true.

In this chapter, we explore how the changing world has forced us to rethink and change our approach to design. We look at the problems that face us as designers, and suggest how to look at waste, materials, and assembly in new ways. If you're an architect, industrial designer, or product designer, this chapter is for you because the next big thing in design will be circular design!

Redesigning Design

Architects, designers, and other creative types represent around 5 percent of the global workforce today. This small fraction is about to play a crucial role in designing the world we will be living in by 2030.

In recent years, businesses have started to understand the value that design brings to their business. Apple, VW, and Nest are examples of companies that use design to drive people to their products. McKinsey & Company, a major global consulting firm, estimates that this new mindset is worth around a trillion dollars and will drive innovation for decades to come — in the process, reshaping everything we produce.

This transformation will require more creativity than ever because we will have to address so many additional concerns that we previously ignored in design. For example, in designing a building, an architect would traditionally consider only the functional needs of the building, their client's budget, and their schedule. They would never consider where the building materials came from or what would happen to them when they were done with them.

Understanding circular design

To be a circular designer means taking much more into consideration beyond what it looks like when coming up with a new design. Picture the following design examples:

>> A toothbrush where the handle gets reused but the bristles are replaced when needed.

>> A water bottle that's redesigned such that it can be reused as a stackable building block when you're done with it.

>> Light bulbs that let you pay for light as a service rather than buying fragile glass bulbs that need replacement. The company takes back their expired bulbs to harvest them for valuable materials for reuse.

>> Laundry detergent that's sold as concentrated small pellets that you mix with water, allowing for smaller packaging, less shipping weight, and less waste.

>> Wall panels that are designed to be easily taken down and rewrapped with a new covering to update the look of the space without the waste and cost of new panels.

>> Instead of using energy-intensive concrete, structural blocks designed to be made from a lab-grown fungus that's all-natural and biodegradable.

>> Carpets redesigned into reusable tiles with a replaceable backing so that you can replace only the damaged areas of carpet and recycle the backing.

>> Cell phones made from modular and easily interchangeable parts to allow anyone to repair or upgrade them so that the useful life of the phone will last for years.

Circular design offers us an opportunity to finally break free from the traditional take-make-waste approach to everything we make. Instead, circular design lets us radically rethink how we use materials and opens up new business models for companies that understand how important this concept is. (See Figure 16-1.)

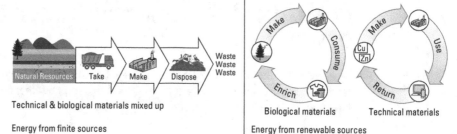

FIGURE 16-1:
The linear economy compared to a circular economy — the difference lies in how it's designed.

Companies are already innovating new types of circular-designed buildings and products:

>> Norwegian tech start-up Othalo (https://othalo.com) has partnered with the United Nations to deliver modular, low-cost homes across Africa, all made from recycled plastic waste.

>> Carpet manufacturer Interface (www.interface.com) produces carbon-neutral carpet tiles with an innovative carbo-storing backing.

>> Italian company Wasp (www.3dwasp.com) is producing giant 3D printers to allow you to print an entire house out of concrete in just 24 hours.

>> Dutch architects Overtreders W (https://en.overtreders-w.nl) designs buildings with reusable components that can be moved or rearranged.

Throughout this book, we talk about the fact that the circular economy relies on these three key principles:

>> Designing out waste

>> Keeping products and materials in use

>> Regenerating natural systems

All these principles are driven by design, and circular design in particular builds on these principles by creating a framework for them, as described in this list:

>> **Design out waste:** By using recycled, reclaimed, or salvaged materials, as well as materials that can be recovered at the end of their life

>> **Keep products and materials in use:** By designing durable products that can be repaired, maintained, and converted to other uses

>> **Regenerate natural systems:** By avoiding toxic or harmful materials and instead sourcing from sustainably harvested, renewable, or natural materials

COMMON MISCONCEPTIONS IN CIRCULAR DESIGN

Since we're talking about how everything needs to be redesigned to make the world more "circular," let's address some of the nagging misconceptions that people usually have around designing for a circular economy (circular design):

Misconception 1: It's only about reducing waste

Though it is true that, in a circular economy, we attempt to design out waste by way of better design, that's not the full story. Circular design encompasses many aspects, including designing for disassembly, designing for durability, designing for future flexibility, and, yes, designing to minimize waste. The focus is on *upstream* innovations (eliminating waste from extracting, producing, manufacturing, or transporting materials) and not just waste reduction.

Misconception 2: It's only about recycling

Using recycled materials is an easy way to keep waste out of the landfill and find an alternative source of raw materials. Unfortunately, even if we exclusively used 100 percent recycled materials in every product today, eventually, at some point in the future, they would still end up in the landfill. What's needed are innovations in materials that are designed to be infinitely renewable and recyclable. In circular design, we're really looking at developing durable, long-lasting products that achieve their highest possible value. Though recycling is part of the circular economy, remember that it only represents the outer loop on the butterfly diagram we talk about in Chapter 10. For this reason, recycling is often referred to as the loop of last resort.

Misconception 3: It's only about efficiency

Efficiency is often linked with good design because it seeks to use the least amount of material to achieve the biggest impact. We try to be energy efficient in our buildings to save money; we try to be resource-efficient in our designs to reduce waste and lower costs. But efficiency isn't our end goal here. In the end, efficiency can only get you so far. Nature, after all, is not efficient. Nature is abundant. You don't look at a field of flowers and think, "Gosh, how many more flowers are enough here?!"

Misconception 4: It's just a fancy, new word for sustainability

The circular economy isn't the latest trend or a slick synonym for sustainability. It's a radically different approach to how to design truly sustainable and endlessly reusable materials. In fact, the circular economy is a departure from traditional sustainability in that we're looking to redesign everything. To be truly circular would mean that we're designing the way nature designs: where everything is in a balanced loop with everything else, instead of trying to get people to consume less or feel guilty about their consumption.

Misconception 5: It's about converting waste to energy

Although many countries, including the United States, incinerate their trash to produce energy, it's really a dumb idea. Burning toxic materials that escape into the air just to get a one-time benefit seems a little shortsighted. A much smarter solution would be to see waste material for what it truly is: valuable resources that could potentially be reused. Doing so would save considerably more energy because it avoids having to produce new materials in the first place.

Designing out waste

Swiss architect and circular designer Walter Stahel once wrote, "The goods of today are the resources of tomorrow at the resource prices of yesterday." The first step in becoming a circular designer is to reimagine how we look at materials and their relationship to waste. Most designers assume that creating waste is inevitable. If we can shift this thinking slightly to realize that all materials are potentially valuable resources, we can stop this endless linear line of pulling things out of the earth and dumping them into a landfill.

Here are some examples of designing out waste:

>> Rather than limit recycling to commonly recycled materials, such as glass and aluminum, consider recycling materials that otherwise would end up in the landfill, such as Styrofoam (expanded polystyrene), which hardly ever gets recycled.

>> Packaging your product in minimal packaging that can be easily recycled or composted reduces shipping weight, or it can be used for another purpose.

>> Redesigning your product so that the more durable parts (like the handle) are reused and only the worn-out parts (like the bristles) are replaced.

You are limited only by your imagination.

Keeping products and materials in use

In circular design, we seek to keep materials and resources in use for as long as possible so that we can extract the maximum value from them. Nothing should be considered a disposable product. Instead, we recover and regenerate materials at the end of the product's life so that it can easily be remade into something else.

Here are some examples of using circular design to keep materials in use:

>> Providing a repair-and-refurbish service (like clothing maker Patagonia does) to extend the life of your products while also connecting to your customers.

>> Redesigning the product or material to allow replacing the outside with new skins, covers, or panels. This allows people to change the look without having to replace the product entirely.

>> Designing the product to be easily disassembled at the end of its use and then taking back the used products so that they can be recovered and reused into new products.

When you see every material as valuable, you start to open up a wealth of design possibilities.

Regenerating natural systems

Circular design offers an approach to building without destroying our environment at the same time. It forces us to look at the impacts of our design decisions. (For more on the negative impacts we cause, see Chapter 2.)

Here are some examples of using circular design to regenerate natural systems:

>> Avoiding energy or carbon-intensive materials such as steel, concrete, and aluminum and instead using low- and zero-carbon alternatives

>> Sourcing your raw materials from places that aren't being exploited through a lack of labor laws, clearcutting practices, or other unethical means

>> Redesigning your product to provide a beneficial function, such as topping your building with a rooftop garden that provides a habitat for the birds and insects while also creating a lovely amenity for its occupants

By approaching your design with the mindset to work with nature (rather than against it), new opportunities will emerge.

For more ideas, check out the suggestions that the folks behind the *Circular Design Guide* came up with at www.circulardesignguide.com.

Recognizing the Problems Designers Face

The construction and real estate sector of the economy is the largest consumer of raw materials worldwide. According to the Organization for Economic Co-operation and Development (www.oecd.org), natural resources are now being consumed at twice the rate they're produced. By 2050, estimates are that it could be three times the rate. According to the United Nations, cities worldwide make up 75 percent of the world's natural resource consumption, 50 percent of global waste production, and 60 to 80 percent of global greenhouse gas emissions. The construction and operation of buildings alone accounts for 50 percent of those total emissions. If we humans are to save the planet, we must radically transform how we build our buildings and cities.

We're being overtaken by trash

Around a third of the waste sent to the landfills globally is construction waste. (In Brazil, it's half.) Most of this construction waste contains valuable and reusable materials that we're in too much of a hurry to collect. Instead, we tear down a building and throw it away, only to build another one in the same place. What's worse, around 10 to 15 percent of building materials are wasted during construction itself. As a result, we're running out of room for landfills, and our oceans contain six times as much plastic as plankton.

Applying circular design principles to construction waste would drastically reduce the volume of materials ending up in the landfill.

We're running out of materials

Worldwide, buildings cover about 2.4 trillion square feet of the earth's surface. By 2060, this number is expected to double. That means that we'll be building an area the equivalent of New York City every 34 days. If we continue building this massive amount of construction the traditional way, we'll quickly run out of natural resources and our ability to meet the needs of the population.

We're choking on carbon

The climate crisis has put humans in a precarious position. Rising global temperatures are causing stronger and more frequent climate-related natural disasters. Increased hurricanes, tornadoes, wildfires, and rising sea levels threaten our way of life. At the time of this writing, 18 of the 20 hottest years on record all occurred in this century. The five hottest years on record have occurred during the past five years (which is sadly a condition that will remain true moving forward). Each year, the climate crisis fuels dozens of disasters, with damage in the billions. The way we design and build our buildings and cities is the biggest culprit.

Despite what people may think about what role our dependence on cars plays in increasing CO_2 emissions, according to the American Institute of Architects (www.aia.org) and the advocacy group Architecture2030 (https://architecture2030.org), cars are responsible for only around 23 percent. (See Figure 16-2.) The construction and operation of buildings and the building material industry cause most of the rest. Just a handful of materials — steel, aluminum, plastic, and cement (used in concrete) — make up most of these impacts. (In fact, cement production alone is responsible for between 8 to 12 percent of all global CO_2 emissions!)

Global CO2 Emissions by Sector

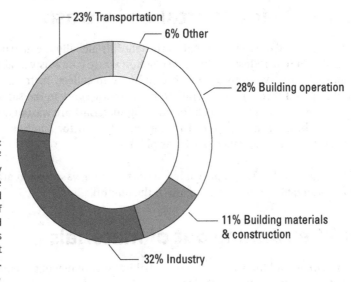

23% Transportation
6% Other
28% Building operation
11% Building materials & construction
32% Industry

FIGURE 16-2: Total CO_2 emissions by sector: The construction and operation of buildings and materials accounts for most of this impact.

All this bad news is a global emergency of our own making. If we don't quickly change how we design our built environment, we'll irreversibly change the planet as we know it. If we don't cut our global CO^2 emissions by 65 percent by 2030 (and then to 0 percent by 2040), climate change will become irreversible. Buildings are the key to this effort.

Yet if we pull this off, we would not only save our planet from becoming uninhabitable but also save billions of dollars a year in energy, labor, materials, and health costs. It seems like a no-brainer, doesn't it?

Creating a Framework for Circular Design

Now that you're excited about the prospects for circular design, let's review some ways to best approach your design project. These seven strategies are a helpful framework to follow when starting a project. Keep in mind that circular design requires you to be innovative around issues that most designers typically ignore. No design is ever perfect, so use these strategies as a way to raise questions and start a discussion:

- » **Preserve and extend what's already made:** For materials and resources that are already in use, find ways to maintain, repair, and upgrade them over time so that you can maximize their useful life or possibly even give them a second life when you're done with them.

- » **Prioritize regenerative resources:** To avoid impacting climate change negatively, use renewable, reusable, nontoxic resources in an efficient way.

- » **Use waste as a resource:** Tap into existing waste streams as a source of secondary materials. Recover waste materials for recycling and reuse.

- » **Rethink the business model:** Uncover opportunities to add value for your clients and end users by incentivizing them to participate in this circular process. Create opportunities for people to interact with the materials and the service it provides.

- » **Design for the future:** Consider future use and flexibility during the design process by exploring durable materials, future possible uses, and appropriate useful life for that material.

- » **Incorporate digital technology:** Use trackers, sensors, and other sources of data to strengthen the connection between where the material came from and what happens to it at the end of its life.

>> **Collaborate to create joint value:** Collaborate throughout your entire supply chain with all your suppliers and manufacturers to increase the transparency of how the product or material is manufactured. Knowing what goes into a product helps inform your decision-making and what you choose during design.

REMEMBER

When you first start out designing with circularity in mind, it might raise more questions than answers. That's okay. Just considering these different strategies is a great start.

Applying the ReSOLVE framework to buildings

Another design framework to consider is ReSOLVE, which stands for *Regenerate, Share, Optimize, Loop, Virtualize, Exchange.* (For more on the ReSOLVE framework, see Chapter 5.)

If we apply this same thinking to the design of buildings, it gives us some interesting questions to rethink our design approach:

>> **Regenerate:** How can we transition from dirty fossil fuels to renewable energy? How can we reclaim or restore land in order to protect ecosystems? In what ways can we return biological resources to nature?

>> **Share:** How can we share little-used materials or spaces to get the full use out of them to eliminate waste and redundancy? How many hours a day will the spaces go empty or unused? Who could we invite in to use these resources when they're not being used?

>> **Optimize:** How can we reduce the waste energy from manufacturing these materials? Where are materials being wasted unnecessarily? Which byproducts are being produced from the manufacturing that could be captured and used in other ways?

>> **Loop:** Where can organic materials be looped back into nature, such as being composted? Where can inorganic technical materials be reused, such as being recycled or remanufactured? What possible linear processes exist that can be bent into circular loops?

>> **Virtualize:** Where can we replace a physical object with a virtual or digital one? What aspects of the design can we dematerialize and make digital?

>> **Exchange:** How can we design in the ability to swap in new technologies or upgrades in the future? What trends or technologies can we assume will change in the future that we can anticipate and design for now?

Here are some examples of how this ReSOLVE framework functions in the real world:

>> Airbnb (www.airbnb.com) allows people to safely rent out their unused extra bedrooms to travelers, creating better use of an unused resource.

>> LiquidSpace (https://liquidspace.com) rents unused conference rooms and offices to business travelers in need of a workspace for a few hours.

>> DIRTT (www.dirtt.com) manufactures beautiful modular, demountable walls that can easily be disassembled and reassembled into new locations. In addition, the front panels can be easily replaced when they become worn or faded. This concept is perfect for hotels or hospitals looking to easily change their layouts in the future without producing waste.

Layers of useful life

Not all items in a building are created equal. People remodel their living rooms every 7 to 10 years, their kitchens every 10 to 15 years, and maybe their whole house every 20 to 30 years. As a result, the expected useful life of any part of a building varies by its use.

To help you understand how to design for an appropriate useful life for your building, Figure 16-3 is a helpful guide — you can see that, although the structure should be designed to last 50 to 100 years (a nice long life), the fixtures can be expected to last only between 5 and 15 years. As a result, we should design with this timeframe in mind.

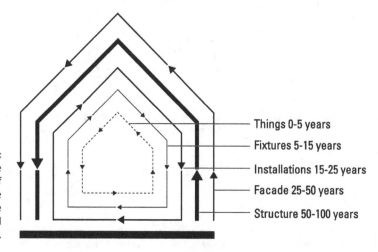

Things 0-5 years
Fixtures 5-15 years
Installations 15-25 years
Facade 25-50 years
Structure 50-100 years

FIGURE 16-3:
Not all the various layers of a building have the same expected useful life.

Here are some helpful construction waste terms to know about:

>> **Demolition:** Traditionally, buildings are torn down in order to clear the site as quickly as possible, to make away for the new building about to be erected. This process reduces any chance of recycling or recovering the materials as they're mixed together into a dusty pile.

>> **Deconstruction:** This process systematically dismantles and disassembles the building for its valuable parts. Watching it happen is like doing the construction in reverse. Most of the salvaged materials can be reused for their original purpose.

>> **Salvage:** This process includes the removal of select building components for refurbishment, restoration, and reuse.

>> **Strip-out:** This quick process harvests only the building's most valuable and easily removable components and is typically limited to equipment, cabinets, fixtures, and doors. The majority of the structure ends up being demolished.

The deconstruction of buildings also helps reduce toxic dust blowing off of construction sites, metal leaching into the soil, waste being dumped into landfills, and the need to produce new building materials.

REMEMBER

One challenge in choosing deconstruction instead of demolition is in how the original building was built in the first place. Though screws are easy to remove, nails damage the material going in and coming out. Dissolvable binders can be easily taken apart, but glues are permanent and prevent the disassembly of building components. Making simple, common-sense decisions when it comes to your construction details will help make it easy for future deconstruction crews to salvage your building. Figure 16-4 summarizes some of the best practices you should follow.

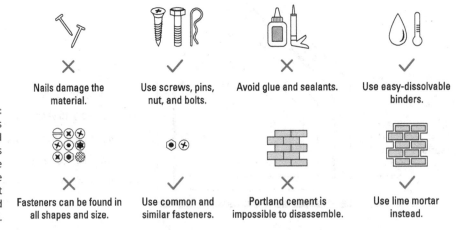

FIGURE 16-4:
Simple changes to how you detail your buildings will improve the chances that the materials get deconstructed and reused.

Nails damage the material.

Use screws, pins, nut, and bolts.

Avoid glue and sealants.

Use easy-dissolvable binders.

Fasteners can be found in all shapes and size.

Use common and similar fasteners.

Portland cement is impossible to disassemble.

Use lime mortar instead.

Putting the pieces together

If we start to think about how this all comes together into a truly circular building, it starts to look like what you see in Table 16-1.

TABLE 16-1   ## Design Goals for a Circular Economy

Value	Health and Well-Being	Culture and Society
• Ensure long-term use through timeless design. • Encourage the sharing of knowledge.	• Avoid toxic or carcinogenic materials. • Ensure an ample quantity of air, daylight, thermal comfort, acoustics, and safety.	• Preserve the unique cultural and social character of a community. • Facilitate shared amenities and communal spaces.
Biodiversity	**Material Use**	**Energy Efficiency**
• Protect and preserve biodiversity. • Integrate ecosystem services. • Stimulate and restore biodiversity.	• Optimize material use for efficiency. • Reuse and reclaim products. • Use circular and biobased materials.	• Minimize energy consumption. • Optimize solar orientation. • Source onsite and offsite renewable energy.
Water Efficiency:		**Waste Reduction:**
• Use low-flow water fixtures. • Incorporate water reuse (graywater and rainwater catchment).		• Design for components to be disassembled. • Design to the width of the material to avoid cutting and waste.

If we look at the various stages of design, from design through construction and use, there are several clear ideas to follow, as shown in Table 16-2.

Though nature is 100 percent circular, only around 9 percent of our current built environment is. Everything needs to be redesigned to incorporate these circular design considerations, making this an exciting time to be a designer.

Given the global crises facing us, we cannot continue designing buildings the way we have been. We need to quickly transform our design process to address the issues of waste, climate change, and resource depletion to factor in opportunities such as material recovery, zero carbon materials, and renewable resources.

This is a huge undertaking and a global challenge, but if we rise up to meet it, we will also save billions a year in construction, health, and labor costs. It's a challenge we can't afford not to meet.

TABLE 16-2   Circular Design First Principles

Design Stage	Circular Design Considerations
Design	Design for disassembly (DfD).
	Design for adaptability and flexibility.
	Design for standardization of parts.
	Design out unnecessary waste.
	Design in modularity.
	Specify reclaimed materials.
	Specify recycled materials.
	Create feedback loops from users back to designers.
	Collect metrics and datasets.
Manufacturing	Adopt ecodesign principles.
	Use fewer materials and optimize material use.
	Avoid hazardous materials.
	Increase the lifespan.
	Use secondary materials.
	Use take-back schemes.
Construction/assembly	Reverse logistics.
	Minimize or recycle construction waste.
	Procure reused or reclaimed or salvaged materials.
	Use off-site construction.
	Use timber instead of steel or concrete for the structure.
	Source low-carbon steel and cement alternatives.
Use/maintenance/operations	Minimize waste from use.
	Minimize the need for maintenance.
	Minimize the need for batteries or other disposables.
	Take proper care to extend useful life.
Repair/upgrade	Take advantage of the simple repair and upgrade of components.
	Quickly replace worn areas to extend life.
	Renovate and remodel instead of demolish.
Adaptability/flexibility	Be adaptable (to a new purpose).
	Be flexible (rearrange the spaces).

Design Stage	Circular Design Considerations
End-of-life	Deconstruct.
	Selectively demolish.
	Reuse products and components.
	Use closed-loop recycling.
	Use open-loop recycling.

BUILDING FOR A LIFECYCLE: USGBC ADVANCES CIRCULARITY THROUGH LEED

The U.S. Green Building Council (USGBC) is a nonprofit organization that supports the development of prosperous, healthy, and resilient communities through the transformation of the built environment. Through its Leadership in Energy and Environmental Design (LEED) green building program, USGBC is committed to transforming how our buildings and communities are designed, constructed, and operated, enabling an environmentally and socially responsible, healthy, and prosperous environment that improves quality of life.

Melanie Colburn is the director of the Northern California Chapter of the U.S. Green Building Council and serves as their director of market transformation & development. She shared her thoughts on how to transform an industry as large as the building industry:

LEED brings circular economy principles to building projects around the world

LEED, which stands for Leadership in Energy and Environmental Design, is the world's most widely used green building certification program. It was first introduced in 1998 and since then has been used by over 106,000 commercial projects in more than 180 countries and territories. A building that is LEED-certified meets the highest sustainability standards when it comes to design, construction, and operations. Given its international reach and adoption, LEED has the capacity to greatly extend the circular economy by guiding building professionals in applying circularity principles to new buildings and major renovations.

The concept and aspiration of a circular economy — that efficient and creative uses for materials will maximize their utility and minimize planetary impacts — aligns with USGBC's mission, to build a greener, healthier future for all.

(continued)

(continued)

Sustainable Materials Selection

Materials matter: where they came from, their toxicity level, their potential for recycling, reuse, and waste.

USGBC's holistic vision for materials and resources comprises three strategies: 1. reduce embodied carbon; 2. protect human and ecological health; and 3. advance the circular economy. The LEED v4.1 credit framework increases market demand for recycled content, responsibly sourced products and raw materials, and healthier materials that can be reused or repurposed in an "infinite loop."

It is most efficient and effective to advance comprehensive circular economy principles at the earliest phase of design and sourcing. But what about buildings that are already built? Existing buildings can also incorporate these lifecycle principles through thoughtful and aligned building operations and maintenance practices. Decisions about what supplies to purchase, how to manage waste and recycling, and the timing and method of cleaning all add up and contribute to the building's lifecycle impact.

Reducing and Zeroing Out Waste

The building industry contributes about 23 percent of landfill waste in the US (or 138 million tons), according to the Environmental Protection Agency (EPA, 2018). Many of the opportunities to eliminate building waste exist before construction even begins. For this reason, a LEED project team can identify opportunities to eliminate waste during project design before materials ever arrive at the project site.

For USGBC, this starts with adaptive reuse of buildings that have outlived their initial purpose, and/or the renovation of abandoned buildings rather than building new. For example, converting an old hospital into an apartment building, rather than knocking down the structure, prevents landfill waste from demolition. Reusing salvaged components from the old structure further reduces the portion of virgin material needed for construction.

If reuse is not possible, project teams can design out waste by eliminating finishes, such as drop ceilings or floor coverings where appropriate, or design structural and enclosure systems that fulfill the same purpose but with less materials.

LEED's Journey Forward

USGBC will continue to evolve LEED, both to adjust for advances in the circular economy and to make circularity more accessible and feasible for teams to implement. Circularity will only become more important as green building and LEED continues to evolve.

The strategies found in LEED work together to not only advance a closed-loop economy, but also protect human health and support corporate social responsibility goals. To learn more about how USGBC's LEED rating system can support a building's circular economy goals, visit www.usgbc.org/.

Chapter **17**

Circular Economy for Builders, Makers, and Manufacturers

C an the circular economy extend beyond products to entire buildings? Of course it can! But it gets hairy in a hurry. In this chapter, we begin by exploring a building's lifecycle and offer some guidance on how to make better choices for building products. Cycling through the full disclosure of product ingredients, responsible material sourcing, and building product choices that don't harm the environment or threaten human health, we'll take you through the necessary steps to optimize your next project!

Why focus on buildings? Well, buildings are a major contributor to various emissions, and they hold great opportunity for improvement. With this in mind, we'll discuss buildings in a broader global context with regard to greenhouse gas emissions with the full realization that a circular economy requires an aggressive strategy to reduce how much carbon linear buildings emit into the atmosphere.

Finally, in order for circular buildings to become less of a futuristic dream and more of a current option, the necessary information and strategies for making that dream a reality *must* be made public for viewing and collaboration. In the last section of this chapter, we look at whether an open-source approach to how we make buildings is ultimately necessary in order to realize true circularity as well as no greenhouse gas emissions.

Assessing a Building's Lifecycle

To understand how you can improve a building's lifecycle, you should first understand what is meant by the term *construction and demolition waste*. From there, you can begin to identify opportunities to not only minimize waste to begin with but also turn waste into a new resource. The first step to understanding where opportunities lie comes from assessing the current status of building lifecycles through the various tools that are now available.

Defining construction and demolition debris

The term *construction and demolition (C&D) waste* encompasses the full range of material waste streams, starting from how we build buildings and ending with how we destroy them. C&D waste streams may include roadwork material, excavated material, demolition waste, construction/renovation waste, and site clearance waste such as trees, stumps, earth, and rock. C&D waste also includes building materials, like concrete, wood, asphalt, gypsum, metals, bricks, glass, plastics, and various salvaged building components (doors, windows, and plumbing fixtures). C&D waste should not include hazardous waste, including materials that contain lead and/or asbestos.

Why address C&D debris? Well, because a lot of waste stems from the architecture, engineering, and construction industries and the circular economy can act as the necessary framework for construction and demolition waste to become a construction and demolition resource. For reference, 600 million tons of C&D debris were generated in the United States in 2018, which is more than twice the amount of generated municipal solid waste. Demolition represents more than 90 percent of total C&D debris generation, whereas construction represents less than 10 percent. Just over 455 million tons of C&D debris were directed to next use, and just under 145 million tons were sent to landfills. A significant amount of materials in the C&D debris gets reused as construction aggregate — particulate matter used to reinforce asphalt and concrete. The Environmental Protection Agency (EPA) also asserts that nonresidential sources accounted for the majority of C&D debris.

The largest building sector that generated C&D materials was nonresidential demolition, followed by the residential renovation.

Gauging the economic opportunities of C&D waste

A number of potential economic benefits are linked to improving building product lifecycles, moving toward circular lifecycles, and reducing the amount of C&D debris sent to landfills or incinerators. The benefits include creating employment and economic activities in recycling industries as well as providing increased business opportunities within the local community, especially when deconstruction and selective demolition methods are used. In addition, a transition to a circular way of managing building materials will aid in reducing overall building project expenses by avoiding purchase and disposal costs and by donating recovered materials to qualified 501(c)(3) charities, which provides a tax benefit. The onsite reuse of materials — rather than throwing away the old junk and buying new junk — also reduces the costs associated with transporting waste and new products, leading to fewer disposal facilities and potentially reducing the associated environmental issues. Offsetting the environmental impact associated with the extraction and consumption of virgin resources and production of new materials will also make an impact!

Measuring C&D waste impact

The lifecycle of a building product comes with a range of associated impacts. Though they're all interrelated, there are three basic types of impacts: environmental, human health, and economic. Historically, lifecycle assessments (LCA) have been developed as a framework to assess and report the environmental impact of a product in a standardized way. However, the building design and construction industry has recently moved toward also integrating an assessment of the human health impact and direct financial costs. Now, there are four basic scopes and four similar acronyms that are worth exploring:

>> **Lifecycle assessment (LCA)** is a procedure for quantifying the total environmental impact of a product across its entire lifetime. This multistep process includes describing the goal and scope of the assessment, examining data about how the product is made, gathering information about the environmental impacts, and interpreting the results in a standardized summary report. LCAs are a snapshot in time, based on the best available information. As the plausibility, quality, and completeness of relevant product information changes over time, LCAs need to be conducted again in order to be accurate and relevant.

- » **Lifecycle inventory (LCI)** is the data-collection phase of an LCA. Basically, an LCI strives to take account of everything involved in the product or service. This inventory considers the total system of the product — including all the resource inputs and outputs involved in making the product. Such a detailed accounting may include raw resources or materials, energy by type, water by source, and the various emissions to air, water, and/or land by substance. An LCI may be extremely complex because it could include any number of individual related processes contributing to the product's supply chains (the extraction of raw materials, various production processes, transportation, and so on) along with any and all constituent substances (for which there could be hundreds).

- » **Lifecycle impact assessment (LCIA)** can be thought of as the what-does-it-mean? step in the lifecycle assessment process. Through an LCIA, the data and information from the previous LCI is assessed in order to figure out the product's environmental impact. The results are typically reported based on one of several standardized methods for categorizing and characterizing the environmental impact of a product's various material/resource flows to and from the environment. There are several internationally recognized methods for conducting an LCIA, but two of the most common methods now utilized for building products are CML and TRACI. The CML methodology, developed by the Institute of Environmental Sciences at the University of Leiden in The Netherlands, is the most widely used method and is often considered the most complete of all LCIA methodologies. (If you're up on your Dutch language skills, you'll be pleased to know that CML stands for Centrum voor Milieuwetenschappen. If your Dutch is weak, just know that CML would be the same thing as the Institute of Environmental Studies.) The TRACI methodology (where TRACI is short for Tool for the Reduction and Assessment of Chemical and Other Environmental Impacts) is an impact assessment methodology developed by the US EPA.

- » **Lifecycle costing (LCC)** is another lifecycle approach through which the direct monetary costs involved with a product or service are examined rather than the environmental impact.

What about the human health impact option we just mentioned? Well, in addition to the environmental impact and financial cost of a product, rising concerns regarding human health and wellness have precipitated the establishment of an international standard to accurately, reliably, and consistently report a building product's contents and associated health information. Health product declarations (HPDs), for instance, adhere to an open standard for reporting a product's lifecycle human health impact. (See the "Straight from the Open Source" section, later in this chapter, for more on this topic.)

Defining lifecycle impacts

In accordance with TRACI, the preeminent domestic methodology for lifecycle impact assessments, environmental impact categories may include these:

>> **Global warming potential:** This is a calculation of the potency of greenhouse gases relative to atmospheric CO^2 contributions. (See the "We All Embody Carbon" section, later in this chapter, for more on this topic.)

>> **Ozone depletion potential:** Depleting ozone isn't good for the environment. Ozone within the stratosphere provides protection from radiation. Compromising that protection can lead to an increased frequency of skin cancers and cataracts in humans.

>> **Acidification potential:** This is a calculation of the product's potential to decrease the pH of land and water. Acidification can cause damage to building materials, paints, and other human-built structures and to lakes, streams, rivers, and various plants and animals.

>> **Eutrophication potential:** Eutrophication — the enrichment of an aquatic ecosystem with nutrients such as nitrates and phosphates — can accelerate biological productivity (for instance, the growth of algae and weeds). This often leads to an undesirable accumulation of algal biomass. Nutrients such as nitrogen and phosphorus play an important role in the fertilization of agricultural lands and other vegetation, but an excessive release into the environment can cause undesired effects on waterways. Generally, phosphorus has a more negative impact on freshwater bodies, and nitrogen is more detrimental to coastal environments.

>> **Smog formation potential:** Ground-level ozone is created by various chemical reactions between nitrogen oxides (NOxs), volatile organic compounds (VOCs), and sunlight. It can cause a variety of respiratory health issues, including permanent lung damage from prolonged exposure. Smog also damages various ecosystems and crops. The primary sources of smog are motor vehicles, electric power utilities, and industrial facilities — all of which come into play when a product is manufactured and delivered to a building site.

>> **Potential damage to human health:** Substances that could pose a cancerous and noncancerous threat to human health are identified and disclosed.

>> **Ecotoxicity potential:** Substances that could pose a threat to ecosystems are identified and disclosed.

>> **Resource depletion potential:** The resource depletion linked to fossil fuel use, land use, and water use are identified and disclosed.

WARNING

Watch out for different units of measurement! The units by which the potential impact of a product is communicated differ, depending on which LCIA methodology is being utilized.

Identifying human health hazards and promoting transparency

In addition to the environmental-impact categories defined by the LCAI methodology, human health impacts are further gauged by examining the type and amount of potentially hazardous substances present in a product. To ensure human health hazards within the built environment are avoided to a high degree, some "best practices" have been developed to aid even a beginner in their selection of healthy materials.

>> **Full disclosure:** For any product, all of its substances should be characterized, screened, and identified. Then the information should be shared in a summary document, such as a health product declaration (HPD).

>> **Everything over the threshold level must be reported.** In reality, it's impractical to report every single substance in a product, because a variety of substances can be present in extremely small *(trace)* amounts. Therefore, a threshold level is identified: If there are more parts of a substance than the threshold level, it must be disclosed; otherwise, it can be ignored as practically insignificant. Common threshold levels are 1,000 parts per mission (ppm) or perhaps even just 100 ppm.

>> **If in doubt, do without — the precautionary principle.** As defined by the World Health Organization (WHO), "[T]he precautionary principle states that, in cases of serious or irreversible threats to the health of humans or ecosystems, acknowledged scientific uncertainty should not be used as a reason to postpone preventive measures." The principle originated as a tool to bridge uncertain scientific information and political responsibility to act in order to prevent damage to human health and to ecosystems.

>> **Always avoid the red list.** The term *red list* has been used by a variety of organizations to explicitly call out chemicals and substances that should never be used for products, because they pose a clear and significant risk to human and/or environmental health.

People, planet and profit

When building product lifecycles are improved to minimize their detrimental environmental and human health impacts, nature and society all benefit. Society benefits by way of improved safety and security, increased workforce productivity, improved satisfaction of building occupants, and improved student cognition performance through toxic material avoidance. Improved and restored ecosystems result in healthier waterways, increased biodiversity, wildlife habitat provision, atmospheric and oceanic carbon sequestration, and energy resource conservation. All this allows nature to exhibit increased *ecosystem services* — the oxygen, air, and water purification and the nutrient cycling that nature provides for us. Healthier materials with improved lifecycles come with a range of direct and indirect economic benefits, including reduced demolition costs, increased job creation, material sourcing stability, offset remediation efforts, and reduced healthcare costs.

THE JOYS OF ADDITIVE MANUFACTURING

Sarah O'Sell is a Digital Manufacturing and Circular Economy strategist located in Seattle, WA, USA. You can learn more about her work at www.sarahosell.com/. She has some ideas about additive manufacturing she would like to share.

In an industrial context, additive manufacturing (AM) is one of an assortment of digital manufacturing tools that are circularity catalysts; agile technologies that enhance product and material systems by using only stock needed for the object, where it is needed, on-demand, customizable, and available in your neighborhood. They are increasingly able to sense and adapt to their material inputs, and owners are more readily able to maintain and improve tool components with the tool itself. With the formation of the Additive Manufacturer Green Trade Association (AMGTA) in November 2019, we see that AM is becoming engaged by the ROI of more efficient hardware, design innovation, and systems thinking.

Additive Manufacturing circularity solutions:

- Design and engineering for energy and assembly efficiency of machines and products

  Marita Sauerwein, PhD, TU Delft, has developed alternative 3D printed joinery and disassembly techniques

- Designing out waste and material reduction through engineering simulation, called lightweighting

  Neri Oxman has defined the new field of material ecology to fuse technology and biology for ecological sustainability using AM to deliver solutions

(continued)

(continued)

- Post-production custom part replacement for product refurbish or enhancement, HP's Multi Jet Fusion is "the printer that prints itself" for 140 components

- Material recovery for reuse or resale channels that capture more value while eliminating waste streams

- A shift to HaaS (hardware as a service) sales models that enable broader market accessibility, extend product or part lifetime, and ensure software deliverability, while driving long-term revenue stability from ongoing license fees

- Ivaldi's company tagline, "send files, not parts" represents a business model that exists by optimizing shipping cost and emissions impact through the shortened go-to-market distance of a distributed additive supply chain

One of industry's greatest circularity challenges is product and material life cycle analysis. This process is manual, cost and time preventative in an iterative development environment, not securely accessible while remaining open to downstream stakeholders, and does not scale for the next generation of mass-custom on-demand applications. When we do not know our supply chains or maintain buyer relationships, we forego visibility to or even disable downstream financial opportunities — and there is value on the table. *Harvard Business Review* found that consumers are willing to pay more for sustainably marketed goods across 90 percent of categories.

Within all of manufacturing, AM is best able to deliver a fully circular hardgood product to the world by existence at innovation origin points; cutting edge material science, emerging digital technologies, and product conception. By existing at the start, additive holds the key (data and design opportunity) for the finish; complete cycle management. If we are able to track materials, assemblies, production processes, use and maintenance throughout a product's lifetime, we can predict next-use material integrity, market value, establish part or whole-product resale or sharing routes, and fine tune our resource planning. Essentially, we create a digital twin or passport record of past, present, and future product life. Through practice, we can grow to build predictive models to inform better processes at the point of product and supply chain development, and even encourage course-corrective downstream adjustments, which holds sweeping implications for investment awards.

Innovations in inventory management mean computing is reaching a point of readiness to develop, deploy, manage, and learn with complex chaotic systems of multidimensional product lifetime data. What we are missing is industry initiative around data-sharing and security protocols, downstream stakeholder communications infrastructure, and collaborative incentive; stock and benefit sharing from the implementation and success of this system. Good news — there are case studies to build on already in progress in softgoods with international buy-in.

This is not about revealing or assigning blame for the climate and supply chain infrastructure collapse dual-crisis, this is about moving forward towards economic strength, distributed agility, and industrial infrastructure evolution. As our energy and production markets shift to satisfy hyper-local demand; this infrastructure build is an opportunity to realize circular value, with AM as a core enabling technology.

A circular economy for hardgoods, starting with AM, is next.

Selecting Appropriate Building Products

It's not hard for us humans to know what's in our food — we can consult an ingredients list. What if building products were the same way? Why not have "nutrition labels" for building products? Wouldn't it be useful if building products came with a simple, consistent way to label what it's made of? Think of a box of cereal: You can grab any type of cereal, and no matter how healthy (or unhealthy) it is, no matter who made it, and no matter how much it costs, all the cereal in the grocery aisle bears a label telling you what (and how much) is in it. These nutrition labels are placed on food sold at grocery stores, because the US government recognized that people need to understand what they're putting in their bodies. Yet, when it comes to what we're putting in our buildings, we haven't yet come to this same sort of resolution. The government doesn't require building product manufacturers to tell you what (and how much) is in their products.

In some cases, if a bad ingredient is in a building product, you may see a warning label — but what about the other substances you're unsure about? What about those who choose to adhere to the Precautionary principle, preferring not to finish an indoor space with products that could emit compounds that may potentially pose a health risk or negatively impact those who manufactured the product? Until the day that building products are required to have their own nutrition labels, so to speak, we will need to depend on the free market to entice manufacturers to share product ingredients and optimize product lifecycles. This is where you come in.

As with most industries, the building products industry is competitive. Manufacturers are looking for an edge; they want to meet the demands of the market. In pursuit of a circular economy for building products, it's important that we prioritize building products from manufacturers who are doing their homework to eliminate waste, achieve cradle-to-cradle processes, and minimize negative lifecycle impacts. There's no way to accomplish this without manufacturers stepping up and being willing to critically assess their processes, improve their supply chains, and publicly share the good, the bad, and the ugly about their activities and products. This *product transparency* isn't required, nor is it a standard practice of building product manufacturers. Product transparency will become more common only if the marketplace demands it.

TIP

Prioritize products from manufacturers who have published ingredient disclosure and lifecycle analysis information. Such information may be presented in a variety of forms; however, an environmental product declaration is a common and internationally recognized form of public disclosure.

Sourcing responsibly

The circular economy will never be fully realized without the responsible sourcing of material inputs used for building products. Recycled materials are preferred, but raw material extraction will always be present to some degree. It must be minimized and optimized because raw material extraction has a direct environmental impact on Earth's ecosystems.

For example, according to the United Nations, conventional logging is the largest source of deforestation in Latin America and subtropical Asia, accounting for more than 70 percent of resource depletion; mining operations clear another 18 percent of the world's forests. Unmanaged raw-material extraction practices can degrade water sources, cause habitat loss, threaten rare and endangered species, release toxic chemicals to damaging effect, and infringe on indigenous peoples' rights. When raw materials are needed in the manufacturing of a building product, responsible sourcing is critical. Always encourage the use of responsibly sourced and extracted materials through reporting and the demonstration of responsible extraction practices.

TIP

Want to learn more? Examine the corporate sustainability reports (CSRs) of the companies you're considering working with. These documents are based on widely recognized frameworks and standards and can shed light on product supply chains as well as identify sources of raw material extraction. CSRs have become increasingly popular among all types of businesses, from retail organizations to product manufacturers. Be sure that the reports are based on internationally sanctioned reporting protocols.

In addition, you should select products that responsibly source materials. Exercising this responsibility may include any combination of the following:

- >> **Reduce (optimize demand):** When it comes to building design and construction, are there opportunities to reduce the amount of material that's necessary? A product not used is material spared.

- >> **Reuse (maximize material reuse):** The term *reuse* can encompass any material that's salvaged, refurbished, or reused. Reused products supplant raw material demand and keep items out of the waste stream. These should be preferred over recycled content and sustainably managed raw material.

- >> **Recycle (prioritize recycled content):** Supplanting raw materials with recycled content minimizes waste and increases circularity. It's much easier for manufacturers to salvage and reconstitute excess and waste materials during their controlled industrial processes than it is to source and take back content after people have used and potentially degraded or contaminated the material. This is why recycled content should be prioritized.

If raw material must be used, see whether the manufacturer participates in an extended producer responsibility program — one which accounts for the total cost of the material's lifecycle, rather than just first costs — or is directly responsible for extended producer responsibility. In addition, bio-based products and materials other than wood should be tested or certified by a third party. Responsibly sourced wood products should be certified by the Forest Stewardship Council (https://fsc.org) or another similarly rigorous third-party organization.

Prioritize product manufacturers who offer evidence of supply chain optimization. By increasing the demand for transparency in mining, quarrying, agriculture, forestry, and other raw material extraction processes, negative environmental impacts will be reduced and eventually may result in positive outcomes. Imagine if an agrifiber-based interior wallboard product could be sustainably managed from regional resources and when used in buildings actually sequester carbon that would otherwise be suspended in the Earth's atmosphere. Then, after the product is no longer in use, it could be completely composted as a natural nutrient and new, sustainably managed raw agrifiber harvested. The circular economy manifests itself through a truly sustainable, natural metabolism.

Something stinks

We humans have a relationship with smells. Let's be honest: We all love that new-building smell, don't we? Just admit it. We've been conditioned to associate certain smells with new-and-clean regardless of the details of the chemical concoction we're inhaling. The automotive industry understands this concept and sells air fresheners designed to emulate that new-car smell. But when we smell something — anything — we're breathing in airborne particles of that which we're smelling. (Let that sink in for a minute.)

Everything lets off gas. It's natural. When a building product emits a smell, it's called *off-gassing.* Virtually all building products off-gas to some degree — admittedly, some more than others. Off-gassing isn't constant — most building products will off-gas less and less over a certain period until the level becomes negligible. However, air temperature, humidity levels, and the chemistry of the air around a product will also impact off-gassing. Many products will off-gas more as temperatures increase and the molecules of the product become more excited. (You have experienced the same effect with food. Ask yourself the following question: Which has a stronger smell — hot or cold pizza?)

Some gas is silent but deadly. Volatile organic compounds (VOCs) are a large group of chemicals found in many products we use to build and maintain our buildings. Once products are inside our buildings, the VOCs are released to the air through off-gassing, and we breathe the chemicals into our bodies. Many VOCs are odorless and potentially quite harmful. Overexposure to VOC emissions can lead to respiratory problems, including lung damage, but other issues that can result from too much exposure may include fatigue, headaches, and eyes, nose, and throat irritation, among other symptoms. Collectively, these acute and less life-threatening issues brought on by VOC exposure are called, collectively, sick building syndrome: The building's contaminated air makes you feel sick, but once you leave and breathe in clean air, the symptoms subside. It's kind of like being allergic to cats" Get away from the cats and you feel better. However, some people may experience harmful effects from breathing in too many (or certain types of) VOCs. For instance, formaldehyde is a colorless, strong-smelling gas used in making building materials and many household products. It's used in pressed-wood products, such as particleboard, plywood, and fiberboard; glues and adhesives; permanent-press fabrics; paper product coatings; and certain insulation materials. According to the American Cancer Society, formaldehyde has been shown to cause cancer in laboratory test animals. Exposure to relatively high amounts of formaldehyde in medical and occupational settings has been linked to some types of cancer in humans, but the effect of exposure to small amounts is less clear.

If a products stinks — either figuratively in terms of containing harmful materials or literally because it's a product known to off-gas excessively — consider looking for alternatives. In many instances, there are alternative solutions to products that result in healthier indoor air quality. For instance, you can choose to go with cork flooring rather than modular carpet tiles.

In addition to looking for alternatives, beware of *greenwashing*, a fairly standard marketing tactic used to convince customers that a product or company is helping the environment. Manufacturers understand that people feel an increasing concern over the health impacts of building products. Some may try to take advantage of this by communicating their products as being green or healthy when they really don't meet the industry's latest standards for touting such qualities. In a

2010 study, TerraChoice investigated the claims of 4,744 green products carried in stores across the United States and Canada, finding that more than 95 percent of these products were guilty of at least one example of greenwashing.

TIP

Many manufacturers have published content inventories of their products — examine this information, which may include publicly available inventories of all ingredients identified, chemical hazard-screening processes such as GreenScreen (www.greenscreenchemicals.org), health product declarations (HPDs) from the Health Product Declaration Collaborative or Declare product label information from the International Living Future Institute.

Going beyond disclosures, some manufacturers have earned industry-recognized certification for having green products in terms of less-harmful ingredients. These certifications should come from third-party evaluations, such as Cradle to Cradle Certified, from the Cradle to Cradle Products Innovation Institute (www.c2ccertified.org/get-certified/product-certification), or the Product Lens certification from UL (www.ul.com/resources/product-lens-certification-program). If certification isn't an option, your product could still achieve a certain result via the third-party disclosure process. For instance, under the GreenScreen benchmark, the product is inventoried to 100 ppm (parts per million) and is determined to have no Benchmark 1 hazards, or chemicals with the highest human health threat(www.greenscreenchemicals.org/learn/full-greenscreen-method).

After you've selected all your products, you still have opportunities for improvement with the use air filters. This may require choosing and maintaining a certain type of air filter in your mechanical air system and/or installing local air purification devices within a space. On top of filters, be sure to complete a building flush-out before occupancy to ensure that any lingering gases and chemicals can be, well, flushed out. When a building is first built, off-gassing levels are at their highest. It makes sense to spend some extra time opening up the building or running the air system at a higher level in order to flush out the most highly contaminated air before people move into the building.

We All Embody Carbon

Carbon is a basic building block of life, playing a unique role among the chemical elements. You may have heard that we humans are all carbon-based lifeforms (although we also contain a lot of hydrogen, oxygen, nitrogen, phosphors, and sulfur as well). This is because carbon is the smallest element that's able to make a covalent bond to four different atoms, which enables carbon compounds to have many different forms and to link to an almost limitless chain with other atoms.

Carbon atoms can bond together to form vast branching networks and are therefore a foundational component of organic chemistry. All organic substances contain carbon. The covalent bonding of carbon is responsible for fossil fuels, DNA, protein, carbohydrates, lipids, and synthetic polymers. Simply put, life on this planet couldn't exist without carbon. We all embody carbon. The problem occurs when too much of it is suspended in the air.

The human's relationship to carbon

As much as we depend on carbon-based chemistry for life on Earth, when certain types of carbon-based molecules are suspended in the upper atmosphere by human activity, there's an unintended consequence. Take carbon dioxide (CO_2) as a prime example: Carbon dioxide is an example of a greenhouse gas (GHG) — it absorbs and radiates heat. When the Earth's land and water bodies receive sunlight, it's warmed. This is necessary for life to exist; however, some of the sun's energy is reflected and/or radiated back to the atmosphere and into space. According to NASA, 71 percent of the total incoming solar energy from the sun is absorbed by the Earth (48 percent by the surface; 23 percent by the atmosphere; the remaining 29 percent is reflected back to space, mostly by clouds). This 71 percent strikes a delicate balance. If too much or too little of the sun's energy is absorbed, it can lead to massive changes in climate patterns and result in altered landforms, shifting water bodies, mass species migration and extinction, and a variety of chronic and acute human health threats, including the displacement of entire populations.

What is the greenhouse effect? This question gets us back to carbon dioxide and other greenhouse gases. If too many molecules of CO_2 are emitted into the skies and become suspended in the upper atmosphere, it causes what scientists call the *greenhouse effect:* Like the glass enclosure on a greenhouse, sunshine pierces through and turns into heat, and the heat waves cannot easily pass back through the glass, so the temperature builds up inside the greenhouse. For a similar analogy, consider your car windows on a sunny day. The temperature might be below freezing outside, but the inside of your car still builds up heat. If you crack your windows, heat escapes and it feels much cooler.

Why do we focus on atmospheric carbon dioxide? The build-up of greenhouse gases in the atmosphere is a slow process. Scientists have been tracking it for years. Many greenhouse gases are in the atmosphere, but scientists who are concerned with the greenhouse effect focus on CO_2. Why? Because carbon dioxide is the most important of Earth's long-lived greenhouse gases. It absorbs less heat per molecule than the other greenhouse gases, but it's more abundant and it stays in the atmosphere much longer. Although carbon dioxide is less abundant and less powerful than water vapor on a molecule-per-molecule basis, it absorbs more heat and adds to the greenhouse effect in quite an effective manner. According to the NOAA, increases in atmospheric carbon dioxide are responsible for about two-thirds of the total energy imbalance that's causing Earth's temperature to rise.

How do we measure atmospheric carbon? The scientific community measures and tracks atmospheric carbon dioxide in a number of parts per million (ppm). This number tells how many "parts" of carbon dioxide are in 1 million parts of air. For example, if atmospheric carbon dioxide is at 350 ppm, that means in 1 million particles of air, there are 350 particles of carbon dioxide. Using various tracing methods, scientists can generally track the amount of CO^2 in the atmosphere going back hundreds of thousands of years. Evidence suggests that the Earth may be about 4.5 billion years old. So, a timeframe of several hundred thousand years gives us only a relatively recent snapshot of the history of carbon dioxide in the Earth's atmosphere; however, over the past 800,000 years, it appears that the carbon dioxide levels have fluctuated between 170 ppm, during the ice age around 650,000 years ago, and 300 ppm, around 360,000 years ago. Many scientists believe that 350 ppm is the upper limit of what the Earth can withstand before we see severe changes in the climate from the greenhouse gas effect. According to the National Oceanic and Atmospheric Administration (NOAA), the global average atmospheric carbon dioxide in 2019 was 409.8 ppm. Carbon dioxide levels today are higher than at any point in at least the past 800,000 years. (See Figure 17-1.) We're in uncharted territory, and nobody truly knows what will happen to our climate and planet as a result.

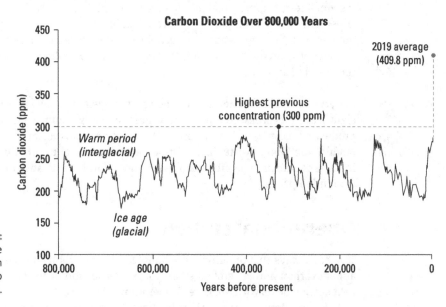

FIGURE 17-1: Carbon dioxide emissions, from 800,000 BCE to the present.

In addition to tracking atmospheric CO_2, scientists keep track of how much carbon dioxide we emit into the skies. For the sake of discussion and convenience, we measure all major greenhouse gases emitted into the atmosphere and lump the figures together to come up with a global CO_2 equivalency.

Total carbon emissions come in huge numbers. Often, total global carbon emissions are presented as gigatons of CO_2 equivalent. One gigaton equals 1 billion, or 1,000,000,000 tons.

Humans are on a carbon binge. To put things in perspective, when the United States was founded in 1776, our global CO_2 emissions were 0.015 gigatons. In 2019, they clocked in at 33 gigatons. Globally, our carbon emissions have been on a precipitous rise since the end of World War II. Again, the amount of human-generated global carbon emissions released into the atmosphere is unprecedented in world history. To stave off a climate catastrophe, the consensus among the scientific community is that we must act quickly by reducing our current peak CO_2 emissions 65 percent in the next ten years and reach zero emissions by 2040.

The building's relationship to carbon

The building sector accounts for about 40 percent of global carbon emissions. According to information from the International Energy Agency, buildings are responsible for approximately 39 percent of global CO_2 emissions. Specifically, 11 percent comes from building materials and construction; 28 percent is attributed to building operations — primarily, energy consumption. (Additionally, 23 percent is attributed to the transportation sector, which can be influenced by the building sector.)

Materials matter. Actions taken to better manage materials and reduce waste can significantly decrease the associated greenhouse gas emissions up and down a product's lifecycle, including resource extraction, transportation, manufacturing, landfill methane, waste incineration, and ocean pollution. Quantifying these impacts is crucial in helping businesses understand, track, and communicate their carbon footprint.

Operational carbon

Two basic ways that buildings contribute to global carbon emissions are via operational carbon and via embodied carbon. (This section deals with the former; the next section deals with the latter.) Operational carbon (28 percent of annual global carbon emissions) is the carbon load created by the use of energy to heat and power a building. Operational carbon is constantly happening — like turning on a water faucet and letting it run forever. It accounts for the carbon contribution from a building's energy consumption. Such accounting is complicated because — depending on the location of a building, its energy sources, its mechanical and electrical systems, and other factors — the ultimate sources and quantity of energy consumption will vary significantly.

An additional complication comes into play when you factor in site energy versus source energy. *Site energy* is the amount of energy consumed by the building property; however, *source energy* accounts for the inefficiencies and losses from the utility plant, through the power lines, to the property itself. This is an important distinction because, according to the US Energy Information Administration, over 60 percent of the energy created from the fuel sources at a power plant is lost in the process of generating and transmitting electricity.

TECHNICAL STUFF

There are various units of measure across different energy fuel sources. A common unit utilized to measure total energy from any fuel source is a British thermal unit, or BTU. One BTU is roughly equivalent to the energy of one kitchen match.

The US building sector has made great strides in energy efficiency as well as in the reduction of emissions from day-to-day building operations, even while adding over 30 billion square feet of building stock over the past 15 years. However, the result is virtually a flat trendline. Over the past decade, the total energy consumption from the US building sector operations went from 39.5 quadrillion BTUs to 39.4. That's a 0.003 percent change in total energy consumption. On the other hand, US building sector carbon emissions have dropped because utility companies have shifted to cleaner energy fuel sources over the same 15-year stretch. In fact, CO_2 emissions from US building sector operations have dropped 18.9 percent to 2.1 gigatons of CO_2. What does this mean? Well, this means a building's energy efficiency matters, but so does its energy fuel source. It's now possible for every new building to have zero-net-carbon (ZNC) operations as long as the correct fuel source is used and the building produces, or procures, enough carbon-free (renewable) energy onsite to meet building operations energy consumption annually.

Embodied carbon

Embodied carbon (11 percent of annual global carbon emissions) is the carbon load released to the atmosphere in the manufacturing, production, transportation, installation, and disposal of our building materials. This book talks about the life-cycle of the things we make — including buildings. Every phase of a product's lifecycle comes with an energy-and-carbon consequence. As it relates here, embodied carbon defines the total amount of equivalent CO_2 emissions from constructing a building.

Similar to operational carbon, embodied carbon can be measured in a weight of CO_2 equivalence. Every year, roughly 66 billion square feet of buildings is constructed. The embodied carbon emissions of that construction is approximately 3.73 gigatons of CO_2 per year. Embodied carbon will be responsible for almost half of total new construction emissions between now and 2050. By the year 2050, accounting for all the new construction in that 30-year span, embodied carbon emissions and operational carbon emissions will be roughly equivalent.

How can we measure the embodied carbon of buildings? The building design and construction industry has a variety of tools emerging in the marketplace to assess the embodied carbon of our buildings using large datasets and aggregated product data from leading manufacturers who have been willing to share information about their building products. Tools such as the Athena EcoCalculator, Tally, One-Click LCA, the Embodied Carbon in Construction Calculator (EC3) tool, and other platforms are allowing the design-and-construction industry to assess and optimize building solutions for low/no-carbon like never before. All these tools have been made available because it's crucial that we dramatically reduce embodied carbon in infrastructure, buildings, and materials over the course of the next ten years. According to industry leaders, we must cut our annual embodied carbon contribution by half. By 2050, we need to achieve zero embodied carbon emissions from buildings, infrastructure, and materials.

Though global carbon emissions may be measured in gigatons of CO_2-equivalent, at the individual building scale, the numbers become much smaller — and more specific. Some parts of the building have more embodied carbon than others. In fact, emerging data is revealing that the building foundation, structure, and envelope account for the majority of a building's embodied carbon. High-density/high-rise structures may be problematic because concrete and steel account for a lot of embodied carbon. A high-density/high-rise structure may dictate more robust, high-carbon materials. With this understanding, innovative engineered wood, concrete, and steel products with lower embodied carbon are emerging in the industry, although there's still a long way to go toward realizing their potential.

For now, note that a stout concrete-and-steel frame for a new high-rise could pose major challenges for lowering embodied carbon. Today, a large, heavy building (60 to 120 lbs. per square foot of CO_2) will come with roughly double the embodied carbon as a small, light building (30 to 70 lbs. per square foot). (See Figure 17-2.) Do keep in mind that the lifespan of interior finishes and building systems are often much shorter than the foundation, structure, and building enclosure and therefore can add up significantly if a building succeeds in having a long lifespan.

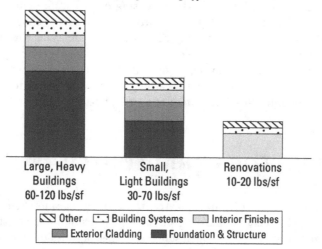

Carbon Emissions by Building Type and Materials

| Large, Heavy Buildings 60-120 lbs/sf | Small, Light Buildings 30-70 lbs/sf | Renovations 10-20 lbs/sf |

Other ⬚ Building Systems ☐ Interior Finishes
▨ Exterior Cladding ■ Foundation & Structure

FIGURE 17-2: Building types and materials affect carbon dioxide emissions.

Carbon influences on building design

Acknowledging the varying carbon impact between different building types incentivizes us humans to prioritize low- and zero-carbon building structures and products. A range of low- and zero-carbon products are in the marketplace, but please don't assume mass timber is always preferable to the latest innovations with concrete or steel — the complexities of reality aren't necessarily so simple. Critically assess proposed design solutions and materials, and then optimize them. Mass timber isn't a messiah material just because it's fully renewable.

To make the biggest impact in the design of buildings, it's clear that architecture, engineering, and construction professionals need to understand that the amount of atmospheric CO^2 emitted and captured by different forms of construction and various products range considerably. When a material is net-carbon negative over its full lifecycle, we consider it a carbon sink. Examples of carbon sinks are cotton, flax, cork, wool, straw, thatch, bamboo, hemp, and other vegetable fibers. Wood, when harvested locally and managed sustainably, can be net-carbon negative. What makes these materials net-carbon negative and truly renewable is that they're sourced from living plants and animals — not from mineral deposits or fossil deposits of organic material.

Using the design-and-construction tools available today, building project teams can go beyond assessment toward optimization of a building's embodied carbon. This will be realized by way of leveraging these tools for better-informed design and construction-related decisions. When you factor transportation-related energy into the embodied carbon equation, it soon becomes clear that we have to prioritize locally sourced materials, because they can significantly reduce transportation-related energy expenditures as well one's carbon footprint.

If there's a silver bullet, it lies in reusing our existing buildings. Buildings are often assumed to have a lifespan of around 60 years. We should insist on a longer lifespan. Renovations of existing structures is a double win. Not only is the embodied carbon of demolition spared but also the embodied carbon of any new foundations, structures, and envelopes. Considering today's standard practices, this can result in a building's embodied carbon being as low as 10 to 20 lbs. per square foot — roughly one-sixth of that of a large, heavy building.

Straight from the Open Source

In the computer software industry, the term *open source* refers to source code that's made freely available for possible modification and redistribution by anyone, anywhere, anytime. Open source includes permission to use the source code, design documents, or other content of the product, make whatever changes you see fit, and make the resulting document available to the same public forum. Today, a broader open-source movement encompasses many industries far beyond computer software — including building design and construction.

Sharing is caring. *Open source* means that the product is shared openly — no legal restrictions or transferred legal exposure. Champions of the open-source movement support a broader spirit of open collaboration. True open-source processes require that no one can discriminate against a group by choosing not to share edits made to a body of work or hinder others from editing their already edited work. Though the open-source movement makes it difficult to establish ownership of a product, it advances the ultimate goal of producing higher-quality products and solutions by working cooperatively with others in a community. The idea is that open-source processes tap into the collective wisdom of a community to advance products or solutions much more efficiently and effectively than any government or corporation could.

Recognizing the benefit

Cooking is a helpful example of how open-source can be beneficial. Cooking is, in many ways, a pure example of open-source design: a social action guided by a community over the course of human history. Culinary traditions reflect and guide social interactions in any community. Such traditions are also altered, transformed, and passed on as a form of open-source cultural genealogy. Information is shared in the form of recipes. As such, any recipe can be easily distributed and modified, taking on a history of its own — and, from a historical perspective, this has always been a communal endeavor at the local level.

You might like to cook, but let's be honest — you're no Wolfgang Puck, the Austro-American chef considered to be one of the highest-earning chefs on Earth. He improved American cooking by integrating elements of Asian, French, and Californian methods into his kitchen as well as various premium-quality ingredients from cuisines all over the world. You can buy food designed by Wolfgang Puck and purchase his cookbooks, yet his culinary genius cannot be duplicated. He could freely share his products because he was always innovating and improving on the information he made available to the public. Open-source design is predicated on constant evolution and improvement. So, by making information, strategies, and ideas open-source, products can be improved on much quicker because of the collective effort involved.

Open-source design is all around you. Our buildings and infrastructure are examples of open-source design. From concrete mixes to methods of using wood framing to how to install windows or hang shingles in such a way that they effectively shed rain — the products and methods in use today are no secret. They're what we call *standard practice*.

Most of the world — 98 percent, in fact — cannot gain access to building-design services. Alastair Parvin, designer and founder of the nonprofit Open Systems Lab, points out that architects and engineers are among the top 2 percent of the richest people in the world and their clients constitute the upper 1 percent of the richest people in the world. In their book *Open Source Architecture*, Carlo Ratti and Matthew Claudel point out that 98 percent of all building in the world happens without the design expertise of architects and engineers. These thought leaders see a huge disconnect. Architects and engineers have the expert know-how to create buildings that tap into the circular economy, but most of the world cannot receive their expertise. There's only one solution: open-source design.

Looking at open source in action

You might think that architecture, engineering, and construction professionals would jealously guard the techniques and methods that have made them a success. Sure, some do keep their trade secrets locked up tight, but some of them out there subscribe to the open-source philosophy. Here are a few to check out:

>> **Bricks:** This company aims to be the GitHub of open-source architecture and construction projects, making it easier to find and contribute to new projects. (https://bricks.medium.com/toolkit-for-open-source-architecture-and-collaborative-design-projects-7764aad7360f)

>> **Elemental:** Through his company, Pritzker Prize laureate Alejandro Aravena has offered numerous open-source plans for low-cost yet upgradable housing. (www.elementalchile.cl)

>> **Open Systems Lab (OSL):** This nonprofit company works on digital innova-
tion in housing using open-source design. One of its most notable offerings is
the WikiHouse, a freely accessible, digitally manufactured housing system
that's adaptable and uses standardized parts. (Nutrition labels for building
products? Wouldn't it be great if our building products came with a simple,
consistent way of labeling what they're made of?) (www.opensystemslab.io)

>> **Open Source Ecology:** Guided by its creators, Marcin Jakubowski and
Catarina Mota, Open Source Ecology is developing open-source industrial
machines that can be made for a fraction of its commercial costs and sharing
its designs online for free. The goal of Open Source Ecology is to create an
open-source economy — an efficient economy that increases innovation by
open collaboration. (www.opensourceecology.org)

A circular economy across the building sector most likely will depend on open-
source design. Much like the cooking example we offered earlier, great architects,
engineers, and builders will continue to lead and innovate. Open-source design
isn't a threat to business, but rather is an emerging opportunity for the building
design and construction industry to reach far more people than ever before and
lead the built environment toward a greater and more effective alignment with
the circular economy.

Chapter **18**

The Circular Economy for Fashion and Clothing

There's a reason that this chapter is one of the longest chapters in this book: The fashion industry is extremely wasteful and has a lot of room for improvement, and the circular economy is the saving grace of this trillion-dollar industry. Every person on Planet Earth needs and uses textiles, especially for clothing. Fashion is a global enterprise that not only allows individuals to creatively express themselves, but also allows them to maintain level of personal comfort as well. Hot weather, cold weather, wet, dry, humid — whatever the climate conditions are, clothes have been made to specifically maintain comfort and protect the user from the elements.

Though technological advancements have allowed for a wider range of materials — each with its own, unique properties — the way we design, manufacture, and manage the material lifecycle of clothing has some severe drawbacks that need to be resolved. The current fashion industry is far from circular — in fact, it's linear to its core. Nonrenewable and nonbiodegradable materials are extracted from the earth and are utilized to make (often) inexpensive clothing. Because of the lack of quality often found in most large-scale clothing production lines, these clothes are typically used for only a short time before eventually ending up in a landfill somewhere. Remember that flannel shirt you bought when you were *totally* into Nirvana? That shirt didn't just go away — it's still here somewhere! It's probably in New Jersey, if we had to guess.

This linear model — take-make-waste — that the fashion industry has embedded into its process possesses many negative environmental effects, such as the 1.2 billion tons of total greenhouse gases it emits annually. In addition to the greenhouse gases emitted, when plastic-based fibers are washed, they emit small microfibers into the environment that eventually end up in the ocean (and in that salmon you enjoy so much). This linear way of managing fashion products is not only a problem for the environment but also (because of the lack of circular methods) a missed business opportunity, because more than USD$500 billion is lost annually.

This chapter encourages a future that has moved away from this harmful make-take-waste business model and instead utilizes the environmental, financial, and social benefits the circular economy has to offer. Within the circular economy framework, clothes and the fibers required to produce them are made to be durable and last much longer than conventional fibers. Once they reach the end of their useful life, proper structures need to be in place to recover these fibers and reintroduce them into the manufacturing process to serve a new purpose. Within this circular economy framework, there is no waste in the fashion industry.

In this chapter, we explore the current position that the textile and fashion industry finds itself in, examine the opportunity for improving the fashion industry by utilizing circular economy practices, and outline the advantages and disadvantages of some of the most common textiles used by the fashion industry.

Sewing Together the Issue: Where Fashion Is and Where It's Headed

The fashion industry connects with everyone. Even if you don't consider yourself fashionable, you still are impacted by, and still rely on, the industry. Try to imagine a world without clothing. Never mind — don't do that. Clothing and fashion allow people to express their creative selves while also shielding themselves from the elements. The $1.3 trillion fashion industry is massive and employs millions of people around the world. These fashion industry employees help drive the engine that extracts, manufactures, and sells the ever-developing clothes you rely on daily. Of the 300 million people working within the fashion industry, nearly 21 million of them — or 7 percent — are busily manufacturing cotton. Although the textile industry is composed of many subgroups, clothing/fashion is the largest piece of the pie and represents 60 percent of the entire textile market.

As the fashion industry and the demand for clothing continue to rise, so does the negative environmental impact associated with its production. A trend can be seen over the past 20 years, where the production of clothing has nearly doubled while the number of times an item of clothing is actually worn maintains a steady state of decline. (See Figure 18-1.) According to the Ellen MacArthur Foundation, this relationship between clothing sales and clothing utilization can be attributed to a phenomenon called *fast fashion*, where the advanced pace at which new trends occur within the fashion industry leads to more purchasing and less clothing utilization. Simply put: Major fashion brands are offering more clothing options more frequently, which motivates consumers to buy and discard a larger amount of clothing.

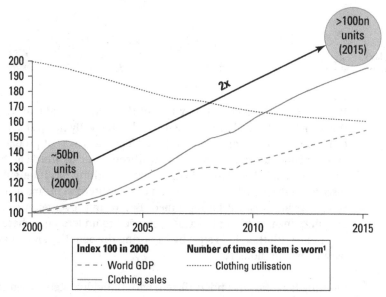

Growth of clothing sales and decline in clothing utilisation since 2000

FIGURE 18-1: Clothing sales are growing, but times worn is declining.

1 Average number of times a garment is worn before it ceases to be used

With this increased purchasing and increased waste, the amount of environmental degradation and pollution tied to the fashion industry is astronomical. To find out how astronomical, we want to dive a bit deeper in the next section into the details of global material flows for clothing and the negative impacts it causes.

Fashion = Waste + Pollution

The current clothing system — and by this we mean the acquiring of raw materials, the manufacturing of advanced fibers, the production of the clothing itself, its distribution, its use, and its removal — is extremely wasteful and pollutes the natural environment in many ways. (See Figure 18-2.) It takes a lot of water and energy to make the array of clothing currently found on the market, and, unfortunately, clothing is used for only a short time before being replaced with the latest-and-greatest trends. After it's discarded, clothing eventually ends up in either a landfill or an incinerator.

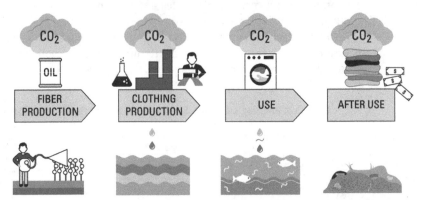

Today's clothing system puts pressure on resources, pollutes the environment, and creates negative societal impacts

CO_2 CO_2 CO_2 CO_2

OIL

FIBER PRODUCTION   CLOTHING PRODUCTION   USE   AFTER USE

FIGURE 18-2: The negative effects of today's clothing "system."

It has been estimated that only half of the clothing and textiles produced within the fashion industry live past their first birthday. By no stretch of the imagination can you call this a long-term strategy. This linear way of producing clothes is not only detrimental to the environment throughout its lifecycle, but it also means that a fortune is being lost along the way. Clothing has inherent value, so simply discarding these materials at the end of their lifetime means discarding that value when it could instead be reclaimed. Before improvements can be made to the existing, linear clothing lifecycle, you need to understand where the current system fails. With that, let's start by exploring the quantity and types of waste caused by the fashion industry.

Clothing is massively underutilized, with individual items used far less often now than they were 20 years ago. According to the Circular Fibres Initiative Analysis from 2016, the global utilization of clothing — the number of times an item of clothing is used before it's discarded, in other words — has dropped on average by 36 percent. Although this is a global percent reduction, the utilization rates of wealthy countries are much lower than disadvantaged countries because of their availability of resources. China, for example, has seen its clothing utilization rate decrease 70 percent from 2000 to 2015.

In addition to being underutilized when in use, only 1 percent of clothing is ever recycled into new clothing. Again, according to Circular Fibres Initiative Analysis from 2016, that accounts for a loss of more than $100 billion in material value each year. In addition to the loss in value from the actual materials, it's *expensive* to dispose of that much material. For the UK economy, for example, disposing of its clothing and other textiles costs around $82 million per year.

REMEMBER

Recycling isn't the only way to extend the whole lifecycle of clothing and textiles. Rather than recycle, these materials can *cascade* — repurpose a valuable material into a lower-value function, in other words. For example, when you've decided that crop top has seen its last day, it can be cut up and used as a rag to be used around the house for cleaning. Or, if sent to the right organization, clothing can be redirected and become insulation or provide other low-value functions. The value of cascading doesn't necessarily come from the new service value of the materials, but instead comes from the lack of energy required to dispose of that material.

In a perfect world, all textiles would be sourced from renewable materials and use minimal amounts of water, and we'd all have toilets made from solid gold, but that's just not in the cards now, is it? In the real world, nearly all (97 percent, to be precise) of the fashion industry relies on nonrenewable resources to some degree — from utilizing oil to produce plastic-based materials to using a range of synthetic fertilizers to grow various crops, like cotton, to utilizing a massive range of toxic chemicals to make any type of clothing any color imaginable. On top of the catastrophic use of nonrenewable resources, the production of textiles requires roughly 93 billion cubic meters of water annually. To add insult to injury, the production of textiles is responsible for the emission of over a billion tons of CO_2 annually, and the chemicals required to produce clothing has severe health effects on not only the farmers who grow the raw materials but also the laborers who are responsible for processing and generating clothing.

Lastly, it's well-known now that the production of textiles results in massive amounts of wastewater. This wastewater isn't clean, by any means, mind you: Textile wastewater typically contains traces of hazardous chemicals, and it's estimated that roughly 20 percent of the total industrial water pollution, on a global scale, can be attributed to the coloring and manufacturing of textiles. In addition to chemical pollution, plastic-based fabrics are responsible for emitting microfibers into natural systems. It has been estimated that half a million tons of microfibers end up finding their way into natural bodies of water — mostly, the ocean. Keep that in mind the next time you order some fresh fish. . . .

Three end goals are tied to the circular economy:

>> Design out waste and pollution.

>> Keep products and materials in use.

>> Regenerate natural systems.

Utilizing cascading as a strategy checks off all three boxes by preventing clothing from being thrown away, keeping material in use, and eliminating the need to extract virgin material, therefore allowing natural systems to regenerate.

There's clearly a problem with business as usual, and, unfortunately, if the fashion-and-textile industry stays on course, the negative impacts of this particular beast will become more severe. The linear system on which the fashion industry is dependent is extremely degenerative and will only get worse if the current trajectory of the industry is maintained.

The current trajectory to catastrophe

If one accepts that the fashion industry is on a highway to hell when it comes to catastrophic effects on the economy, it's critical that its linear way of thinking and producing fabrics/clothing shifts to a circular framework of production. Populations will only continue to increase, as will the demand for clothing. This pressure will result in a higher dependency on nonrenewable resources and an increase in CO_2 emissions, and will aid in the increase of microplastic release into the oceans.

Based on the current trend of the fashion-and-textile industry, it has been calculated that the demand for resources will grow from the 2015 baseline of 98 million tons to roughly 300 million tons in 2050. (See Figure 18-3.) Similarly, textile's share of the global CO_2 budget required to avoid an average temperature rise of 2 degrees Celsius will have advanced from 2 percent to roughly 26 percent by 2050. Lastly, the quantity of microfibers emitted into the ocean is anticipated to increase by 22 million tons from 2015 to 2050.

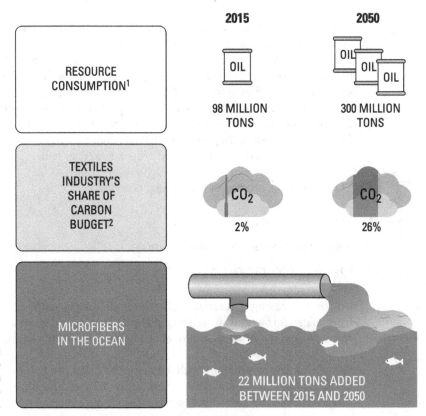

FIGURE 18-3: Future resource consumption in the fashion-and-textile industry.

These projections are quite terrifying, to be completely honest. The future isn't looking bright for the fashion industry if it maintains its current course. The planet will continue to be stripped of its resources, causing catastrophic levels of environmental degradation. The amount of CO_2 emitted will continue to change the conditions that define our global climates, and our oceans will have more plastic in them than fish. Despite these concerns, with their accompanying doom-and-gloom, fortunately, there is hope and it's called the circular economy.

Making It Circular: A Future Forecast for Fashion

That the fashion industry is harmful is old news. The people who produce clothes know it, and the people who buy the clothes know it, so we don't waste your time beating a dead horse. With that said, though, we'd be lying if we didn't say that improvements are being made to the current linear system, and it is improving — manufacturers are focusing on using simpler and better-organized ways to produce clothes and selecting better materials as well. Although these intentions are good, they aren't really solving the problem. Trying to optimize a linear textile lifecycle is equivalent to applying a Band-aid to a stab wound: It slightly slows down the inevitable road to a catastrophe, but doesn't ever prevent it from happening, because a linear lifecycle will never fix the issues we're trying to solve: eliminating waste, keeping products in use for longer periods, and regenerating natural systems.

The true resolution to the problem has to take place on a much larger scale: We have to transition this linear process to a circular process. By doing so, we will keep clothing items in use at their highest value and have avenues set up for these products to be recaptured and recycled after they reach the end of their useful life. Transitioning from a linear process to a circular process would eliminate the costs associated with extracting and processing virgin materials, making access to clothing more affordable. Transitioning from a linear process to a circular process would also reduce the demand for raw materials we've placed on our natural environments and allow for natural ecosystems to regenerate themselves.

To allow the fashion industry to make this transition from a linear process to a circular process, we need to address four major steps. Figure 18-4 shows the steps in graphical form; the following sections describe them in greater detail.

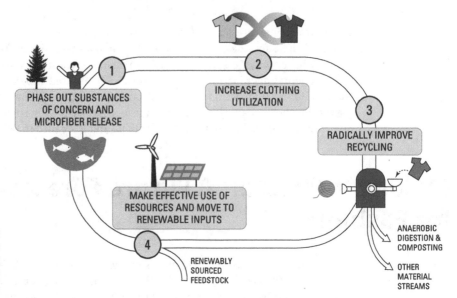

The Phase Out phase

The first step involved in making the fashion industry circular involves ensuring that the materials used are selected based on their ability to be recycled. Doing so would design out materials that act as negative influences on human and environmental health while also eliminating pollution. The two key steps needed to achieve this transition are creating safe material cycles and reducing microfiber release.

By creating safe material cycles, you're eliminating materials that negatively impact human as well as environmental health. Making this transition also simplifies the types of materials in flow, empowering the system to adopt large-scale recycling efforts. The more variety of materials you have in flow, the harder it is to separate and appropriately recycle them. By increasing the transparency of product contents — by clearly stating "this material contains bad things," in other words — would also be a great help when it comes to phasing out unhealthy and nonrenewable materials.

REMEMBER

Although some materials would be easy to phase out, this isn't an overnight change you can expect to see. A lot of work will be required to generate healthy materials and the means of production necessary to successfully design out degenerative materials.

In addition to creating safe material cycles, achieving a circular fashion industry would also require reducing microfiber release into natural systems. Facilitating this reduction would involve the removal of some materials altogether as well as the adjustment of manufacturing processes and the use of enhanced technologies to harvest those microfibers from waste before being emitted into the environment.

Redesigning how clothes are used

The next step involved in making the fashion industry circular involves transforming the various elements of clothing items' lifecycle to make them circular. As we mention earlier in this chapter, the global utilization rate of clothing continues to drop over time, resulting in more waste. Increasing that utilization rate is the most effective strategy when it comes to increasing the value of clothes while designing out waste and pollution. In addition, creating clothes that are higher in quality (and therefore longer-lasting) while also getting creative about how the global population acquires their clothes via innovative business models would also aid in this transformation. Many new business models that have acknowledged the value of these strategies are emerging as part of the fashion industry, and they've proven to be successful. The three key steps to transforming the elements of clothing items' lifecycle in order to make them circular involve scaling up clothing rentals, increasing the durability of clothing, and encouraging brand leadership.

Understanding that short-term rentals play a major role in creating a circular fashion industry is critical. Imagine if every wedding bride and groom purchased, rather than rented, their wedding gown and tuxedo — it doesn't make sense. Although daywear is worn more frequently than wedding gowns, there's still an opportunity at hand for the clothing rental industry. Customers may be interested in updating their wardrobe often to keep it fresh, but don't want to invest the amount of money that would be required to do so. Renting would be an attractive option for them. Other customers may realize that babies grow, but their clothes don't. Renting would also be an attractive option for them, and that's why companies like Borobabi (www.borobabi.com) exist. This children's clothing company allows parents to rent clothes rather than buy them. Children grow so quickly that it often doesn't make sense to purchase these products new and simply store them away when they're too small for your child. Borobabi recognized this problem and capitalized on the opportunity. The bottom line is that clothing rental is a win-win situation for both the customer and the business organization, and it aids in transitioning the fashion industry toward a circular economy framework.

In addition to clothing rentals, clothing durability will play a major role in creating a circular fashion industry. Although the clothing rental model can harness the value of durability by expanding the utilization rate of clothing, the value of durability can also be harnessed by a single user. "You get what you pay for" is a common piece of advice you hear when buying a new item, and it's quite often true. For used clothing that's still durable and available for a new owner, resale models allow durability-focused customers to acquire the durable clothes they're after but at a fraction of the price. By incorporating durability as a key driving force behind the development of clothes, customers will anticipate owning their garments for longer periods and will begin to demand further customization options from the manufacturers to allow customers to truly invest in their clothing and make it unique to them.

Lastly, on top of short-term rental and increased durability, encouraging brand leadership will also contribute toward making the fashion industry circular. Encouraging higher rates of clothing utilization requires clothes that are designed from the start to be durable and effective. Some companies understand and support this initiative, while others are simply focused on their bottom line and profit. By supporting companies who are leading their portion of the market toward a circular economy, customers can begin to transform how the market aims to sell you their products. Take Patagonia, for example. Patagonia prioritized the circular economy by designing products that can easily be repaired. Once their clothing can no longer be repaired, Patagonia will reclaim their product and issue the customer a voucher worth the amount of their product. Not only does incentivizing customers to repair and maintain their items ensure their products are used for as long as possible, but by providing a lifetime guarantee included in the purpose of their gear, Patagonia is encouraging their customers to be customers for life. Replaced quote with other text that doesn't require

Optimizing collection and recycling

The next step involved in making the fashion industry circular involves optimization of clothing collection and recycling. We mention earlier in this chapter that disposing of clothing is not only costly due to the inherent value of the clothes being thrown away, but just getting rid of the "trash" itself is costly. By optimizing the collection and recycling of clothing, the fashion industry can recapture the value associated with processing waste and invest it internally to further develop circular economy practices. Promoting this optimization of collection and recycling of clothing will require efforts from both the consumer and the fashion industry. These optimizations include designing clothes with the entire lifecycle in mind, innovation in recycling technologies, increased demand for recycled materials, and large-scale clothing collection.

Clothing is rarely designed with the entire lifecycle in mind. For most companies, once the product is purchased, they couldn't care less what happens to that material. Whether or not the material used for the clothing is easily recyclable is of no concern to the manufacturer. By designing clothing in ways that encourage recycling with ease, we can enhance the rate of material reuse and eliminate waste. Developing clothes that can be easily recycled is the first step in developing the ability to recycle materials on a massive scale to make a massive impact.

In addition to designing clothes with the entire lifecycle in mind, innovation in recycling technologies will prove beneficial in making the transition to circular. The current recycling technology doesn't fully capture the value of the materials being processed, resulting in large amounts of waste. That's kind of the opposite of what we're looking for by recycling, right? By improving the efficiency of recycling for common materials, the quality of that recaptured material would also increase and allow that base material to stay in circulation for a longer period. Designing clothes properly from the beginning by specifying materials that can be easily recycled compounds the benefit of investing in recycling technologies.

From a consumer's perspective, you also have the power to create change. Businesses spend billions of dollars on research and development to ensure that their products meet the needs of the consumer better than their competitor's product. By rejecting clothing that is not made with 100 percent recycled content, you're indirectly influencing the operational guidelines the company has set to meet market demand. By increasing product transparency, these companies can begin to better communicate the clothing's innate properties and empower their customers to make better choices.

In order for clothing to be recycled, it first has to be collected, right? And that's actually one of the major barriers between getting clothing to the proper location for recycling: collection. Clothing collection needs to be scaled dramatically so that the investment in recycling technologies can be properly utilized to create the circular flow of raw materials. inherent value lies in the materials themselves, and businesses are already jumping at the opportunity to provide the necessary capital to facilitate the collection of recyclable clothing.

Relying on renewable resources

The last step involved in making the fashion industry circular involves relying on renewable resources to meet the need for raw materials when increased clothing utilization and recycling doesn't meet industry demand. The need for raw material will always exist within the fashion industry, and that's okay if the production of new materials is fueled by the waste material from previous clothing lifecycles. When recycled materials can't meet the demand for clothing manufacturers, new material will be required. This need for new materials must be met by only the production of *renewable* resources — fibers that can be broken down into their base elements and reassembled to make new fibers. In addition to utilizing regenerative farming methods, renewable feedstock management can be utilized for plastic-based fibers. (For more information on regenerative farming methods, see Chapter 15.)

JEFF DENBY SPEAKS

Eric had a chat with Jeff Denby, co-founder of the Renewal Workshop, a company offering industry-wide solutions to optimize the value of resources invested in apparel. Here's what Jeff had to say:

Eric Corey Freed: In writing this book on the circular economy I've discovered that the fashion industry is perhaps the most . . . let's say in need of a make-over.

Jeff Denby: Yes, so in a closed-loop world we would make new things out of old things and sell them. Then when customers were truly done with them, we turn them back into fiber to make fabric, to make new things again. Then we've got this system that is truly circular. It's going to take time because of the current financial incentives in the apparel industry.

The industry has spent decades perfecting the linear business model. In the early eighties they sent all the work overseas to access lower labor rates. They developed this incredible global supply chain that creates new things very cheaply. That makes profit margins in selling new things extremely high. Most large fashion companies are public. We know innovation plummets inside public companies because circularity requires technological and infrastructure change.

Eric Corey Freed: All these 're-words' — renewed, refreshed, retread. All these fancy words right? You said something I've been thinking about ever since. That the fashion and apparel industry needs to think like the car industry in that they have a depreciating asset, but it has value. You can buy a certified pre-owned car, which is really a fancy word for used. The apparel industry needs to do the same thing and make money a second time from a single resource.

Jeff Denby: Absolutely! We want to figure out a way to keep this customer as a customer forever, which means they're going to buy a car (apparel) from us. We're going to buy it back from them. We're going to sell that person another car (more apparel). And then we're going to sell that car(apparel) to someone new.

And we will get them into this cycle because now this is a long-term engagement, not a single first sale. Apparel brands have spent all their time believing that every sale is the final interaction with that customer. It's a transactional model, rather than a relational one. That needs to change.

It's all about how every piece of your life is connected to every other piece. People approaching it holistically, choosing to live a particular lifestyle. Some brands have really caught on to this, and then there are a whole bunch who wish it wasn't true.

Eric Corey Freed: One of the most interesting parts of the circular economy is how it shows that normal principles of business are still relatively true. You need to produce revenue, you need to make customers happy, you need to source raw materials and you need to minimize liabilities. Now, delving into this to uncover what are the things that you thought were assets that are actually liabilities like your waste stream? Aren't you really saying that one of the new metrics of success would be a decline in new production, a decoupling of revenue from new production, and creating new revenue streams through re-use and re-purposing?

Jeff Denby: Exactly. I want apparel brands to stand up at conferences and say in 2019, we made X amount of product. In 2020 we reduced the amount of product we made and our revenues grew by Z percent. This is the shift that we want to see brands proudly making.

Eric Corey Freed: All of these mixed materials are difficult to recycle and reuse. Is there a push towards a mono material — a simple, singular material that can then be repurposed or refreshed.

Jeff Denby: That's exactly right. We've been working on it. We've been doing design for circularity workshops with a number of our brand partners. We've had a number of them send some of their designers to the Renewal Workshop for a whole week to embed them in our process, in our renewal operations. Then they see why product ends up as waste first-hand. One might say "Oh, that's the jacket I designed." And we can explain to them, "Oh, here's the reason why this is not repairable because it was constructed in such a way, or with a certain material." This becomes learning feedback that goes back to the very beginning of the design process.

Everything used to have a tiny little bit of like 1 percent, 2 percent spandex in it. And that made it garbage at the end of the life, because we can't recycle that. We can't turn that back into a fiber. Well, if we just made it a hundred percent cotton or even a 100 percent polyester there are recycling technologies today that can recycle that back to a fiber.

These design decisions have huge effects, especially when you're making hundreds of millions of products a year that eventually end up in a waste stream or hopefully in a recycling stream.

Eric Corey Freed: You're sounding hopeful about this overall shift.

Jeff Denby: Circularity is a true business model. I think that companies are going to adopt it and flourish, and then other companies won't adopt it and they'll fail. It's survival of the fittest.

Comparing Common Fashion Fabrics

Ever since the beginning of the fashion industry, cotton has played a dominant role in the market. Although it still makes up a very large percentage of the total materials used in the industry today, the evolution of technology and the material sciences has meant that cotton has gradually been replaced as the alpha material with a plastic-based fiber called polyester. Polyester now leads the industry and makes up a total of 55 percent of the textile fiber production, whereas cotton makes up a total of only 22 percent. The remaining 23 percent is shared by other, tertiary materials.

Why are some materials preferred over others? More specifically, why is polyester chosen over cotton? Well, it comes down to the innate advantages and disadvantages of these materials, such as durability, cost, and flexibility of application. To fully understand the impact of these materials within a circular economy framework, however, you need to look at the entire lifecycle of these textiles. The lifecycle of materials used in the fashion industry consists of the feedstock for the base material, production methodologies used by manufacturers, the lifespan during its actual use, and the post-use phase where most clothes are typically discarded to the landfill. To help gain a better grasp of the range of material types circulating through the fashion industry at this very minute, we've provided a collective breakdown, in the form of Figure 18-5. For more detail on the advantages and disadvantages of these material types, check out the next few sections.

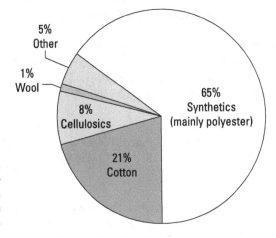

FIGURE 18-5: The major material types in the fashion industry.

Plastic

The first family of fabric we explore is plastics. Although you don't see the word *plastic* written on the tag of shirts, plastic clothing dominates the fashion industry. Often referred to as *synthetic* rather than *plastic,* these oil-based products account for roughly two-thirds of the total material input used in textile production.

Plastic textiles have exploded in popularity, for several reasons. First and foremost, the production of plastics doesn't rely on farmland to source the base material — which means that manufacturers don't have to wait for plastics to be in season to get hold of some. In addition, when compared to the lifecycle of other materials common in the fashion industry, producing and processing plastic-based materials produces very little wastewater. And, finally, when plastic clothes are washed, it takes very little time for them to dry completely, because plastic doesn't absorb water, like most of its competition. This unique property also makes plastic-based textiles resistant to staining, which is also a strong advantage.

Although clearly there are a lot of benefits to plastic-based clothing, it has some major downsides as well. Because plastic-based textiles don't require farmland or rely on the farming process to source raw materials, the raw material is, by definition, finite — nonrenewable, in other words. (Check out Chapter 10 for more on how renewable and nonrenewable material lifecycles must function differently within a circular economy framework.) In addition to being supported by a finite material, the fact that extracting and processing petroleum-based fashion materials is extremely energy-intensive is an additional disadvantage. Lastly, because plastic fibers are nonrenewable, they won't break down to organic components in the natural environment, which leads to high levels of pollution. During their use as clothing, these products shed microfibers into the environment, which end up polluting soils and bodies of water. Because they aren't biodegradable, these microfibers will remain in the environment indefinitely and can even wind up in that lobster you've been looking forward to all week.

Overall, plastic fashion textiles offer a wide range of advantages and disadvantages to its user group. Although it's durable, requires a low-water investment, and can dry quickly, it's also extremely energy intensive and pollutes the natural environment we rely on for survival. Although all petroleum-based textiles share these properties, by diving in deeper, we explore the unique advantages and disadvantages of four different plastic textiles: polyester, nylon, acrylic, and elastane.

Polyester

Polyester is the most prominent plastic textile in the fashion industry, making up 55 percent of the market. For those of you who consider yourself athletic (and no, the walk from your couch to the refrigerator doesn't count as exercise), you're no stranger to polyester, because it's commonly used to make sportswear. (In addition to sportswear, polyester is often utilized to make womenswear.)

When compared to other textiles that are quite fragile, polyester is relatively strong, which makes it great for activewear, when you want to provide for a wide range of motion during use. In addition to being strong and durable, polyester is inexpensive. On top of that, minimal chemical input is required in order to dye polyester and, when collected and processed correctly, polyester can be recycled back to its virgin state and made available for reuse. On the downside of things, producing this flexible material requires the use of heavy, toxic metals and is extremely energy intensive.

Nylon

Nylon? More like why-lon, right? Anyway, got sidetracked there. Nylon is also a common plastic-based textile that is often used to make various types of underwear and hosiery, socks, sportswear, and average day wear, like dresses and shorts. It shares a lot of similar characteristics to polyester — because of the innate properties found in all plastic-based fabric — such as strength and resistance to creasing and wrinkles. One benefit of nylon, however, is its ability to be fully recycled through a combined process of depolymerization and repolymerization. During this process, the plastic fiber is broken down into monomers (the smaller, base unit of the textile) and then reconstructed to form larger, chainlike networks to be used again.

On the downside, the production of nylon emits extremely harmful chemicals and gases such as nitrous oxide. This destructive chemical acts as a greenhouse gas and affects environmental air quality. In addition — even when compared to other plastic-based textiles, like polyester — the production of nylon requires massive amounts of energy.

Acrylic

Popular in the production of sportswear and fleece, acrylic has a wool-like texture and does a great job at keeping the user warm, unlike other plastic-based materials which don't have insulation properties. Well . . . why not just buy wool if you can but acrylic? As we mentioned, acrylic is popular amongst sportswear clothing, which means it will — without a doubt — come in contact with sweat. Because acrylic doesn't hold on to scents as well as wool would and it dries much quicker, there are some clear reasons as to why it would be chosen over wool. Aside from sharing the common negative trait as all other plastic-based textiles — it's extremely energy-intensive to produce — there are no other notable downsides of acrylic.

Plants

Cellulose fabrics can be sourced from plants in a raw state or acquired by way of chemical extraction processes. They come in various forms, like cotton, viscose, lyocell and linen/hemp. Plant-sourced fibers make up roughly 33 percent of the textile industry, with cotton leading the way with 27 percent. The absolute best quality of protein-based fabrics is their ability to fully decompose, assuming that no synthetic materials have been combined with them during the manufacturing process.

Cotton

There's a pretty decent chance that you're wearing something made of cotton right now. Why is that a good assumption? Because cotton is used to make so many different items of clothes — shirts, pants, underwear, and more. Go ahead! Take a look at the tags — is anything made with cotton? (PSA from the authors: Please don't check your tags while in public.)

Cotton is a popular material in the fashion industry because it's extremely lightweight yet very strong. It's also quite absorbent and nonallergenic, and can be utilized to create other fabrics post-recycling — like viscose and lyocell — because its cellulose content is so high. This ability of the material helps to extend the lifecycle of the material, which satisfies the circular economy's goal of keeping materials in use for longer periods.

Because cotton has to be grown in fields, the production of this useful material requires a lot of time, water, fertilizers, and pesticides. In addition, because of its properties, it takes a lot of chemicals to properly dye cotton. Not only does this dying process require a lot of resources, but the actual cotton-spinning process is also energy-intensive.

Viscose

Cotton can be chemically treated at the end of its useful life to extract the cellulose necessary to produce viscose. Viscose — also is known as *rayon*, in some arenas — can also be manufactured from cellulose that has been chemically extracted from wood. *Viscose* is a soft material and acts as an affordable alternative to silk (which we all know typically comes with a hefty price tag). Though the advantages of viscose are limited, the disadvantages, unfortunately, are quite vast.

The first downside of this material can be traced to its production. Under conventional methods, the chemical used to extract the cellulose required to make viscose (carbon disulphide) is not only extremely hard to recapture and reuse but it's also extremely toxic and causes major concern as an environmental pollution hazard. However, current methods of extracting cellulose have improved the efficiency of recovering these chemicals, which greatly reduces the potential pollution hazards associated with production. Aside from the chemical, energy, and water requirements associated with the production of viscose — because this material is sourced from wood — there are major concerns associated with the proper sourcing of the timber necessary for production.

Lyocell

Like viscose, cotton can be chemically treated at the end of its useful life to extract the cellulose necessary to produce Lyocell as well. In addition to cotton, wood is a major source of the cellulose required to produce lyocell. Unlike the harmful chemicals required to produce viscose, the chemicals used to produce lyocell are nontoxic and can be kept within a closed-loop process. Although it's a much better choice than viscose, lyocell still requires high amounts of energy to produce.

Linen and industrial hemp

Linen (made from the fibers of the flax plant) and industrial hemp (a variety of cannabis plant) are most often used to make shirts and pants and are mostly used in warmer climates because of their ability to dry quickly. Both linen and hemp are absorbent, like cotton, and require minimal resources to grow when compared to the alternatives. One of the best qualities of these products is their ability to grow in soils that aren't adequate to produce food. This is a critical opportunity to acknowledge because our modern food production system often depletes soils — they're no longer good for growing food crops, but can be used for the production of linen and hemp. (For more on the degenerative nature of modern food production, see Chapter 15.) Although these fabrics tend to soften continuously throughout their lifecycle, linen and hemp products start off by being extremely rigid and uncomfortable. In addition, the production of hemp is commonly banned in most areas around the world because of the psychoactive properties of the compound THC to be found in any cannabis plant. Although the levels of THC found in industrial hemp are extremely low, many governments still refuse to allow its production, regardless of the countless benefits.

Animals

Animal-sourced fabrics are often referred to as *protein* fabrics because they're sourced from livestock. Protein-based textiles make up a very small percentage of the total fabric industry — only 2 percent — most of which has been claimed by wool. Like plant-sourced fibers, the absolute best quality of protein-based fabrics is their ability to fully decompose, assuming no synthetic materials have been combined with them during the manufacturing process.

Wool

Wool — although it makes up a very small percentage of the fashion industry — is used to make a wide array of clothing, including jackets, suits, and even other soft items like blankets and rugs. Because it's made from animal fur — most often from sheep — it's fully biodegradable. As you can assume from the list of products wool is typically used for, this warm fabric is quite breathable. In addition, wool can easily be dyed (which reduces the amount of dye required to complete the process) and, given the fact that wool fibers are typically longer than other fabrics, it's well-suited to being mechanically recycled.

Aside from the benefits of wool, there are some major downsides that influence its small market share. First and foremost, wool is an *expensive* material to develop. Raising the number of sheep necessary to meet the demand for wool requires extensive amounts of land and resources, like water and feed for the sheep. In addition, like all livestock, sheep are responsible for releasing large amounts of methane into the atmosphere. Because sheep don't stay in a 5-star hotel while growing their coats, chemical-intensive processing must occur post-harvest to ensure that all dirt and pests have been removed from the raw material before it can be sent off for processing.

Silk

Silk, which is an uncommon material, is typically saved for producing higher-quality products. Used in anything from blouses and scarves to bedspreads and dresses, silk is widely known for being soft to the touch. Just like wool, silk is easily dyed because it's a biobased product, which means less dye is required to complete the coloring process. In addition, silk feels cool against the skin in the warm months and can provide a sense of heat during the cool months. One of the unique qualities of silk, which sets it aside from wool, is its ability to absorb a significant amount of moisture before feeling wet. The major disadvantage of using silk is that producing it is no easy feat; growing silkworms and extracting the filament is an extremely laborious process. This explains why it comes at such a high cost when compared to other fashion materials and is quite often reserved for expensive garments.

5

Creating a Circular Economy for All

Chapter **19**

Understanding an Individual's Circular Opportunities

The individual — as just a single action point among the billions that exist within a global economy — plays a miniscule role when it comes to transitioning from a linear economy to a circular economy. By that, we mean that the amount of change stemming from one person's actions is minimal when compared to the actions of a larger, collective group or an organized body. When working together toward a common goal, however, individuals as a collective can play a significant role. Through your choices, the consumer can supply the force needed to make the shift from linear to circular. However, none of the large, global changes that can happen will be of any value if the actions required by the individual aren't the most convenient options.

Most individuals can agree that the convenience and ease of access of an item immediately add a competitive edge. Entire stores in the United States are created with this understanding. Drive down any major road and you'll see them lined up like dominoes — fast-food chains that get you what you need quickly, at little cost, with little nutritional value and lots of unintended health consequences down the road, for example, or drive-through pharmacies or streaming services or Amazon Prime delivery. The message is clear — nothing dare make the customer wait. This is a representative principle of the linear economy: instant gratification with little consideration of unintended, future consequences.

Once a product or material has been used and it's no longer needed, it's quite convenient to have a single bin capable of receiving all these items. Not only that, but it's also quite convenient to roll a can out to the sidewalk each week and have those discarded items thrown away from our reality completely. Where is "away," anyway? We seem to throw a lot of things there. Quite often, the most convenient way to dispose of an item isn't the best way. Materials can be reused, products can be shared, energy can be recaptured, and things can stay in use for longer periods. It's just not convenient to make it happen. Herein lies the major barrier to individuals making a bigger impact.

Until it becomes convenient for you to support a circular economy, there's only a small chance that it'll happen. While we wait for that day, however, you can address some critical areas of your life that will help influence the transition from a linear economy to a circular economy — even if it's not convenient. And that topic is the one we explore in this chapter.

Looking at the Food You Eat

Though most of the variables included in the food you eat are out of your control, two different food-growing strategies can be either supported or discouraged, depending on where you source your products. You support large-scale, industrialized methods — which rely on the heavy use of fossil fuels and artificial fertilizers (resulting in significant environment degeneration) — if you buy from nonlocal sources. You support small-scale, farming methods — which rely on the efforts of environmental systems to offset the need for fossil fuels and artificial fertilizers and instead result in environment regeneration — if you buy from local sources. In addition to selecting local food versus global food, ensuring first that food waste is prevented, and then is properly managed after it becomes waste, are other actions you can take to support the circular economy.

Sourcing

Sourcing your food locally isn't just about keeping your money flowing through the local economy. It's much more than that. Sourcing local food ensures that your dollars aren't funding industrialized farming methods that global economies have depended on for far too long. Sourcing your food locally can mean participating in a community supported agriculture (CSA) program, making a weekly trip to the farmers market, or swapping the extra tomatoes from your garden for some of the extra peppers from your neighbor's garden.

Though not all small-scale food production uses regenerative farming techniques and not all large-scale farming uses industrialized farming techniques — it's not black-and-white — it's safe to say that local produce is most often not produced within an industrialized framework. Local food production doesn't require the same industrialized methods on which the global food production has grown dependent. Regenerative farming methods, however, do work to harness the working power of natural systems rather than fight against them. Regenerative farming has the potential to rehabilitate soils, improve the nutrient levels found within the soil, strengthen soil structures to prevent erosion, captures and stores carbon, and much more. Local, small-scale food production also tends to maintain soil stability, by avoiding the tilling of soils, and introduces crop rotations and cover crops to reintroduce nutrients into the soil, which all lead to a healthier and more resilient platform for food production.

So, when it comes to food, sourcing it locally supports the regeneration of natural capital while also eliminating many sources of waste associated with industrialized methods.

Managing food waste

You might be surprised to find out that nearly one-third of the entire US food supply goes to waste. This fact alone supports the idea that the proper management, storage, and distribution of food can have a major impact in eliminating waste, keeping products in use for longer periods, and allowing natural capital to regenerate — all goals of a circular economy framework.

Once food is harvested, there's only a limited amount of time for that food to be consumed. After that point, it's considered waste. It is therefore important to preserve that food in natural ways to avoid waste. Whether it's by freezing, fermenting, processing, or storing, we have many ways to delay the rotting of food.

After food inevitably does become waste, there are strategies available to still extract some of the innate value of that food to serve another purpose. Once food can no longer be consumed by humans, it may still be fit to be eaten by other living forms that can then be consumed by humans instead. Both plants and livestock can benefit from food waste, if managed properly. Spent grain — the byproduct of the brewing process — is often a waste that's collected by farmers and fed to their livestock. At home, many people who keep chickens will take their table scraps and simply toss them into the coop for the chickens to eat. Or, for food that isn't suitable for animal consumption, composting can be used to break down foods into their basic elements and utilized as a fertilizer for new crops. No matter what the food waste may be, are opportunities are available for either preventing it in the first place or letting it be consumed by other living organisms.

There is no such thing as waste. Waste is simply an unused resource.

REMEMBER

RORY USHER SPEAKS

Rory Usher is the public relations manager for DeepGreen Metals. He is an experienced strategy and policy consultant who has lived and studied in both Europe and on the African continent.

Eric Corey Freed: Tell us about DeepGreen Metals, how does it work?

Rory Usher: It's been controversial up to this point, primarily because there is a lack of public awareness around these resources. But particularly because the detractors are good at not pointing out the fact that there are three different types of resources that make up this broader industry. For example, there are the seafloor massive sulfides and cobalt crusts. Then there is the polymetallic nodules, which DeepGreen is very interested in.

The problem with the first two is that they essentially form integral parts of the sea floor and can only be accessed through destructive cutting, blasting, and drilling. The beauty of polymetallic nodules is that they lie there unattached, ready to be collected using some pretty cool engineering. Essentially, we blow a jet of sea water parallel with the sea floor without touching it. When the water hits a curved piece of polymetallic nodule (rock), it follows the curve and lifts the rock up without touching anything else. The process has a similar effect to a jet wing. The process does lift up a bit of sediment, approximately 8%. Obviously, we're working to ensure that even less sediment is disturbed.

It completely changes the narrative when you consider the industry has three distinct resources. The two other resources are largely not being considered because of potential impacts. They're also in shallower waters, which represents greater loss of life, whereas our process is at a much greater depth. There's no sunlight at that depth; 80% of the life is bacteria. Everything is smaller than four centimeters and there are very few fish. It completely changes the game in terms of sea resources. We're constantly getting the word out to the public to stop looking at our process as monolithic industry, because it just isn't.

Eric Corey Freed: There's an old expression: "Perfect is the enemy of good." In hearing you talk about your process, which is fascinating, it already sounds so much better than the traditional way of sourcing some of these minerals and metals. Do you feel pressure to get it right? You said 92 percent of the environment remains undisturbed. It already sounds pretty perfect. Yeah, I know that among environmentalists, including myself, it's easy to fall into that trap of, "Well, gosh, solar panels have a little bit of an environmental impact and wind turbines kill four birds a year, and so on and so forth." We have this idea that we have to be held to a higher standard where we have to be perfect. But nothing's perfect.

Rory Usher: Yeah, definitely. There were a few things that need to be unpacked in that.

Wherever we get this metal, we need a lot of it. That's undeniable. It's impossible to extract metal without any impact. Whatever we do, we will realize an impact. It's the same for any industry. We buy a new t-shirt and that has an impact somewhere. Thankfully people are becoming more aware of that.

We can absolutely reduce the impacts of producing metals, particularly for battery metals used in electric vehicles. DeepGreen produced a white paper that broke down and compared the impacts of producing metals for a billion electric vehicles. It included 18 or 19 impact indicators. Not just carbon emissions, but also disruptions to carbon sequestration, disruptions to stored carbon, waste streams' impacts on biodiversity, fresh water usage toxicity, you name it. We looked at the whole life cycle of producing these metals. From the initial research standpoint, we are absolutely determined to reduce these as far as possible.

It's interesting to look at the European Union at the moment, which obviously has a very strong focus on sustainable batteries. It's quite telling that the only indicator that they are looking at in sustainable batteries is the carbon emissions. They don't look at impacts to carbon sequestration, impacts to stored carbon, or energy expended in harvesting and production. There's a lot more that needs to be done in that aspect. There's a case to make that Europe, if it doesn't wake up and look at these other indicators, they could sleepwalk into a ticking time bomb.

We know that recycling can only take us so far. There is simply not enough metal available to recycle. We can recycle 80-plus percent of copper at the moment, but even if recycling rates hit a hundred percent, we're looking at a demand reduction in copper of around 25 percent, just because demand is so great. And that's similar for a number of metals — nickel, you name it — it's all necessary. It's an exponential increase, and it's got to come from somewhere.

(continued)

(continued)

One thing that we will be implementing in the wider context of resource production is an adaptive management system. Because it's something of a two-dimensional resource, a carpet of these nodules, we don't have to dig down. This gives us flexibility to avoid more ecologically sensitive areas. This adaptive management system is comprised of drones and subsea sensors that will allow us to adapt and manage our impact in real time. There will be a 24/7 live feed that exists as a website that you can view in real time. That way, anyone who wants access to what we are doing has access, for instance, stakeholders, shareholders. NGOs, you name it. That kind of transparency is pretty radical in this industry.

If you've ever done any kind of natural resource supply chain research, you know about the sort of shady deals that have gone on between companies, particularly in certain countries. Transparency has definitely not been the main priority. So it's pretty revolutionary in that aspect.

To backtrack, this industry has just started, and there are two ways in which it can begin. First, there needs to be a regulatory regime in place. It was supposed to be settled last year, but COVID-19 went around the world and threw things out of whack. We expect it to be in place by the end of the year, or more likely sometime next year.

Eric Corey Freed: You're welcoming the regulation?

Rory Usher: Absolutely. The beauty of this is that it will be a regulatory regime in place before an extractive industry begins, which has never happened in history. We're going to set the bar as high as possible. In doing so, that requires every other contractor that is working in this area has to abide by that heightened and stringent standard. So that's the one side. And then on the other side, as a contractor, you are required to submit an environmental impact assessment. So particularly NGOs see it as this rush to the seabed as they call it. The fact is, they will first have to submit these environmental impact assessments, which take two, three, four years.

We started last year. We're spending $75 million on it. It could very well be that at the three-year mark when we submit our environmental impact assessment that the result comes back and they say, "No, you can't do this." If that happens, we are committed and have said to our shareholders that if we find anything that shows the impact and risks are too great, we will completely stop and find a better solution. Which again is a radical notion.

That multi-year environmental, social impact assessment is being conducted with the world's leading researchers. We've got the Natural History Museum in the UK, the UK National Oceanography Center, the University of Hawaii, University of Texas at Austin, University of Florida, University of Gothenburg, JAMSTEC in Japan, and more. We are making sure we get this right. We take pride in doing everything we can.

It's not just an offshore business that we're looking at. We're very much focused on the onshore side as well. This isn't true of all contractors, but we see ourselves as integrating across the whole process. For example, in our transport ships, we will prioritize the use of either hydrogen fuel or ammonia. Electrofuels dramatically reduce our carbon footprint.

Once we're on shore, we're committed to processing these nodules with zero solid waste. We can do that because these nodules contain no toxic elements like you get with terrestrial resources. There's no mercury, cadmium, arsenic, you name it. Everything in a nodule is usable, not just the metal. About one-third of each nodule is usable metal. The rest of it can be converted into byproducts that are eminently salable to society. For example, we'll produce a hell of a lot of agricultural grade fertilizer. We'll also produce a lot of aggregate that can be used in construction. We'll produce no solid waste and 90 percent less CO_2 emissions. When multiplied across a billion vehicles, you're looking at a savings of around 7 to 9 percent of the planet's remaining carbon budget. Also we're not using coking coal in the smelting process. Instead, we'll use carbon-negative reductants.

Eric Corey Freed: So you're saying we foresee a surging demand for all types of batteries, especially for electric vehicles, poised to explode in the next year.

Rory Usher: Yes, Polestar is obviously an electric vehicle company. The big ones recently, like Volvo and GM. Ford recently launched this week, actually. They intend to sell only electric vehicles in Europe, admittedly for now, by 2030. Jaguar is committed. Obviously, they don't produce as many cars, but still, it's all welcome. Audi, VW, you name it. They're all committed, and if they're not committed to it yet, the big boys are all getting to it. Once one falls, it's a domino effect, and they all go. Tesla wants to be producing 20 million vehicles a year by 2030. There isn't enough supply at the moment. The beauty of nodules in particular is that they contain everything in an electric vehicle battery in the exact ratios that are required for an electric vehicle battery.

This is the chemistry that Tesla is using in the U.S. In China at the moment, they're doing LFP batteries, but they're less energy dense. They're just not as suitable.

So nickel for batteries alone, the requirements need to jump 40 times in the coming years just to meet nickel demand for batteries. Currently 7 percent of nickel goes into batteries. Of the total nickel production on the planet every year, only 45 percent of it is suitable for batteries. Because it's got to be of a certain quality. The majority of new supply is coming from Indonesia, which just happens to be one of the most biodiverse places on earth. If you've ever been there, they have incredible rainforests. The problem is that the nickel resource in Indonesia requires clearing every bit of rainforest. You can see it's just horrific.

(continued)

Again, it comes back to impact reductions. If you were to measure life in an environment as carbon, almost everything is made mostly of carbon. There is roughly 300 times more biomass contained as carbon in a terrestrial environment, compared to the sea floor, where we're going to be operating. But if you compare that to a nickel mine in Indonesia, you're looking at upwards of between 1500 and 3000 times more life in that Indonesia ecosystem than where we're going to be operating. So, when it comes to abundance of life, these material things are what we need to be thinking about.

When people say, "You will have an impact on the seafloor." Yes, we will. But we own that because, again, it's impossible to produce anything without an impact. But the difference is, the impact will be far less.

There are difficult trade-offs to get where we need to go, but this seems like a pretty good trade-off, particularly when you consider that the area being considered represents 1% of the global ocean. And even then, within that 1%, approximately 46% of that area is being considered for exploration. So essentially that's 0.5% of the global ocean to electrify the entire electric vehicle fleet four times over. In our contracts alone, we're looking at 280 million electric vehicle batteries that could be made.

Eric Corey Freed: It sounds like what you're saying is, we're all excited about electric vehicles removing all those carbon emissions from internal combustion engines, but we're not going to have enough batteries. And so you're already seeing this demand about to explode.

Rory Usher: Yeah. The initial consideration of just batteries is obviously a massively hot topic and of great interest. Also, it's the unique alignment in terms of ratios of the metals. It's so convenient, but it's almost like you couldn't write that, and you couldn't make it up.

Eric Corey Freed: In the circular economy, one of the principles we talk about is using the material to its highest and best use. You're getting all these valuable materials: cobalt, nickel, copper manganese. Is this the highest and best use?

Rory Usher: No, I don't think it's the best use, but it's a better use than how we get metals already. That's indisputable. However, they are absolutely great for electrifying vehicles as quickly as possible and producing the metals for electrical vehicles as quickly as possible.

We really do need to think differently about how we use these resources. The circular economy is of prime consideration. There are conversations around intergenerational equity: the property of the people who are alive now. What about people who live in the future? Who should have had the rights to benefit from those? From DeepGreen's perspective, we absolutely believe that mining must come to an end. We need to stop extracting nonrenewable resources from the ground now. The beauty of metals is that they are indestructible. We are completely committed to this. We absolutely want to be recycling everything we produce. As an indestructible resource, if we put some pretty innovative business models in place, we ensure that not a single atom of metal is lost.

When the battery in a vehicle has come to the end of its life, it's then gone through stationary storage, which is often considered afterwards. Once we know it's really at the end of its life, we will take them back, dismantle them, and recycle them. Once they've been recycled, they can be reinjected back into that circulation of metal in perpetuity, because they're indestructible. So that's when you start to see that the metal we produced this year could, in theory, go to build a battery for my great, great grandchildren in 100 to 200 years.

The impact reductions that come across with recycling metal in perpetuity and ending mining in the future are enormous. We move to a model where we rent metals to companies and then they return them to us. We've produced a white paper on how we intend to use blockchain for this.

If we build our climate infrastructure, our zero carbon climate infrastructure, using these metals and then recycling them, that's a massive contribution to combating climate change. That's our kind of North Star. That's what we're aiming for.

Sizing Up the Products You Buy

Within a circular economy framework, companies and manufacturers will not only need to identify ways to meet consumer demand while also eliminating waste from their processes — they will also need to figure out how to keep products in use for longer periods while also allowing natural capital to regenerate. Fortunately, the last step is a result of successfully implementing the first two steps. The current linear way of producing products isn't *sustainable* (it can't last forever), which means that a transition to a circular economy framework is critical.

Recycling: The last resort

Recycling has always been marketed as a good thing. And it is — don't get us wrong. A thousand dollars is a lot of dough when held up next to a single penny. But saying that $1,000 is a lot of money seems wrong when you're holding $10,000 next to it. The point here is that recycling is good when waste is the only alternative. But it's not.

Though recycling has encouraged the market to shift in the right direction, it hasn't shifted far enough to realize that recycling should be a last resort; a destination for a material or product when no other use or value can be sourced from it. The goal within a circular economy is to keep materials and products in use for as long as possible and not to produce waste. Recycling doesn't aid in achieving this goal — only avoiding the need to recycle does. Reusing, repairing, and remanufacturing a product is much more efficient than recycling a product, because the value of a product most often comes from the function of that product. Recycling a product into the same product, instead of keeping it in use, is like freezing a cup of water to only then let it thaw out again. There's no value in the act of recycling a product if it will be recycled to serve a function of equal or lesser value. Therefore, maximizing the life of a product and seeing recycling as a last resort holds true value by eliminating waste and eliminating the need for raw material inputs.

Selecting products with reuse potential

Whether we're talking about a product that's made from renewable materials or finite materials, you have options when it comes to extending that product's rate of use while avoiding the need for recycling. For finite materials, you can achieve this by way of sharing, material reuse, repair/refurbishment, and remanufacturing. For renewable materials, cascading and biochemical extraction make more sense. No matter the type of material in play, there's a potential for reuse before recycling.

Many products will be used one time and then stored for years, sometimes, before they're used again. For products like these — with minimal use rate — it often makes more sense to rent or share rather than purchase outright. By utilizing community tool hubs or sharing various products with your friends and family, you're avoiding the initial cost of purchase as well as the additional cost associated with maintaining the product and eventually replacing it. If you absolutely have to purchase a product, look for items that are durable and resilient and won't break after their first use. (Think of a metal knife rather than one made from plastic.) The ability for a product to be repaired by the owner, or by a third party in exchange for a small fee, will also aid in supporting a circular economy, because keeping products in use for as long as possible is one of the key conditions of the practice.

Evaluating the House You Live In

Green buildings have been designed and built to benefit not only the occupants but the environment as well. Living in a green building is a smart choice. We don't say this just because it's good for the environment — which it is — but because it also makes economic sense. Using fewer resources by way of conservation and efficiency means less money you'll need to spend to attain those resources. In addition, by prioritizing healthy materials inside your home, you'll potentially avoid countless medical bills and save yourself a small fortune.

REMEMBER

A green building is defined by its performance in energy and water usage, its use of appropriate technologies, the reduction in construction and demolition waste, the selection and use of human-health-focused interior materials, the use of renewable energy sourcing strategies, and the building's total lifespan.

Considering lifecycle costs

The total lifecycle costs of a product — the costs embedded in its sourcing of materials, manufacturing, shipment, and recycling, in other words — are rarely considered when selections are made. Most often, the products with the cheapest initial cost and an acceptable lifespan will win the buyer's interest and end up incorporated into the home. This is a mistake that disregards the costs associated with maintenance, repair, and eventual replacement.

The goal of green buildings is to offset the costs of their purchase and installation via indirect environmental, social, and economic savings. Take an array of solar panels, for example. Solar panels make sense only if the environmental, social, and economic savings outweigh their initial purchase, installation, and maintenance costs. A return on investment is the rate at which, over the total duration of time required, the purchased product pays for itself. Unfortunately, many of the environmental and social costs associated with building products aren't acknowledged and incorporated into the initial cost to the user. As such, the system is out of balance, which leads to a misrepresentation of total costs to the user and most often encourages the purchase of products that will cost more in the long run.

Green buildings also prioritize the use of materials that will withstand the test of time. Yes, a timber frame home with cheap finishing materials may result in a more affordable home, but those materials will require more maintenance over their very short lifespan and will eventually need to be replaced altogether. It's better to make the investment up-front and save money later. From paints and roofing to light bulbs and finishes, green materials may not always be competitive with their up-front price, but their lifecycle cost will be competitive.

Building better

The circular economy is all about eliminating waste, keeping materials in use for longer periods, and allowing natural capital to regenerate. We can address all these areas by designing and constructing better buildings through these five key stages:

>> Analysis

>> Conservation

>> Efficiency

>> Time-of-use management

>> Renewables promotion

Before any improvements can be made, it's critical to know where improvements will have the biggest impact. By analyzing total costs, energy usage, water usage, maintenance costs, replacement costs, and a host of other lifecycle variables, you can better identify where the biggest impacts can be made to reduce waste, keep materials in use for longer periods, and allow natural capital to regenerate.

After these areas have been identified, you can identify where conservation can come into play. Can you design spaces that can be multifunctional? Maybe the home office can double as a guest room and you can avoid the extra square footage that will only be used 1 percent of the time. Can you make the size of the home smaller, to reduce the total amount of building material needed? By reducing the size of the home, it also costs much less to heat, cool, and maintain. Is there room for a clothesline outside? Installing one will reduce much of the cost associated with a conventional dryer. What about the materials themselves? Are they fully recyclable or reusable at the end of their lives? Selecting materials that can be cycled back into the system will conserve the amount of raw materials required.

Once opportunities for conservation have been addressed, efficiency can become the focus. When water and energy are needed, select the proper fittings and fixtures required to use them as efficiently as possible. Consider building a two-story home rather than a sprawling, range-style home. Two-story homes not only use land more efficiently but also manage heat better. (Heat rises, so heat headed upward is cheaper than heat spreading out horizontally.) Get the right team involved, if you can. Select designers and contractors with green building credentials to ensure that your home is designed and constructed with proper levels of insulation, efficient heating, ventilation, air conditioning units, and an airtight building skin.

Time-of-use management is all about using energy and the space within your home at the best possible times to account for natural energy systems. By placing your bedroom on the south side of your home (in the northern hemisphere, that is), you can offset the need for artificial lighting in the morning by relying on the sun. If you're able to install a full-house home battery in your residence, you can draw energy from it during high-demand periods (when energy costs the most) and draw from the grid during low-demand periods (when energy costs the least amount). When it comes to time-of-use management, savings are limited only by your creativity!

Last but not least, you have the option of using a renewable energy system. If it makes sense, utilize some form of renewable energy to power your home by either generating it yourself or buying renewable energy from your energy provider. If you're generating it yourself, pair it with a home battery to be used during high-demand periods or emergency situations.

Following all these strategies will lead to living in a home that eliminates waste, keeps materials and products in use for longer periods, and allows natural capital to regenerate. See Chapter 16 for more details on circularity for design, and see Eric's *Green Building & Remodeling For Dummies* (published by Wiley) for a deeper dive on how to build responsibly, reduce waste, and help preserve the environment.

Thinking About the Way You Commute

Although we're now living in a world that seems mostly digital and delivery-oriented, we still have plenty of reasons to travel — to pick up groceries, visit with friends and family, and check in at the office during the week, for example. Although some travel is necessary, strategies are still available for you to eliminate the waste associated with commuting, keep materials and products associated with travel in use for longer periods, and allow natural capital to regenerate. From not using a car to choosing the most efficient vehicle available, we use the next few sections to review your range of commuter strategies.

Be car-less for once

For those living in a country setting, a single-user vehicle is more than likely the only way you have to get around. But if you happen to be living within a city, you have many transportation options available to you other than a single-user vehicle. If you have the time, the weather cooperates, and your destination is close enough, keep your keys on the hook and walk to wherever you need to go. It's healthy and you won't have to worry about finding a parking spot. Instead of walking, why not ride a bike instead? Bicycles are quite often the fastest way to reach your destination within a city setting. If you have the option available, find a way for a group of colleagues to carpool to work. This strategy reduces the fuel needed and the miles put on the car and can often be a more enjoyable way to commute to work. If trains and buses are available, take public transit. Aside from public transit, if you really want to take a car, check out car services like Lyft, which is cheaper than paying for gas, insurance, and maintenance of your own vehicle — by a long shot.

Choose more efficient options

If you find that driving a single-user vehicle is truly the necessary mode of transportation for you, a range of hybrid and fully electric vehicles are available on the market. Batteries are lasting longer, more companies are producing electric vehicles, and charging stations are popping up left and right. Tesla even offers charging for its vehicles at no extra cost to the user.

Sometimes, something new can scare people. And that's okay. If you want to hold on to fossil-fueled-powered vehicles until you run out of gas, there are still some driving practices you can implement that will improve your fuel efficiency, leading to less fuel needed, fewer emissions, and fewer costs. Check your tire pressure and make sure it's within the recommended range for the tire. Underinflated tires have a shorter lifespan, so you need to replace them sooner. In addition, underinflated tires reduce the efficiency of the tire (because more of it is touching the pavement) and results in higher rates of fuel consumption. Also, maintain the speed limit — you'll save gas and lose only a minute or two of your time. On top of it all, drive smoothly. Starting and stopping quickly results in a higher rate of fuel consumption and puts your car (and brakes) under unnecessary levels of stress.

Revisiting the Way You Work

Offices require a lot of electricity and a lot of materials. Though the products used within an office setting are often dependent on the business being run, you can take some steps to help eliminate waste, keep materials in use for longer periods, and allow natural capital to regenerate. You can support a circular economy with some simple adjustments to your business practice. Strategies such as supporting the telecommuting and teleconferencing of your staff, minimizing the amount of "stuff" you use, using better products, and cutting down on business travel all make a big impact at the end of the day.

Promoting telecommuting and teleconferencing

As the coronavirus has shown us, telecommuting and teleconferencing are both realistic alternatives to either working in a typical office setting or traveling around the country and the world for meetings. Many who believed that having people working from their homes would reduce productivity are now seeing that that's not the case. Telecommuting allows for cost savings by downsizing the amount of office space provided for employees and eliminates the travel necessary to commute between home and work every day. Even if it's critical to have some people in the office, there may not be a need to have them there 40 hours per week. (Skipping the office just one day a week still makes a big difference in total emissions.) By setting up teleconferencing meetings, the costs and emissions associated with traveling to and from meetings around the globe can be eliminated altogether, with minimal costs to the social side of meetings. Platforms such as Zoom, Skype, and Microsoft Teams have allowed for an easy transition to virtual meetings.

Managing office supplies

You can implement many strategies to support a circular economy within an office setting, ranging from the efficient use of electricity to the reduction, reuse, and recycling of the materials needed for office administration to the use of eco-friendly products and nontoxic cleaning materials. Though it's difficult to implement all these initiatives at one time, you can start with what's easily manageable and work toward the more difficult efforts over time.

The efficient use of electricity is one of the easiest ways to begin improving office operations; most of the time, these changes can be made with the use of timers and occupancy sensors. Make sure that all the technology and equipment used during the day is fully shut off when not in use. (This includes printers, scanners, computers, and even space heaters at individual workstations.) By placing these items on a timer, which automatically cuts power to them outside of working hours, it takes next to no effort to see the energy savings tied to the efficient use of electricity. In addition, use natural daylight whenever possible and swap your old incandescent light bulbs with compact fluorescent lamps (CFLs) or light-emitting diodes (LEDs). You'll soon see additional drops in energy usage.

Most of us grew up with the "reduce, reuse, recycle" mantra burnt into our minds, but these practices still aren't often applied in an office setting. Documents are printed that could have remained in digital form, paper products still end up in the garbage can, Styrofoam cups and plates are freely used, and water bottles are offered to every guest who enters the front door. Although you may incur an additional up-front cost to buying 100 percent recycled paper, buying reusable plates and utensils for staff and nontoxic versions of common office supplies, like markers and glue, the environmental and social benefits that stem from that economic cost will brings things into balance.

When you have reduced, reused, and recycled what you can, you still need to buy new products at some point. When you do, do your best to purchase only environmentally friendly office products. By "environmentally friendly," we mean that the product has been designed to minimize the negative impact on the environment when compared to a standard product of similar purpose. Buy fair trade coffees for the office rather than coffees that undermine the value of those who harvest it. Find a printer service that will collect and reuse the ink cartridges you use in your printers. Finally, buy durable furniture that you won't have to replace after a couple years of use and buy products that hold the capacity to be repaired and eventually fully recycled.

Chapter **20**

Creating a Career in the Circular Economy

The circular economy offers a new paradigm and model for how we humans can live in balance with our natural resources and break away from the traditional take-make-waste model of business. Rethinking, reimagining, and reinventing how to produce everything won't be easy. It will definitely require a range of new skills and approaches to business. That's where you come in!

The transition to the circular economy is expected to create an incredible demand for new combinations of skills and talents that aren't now widely available. Reusing and recycling materials requires skilled trade hands and an engineering mindset. Sourcing new and sustainable raw materials for making innovative new products will require new models of chemistry. Redesigning and reimagining products to be adaptable and repairable will require new design and problem-solving skills.

As pressure from environmental issues starts to build, companies will begin to feel more pressure from their customers and employees to adopt a more circular approach. For this reason, you can expect to see many new-and-exciting career opportunities for people looking to work in the circular economy.

For some companies, the circular economy represents an opportunity to reduce costs, improve quality, or provide a more ethical and sustainable product to the customers. For example, Schneider Electric (www.se.com) produces a wide array of power-and-energy systems for everything from buildings to cities. In addition to using recycled content and recyclable materials in its products, this industrial equipment manufacturing giant started helping its customers discover how to extend the life of their aging products. By offering new pricing models, including pay-per-use and leasing options — plus, offering new take-back programs to ensure that their products don't end up in the landfill — Schneider Electric now sees circular economy solutions representing 12 percent of its revenues, while preventing 132 million tons of greenhouse gas emissions from being released.

Other companies will place circularity as the central framework of their entire business. Global furniture company IKEA (www.ikea.com) has committed to being 100 percent circular by 2030, which is already requiring company leaders to rethink their stores, products, supply chain, materials, and entire business model. They're seeking to eliminate waste by committing to using only renewable or salvageable materials across the entire product line.

As big-name companies like Schneider Electric and IKEA succeed in using the circular economy, you can expect to see hundreds of others copy them, which means that the demand for those individuals skilled in circular economy approaches will increase as well.

Looking at the Future of Jobs

In summarizing the book *Waste to Wealth: The Circular Economy Advantage*, by Peter Lacy and Jakob Rutqvist, global accounting firm Accenture (www.accenture.com) estimated that the value of the circular economy would reach $4.5 trillion by 2030, just when IKEA is expected to meet its goal of being 100 percent circular. In that same report, Accenture found that the consumer goods industry could recoup up to $110 billion by 2030 by simply optimizing its packaging for circularity and for reducing waste. Those companies will need designers to redesign that packaging in creative and insightful ways.

While all this is going on, you can also expect to see a decline in employment across all the legacy sectors and industries, including mining and excavation. Large, centralized manufacturing plants will be replaced by localized and regional versions of smaller plants, meaning that new jobs will be available in different areas of the world.

Because the circular economy represents this huge, trillion-dollar opportunity to reimagine all of business and industry, no career path will remain affected by this. After all, someone needs to reinvent all the processes, systems, products, and services to design out waste.

Companies not yet embracing the circular economy won't be left out. In fact, these holdouts might represent the biggest opportunity of all. Though there's only one IKEA, hundreds of thousands of other companies out there need smart, skilled people to reimagine and reinvent their entire supply chain. The circular economy could be your secret weapon to uncovering hidden savings for these companies without their ever knowing what you were doing — transforming them!

Just as jobs in the solar-and-wind renewable energy sector overtook the number of jobs in the coal industry in just a couple of decades, so too will you see an entire generation of skilled, circular workforce folks begin to replace the old legacy jobs of the fossil fuel and high-waste industries.

REMEMBER

The circular economy involves a lot more than just recycling, as Figure 20-1 makes clear. It's really about the sustainability, reuse, and extension of the useful life of your products — all while insisting on using non-toxic materials. Because of all this, the circular economy isn't limited to any single industry or location. It can be used in any industry and in every country.

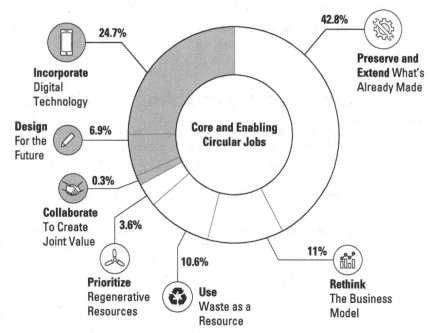

FIGURE 20-1: A Dutch think tank's circular economy report highlights seven areas of jobs within the circular economy.

The Dutch think tank Circle Economy (www.circle-economy.com) came up with the chart shown in Figure 20-1. It has three main circular economy job categories: jobs that are essential to the circular economy, jobs that enable the circular economy, and jobs that are indirectly related to the circular economy. In the next few sections, we explore each of these categories in greater detail.

Jobs that are central to the circular economy

At the core of the circular economy lie jobs that focus specifically on the various technical and nutrient loops we return to time and again in this book. These jobs focus on all the lifecycle and raw material processes needed to convert from linear to circular in order to create a circular economy.

This group might have the term *circular economy* in their job title. Here are some examples:

» **Repair technicians:** These fix-it wizards have strong technical and manual abilities acquired through trade skills. This new generation can also advise you on how to make your products more repairable.

» **Sustainability managers:** These thought leaders in sustainable design oversee many of the topics discussed throughout this book. They seek out ways to bend all those linear loops into circular ones by leading the development of lifecycle assessments and strategies.

» **Zero waste consultant:** These experts in materials and recycling advise companies on the best ways to minimize their waste footprint.

Jobs that are enabling the circular economy

These jobs include people who are speeding up and enabling the adoption of a circular economy. They include supply chain experts, production experts, and scientists who will solve the problems that no one has solved yet.

Here are some examples:

» **Supply chain and procurement experts:** These include skilled professionals who understand the cultural, financial, and geopolitical issues around harvesting materials across the world. Their job involves discovering and sourcing new opportunities for more circular materials, including recycled and reclaimed materials from the waste stream.

» **Biochemists:** These professionals are trained chemists focused on using biology, chemistry, and genetics to discover new approaches for renewable, natural, and healthy bio-based materials.

- » **Production stewardship:** These analysts oversee the supply and demand in order to ensure that you always have enough of a supply of any of your materials. This person must have a keen mind and engage in logical reasoning and thinking.

- » **Industrial engineers:** These talented designers balance both art and science to imagine new manufacturing equipment to produce circular products. They are expert problem solvers and designers.

- » **Pricing analysts:** This person determines how to price your products and evaluates the differences from various sources so that the company can make an informed purchasing decision. These financial wizards supply you with the information you need to transform your company's supply chain.

Jobs that are indirectly related to the circular economy

These folks are the ones working in logistics and education who comprise the last piece of this circular puzzle. This is anyone who is making a reuse-, sharing-, or skills-based economy possible.

Here are some examples:

- » **Teachers:** Teachers play a vital role in any economy as they prepare the future workforce. In the context of a circular economy, teachers can prepare and equip their students with all the skills needed for these new circular business models, including design, creativity, whole systems thinking, and a love of the environment.

- » **Couriers:** The push for take-back, reuse, and crowd-sharing will require messengers and couriers to carry materials and products back-and-forth locally.

- » **Collection centers:** If the goal is to no longer throw anything away, you'll start to see various ways to drop off or donate materials that are unwanted but still useful. These local collection centers will become miniature economic engines for gathering valuable resources.

KICKING OFF INNOVATION IN SPORTSWEAR

Kara Solomonides Brody is a senior sustainability consultant helping large sportswear brands with their sustainability strategies. She's led the marketing, PR, and training for massive sustainability programs in both the U.S. and Europe and shared her insights into how to look at a material-intensive industry like apparel and sportswear:

Sustainability in the apparel and footwear sector is a complex and nuanced topic. Should I get rid of everything and buy all recycled or organic clothing? Should I keep everything? Should I buy from sustainable brands? Is there such thing as a sustainable brand?

Consumers are confused and are constantly bombarded with different — and sometimes conflicting — messages. One message that has been resonating with consumers is the desire to eliminate waste — most of this is focused on eliminating plastic waste and single use items but there are also messages about buying high quality so one does not need to replace items as often. For the majority of consumer goods, including clothing, the most sustainable options are the ones already in the consumer's closet. This begs the question — how can a consumer who wants to look stylish and have new clothing also be sustainable? The answer lies in circularity. While many consumers focus on the elimination of waste at the end of life as a reason to engage in circular business models such as product take back, re-commerce, swapping, the true impact lies in the decrease of more goods created. The majority of the environmental impacts throughout the life of a product are focused in the supply chain and the product creation phase, with some large impacts in the use phase due to the laundering of products. Brands and business can advise consumers to wash their clothing on cold and advise consumers to hang items to dry, but the challenge is that brands and businesses cannot accurately predict consumer behavior, nor would it be appropriate for brands to take credit for a consumer's more sustainable actions.

One action that brands can do is to encourage consumers to buy secondhand clothing instead of new. There are many readily available B2B solutions on the market where consumers can return used clothing and this clothing can be cleaned, repaired if needed, and then resold secondhand under a marketplace type consumer platform that still recognizes the brand. Engaging in circular business models allows brands to accurately measure consumer engagement and allows brands to directly engage with consumers to keep them connected to the brand even though they are not buying new items. Circular business models decrease the environmental impact of a product, allow consumers to acquire new-to-them products, and still allows brands to be a part of the conversation.

In addition to brand led initiatives such as Patagonia Worn Wear, the REI garage, and NorthFace Renewed, there are also consumer C2C platforms such as Poshmark and eBay, that allow consumers to directly purchase other consumers' used items.

The current linear make, use, throw away model is outdated, wasteful, and doesn't account for the true cost of creating products. A circular model uses outputs as inputs to, in the academic model, create an endless system with no waste. Real life circular models do, of course, have waste but are moving in the right direction to create successful business models within a closed and limited system.

Skills required for a circular economy

The transition to a circular economy that we're describing requires skills normally not associated with traditional business practices, as well as critical thinking to reimagine and redesign these systems. Circular economy jobs will most likely require a combination of skills that aren't normally paired, such as manual repair skills mixed with design skills. (Just look at the recent maker movement, where artists create and invent artwork using 3d printers or other tools, as an example of smart people who tinker with their hands.)

Hard technical skills, such as computer programming and machine work, are also required. In addition, you'll see demand for a series of soft skills around collaboration, communication, marketing, and storytelling to connect with customers and share your efforts.

In a truly circular economy, any skills that help people preserve and extend resources will be highly valued and sought-after. Although today certain hobby skills — such as sewing, craft-making, and refinishing — aren't considered career enhancements, they'll be valuable in a circular world, which will need people who can use their hands to make things useful again.

Where to Go for More Education

If you're looking to get started now on building your circularity skills and résumé, we've compiled a list of ideas for where to acquire more skills and training.

Earning certifications

Given that the circular economy is still a new and emerging field, it isn't easy to gain direct experience in a job with the term *circular economy* in the job description. Earning an accreditation or certification in a new field is a fast and reliable way to convince people that you're qualified to do the things you say you can do.

Check out the following certifications available now, most with online training available:

>> **The Global Sustainable Enterprise System** (www.gses-system.com) is an international standard for sustainable enterprises. Certification is based on the internationally recognized ISO standards.

>> **The Circular Economy Institute** (www.circulareconomyclub.com) offers a certification program in becoming a circular economy expert.

>> **The Underwriters Laboratories** (www.ul.com) is typically known for safety standards around electrical products, but also offers a certification for companies to measure and report the circular economy aspects of their products, sites, and organizations.

>> **NSF International** (www.nsf.org, earlier known as the National Sanitation Foundation) is an independent administrator of sanitation and food safety requirements. Its e-waste recycling certifications — responsible recycling (R2), recycling industry operating standard (RIOS), and e-stewards certifications — establish clear standards on how to recycle electronic waste.

>> **SGS** (established in Geneva, Switzerland, as the Société Générale de Surveillance, www.sgsgroup.us.com) is a global inspection, verification, testing, and certification company. Its cradle-to-cradle certification verifies that a product has met the rigorous standards of the Cradle-to-Cradle Institute (www.c2ccertified.org).

>> **BSI Group** (www.bsigroup.com/en-GB), originally known as the British Standards Institution, has established its BS 8001 standard for creating a circular economy framework to reduce waste and encourage resource efficiency.

>> **The International Sustainability and Carbon Certification** (ISCC) (www.iscc-system.org) developed standards for a more sustainable world. Its ISCC Plus standard tracks the entire supply chain of a product to confirm the content of recycled material in bio-based products.

Earning degrees and diplomas

As an emerging field within sustainability studies, the idea of earning a degree in circular economy doesn't exist yet — at least not officially. Of course, 20 years ago, there were no degree programs in sustainable design, either, and dozens of schools now offer specialized degrees in just that field.

Check out the following degrees related to the circular economy. Most are massive open online courses (MOOCs) involving hundreds of people around the world:

>> **TU Delft** (https://ocw.tudelft.nl/courses/circular-economy) is the Delft University of Technology in the Netherlands. It provides some of the best courses on the circular economy, and most are completely free.

>> **edX** (www.edx.org) is an online learning platform, founded by Harvard and MIT. It hosts several courses on the circular economy, and many might qualify for college credits at your school.

>> **Coursera** (www.coursera.org/learn/circular-economy) offers thousands of online courses, including one entitled Circular Economy — Sustainable Materials Management, which explores where important materials in products come from and how these materials can be used more efficiently, longer, and in closed loops.

>> **Ellen MacArthur Foundation (EMF)** (www.ellenmacarthurfoundation. org) is a nonprofit leading the discussion of all topics related to the circular economy. Its *Circular Design Guide* (www.circulardesignguide.com), developed in collaboration with the design firm IDEO, provides approaches to circular innovation as well as interviews with designers, creative exercises, case studies, and tools.

>> **Arizona State University's Global Institute of Sustainability and Innovation** (https://sustainability-innovation.asu.edu) offers an executive certificate in the Ethical Circular Economy in partnership with the Ellen MacArthur Foundation.

>> **Georgia Tech's Ray C. Anderson Center for Sustainable Business** (www.scheller.gatech.edu/centers-initiatives/ray-c-anderson-center-for-sustainable-business/index.html) focuses on the circular economy as a key theme for research on business innovation.

>> **McMaster University** (www.mcmaster.ca) offers a professional certificate of completion in circular economy. This beginning course was Canada's first university-level professional training program in the circular economy.

>> **The University of Exeter Business School** (http://business-school. exeter.ac.uk) offers a circular economy master class — a 6-week distance learning program designed to improve the circular approach of decision-makers and business leaders.

In addition, the Ellen MacArthur Foundation offers a list of higher education options to help schools and educators implement and develop circular economy courses. You can access this list at www.ellenmacarthurfoundation.org/assets/downloads/Higher-Education-Resource.pdf. It also maintains a database of universities across the world that integrate circular economy principles into their curriculums (www.ellenmacarthurfoundation.org/our-work/activities/universities/profiled-universities).

The jobs of the (near) future will be circular and will require the skills and talents across a variety of disciplines to take on the challenges of transitioning from a linear economy to a circular one. Now is a great time to prepare yourself for this inevitable future.

Chapter **21**

A Global Vision of a Circular Economy

aking time to imagine what the future might look like is exciting. There are so many opportunities available for improvement, and the authors of this book, become giddy just thinking about a circular world. Imagine how different things might look when compared to how things are today. The communities that we humans live in, the universities we attend, and the food service industry we rely on would all be quite different than they are today.

The communities that we humans live in will need to provide community resources and aid in order to support the proper sourcing, use, and disposal of the materials and resources we rely on. The way we manage food systems and transportation systems will also be critical when it comes to creating a circular city. It's hard for a collective group to make an impact if the necessary community structural support isn't available. The same goes for university settings: Universities are similar to communities but hold a much better potential for performing as living laboratories and utilizing data to encourage higher performance. Aside from communities and universities, the restaurant-and-brewery industry can also benefit from transitioning from linear to circular by strategically sourcing and preparing their products, establishing service standards that minimize waste, and utilizing the waste they do produce as a resource for other products.

The world can look much different if the proper structures and strategies are implemented. We'd be living in a world that minimizes the extraction of raw materials by keeping materials and products in use for longer periods and rethinking how waste can act as a new resource. The future is bright and the future is circular.

Seeing What a Circular Community Looks Like

Within the natural world, a community acts as an interrelationship between two separate elements who both benefit from the exchange of goods or services. For example, the three sisters — squash, corn, and beans — act as a community, with each one providing services for the others. Corn provides the necessary structure for beans to climb, the beans add nitrogen to the soil for the corn and squash, and the squash's massive leaves provide shade to maintain moist soils. Together, this community thrives. Apart, these individual elements would struggle to obtain the same level of produce.

Humans must realize that we act as an element of this community, not separate from it. We must be willing to provide the necessary structure for other elements to thrive in exchange for other environmental services, such as raw materials, water, and energy. Unless our communities act as a positive force within the environment in which they live, they will forever be degenerative in nature. When designing for a circular community — rather than a linear one — the health and well-being of all species must be considered. To support nature, our communities need to reestablish themselves as members of nature.

Designing a community within a circular economy framework may at first seem like overkill, given that most communities are relatively small, but there are many opportunities for single elements of a system to influence the operations of the entire system. Different tiers of governing bodies are involved in shaping the world we live in, and even the smallest of communities should have a say. These communities are important platforms for individuals to express their needs and concerns to the governing bodies at higher tiers. By establishing circular processes at a community level, the successes of those communities can be extracted and applied all around the world. Exploring how the circular economy can benefit local communities will fuel the ability for similar communities to benefit as well.

We need to address various layers of our community operations in order to successfully transition from a linear way of life to a circular one. First and foremost, we need to efficiently source our community resources and aid and then ensure that they're effectively made available to those who require them. Energy, material, business support, and tools are all required for a thriving community. In addition, the effective production and distribution of food is a critical component of a circular community. And lastly, the way people and resources are distributed throughout the community is critical. Read on to learn more about how community resources and aid, food management, and transportation all play key roles in a community's transition to a circular economy.

Sourcing community resources and aid

Communities have opportunities to support local businesses while also improving the quality of the environment within that community. By offering convenient opportunities to collect, share, trade, and dispose of resources, materials can be kept in use for longer periods, and the amount of waste produced by the community can be greatly reduced. It takes a collective effort to maintain the health of a community, and clean-up and recycling events can act as a means to harness that collective effort.

Communities can reduce the amount of resources they require by maintaining the value of the resources they have via sharing. Maker spaces, reuse centers, and other strategies can be supported to repurpose many of the products commonly sent to the landfill. This encourages small businesses to thrive by increasing the value of products that are typically seen as waste. These spaces also provide opportunities for education within the community, by offering clinics and courses on how to repair and fix common household items. We can increase the rate of repair, reuse, and remanufacturing by providing opportunities for the community to learn how to do so. In addition to education, these community resource spaces can provide lending libraries to the general public for a small annual membership. Through lending libraries, each member of the community can have access to a wider range of tools than they'd be able to afford on their own. This means Average Joe down the road doesn't need to spend $30 on a pipe wrench that he'll only use once. He can simply borrow it at no additional cost beyond a yearly membership. These lending libraries reduce the consumption of products and greatly reduce the cost of having access to tools and a proper education.

REMEMBER

Sometimes materials don't end up where they should. Drive down any road and you'll see a range of trash lining the streets that could be put to use elsewhere. Aside from pollution on the roads, each homeowner's garbage also contains waste that can be put to use elsewhere, if properly collected. By offering organized community clean-up and recycling events, members of the community can help to clean the environment while also receiving assistance in the proper collection and recycling of the waste they collect as well as the waste from their homes. By offering these community events, neighbors can greatly reduce the amount of waste that's directed to landfills, improve the quality of the environment around them, and save the time and energy required to extract raw materials by recycling materials back to the start of the material lifecycle.

Looking at food management

Everyone likes food and everyone needs food, so communities have an opportunity to make food access and its disposal as convenient and efficient as possible in order to benefit the community as a whole. By creating opportunities for communities to buy food in bulk, establishing community composting programs with incentives, and creating opportunities for community gardens to fill the margins of the city, food can become a valuable commodity within a circular community.

Buying products in bulk is commonly tied to lower prices per product. Often, buying more of a product at one time results in not only lower prices but also a lower amount of packaging. Visit any buy-in-bulk store (Costco or Sam's Club, for example) and you'll see why members are willing to pay a premium for a membership to gain access to the value of bulk purchasing.

REMEMBER

You don't have to rely on these large, commercialized sources to gain the savings associated with buying bulk. Go to your local butcher, CSA-partnering farmer, or other vendors to see what value you can obtain by buying in bulk.

Once food is purchased within a community, chances are good that some of that food will spoil and become inedible. The nutrient value and raw material are still there — it's just no longer in an edible form that can safely be consumed. To allow that material to maintain its value, you need to make community composting programs available. Persuading members of the community to complete the necessary steps to compost their food waste can be achieved only if the proper incentives are built into the system. Not every member of a community is the hug-a-tree type, so we can't expect all of them to take the time to care for the environment and save their food scraps. By installing large collection centers in neighborhoods, members of the community can exchange their food scraps for access to community garden space or discounts on produce their neighbors have collected. Ensuring that the value that comes from food waste is returned to those who are delivering the food waste to begin with is the best possible strategy to motivate this type of activity. Over time, with an entire neighborhood fueling a composting system, the food waste will decompose and provide nutrient-dense soil that can be used to grow more food for those neighbors. This reduces the amount of fertilizers required to be purchased each year, keeps organic material in use longer, and eliminates food waste.

Ensuring that this compost has a place to go is also critical for the development of a composting system. What is a community supposed to do with massive piles of compost and no community vegetable gardens in which to use it? Some members of the community will have more garden space than they know what to do with, and others won't have enough. Creating partnerships between these two groups ensures that land use is optimized and everyone benefits. Cooperatives — *co-ops*, for short — can also be established within a community. Within a co-op, members are paid with fresh vegetables for the work they do planting, maintaining, and harvesting vegetables for the entire co-op. This form of a *micro* food hub (where food is sourced from local regions) is preferable when compared to *macro* food hubs (where food is imported into a community from sources outside of the community) for many reasons. Having to import food requires the transportation of that food and, during the time it takes to transport the food, it loses freshness. To maintain freshness, packaging and preservatives are introduced into the process to make up for transportation delays. Maintaining a micro food hub, however, eliminates the need for transportation and packaging (and the waste associated with them) by keeping the production of food local and circular. In a circular food network, those who rely on local food also take part in (and ownership of) the production, maintenance, consumption, and waste recycling of food and its waste.

Eyeing transportation

The transportation options made available to a community should reflect the size and scale of that community. It makes no sense to incorporate a bullet train within a rural setting, because the demand isn't there. Instead, it makes sense to install a bullet train on the east coast, where it can connect Boston, New York, Philadelphia, and Baltimore and allow for ease of transport between these major cities. In smaller communities, as well as within the central core of major cities, it makes sense to incorporate alternative forms of transportation, like electric scooters and bicycles. Ride sharing also needs to be supported because it promotes the elimination of individually owned cars and promotes the use of one car to service thousands of individuals

The transportation strategies set by a community need to be relevant and service the demand of that community. Sidewalks need to be provided within a city to promote walking — this simple act comes with economic, social, and environmental benefits. We also need to encourage bicycling, because it's a faster mode of transportation than walking that holds all of walking's benefits — but only where it makes sense. You wouldn't expect to see a dedicated bike lane in rural Indiana, but you would expect to see one on every street in New York City. Similarly, you would expect to see a dedicated carpool lane in rural Indiana, but not in downtown New York City. The transportation options we provide need to make sense for the community they're serving so that we can eliminate the waste and pollution associated with transportation where it can be prevented.

Ride sharing is becoming a popular option within cities big and small alike because it brings mutual benefit to the rider, the driver, and the general public. The driver benefits by receiving an additional source of income to cover their monthly payment, insurance and general maintenance; the rider benefits by not having to pay a monthly car loan as well as insurance and maintenance payments; and the general public benefits by having a city with less congestion and emissions caused by internal combustion engines. Ride sharing companies like Lyft and Uber have created a new market that minimizes the amount of material input that's required by minimizing the number of cars on the road, maximizing the value that comes from the cars on the road by increasing their rate of usage, and eliminating the amount of waste by reducing the total number of cars on the road that require constant repair and maintenance.

Seeing What a Circular University Looks Like

The beauty of making a university circular is that the staff doesn't need to do it alone. At any point in time, numerous faculty members, researchers, graduate students, and professionals are at work, trying to make the world a better place. In a sense, a university should be the mecca of discovery. A university should understand the value of student and staff research and develop a platform to utilize this range of learning, research, and data as a tool for transitioning university operations toward a circular future.

By generating the necessary infrastructure and incorporating the range of studies that takes place within a university setting, campuses can act as a living laboratory, tasked with discovering the best way to transition campus operation, classroom activities, and student learning toward a circular future. A circular university will use the living laboratory structure as a tool to constantly exposure the "better" way to live and learn. By harnessing data-driven education programs, faculty, staff, and students can generate the data necessary to fuel critical decision-making around capital investments, educational platforms, and student success.

REMEMBER

Generating data will aid in transitioning universities from a linear way of operation to a circular one. Without data, there is no opportunity to conserve waste, to efficiently use the waste that's produced, or to understand how waste can be eliminated. Generating data (and analyzing that data) is what faculty and students do best. A circular university will harness the power of these groups to map out the future. Data will not only be extracted and utilized by university staff, either. Data derived from building metering will also fuel the activity of students and staff. By providing transparency of material, energy, and water usage, students and staff will be motivated to optimize their impact within the university setting. Extracting the value of academics and data will allow for universities to lead the rest of the world toward a circular future.

Learning from living laboratories

Living laboratories are research-based settings that are user-centered, and the research that's completed is applied within the same setting in which the research is taking place. Universities act as a prime platform for living laboratories to work. The benefits of using universities as the location of living laboratories is that the campus often acts as a *think tank* — a dense hub of research and knowledge creation. In other words, plenty of opportunities are available for research to take place. Within a university setting, the campus itself can support not only the research of studies related to the circular economy — sustainable food production, business ethics, material lifecycles, and natural resource management, for example — but also the application of this research in a real-world setting.

Living laboratories within a university setting are the key to developing the data required to make smart changes. Building operations, academic structures, student engagement, food sourcing and management, transportation, utility services, water use, and so many other areas of a university setting can be improved by way of research partnerships between faculty and students. By utilizing classrooms as the overlap between student learning and real-world application, the data derived from faculty and student research benefits not only the university but the surrounding community as well.

Colby College, located in Waterville, Maine, built a new student dorm in 2018 that demonstrates the value of a living laboratory and making an impact on the community in which you live. Roughly 200 students of Colby College — in addition to a handful of faculty members, acting as mentors — now live in Downtown Waterville, Maine, and participate within the Program for Civil Engagement and Community Partnership. This program helps to build relationships between members of the community and Colby College students and provides the necessary space for academics to impact the real world. The main goal of this building was to offer space for students and the community to work together. On the first floor, the Chase Community Forum will support an array of programs such as workshops and lectures, which will be aimed to facilitate change within the community. The college not only provided the necessary space for the community and students to collaborate but also built in academic requirements to allow for students to apply the knowledge they're developing in a real-world setting through volunteer requirements.

Insisting on data visibility

What gets measured gets managed. This fact alone is why data is such a critical component of any transitioning effort towards circular operations on a university campus. Don't limit your thinking and assume that only those who are in charge of campus operations will be the ones who have access to this data, either. That is not a recipe for success. The students, staff, faculty, and administration all need access to this data for the transition from linear to circular to work. Data about everything (we mean it, everything) should be fully incorporated into the environment in which each member of the university learns, sleeps, eats, and teaches. Imagine dormitories, labs, cafeterias, and bathrooms all communicating relevant data to the users of those spaces. "Your dormitory has used 25 percent more water than other dormitories on campus." By exposing these data points to users and providing incentives for better performance, data can act as the driving force behind improved operations on campus. Exposing the data behind the world around us reminds everyone that they play a major part in affecting those data points.

Not only can data impact the choices building occupants make, but it can also help building occupants be proud of the buildings in which they live and study. Imagine walking down a hallway to your next class and reading "300 trees were saved by reusing the old gymnasium floor in this new medical center" on a newly posted sign. Those students and staff would proudly embrace the fact that their building holds character and has diverted waste from the landfill by making old materials new again.

Imagine you are taking your high school senior on their first campus tour and it seems a bit different from when you were last on campus. As you walk through campus, you notice that data is influencing decisions. You walk into the student center and realize that air monitors are reporting the air quality to occupants in real time. As you go through the bathrooms, you realize that the fixtures chosen reduce water consumption by 25 percent when compared to baseline fixtures in the market. During your lunch break, you learn that the food you are consuming has been sourced from farms within 10 miles of the campus and all food waste you produce will be sent back to the farm to either be composed or used as livestock feed. You learn that the electric shuttles on campus are completely fueled by an array of renewable energy sources placed around the university and you come to find out that all of these elements are constantly improving thanks to student and faculty research.

REMEMBER

What gets measured, gets managed, and exposing university occupants to this data not only helps to improve their decisions, but it also creates a sense of place and ownership. Combining the living laboratory framework with data visibility is the perfect recipe for transitioning campus operations from a historically linear way of a life to a futuristic, circular one.

Seeing What a Circular Restaurant and Brewery Look Like

Food and beer hold a close relationship worldwide. These two products are quite often paired and served together. A hot-and-spicy dish would pair well with an ice-cold lager, and a warm-and-rich dish would pair well with a dark and earthy stout. Not only are they complementary, but food and beer also require an array of ingredients and techniques — and also result in a substantial amount of waste. However, through effective and efficient sourcing and processing, service standards, and utilizing waste as a resource, these two giant industries can have a brighter future.

Why focus on the restaurant industry? Well, every person on this planet requires food daily, and most of us enjoy exploring the wide variety of flavors that cultures and restaurants have to offer. Though you may have found your red meat and potatoes and are content with that option moving forward, others see the rainbow of flavors available around the world and salivate at the idea of trying them all. This need for food isn't slowing down, either. According to the Bureau of Labor Statistics, over $3,000 per year is spent by the average American household eating "out." And, as the population continues to grow, so will that demand for food and the resulting waste. According to a report developed by the Food Waste Reduction Alliance, roughly half a pound of food is wasted for every meal served in a restaurant. On top of that, of the food that isn't consumed in a restaurant, 85 percent of it remains unused. This equates to massive amounts of waste that could otherwise be utilized if properly sourced and prepared.

Beer is, by far, the most common low-alcohol beverage purchased and consumed around the world. The brewery industry — composed of both microbreweries and macrobreweries — acts as a source of substantial revenues, requires a large amount of resources, and produces extensive amounts of waste. Identifying these byproducts as resources instead of waste can lead to additional sources of revenue while also offsetting the negative environmental impacts associated with the disposal of these byproducts.

REMEMBER

One place where brewing byproducts can be utilized as inputs is within the restaurant industry. Brewery byproducts hold the opportunity to act as cheaper alternatives to raw material sourcing and an additional source of nutrients within various types of food.

Given their global reach and the nature of the restaurant and brewery businesses, it's evident that they're extremely dependent on raw materials to fuel the demand of restaurant- and brewery-goers worldwide. These markets extract billions of pounds of resources from the earth every year in the form of livestock, water, energy, and produce, and (unfortunately) are also responsible for producing large amounts of waste during both the preparation and post-consumption of food and beer. Luckily, given the relationship between the two industries — who doesn't enjoy a nice, cold beer with their meal? —a lot of opportunities are available to reduce the amount of raw materials required within each industry by harnessing the waste of the other industry as a resource. Keep reading to find out which opportunities are out there.

Fostering effective and efficient sourcing and prep

When it comes to sourcing and preparing the range of food and beverages being provided in the service industry, the role of the chef or brewer is to generate a circular system that lifts up the process and the goods served rather than limits them. A chef shouldn't see the proper sourcing and preparation of a chicken as a hurdle to overcome, but rather as an opportunity to source fresh resources for their customers and fully utilize the value of their investment in the entire chicken — and not just the edible parts. And a brewer shouldn't see the proper sourcing and preparation of their grain, hops, and yeast as a cost to swallow, but rather as an opportunity to source local flavors while maximizing the value of the resources, even after the brewery process is complete.

Where restaurant and brewery ingredients come from matters. By sourcing ingredients locally, you can ensure their freshness and eliminate a lot of the costs associated with national or international shipment of goods. Also, by sourcing products locally, you are supporting local businesses and very likely serving those local ingredients to local customers — maybe even the people who sold you your ingredients in the first place! Though ingredients sourced locally are often assumed to be more expensive than those sold by industrialized institutions, make sure that's the case before deciding where you get your ingredients. Quite often, local ingredients cost less because they don't require national or international shipment and do not rely on heavy, industrialized equipment to be harvested.

In addition to eliminating waste by sourcing food and brewing ingredients effectively and efficiently, preparing food and beer efficiently can assist in the transition from a linear restaurant-and-brewery industry to a circular one. Chef Kim Wejendorp, of Amass Restaurant in Copenhagen, is a master of eliminating food waste through proper resource preparation and utilization. Creativity and resourcefulness act as tools to utilize every bit of an ingredient, and this creativity and resourcefulness can be applied in the kitchen and the brewery. Through effective and efficient processing, Chef Wejendorp strategically aims to extract a range of flavors from kitchen byproducts that would be destined for the garbage can in common, commercial kitchen settings. Anyone who has diced up carrots or bell peppers, or who has brewed a batch of beer, knows that certain parts of the ingredients are often discarded. Many chefs, including Chef Wejendorp, understand that there is remaining value in those "scraps" and that value can be utilized as additional flavor, or composted to support the growth of new ingredients.

Revising service standards

The way restaurants serve their meals — that point of connection between customer and food — is critical. With flavors, scents, and aesthetics all at play, the service standards set by a restaurant are critical to ensure that customers enjoy their experience and want to come back again. The same applies to the brewery industry. The way a brewery serves its beer — that point of connection between the customer and the brew — is critical. Aside from maintaining customers and ensuring the future of your business, there are economic and environmental impacts tied to service standards that also play a role. Take your pick: Do you want to serve your food via disposable methods? Or are reusable plates, cups, utensils, and napkins in order? There are certainly economic and environmental advantages and drawbacks to both.

By using disposable methods — like those white, plastic forks and knives that bend and snap in half — it's true that you're eliminating the need to have a standard 3-sink commercial kitchen setup required to wash, rinse, and sanitize reusable dishes and silverware. All that does save time and water, but you're also continuously buying a disposable material, generating waste, and giving your customers the idea that the meals they're buying from you are only worth being eaten with the help of solidified oil. Great sales pitch, right?

Though incorporating reusable plates, cups, utensils, and napkins does require time and space for the three-sink commercial kitchen setup, water, and cleaning solutions, you can develop your meals in a way that minimizes the use of reusable utensils — by designing meals that are eaten with one's hands. By getting creative with delivery of your meals, items that were once served on individual plates to a table of four could be consolidated to one plate, from which the entire table can share. Maybe a plate isn't even necessary. Rather than serve meals on either a disposable or reusable plate, why not use parchment paper? This material adds a rustic element to the meal and can be properly composed after use rather than be thrown away. Compostable yet disposable, products are a happy middle ground for restaurants that can't afford to fully transition from disposable service standards to reusable. The Under Armor global headquarters food service cafeterias now serve their meals to employees with the help of compostable products — compostable containers, utensils, and cups — and offer free beverages to those who bring their own reusable cups and thermoses.

Serving beer to customers is no different from serving food. How breweries serve their beverages is just as critical. Developing service standards to minimize material input, keep materials and products in use for longer periods, and eliminate unnecessary waste is critical for the brewery industry's transition from a linear process to a circular one. Fortunately, a lot of great strategies are already being implemented at an industry level to keep materials and products in use for longer periods and to eliminate waste. Great breweries don't use plastic cups — clearly, brewery-goers are there to appreciate the craft of beer, not participate in a ridiculous frat party. Instead, great breweries serve their beer in glasses, which can be used thousands of times and recycled when damaged beyond repair. For the regulars, mug clubs are available that offer — for a small annual fee — a custom mug to be used only by that customer. Extending the ownership of the mug to the customer ensures that they have a reason to maintain its quality, which maximizes the life and use of the product to avoid replacement. For those who want to enjoy beer but don't have time to sit inside the pub, takeaway options are growing in popularity. Plastic bottles should be avoided, and the use of cans and growlers should be supported. Plastic bottles are intended to be thrown away, whereas cans can be recycled and growlers can be reused. To eliminate the need to buy new containers, keep products in use longer, and eliminate waste, growlers are by far the best option.

Viewing waste as a resource

In terms of resource management, there are also a lot of opportunities for the waste of one industry to serve as a resource for the other. And vice versa. Identifying these areas of overlap between the restaurant and brewery industries offers opportunities to not only reduce the amount of waste from one industry but also reduce the amount of raw materials required within the other industry. Food waste can act as an input in the brewery process, and brewery waste can act as an input in the restaurant business.

Food and brewery waste comes in these two forms:

>> **Pre-consumer waste** stems from the preparation of food and beer — before it's served to the customer, in other words.

>> **Post-consumer waste** stems from the customer's plate or glass. Either they didn't like what you had to offer or you gave them too much.

Dealing with pre-consumer waste is pretty simple: Minimize scraps during preparation by processing raw ingredients more efficiently, and use what scraps you produce as a new source of flavor for something else. Though you may be serving only chicken breast and legs to your customer, the rest of the raw chicken can be boiled to create a broth. This broth can either be used as the base for a soup or concentrated to form a sauce. Those sweet potato scraps you have in the kitchen don't have to be thrown out, but can act as a source of flavor for that new fall beer you're planning to offer when Thanksgiving rolls around. Utilizing waste as a resource offers two benefits: It eliminates the need to buy more raw materials, and it eliminates the amount of waste produced by the kitchen. Both outcomes save you, the restaurant manager, money.

Dealing with post-consumer food isn't as simple, unfortunately: Post-consumer food isn't as simple as the raw ingredients that went into making the meal. It's all blended together and made up of fats, salts, vegetables, and meats, and therefore it's harder to sort through and extract value from it. Due to sanitary constraints, offering post-consumer waste to food banks is quite often prohibited, even if the food was untouched by anyone. So, what can we do with post-consumer waste? Direct food waste to a food bank whenever possible, food-and-brewery waste to a farmer to feed livestock, and/or compost it if the ingredients allow for it. All these alternatives to waste should be seen as available strategies for eliminating post-consumer food waste. Any of these solutions would reduce the amount of food that would have ended up in a landfill. Composting may become a more popular option for restaurant and brewery owners as the number of composting facilities across the United States continues to increase. A company by the name of Black Bear Composting — located in Charlottesville, Virginia — is an emerging example of how composting can act as a successful business venture by servicing local schools and restaurants.

6

The Part of Tens

Chapter **22**

Ten Questions to Ask About Your Material Lifecycle

E very material has what's called a *lifecycle*. That is to say, every material has some type of *birth* (where it's initially extracted, processed, manufactured, packaged, and delivered); it has a *life* (where it's used, cleaned, maintained, and repaired); and it has a *death* (where it's disposed of, repurposed, or reused). Every one of these stages has potentially negative environmental impacts, but the more you understand the lifecycle, the easier it to identify ways to improve it. (We cover this topic in more detail in Chapter 10.)

This chapter lists the questions you should be asking regarding your material in order to better understand the full picture of this lifecycle. By finding answers to these questions, you'll be able to recognize the environmental impacts of each stage of your material's lifecycle and, more importantly, how to find ways to reduce or mitigate these negative impacts.

REMEMBER

When we talk about *materials,* we might be talking about raw materials. natural materials, synthetic materials, or even an entire product.

Where Did This Material Come From?

Although this question seems like an easy, straightforward one, asking the source of a material or product can be complicated. Whether it's mined from the earth, cut from a forest, or mixed together from chemicals, some type of raw materials are assembled to produce a final product. Discovering the source of a material helps you understand how much effort goes into making it. For example, glass is made from heating silica (sand), an abundant and common material. Vinyl, on the other hand, commonly known as polyvinyl chloride (PVC), is a thermoplastic made from a polymer of toxic, oil-based chemicals and chlorine (salt).

REMEMBER

Knowing the source of a material starts to shape how you view its impact.

What Are the By-Products of Harvesting This Material?

Collecting and harvesting any material will have some sort of by-product (which isn't necessarily good or bad). Harvesting apples produces jobs, keeps the apples from rotting on the ground, and (most importantly) provides apples to eat! The more complex the material, however, the more complex (typically) the by-products of harvesting it.

Commonly used materials often can have surprisingly terrible by-products. For example, drywall, the building material used for the interior of walls in countless buildings, comes from the mining of gypsum from the earth. Mining all that raw gypsum destroys the surrounding landscape, contributing to soil degradation, biohabitat loss, and destruction of biodiversity.

REMEMBER

Mapping out the extent of these by-products helps start the thought process to avoid them in a more circular approach.

What Are the By-Products of Manufacturing This Material?

After the raw materials have been harvested, they have to undergo some sort of manufacturing and processing to make them into a final product. This processing is often the stage with the most negative environmental impact.

Continuing with the earlier drywall example, all that mined gypsum is heated at a high temperate to treat and convert the materials into a stable mix. This gypsum mix is then ground up and mixed with several chemical additives to add fire, water, and mold resistance. The wet plaster gypsum mix is formed into a panel and sandwiched between two layers of heavy, recycled paper. This panel is then heated again in a giant kiln oven, where it hardens until it's strong enough to be used as a wall panel.

All this manufacturing, including heating the raw mix and firing the panels, consumes almost 1 percent of all US energy. Over 30 billion square feet of new drywall is produced every year. Producing 1,000 square feet of drywall needed for a typical home requires around 2 million BTUs of natural gas and generates 234 pounds of carbon dioxide. The manufacturing of drywall produces 51 million tons of greenhouse gases every year, contributing to climate change.

REMEMBER

Understanding the impacts generated from manufacturing helps to uncover ways to embrace more circular processes and reduce those impacts.

How Is the Material Delivered?

After the materials or products have been produced, they have to get to where they're needed. The packaging, shipping, transporting, delivery, and receiving of materials is typically done with massive amounts of energy from the use of ships, trains, or trucks powered by fossil fuels. (Even electric trains are still powered by fossil-fuel-powered electricity. Solar-powered trains and trucks don't quite exist yet.)

After the materials or products arrive, they usually sit in a warehouse, where they're often shipped again to another warehouse or store or directly to the end user. The distance these materials or products travel affects the amount of carbon emissions that are produced along the way.

REMEMBER

Selecting and sourcing local (or, at least, closer) materials reduces these carbon emissions and moves you closer to the circular approach.

How Is the Material Installed?

After the materials or products arrive at their final destination, they might not require any sort of installation. If you order a set of dishes for your kitchen, they arrive and you use the plates anytime you want. Other materials might require assembly or installation.

Depending on the material, this installation may need adhesives, sealants, urethanes, cutting, or sanding. These typically involve the use of harmful chemicals or require labor-intensive methods.

REMEMBER

Considering the installation needs for a material helps to identify ways to have less dependency on chemicals or labor, and might even create opportunities to allow the material to be more easily recycled later, at the end of its life.

How Is the Material Maintained, Powered, or Operated?

Certain materials don't require much maintenance or care. A piece of clothing needs only to be washed, dried, and hung back in the closet. A sofa really only needs a light vacuuming and the good sense to avoid spilling wine on it. Other materials don't get off so easily.

Those hardwood floors in your kitchen may eventually need to be sanded and refinished. Your beloved cell phone needs constant recharging in order to be useful. That computer printer consumes expensive inkjet cartridges in order to work. These consumables add to the lifecycle impact and cost of owning that material.

REMEMBER

Knowing how much power or maintenance is required to keep a product in good working order can inform your decision on whether you even want it. A truly circular material wouldn't need massive amounts of energy or a steady supply of disposable cartridges.

How Healthy Are the Materials?

Our modern lives are surrounded by products made from an unhealthy concoction of carcinogens, toxins, and chemicals. The average household contains over 17,000 petrochemicals known to affect human health.

The collective impact of this chemical exposure is still up for debate among doctors but one thing is clear — it's harmful to your health.

That new-paint smell in your recently painted bedroom? It comes from volatile organic compounds (VOCs), a variety of chemicals that can cause eye, nose, and throat irritation, shortness of breath, headaches, fatigue, nausea, dizziness, and skin problems.

That new-car smell in your fancy, new vehicle? That comes from more carcinogens, phthalates, and endocrine disruptors, which have a direct impact on human health.

(Not to get too science-y here, but carcinogens are chemicals that are tied to causing cancer in humans; phthalates are groups of chemicals typically used to make plastics harder, but are linked to neurodevelopmental and fertility problems; and endocrine disruptors interfere with the body's hormones. They are trouble!)

REMEMBER

Pushing for organic, natural, unfinished, or healthy materials reduces your exposure to these harmful chemicals. Reducing or avoiding toxic materials not only improves health, but makes it easier to recycle and reuse.

What Can We Do with These Materials After We're Done with Them?

The common approach to discarding used up or unwanted materials is to simply throw them away. The trouble is that there really is no place called "away." Instead, discarded items end up in landfills where they leech toxic chemicals into the soil and groundwater. In addition, most of these items contain valuable natural resources that have been overharvested to the point that we cannot simply keep consuming them.

Some materials can be easily disassembled and recycled or repurposed into other products. Glass and aluminum and certain plastics are examples of materials that can be sorted and recycled into other (often less complex) products.

Other materials can be collected and remade into exactly the same product. For example, manufacturers can offer take-back programs, where they collect your discarded products (furniture or ceiling tiles, for example) and remake them into new versions of the same product.

REMEMBER

Any material that can't be recycled or remanufactured should be made from bio-degradable materials. This way, if you think you'll just end up throwing the product in the trash, at least the product can break down naturally and not spread toxins into the ground. Biodegradable materials should be the last option, as they still release greenhouse gas emissions while breaking down.

What Can Be Done to Extend, Prolong, or Maintain the Material?

Given that most materials and products are treated as disposable and end up in landfills, this question seeks to find ways to increase the useful life of a material. The possible answers to this question can be fun and creative.

Imagine a computer laptop that's designed with swappable components to allow for easy upgrades. Imagine a carpet tile that's durable and stain resistant, so it's used well beyond the typical carpet life of five years. Imagine a pair of pants that comes with matching patches so that you repair them and extend their useful life.

REMEMBER

Rethinking our approach to disposal is the key to redesigning for a circular economy.

What Can We Do to Encourage the Reuse, Refurbishment, Redistribution, or Remanufacture of the Material?

Regardless of how durable someone makes a material as part of a strategy to extend its useful life, eventually the time will come when consumers no longer want or need it. To prevent the typical take-make-waste approach to materials so common in traditional linear economies, this question uncovers opportunities to divert and direct materials to stay circular and remain useful.

Solutions designed to answer this question require some creative thinking. It might require financial incentives, such as rebates or partial refunds for returning old materials. Another approach might be to design for reconfiguration so that a cabinet can be arranged in new ways that updates its appearance or functionality. Alternatively, the material might be made with a replaceable top layer so that you can peel off one color, apply a new one, and suddenly have the appearance of a new material without creating all the waste that goes with it.

Chapter **23**

Ten Questions to Foster Innovative Thinking

Every year, humans throw away over 14 billon tons of *stuff*. That's over 4,400 pounds of material that will sit in a landfill and leech chemicals into the ground and then never get used again. Although our planet is big, it's not big enough for an endless pile of waste.

The whole idea of building a circular economy aims to address this situation by rejecting an outdated take-make-waste model of endlessly extracting, producing, and consuming that has dominated our approach to manufacturing for centuries. To design-out waste, so to speak, we need to reinvent our models of business, manufacturing, and use. A paradigm shift like this one requires some innovative thinking and asking some really big questions (that normally aren't asked).

This chapter presents ten questions to get your innovative and creative juices flowing so that you can start the process of creating a more circular product or service.

Figure 23-1 shows the order of strategies to make something circular and are in order from the most circular to the least circular. While every improvement is useful, Figure 23-1 is a great reference for seeing how refusing or rethinking a product (at the top) is much more impactful than simply recycling or using energy recovery (at the bottom).

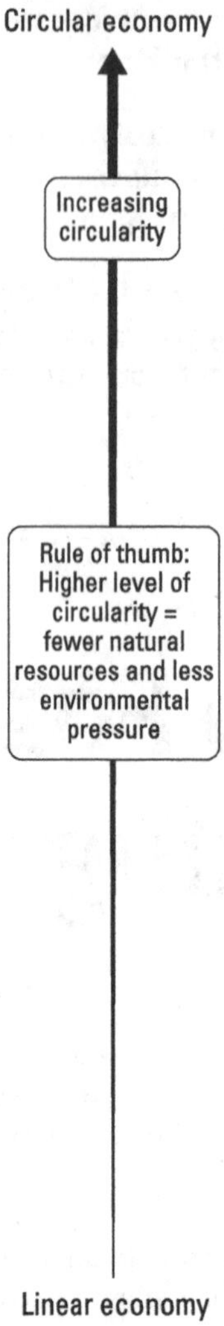

		Strategies	
Increasing circularity ↑	Smarter product use and manufacture	R0 Refuse	Make product redundant by abandoning its function or by offering the same function with a radically different product
		R1 Rethink	Make product use more intensive (e.g. through sharing products, or by putting multi-functional products on the market)
		R2 Reduce	Increase efficiency in product manufacture or use by consuming fewer natural resources and materials
Rule of thumb: Higher level of circularity = fewer natural resources and less environmental pressure	Extend lifespan of product and its parts	R3 Re-use	Re-use by another consumer of discarded product which is still in good condition and fulfills its original function
		R4 Repair	Repair and maintenance of defective product so it can be used with its original function
		R5 Refurbish	Restore an old product and bring it up to date
		R6 Remanufacture	Use parts of discarded product in a new product with the same function
		R7 Repurpose	Use discarded product or its parts in a new product with a different function
	Useful application of materials	R8 Recycle	Process materials to obtain the same (high grade) or lower (low grade) quality
		R9 Recover	Incineration of materials with energy recovery

FIGURE 23-1: Circularity and the 10 Rs.

Linear economy ↓

How Can We Make This Product Redundant?

So many products simply don't need to exist, whether they're single-use disposable products (like water bottles) or single-function products (like that avocado slicer that can be replaced by a kitchen knife). Exploring ways to make a product redundant by offering the same function with a radically different product or abandoning the function altogether might eliminate the need for it to exist.

How Can We Rethink How This Product Is Used?

Most products are designed around a set of assumptions that are never questioned — assuming that they will be used by only one person or stored in only one household, for example. If we rethink how, where, and by whom this product will be used, new possibilities begin to open up. Consider how car- and bike-share programs work and how we might rethink those products to encourage increased use by more people. Could this product instead be provided as a service that is shared among many people?

How Can We Reduce the Resources or Materials Used?

Most disposable products contain some type of plastic (in the packaging or the product), all of which comes from oil. Even products without plastic still depend on the extraction of the planet's dwindling natural resources. Rather than assume that these impacts are simply a result of the cost of doing business, are there ways to increase the efficiency of how the raw materials are used (less material); how they're manufactured (less energy); or how they're produced (less waste)?

In What Ways Can This Product Be Reused by Another Consumer?

Most products are designed around individual ownership. (You own a lawn mower and I own a lawn mower.) As a result, most products sit unused most of the time. (Your lawn mower is probably used an hour a week and sits idle the remaining 167 hours.) Instead, we should consider approaches that encourage sharing or encourage people to recycle discarded products in good condition in order to reuse them. This might influence the design to have objects such as wheels and a handle (encourages sharing) or user settings (encourages multiple users).

In What Ways Can This Product Be More Easily Maintained and Repaired?

Used long enough, any product eventually wears out, breaks down, or needs some type of repair. Rather than throw the product away, we should instead see all materials as having value and redesign them to allow for their repair and ongoing maintenance. Perhaps that button that always wears out is designed to be replaced, or that handle that typically cracks is designed to pop off and be replaced.

In What Ways Can This Product Be Restored or Kept Up-to-Date?

Even the most beloved products will pick up the patina of scratches and aging. Once we decide to redesign objects to last longer, we might use materials that can be refinished, repainted, or restored. For tech products, we might redesign them so that it's easier to swap out circuits, memory, or storage to bring them back up-to-date. All these strategies extend the useful life of a product.

How Can Discarded Parts Be Remade into a New Version of the Same Product?

For certain products, only parts of them wear out and need replacement (like the top layer of carpet tile). The other parts might still be in good condition. We can redesign products to allow for them to be separated back into parts, to allow the manufacturer to remake them into new versions of the same product. One example is separating the carpet backing from the worn-out top surface to be remade into new backing.

While most recycling takes a product and downgrades it into something less useful (a plastic bottle is recycled into a trash can), this question is asking to remake the product into the same product and preserves its value.

How Can Discarded Parts Be Remade Into a New Product?

For certain other products, their parts cannot be remade into the same product but can potentially be made into another one. Automobile tires are difficult to make into new tires because of their chemical composition, but those same tires can be easily collected and formed into a new product, such as rubber flooring. Remaking discarded parts into new materials reduces waste and the demand for virgin materials.

If the product cannot be remade into the same product, perhaps it can at least be made into something useful. To help facilitate this, the product or material should be redesigned to be disassembled.

In What Ways Can We Recycle These Materials into Quality Products?

Each year, millions of tons of plastic end up in local landfills and then head downstream into our oceans, where you can find 6 times more plastic than phytoplankton and 50 times more plastic than zooplankton (by weight). We can redesign and use products that are recyclable. The comingling of recycled plastic water bottles with other materials makes them difficult to turn into new plastic water bottles, but those same bottles can be made into thousands of other useful products. Only around a third of plastic water bottles are recycled; the rest end up in landfills.

How Can We Dispose of This Material in a Manner That Recovers Energy?

Although we can redesign a product to be infinitely reused, remade, or recycled, certain materials can still end up being thrown "away" or discarded. We can prepare for this by redesigning the products to use materials that can be converted into energy — incinerating organic materials can generate a form of clean energy, for example. Though not the ideal reuse of a product, it does wring one last bit of usefulness from it, and it's certainly better than ending up in a landfill.

Chapter **24**

Ten Questions to Ask about Your Supply Chain

E very product has a lifecycle, or a series of steps that make up its life. This path of a product — from the design of the product itself and production of that product to the manufacturing process and from the packaging and distribution to the eventual sale — requires high levels of planning and organization to ensure that it reaches its intended customer. The sale of a product, for most businesses, is where their involvement ends, unfortunately. By not participating in the life of the product *post-sale*, businesses are missing out on an array of opportunities to eliminate the amount of waste they produce during the manufacturing process, improve the durability and resilience of their product, and eliminate costs associated with raw material extraction by recapturing the product after the consumer no longer needs or wants it.

In this chapter, we two coauthors help you explore the questions you can ask about your supply chain to maximize the value of a circular economy framework. By doing this, you can then either critically assess an existing supply chain and identify key intervention opportunities for improvement or let these questions aid in the creation of a new supply chain. In addition, we'll explain why addressing the entire supply chain is critical in order to pinpoint opportunities for efficiency. and value creation Don't view the following steps, which are laid out in a specific order, as a linear process — view them instead as a circular one. By *circular*, we mean that the last step of the supply chain (reclaiming the product) influences the first step of the supply chain (product design). If, after completing each step, there's still room for improvement, complete the cycle again until waste has been eliminated, the product's use rate has been maximized, and the demand for raw materials has nearly vanished.

REMEMBER

A material lifecycle and a product supply chain are not the same thing. A material lifecycle addresses the life of a material, and a supply chain addresses the process of producing, using, and discarding the product itself. Many material lifecycles can be involved within a single product supply chain. Although there are obviously some points of overlap, addressing these two areas separately is the key to fostering a circular system.

What Drives Your Product Design?

No one can focus only on profit any more. Seriously. We mean it. When we say *profit*, we are referring to initial profit, not future savings. This short-term, surface-level way of thinking about product design is responsible for our presence in a society that supports a linear economy to begin with. It's the reason landfills exist. It's the reason the oceans now hold more plastic than fish. It's the reason that everything costs more than it needs to. By prioritizing initial profit, we're ignoring the opportunity to create future value. Product designs obviously need to account for initial profitability to allow the company to survive and maintain the services provided, but it's also important to realize that there's more to account for. Profit can be increased indirectly by reducing future costs.

The question "What drives your product design?" acts as the first of ten questions to ask about the supply chain within this chapter because it forces you to consider what is often dismissed: the other variables outlined within this chapter that contribute to the creation of a circular supply chain. What drives your product design should be driven by customer needs, the interaction between the product and user (direct sale or lease?), the stakeholders involved (are wholesalers required?), the materials involved (and how many), and the production, sale, delivery, repair, maintenance, and eventual recovery of your product. When these issues are all properly addressed, profit is a natural outcome. So, what drives your design?

What Are Your Users' Needs?

Initial cost isn't the only variable when it comes to your users' needs. Product designs typically assume that low cost is the primary user need, whereas the durability and ease of maintenance of the product are dismissed. Although users do find competitive pricing attractive, it certainly isn't the only variable at play.

Consider how other user needs can potentially influence a purchasing decision and determine how these needs can contribute to developing a circular supply chain. Will the user need to lease or purchase the product? Will they need support in the repair or maintenance of the product after they've received it? Will the user have the option to sell your own product back to you or easily replace it after the product reaches its end of life? Consider how you can optimize all these areas to benefit the user.

Discovering the user's needs greatly impacts how the product itself is shaped — size, weight, color, material, texture, and so on — but it also impacts other areas of the supply chain that will lead to the reduction of waste, an increased rate of use, and the effect it has on the surrounding environment.

Will Your Customers Access or Will They Own Your Product?

Determining whether you will sell or lease a product greatly influences the product's supply chain. If products have a high use rate — a cell phone, for example — it makes sense to design the supply chain with the intention of selling this product. If a product has a relatively low use rate — like an automobile, which on average spends 95 percent of its life parked in the garage or on the street — it makes sense to design the supply chain with the intention of renting this product instead. Since one of the goals of the circular economy is to increase the usage of a product during its lifetime, by determining the use rate of a product, we can determine what the most attractive business/customer transaction might be and maximize the use rate of a single product before it reaches the end of its life.

You might be wondering how leasing a product, rather than selling it, would affect the supply chain. Well, let's use a moving truck as an example. When families move from one house to another, they often need a large moving truck to transport their furniture and the endless boxes of keepsakes they've been storing in their basements for the past decade. Because the use rate for a moving truck is low, we wouldn't expect a family to purchase the truck and store it until their next move. The value isn't there. Instead, moving trucks are leased, which allows the product's use rate to grow drastically and generate revenue for the leasing agent. Determining that this particular product will primarily be leased would then encourage you to design this product — the moving truck — so that it's simple to use, with instructions available on how to use the built-in ramp, properly secure items in the back, and contact the company to hire third-party movers (another service that may be available). Knowing that this product will be leased might also motivate the manufacture to make the vehicle more durable so it will last longer, and therefore, hold the capacity to generate more revenue throughout its life. Knowing that this product will be leased might also encourage the product to prominently display, on its side panels, details about the company website, the costs associated with renting, and the unique features of the vehicle, in order to market the product to other potential customers while in use. It is a *mobile* billboard, after all.

If someone were to tell me ten years ago that I could list my house on a website named Airbnb and make money renting out my home, I would have called them nuts! That's what hotels are for, right? And who would want to stay in a stranger's home, anyway? But the world is changing. Examples like Airbnb perfectly illustrate how user needs have shifted and new business opportunities are emerging in response. An item that was typically sold — such as a home — now has opportunities to be leased instead.

TIP

Determining whether your product will be sold or leased allows you to analyze the supply chain and identify ways to incorporate circular processes.

Who Are Your Partners?

Determining whether your product will be sold or leased (or perhaps both) is crucial, but it's also important to identify who else needs to be involved in the supply chain. Even if you own your own small business selling produce on the side of the road, you'll still have partners who support your operations

Not only is identifying your partners important for logistical reasons, like who produces the packing in which the product will be delivered or even who is responsible for delivering the product to the user's front door, but selecting the right partners also determines your ability to optimize the supply chain. It's extremely unlikely that you will be in control of the entire supply chain on which your product depends, which is why it's vital to identify the partners who are willing to work with you and adjust their services to meet your interests in eliminating waste, increasing the rate of use, or eliminating the need for raw materials.

REMEMBER

The best partners are the ones who are willing to improve their operations not only with you but also for you.

What Materials Are Required?

Many variables come into play when determining which materials are required for your product. Aside from the materials required to produce the product itself, other materials are essential in the processing, manufacturing, and shipping of the product. By first identifying which materials are required, you have the opportunity to make improvements when possible.

Once all materials and areas of improvement are identified, these four priority steps lead to the optimization of those materials:

1. Phase out materials and substances that are harmful to the environment and humans. Only materials that have a net-neutral or net-positive impact on the environment health, on human health, and have an ethical supply chain should be used within a circular economy framework.

2. Use durable materials that allow for heavy use. By relying on cheap materials that fail soon after they're used, the value of durability is lost to the capture, recycling, and remanufacturing of that material.

3. When a material has reached the end of its first life, it should be easily reusable, repairable and lastly recyclable. This means that not only does the material itself need to be recyclable but also the other materials it's paired with.

4. Prioritize the use of renewable materials.

Although finite materials are a critical component of the global economy, they cannot be generated and therefore should be considered a last resort. Check out Chapter 13 for more about selecting the right materials.

TIP

Consider what impact the materials you choose will have on the other steps of the supply chain. The durability of the selected material determines the amount of maintenance required. The weight affects shipping costs, and the recyclability of the material affects your ability to reclaim the value of that material at the end of its life.

How Will You Produce Your Product?

To allow for a circular supply chain to exist, a product *must* be produced with reclaimed materials, not raw materials. Any product that can't be produced with reclaimed materials will be forever dependent on raw materials, and, with no opportunity for recycling, the product will have no value at the end of its life. If some raw materials are absolutely necessary, be sure that that they're renewable rather than finite.

Processing should limit the use of harmful materials and chemicals. Given that one goal of the circular economy is to provide the natural environment with the chance to regenerate itself, relying on harmful substances that hold the potential to pollute the natural environment is counterintuitive. Reconsider how the same product can be manufactured without the use of harmful substances. This may be done successfully via the generation of a new process or an alternative material.

To facilitate frequent usage, the production of your product should embody a commitment to durability and ease of maintenance. The value of a product is determined by its ability to provide a service over a long period and avoid unnecessary replacement costs. By producing a durable product in a way that allows it to be easily maintained, your competitive edge will increase *and* your users will have a reason for continuing to buy your product, by relying on you for maintenance education.

How Will Users Receive Your Product?

For several reasons, bricks and mortar shopping still exists. It allows you to physically review the item you're interested in purchasing, to make sure it's undamaged and it facilitates the one-on-one interaction that some humans enjoy. However, shipping is undeniably becoming the standard way to receive products. Even products that were once considered too large to ship — like cars — are now considered shippable. Carvana, for example, lets users select a car online and have it delivered to their door. What's next? Houses? Knowing that people increasingly prefer the shipping strategy will shape other areas of the supply chain, like which partners you'll need to deliver your product and in which state of assembly it's delivered.

REMEMBER

Preassembled versus assembly required — that is the question. Though the assembly-required option reduces packaging requirements because the individual components can be consolidated into a much smaller package, the assembly of certain products may be so complex that you have no option but to send it preassembled. In this situation, although the ability to reduce the quantity of packing required for delivery is limited, the ability to appropriately size the packaging and select renewable packaging material is not.

TIP

Many companies are realizing that at-home delivery is becoming the go-to route for users to acquire their products, which means that packaging and shipping considerations hold a new level of importance. Many companies are investing large amounts of money to ensure that the job is done right. Amazon, for example, now combines lab testing, machine learning, material science, and manufacturing partnerships to ensure that its packaging is right-sized and fully recyclable.

How Will You Support the Repair and Maintenance of Your Product?

It may seem like you'd be drilling a hole in the bottom of your own ship by providing users with the ability to repair and maintain their own products — rather than have them simply buy new ones. But in reality, the benefits outweigh the costs. By empowering users to extend the lifespan of the products they purchase, you create new markets related to maintenance and repair education. On top of that, not only does building in ease of repair and maintenance reduce the overall cost imposed on users — they won't have to keep replacing a broken product with a brand-new one — but it also embeds reliability into your business practice. And creates a stronger and potentially longer customer/manufacturer relationship.

The Empowering Repair Co. Project — a collaborative effort between eBay, HP, and iFixit — helps to address the need for more products that are easier to repair and the various levels of support to make it happen. Clearly, an increased level of repair is required in order to extend product lifespans and essentially increase the value of the energy and material embedded in products by keeping them in use for longer periods. This project outlines many barriers that limit the potential for a larger, fixer movement to occur — a complementary movement running adjacent to the maker movement — such as a lack of repair information, lack of affordable spare parts, and limited repair capabilities stemming from poor product design. A product can be repaired only if it's designed to be easy to repair.

TIP

The Ellen MacArthur Foundation explains the Empowering Repair Co. Project here:

```
www.ellenmacarthurfoundation.org/assets/downloads/ce100/Empowering-
    Repair-Final-Public1.pdf
```

What Refurbishment Options Will You Offer for Your Product?

When one element of a product no longer works, often the entire product is considered broken, which is far from reality. Imagine if you break your leg and the doctor says, "Well, this patient is a goner — pull the plug." It doesn't make sense! Although a stigma is commonly applied against refurbished items, they're critical components of the circular economy. If you're unfamiliar with the concept, the *refurbishment* of an item involves extracting the still-functional elements of a product and reincorporating them into a new product. Although the parts them-selves aren't new, they still function as they should and therefore still have value.

REMEMBER

Utilizing refurbished elements of a product requires a high level of quality assur-ance, cleaning, and repair. Once a product is disassembled, the failing elements have been removed, and the functioning elements are identified, you should ensure that those functioning elements are in a truly reusable state before rein-corporating them into a new product. If those pieces have no major flaws, they can be cleaned and minor imperfections can be repaired before those elements are used again.

Selling refurbished products at a lower price than a new product price is valuable for both the business and the customer. For the business, a large percentage of the costs associated with producing a product has been eliminated by using existing pieces. The cost difference between a new product and a refurbished one can be offset by the savings harnessed during the refurbishment process. From the cus-tomer's side, they get a relatively new product at a fraction of the price. Both sides win, waste is eliminated, and materials are in use for longer periods.

How Will You Reclaim Your Product at Its End of Life?

All products still have innate value at the end of their lives, via their functionality or just their material content, and therefore there is value in developing a supply chain that recaptures products at the end of their lifecycle and reincorporates those elements back into the system. If the product is beyond the point of being refurbished, there is still innate value in the materials themselves.

The biggest roadblock to reclaiming products at the end of their lives is setting up a system that properly incentivizes users to return their products to the supply chain after the product is broken or they no longer want or need it. IKEA is attempting to create such a system by offering the Buyback Program, which distributes payments to customers who return their previously purchased IKEA items. These items are then repaired, as needed, and resold to future users. Items that aren't resold are either recycled or donated to local community projects. IKEA is committed to being 100 percent circular by 2030, and this buyback program is a critical step.

As shown in the IKEA example, reincorporating elements requires the repair of products and the recycling of materials — as a last resort — if elements of a prod-uct are beyond repair. Although recycling is a last resort and there is little value in recycling materials, the true value stems from the efforts made early on in the supply chain to increase durability and repairability of the product to begin with.

Chapter **25**

Ten Questions That Reveal How Much Your Waste Is Costing You

Waste is often seen as valueless. That's why you throw it out to begin with: It serves no purpose and therefore should be disposed of, right? The entire system on which our lives as consumers function has been designed under a false premise: Waste is inevitable and holds no value. But that's not reality. Waste still holds value, in many ways, and in the end, it's costing you much more than you think. Dealing with waste is time consuming; it harms not only human health but environmental health as well. Also, ensuring waste is properly sorted between recyclables and non-recyclables requires a lot of human effort! The cost of waste is often ignored, misrepresented, or separated from the waste itself. It doesn't matter how the truth is bent and shifted — waste is costing you.

In this chapter, we help you explore the ten ways that waste is costing you, and we offer some new perspectives. Waste doesn't need to cost you. Instead, it can be of value to you. By addressing how waste costs you, we hope to help you uncover opportunities for your trash to become your treasure.

What Labor Costs Are Tied to Waste Disposal?

It takes human labor to collect waste from homes, businesses, and communities. It also takes human labor to transport that waste from these various sources to the local or regional landfill. And the need for human involvement doesn't stop there, either — no, it also takes human labor to properly dispose of and maintain this collection of waste after it arrives at its destination. Waste doesn't stop costing us once it arrives at the landfill. It costs us for as long as it's there.

Waste management generally requires human labor regardless of what you decide to do with it — whether you're disposing of waste, sorting out and recycling waste, or even burning waste. In each case, human hours will be a variable at play. By exploring how we spend those hours, we can usher in real change and provide a proper transition from a linear economy to a circular one. Through this lens — the idea that human labor and time are required in order to deal with waste, no matter what we do — we can start to explore how each investment of human time compares against the others in terms of cost and then select the option that eliminates waste altogether. You'll find that, by directing human labor toward circular processes, waste actually holds a lot of value.

Human labor is often seen as a cost rather than a source of value. This view can change, however. For example, though human labor is required in order to collect waste from the homes, businesses, and communities that produce it, some of that labor can be redirected instead toward the separation, cleaning, and recycling of waste. By redefining human labor as investment rather than as overhead and lost time, it becomes clear that human hours can be directed toward the reclamation of value from waste rather than simply added in as a source of waste itself. What was once a cost is now a new source of value.

What Is the Real Cost of Waste Disposal?

Imagine for a minute how much energy goes into disposing of waste: a global fleet of (most often) diesel-powered vehicles driving thousands of miles daily to collect waste from homes, businesses, and other sources, only then to travel further to transport waste to its final stop: the landfill or incinerator. Our waste travels more than we do!

After the waste has been delivered to its final destination, entire teams are employed on a full-time basis to manage, process, or burn this collection of waste. These individuals require payment, insurance, and other benefits to perform these services. An entire section of the global economy is fueled to bury or burn the inefficiencies produced from the other segments of the global economy — at an alarming cost. How can this cost continue to be supported when much of the material seen as waste doesn't need to be disposed of? Rather, it simply needs to be redirected to another purpose. By reclaiming materials rather than disposing of them, the costs of waste disposal become the revenue of reclamation.

What Is the Impact on Human Health?

A secondary cost of waste is its impact on human health. The impact of waste on human health is directly related to the impact of waste on environmental health. Waste equals pollution, and pollution harms human health by negatively impacting the many resources on which we are dependent: air, water, and soil, for example. Exposure to the many hazardous chemicals that stem from waste can be lethal, especially for children who are more vulnerable to these toxins. Multiple studies conducted by the Environmental Working Group found an average of some two hundred chemicals and pollutants within umbilical cords — evidence that waste clearly has a negative impact on human health even before a child is even born.

REMEMBER

Although it's difficult to make an overall declaration about the health impacts of waste and its management, the evidence that is available suggests that exposure to waste — throughout its lifecycle — can lead to many serious health outcomes, including an array of cancers, respiratory infections, and birth defects.

So, by continuously producing more waste, we're continuously harming human health. This cost is listed not on your monthly waste management bill but rather on your medical bills. (It's just a thought, but perhaps your waste management bill would be a better location for it.)

How Does Waste Impact Ecosystem Services?

Ecosystem services are environmental functions that provide value to human society. Mycelium (mushrooms) break down complex biomaterials into smaller particles, allowing the surrounding environment to thrive. Birds eat fruit from trees and then distribute those seeds around the local environment by way of their droppings. Bees travel numerous miles to pollinate a wide array of crops that humans consume. These services are provided at no cost to humans, but humans benefit from these services greatly.

When waste is produced, materials that were once in use are removed from the global economy and a demand for new, raw materials is created. This requires damaging ecosystems by extracting materials from the earth, and some of these natural materials provide ecosystem services. Trees, for example, capture stormwater, conserve home energy use by providing shade, and remove pollutants and gases from the air. Completing these services via manmade routes would cost a lot of money. Therefore, these ecosystem services provide society with a lot of value by eliminating the need for humans to complete the service. New York City is aware of the value of ecosystem services and has accounted for each tree's service within the city, via the New York City Street Tree Map, listing, for example, the amount of stormwater intercepted each year as well as the amount of air pollutants that trees filter.

REMEMBER

By wasting materials that can be reused or recycled, we are not only accepting the innate cost of collecting, transporting, and managing waste but also eliminating the value that comes from ecosystem services on top of it. A tree that is harvested for paper can no longer capture stormwater.

What Is the Innate Value of Waste?

Waste isn't just a big mound of black, stinky sludge that sits in a landfill. Well, sometimes it is, but the majority of it is made up of useful materials — like metal, plastic, and glass — that still hold innate value and are only inches away from serving another purpose. On top of basic materials, many products are disposed of when a simple element or component of a product stops working while much of the product is still in working order. It is not just by accident that products fail, either. When a product is designed to fail after a certain amount of time, planned obsolescence has been embedded into the very product itself. This is a defining feature of the linear economy.

Metals, glass, paper products, plastics — all require extraction, processing, and manufacturing to become useful to society. A lot of resources and time go into this process, but these materials (and their embodied energy) are quickly discarded after they have been used once. These materials still hold innate value, and it's nearly always more cost-effective to maintain an existing material rather than discard it and then replace it. Any cost comparison exercise that arrives at an alternative finding surely doesn't include all the lifecycle costs involved.

As for products (essentially, a combination of distinct materials that, when joined together, serve a purpose), in many cases a simple repair is all that's needed for something that's considered waste to be transformed back into a useful function. Within a broken product, functional components still work. Unfortunately, the global economy just isn't set up to acknowledge and value products that need repair, which is why they get thrown away in the first place.

How Much Raw Material Is Required to Offset Waste?

Throwing away a material means that a void is created in the universe. And by *universe*, we mean the supply-and-demand chain. The demand hasn't diminished, so a new source of supply needs to be generated. Since we've thrown out the perfectly functional option, to sit aimlessly for decades with that sweater you bought at Kohl's three years ago that turned out to be a huge mistake (do you remember — during your building-a-better-me phase?), a new resource needs to replace it.

Replacing that material comes at a steep price. The material needs to be extracted from where it originates, processed into the proper shape and form, and then shipped between each stage to eventually replace an item that needed only a proper reuse framework.

REMEMBER

The effort required to source something brand-new is so much greater than creating a system that allows existing materials to be reused, repaired, remanufactured, or recycled. When we avoid raw materials, the embodied energy and value of a material or product can be maintained. The longer a product or material stays in use, the more valuable it becomes.

What Are the Indirect Costs of Waste?

There's an entire industry behind waste management, and that management requires a lot to stay afloat. The business of waste management is no simple task. A lot of organization and coordination are required in order to ensure that waste is managed appropriately, effectively, and efficiently. The companies and institutions responsible for collecting and properly managing your waste have administration requirements that demand packaging, office consumables, human resources, and much more to stay in motion.

Aside from administration and organizational requirements, from a business perspective, waste can cost you not only revenue but also customers. Now, more than ever, the user cares about how companies are developing the goods they're selling. Customers care about corporate responsibility, and those businesses that don't take their social and environmental impacts as seriously as their customers do may find themselves without patrons. Businesses such as Patagonia and Amazon understand that their corporate responsibilities are growing, and their businesses are responding by reassessing the way they create and ship products.

How Much Does Poor Efficiency Cost?

Waste is a result of poor efficiency of process. By this, we mean that the process of manufacturing, creating, producing, or making whatever product has been designed has been done inefficiently. Producing waste as an outcome of a process means that waste — or a collection of material that has no automatic next step in its lifecycle — hasn't been used to generate something of value.

This inefficiency comes at a cost, and the management of waste is only half the problem. Waste requires collection, processing, shipping, and eventual disposal at a landfill or burning at an incinerator. Even if electricity is generated by burning waste, the value obtained never is greater than or equal to the innate value that the collection of waste embodies.

The other half of the problem that is rarely accounted for is the absence of value that could have been obtained if the waste were redirected toward another purpose. A garbage can isn't an alternative dimension where all materials become obsolete. Materials themselves have embodied value — the value tied to the resources and efforts required to extract, process, and ship to you for use — and are also valuable in the sense that they can be redirected to serve another purpose.

What Natural Resources Are Required for Waste?

Natural resources — energy, water, and other materials — are required during all stages of a product's lifecycle. The sourcing of materials, the processing and shipment of those materials, the use of those materials, and the eventual disposal of those materials all require natural resources.

Waste itself, even, requires natural resources to be collected, shipped, and processed. With waste comes pollution, which also holds an environmental cost. The methane released from landfills and the burning of trash emit harmful chemicals and gases that pollute the world's natural resource base and contribute to anthropogenic-sourced climate change. Much of the solid waste that fails to reach the landfill or incinerator finds its way into bodies of water and eventually into the ocean. Here, an array of aquatic animals ingest this trash and die from it. This mismanagement of waste has severe impacts on the natural resources we depend on.

On top of it all, waste is an unused resource that has forever been removed from global circulation. By allowing this situation, we are creating a demand for raw materials to replace the previous materials. This ever-growing demand for resources continues to decimate natural landscapes via deforestation, mining, and other harmful actions.

What Waste Remediation Will Be Required?

Human demand for new resources already exceeds the carrying capacity of the planet, so materials that were once considered waste will soon need to be recaptured in order to meet the ever-growing demand for resources. This need for materials, which will come at great cost, will be the true primary motivation behind environmental remediation — not some hoped-for global shift in mindfulness or calls for environmental stewardship.

The day will come when landfills are mined for valuable resources, just like natural landscapes are today. Sorting through fields of decades-old debris will require extensive amounts of energy, water, and materials, but will be more cost-effective than sourcing raw materials from the natural environment. In addition to landfills, oceans will become a source of valuable resources — especially plastics — and will be widely screened and filtered to recapture the materials that have been polluting them for decades.

Every element of the natural landscape — soils, bodies of water, habitats in general — will be allowed to regenerate themselves when human society successfully finds a way to substitute the current use of ecological services with lab-based or alternative growing methods. Commercial foods of high demand, such as greens and other vegetables, will no longer be grown in soil, but will be sourced from artificial environments where all variables can be controlled and altered to create a nutrient-dense product. This strategy will use minimal amounts of water and will substitute simple growth mediums paired with nutrient-dense water for soil. Also, soil-grown crops will mostly stem from individual properties through gardening.

Index

International Organization for Standardization (ISO), 92
International Sustainability and Carbon Certification (ISCC), 342
inventory, hidden cost of, 104–105
iPhone, 73–74, 131
iron, 213
Ivaldi, 282

J

jargon, greenwashing and, 108
jobs
  central to the circular economy, 338
  enabling the circular economy, 338–339
  future of, 336–341
  indirectly related to circular economy, 339
joining business networking support groups, 151–152
junk cars, selling for scrap, 147

K

Keen, 203
Keynes, John Maynard (economist), 31
Kidizen, 189
Koch Industries, 50
Kohl's, 385

L

labor costs, 250, 382
Lacy, Peter (author)
  Waste to Wealth: The Circular Economy Advantage, 336
landfills, 35, 155, 265
launch stage, in business lifecycles, 97
leaders for change, 14–16
Leadership in Energy and Environmental Design (LEED), 224, 273
legumes, 252
Levi's, 142
liability, 44–45
lifecycle assessment (LCA) tools, 118, 199, 277

Lifecycle Costing (LCC), 278
Lifecycle Impact Assessment (LCIA), 278
Lifecycle Inventory (LCI), 278
lifecycles
  assessing for buildings, 276–281
  building for a, 273–274
  of businesses, 97
  costs of products, 329
lifespans, for products, 86
lifestyle of health and sustainability (LOHAS), 46
lifestyles, that foster health and sustainability, 46
Lindeblad, Abrahamsson (designer), 204–205
linear economy
  about, 23–25
  circular economy *versus,* 60–64
  compared with circular economy, 36–37
  difficulty of change, 36–40
  making wrong materials, 31–34
  taking wrong materials, 25–31
  waste and, 144–145
  wasting wrong materials, 34–36
linen, 314
LiquidSpace, 269
listening, to customers, 109–110
livestock waste, 191
Living Building Challenge, 225
living laboratories, 351
local production, 234–241
logging, 284
Loliware, 143
Loop, in ReSOLVE framework, 42, 82, 268
Looptworks, 143
Lovins, Amory (author)
  Natural Capitalism, 52
Lovins, Hunter (author)
  Natural Capitalism, 52
Lush Cosmetics, 91, 109
Lyft, 115–116, 119, 188, 350
LyftUp, 116
Lyle, John T. (architect), 51
Lyle Center for Regenerative Studies, 51
lyocell, 314

M

macro food hub, 349

Made Safe, 224

maintenance
  of materials, 364
  of products, 370, 379

makers, circular economy for, 275–296

management zones, permaculture, 256–257

managing
  demand for business services, 81–83
  food, 348–349
  food waste, 321–322
  material lifecycle performance, 128–131
  office supplies, 333–334

manufacturability, 131

manufactured capital, 86

manufacturing
  additive, 281–283
  circular economy for, 275–296
  as a design stage, 272
  designing products to be remanufactured, 130
  material lifecycles and, 362–363
  product stewardship and, 70–71
  reducing waste generated by, 141

markets
  developing new, 150–151
  failure of, 59
  product obsoletion and saturation of, 104

massive open online courses (MOOCs), 343–344

Material Circularity Indicators (MCIs), 48–49

material lifecycles
  about, 16, 165–166, 179–181, 195–196, 361
  analyzing materials, 198–200
  analyzing operations, 201–202
  analyzing process of, 179–193
  biological materials, 18–19
  byproducts, 362–363
  compared with supply chain, 374
  delivery of material, 363
  Ellen MacArthur Foundation's Butterfly Diagram, 169–176
  end-of-life, 365–366

environmental impact, 166–169

extending materials, 366

function of, 196–198

harvesting, 362

health of materials, 364–365

identifying where change can occur, 184–187

improving, 195–205

installation of material, 364

maintenance of materials, 364

managing performance of, 128–131

manufacturing, 362–363

opportunities for optimization, 187–191

processes for, 181–184

reusing materials, 366

source of materials, 362

sourcing, suppliers, and customers, 202–203

take-make-waste, 17

technical materials, 17–18, 19

upcycling *versus* downcycling, 19

material loops, 118

material metrics, 42

materials
  about, 207–208, 227–228
  cardboard, 214–217
  certifications and standards, 223–225
  concrete, 218–219
  disposing of, 371
  diversity of, 89
  ethics and, 223
  exploring, 208
  glass, 217–218
  hazardous, 219–222
  hemp, 219
  keeping in use, 231–234, 264
  metals, 212–213
  oil compared with plastics, 208–212
  paper products, 214–217
  red list, 220
  red list alternatives, 221
  redesigning, 228–231
  reducing, 369
  requirements for, 377

About the Authors

Eric Corey Freed is an award-winning architect, 12-time author, global speaker, and notorious comedian. As a sought-out lecturer, he has educated more than 300,000 people across all 50 states and 7 countries on issues related to sustainability, high-performance building, and the built environment. His books and videos have been viewed by over a million people worldwide.

As a licensed architect, Eric brings nearly 30 years of experience in helping architects, builders, and owners use sustainability to improve the design and operational savings for thousands of buildings around the country. Companies such as Autodesk, Pixar, Apple, and Lowe's have hired him to help them incorporate deeper sustainability into their businesses.

Eric is a returning *For Dummies* author, having written his award-winning *Green Building & Remodeling For Dummies* (2007) as well as *Green Your Home For Dummies* (2008). He coauthored another Wiley title, *Sustainable School Architecture* (2010) as well as *Green$ense for the Home: Rating the Payoff from 50 Green Home Projects* (from Taunton Press). The latter won the 2011 Outstanding Book Award from the American Society of Journalists and Authors.

Eric has served on the boards and advisory boards of dozens of companies and nonprofits throughout his career, focused on helping them get "unstuck" through strategy, planning, and implementation for next-stage planning. His real skill lies in helping these organizations connect the dots and uncover new opportunities to raise funding, generate revenue, attract customers, and streamline operations. He does this through the lens of sustainability: return on investment, lifecycle costing, carbon accounting, social equity, and supply chain optimization.

Considered a leader in his field, Eric was named by *San Francisco* magazine Best Green Architect in 2005 and Best Visionary in 2007. In 2012, he was named one of the 25 Best Green Architecture Firms in the United States, and one of the Top 10 Most Influential Green Architects. In 2017 he was named one of Build's American Architecture Top 25, and the following year he was one of Fixr's Top 200 Influencers in the Construction Industry. He also holds a prestigious LEED Fellow award from the US Green Building Council.

Eric loves talking with people about sustainability and design. For more information on his work and activities, visit circulareconomyfordummies.com or follow him on Twitter: @EricCoreyFreed.

Kyle Ritchie is a trained environmental scientist, circular economy expert, and sustainable design consultant who combines his array of natural resources and environmental management expertise with his passion for optimizing the Architecture, Engineering, and Construction (AEC) industry.

As a sustainable design consultant, Kyle has impacted over a million square feet of building area for award-winning universities and institutions in North America, the Middle East, and Eastern Asia and has improved on the design and operations of student housing facilities, hospitals, laboratories, libraries, and entire campuses. Indiana University, Butler University, Colby College, Duke University, Arizona State University, UCLA, The American University of Bahrain, and dozens of other universities around the world have benefited from Kyle's insight and sustainable design leadership. He provides architectural design reviews and project management for projects pursuing various rating systems, including LEED, WELL, CHPS, Living Building Challenge, and is a LEED BD+C, ID+C, WELL AP, and EcoDistrics accredited professional.

In addition to working with institutions to optimize the built environment, Kyle supports the growth of the sustainable design industry as an adjunct professor at the Boston Architectural College, where he teaches both Energy in The Built Environment II and Resilient Design to graduate students enrolled in the college's sustainable design program. In addition, Kyle speaks internationally on the circular economy movement and partners with non-profits and other organizations world-wide to help motivate a global transition to a circular way of living. He also started the Circular Economy Studio which further aims to facilitate the circular economy practice within the built environment. For circular economy consultation and other services, visit `www.circulareconomy.studio` for more information.

Dedication

Eric: My beautiful wife, Laurie, and I dedicate this book to our powerful daughter, Grayson. The world she'll inherit will need people who can implement the circularity solutions outlined in this book. I strive to make the world a better place for her. (I also want to thank my coauthor, Kyle, for talking me into writing this book.)

Kyle: I dedicate this book to my parents, Alan and Pamela; my brilliant coauthor, Eric; my loving partner, Manasvi; and my dearest friends, who have all shown nothing but confidence in me. None of this would have been possible without you all.

Authors' Acknowledgments

"Although the problems of the world are increasingly complex, the solutions remain embarrassingly simple."

—BILL MOLLISON

As teachers and mentors, we are fortunate to work with hundreds of talented students a year. Their questions, enthusiasm, and energy inspire us daily.

The following people must be thanked by name, and you can just assume that they know what they did to deserve mention:

Daniel Overbey, Ball State University

Krista Stark

Bob Leonard

Maureen Addington

Reniera O'Donnell, The Ellen MacArthur Foundation

We would particularly like to thank our editor, Kristie Pyles, for being such a strict taskmaster and keeping us on schedule through a strategy of fear and intimidation. The staff at Wiley Publishing, Inc., is incredibly impressive, and we are appreciative of their support and vision.

This book could not have been possible without our clients, the generous patrons providing the canvas on which we paint.

Publisher's Acknowledgments

Acquisitions Editor: Tracy Boggier

Senior Managing Editor: Kristie Pyles

Copy Editor: Becky Whitney

Technical Editors: Ashleigh and Jaine Morris

Production Editor: Tamilmani Varadharaj

Cover Image: © efetova/Getty Images

Take dummies with you everywhere you go!

Whether you are excited about e-books, want more from the web, must have your mobile apps, or are swept up in social media, dummies makes everything easier.

Find us online!

dummies.com

dummies®
A Wiley Brand

Leverage the power

Dummies is the global leader in the reference category and one of the most trusted and highly regarded brands in the world. No longer just focused on books, customers now have access to the dummies content they need in the format they want. Together we'll craft a solution that engages your customers, stands out from the competition, and helps you meet your goals.

Advertising & Sponsorships

Connect with an engaged audience on a powerful multimedia site, and position your message alongside expert how-to content. Dummies.com is a one-stop shop for free, online information and know-how curated by a team of experts.

- Targeted ads
- Video
- Email Marketing
- Microsites
- Sweepstakes sponsorship

20 MILLION PAGE VIEWS EVERY SINGLE MONTH

15 MILLION UNIQUE VISITORS PER MONTH

43% OF ALL VISITORS ACCESS THE SITE VIA THEIR MOBILE DEVICES

700,000 NEWSLETTER SUBSCRIPTIONS TO THE INBOXES OF

300,000 UNIQUE INDIVIDUALS EVERY WEEK

# of dummies

Custom Publishing

Reach a global audience in any language by creating a solution that will differentiate you from competitors, amplify your message, and encourage customers to make a buying decision.

- Apps
- Books
- eBooks
- Video
- Audio
- Webinars

Brand Licensing & Content

Leverage the strength of the world's most popular reference brand to reach new audiences and channels of distribution.

For more information, visit **dummies.com/biz**

PERSONAL ENRICHMENT

Staying Sharp dummies
9781119187790
USA $26.00
CAN $31.99
UK £19.99

Facebook dummies
Carolyn Abram
9781119179030
USA $21.99
CAN $25.99
UK £16.99

Guitar dummies
Mark Phillips, Jon Chappell
9781119293354
USA $24.99
CAN $29.99
UK £17.99

Investing dummies
Eric Tyson, MBA
9781119293347
USA $22.99
CAN $27.99
UK £16.99

Beekeeping dummies
Howland Blackiston
9781119310068
USA $22.99
CAN $27.99
UK £16.99

Digital Photography dummies
Julie Adair King
9781119235606
USA $24.99
CAN $29.99
UK £17.99

Meditation dummies
Stephan Bodian
9781119251163
USA $24.99
CAN $29.99
UK £17.99

Pregnancy ALL-IN-ONE dummies
9781119235491
USA $26.99
CAN $31.99
UK £19.99

Samsung Galaxy S7 dummies
Bill Hughes
9781119279952
USA $24.99
CAN $29.99
UK £17.99

iPhone dummies
Edward C. Baig, Bob "Dr. Mac" LeVitus
9781119283133
USA $24.99
CAN $29.99
UK £17.99

Crocheting dummies
Karen Manthey, Susan Brittain
9781119287117
USA $24.99
CAN $29.99
UK £16.99

Nutrition dummies
Carol Ann Rinzler
9781119130246
USA $22.99
CAN $27.99
UK £16.99

PROFESSIONAL DEVELOPMENT

Windows 10 dummies
Andy Rathbone
9781119311041
USA $24.99
CAN $29.99
UK £17.99

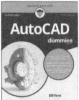
AutoCAD dummies
Bill Fane
9781119255796
USA $39.99
CAN $47.99
UK £27.99

Excel 2016 dummies
Greg Harvey, PhD
9781119293439
USA $26.99
CAN $31.99
UK £19.99

QuickBooks 2017 dummies
Stephen L. Nelson, MBA, CPA, MS in Taxation
9781119281467
USA $26.99
CAN $31.99
UK £19.99

macOS Sierra dummies
Bob "Dr. Mac" LeVitus
9781119280651
USA $29.99
CAN $35.99
UK £21.99

LinkedIn dummies
Joel Elad, MBA's
9781119251132
USA $24.99
CAN $29.99
UK £17.99

Windows 10 ALL-IN-ONE dummies
Woody Leonhard
9781119310563
USA $34.00
CAN $41.99
UK £24.99

SharePoint 2016 dummies
Rosemarie Withee, Ken Withee
9781119181705
USA $29.99
CAN $35.99
UK £21.99

Fundamental Analysis dummies
Matt Krantz
9781119263593
USA $26.99
CAN $31.99
UK £19.99

Networking dummies
Doug Lowe
9781119257769
USA $29.99
CAN $35.99
UK £21.99

Office 2016 dummies
Wallace Wang
9781119293477
USA $26.99
CAN $31.99
UK £19.99

Office 365 dummies
Rosemarie Withee, Ken Withee, Jennifer Reed
9781119265313
USA $24.99
CAN $29.99
UK £17.99

Salesforce.com dummies
Liz Kao, Jon Paz
9781119239314
USA $29.99
CAN $35.99
UK £21.99

Coding dummies
Nikhil Abraham
9781119293323
USA $29.99
CAN $35.99
UK £21.99

Learning Made Easy

ACADEMIC

9781119293576
USA $19.99
CAN $23.99
UK £15.99

9781119293637
USA $19.99
CAN $23.99
UK £15.99

9781119293491
USA $19.99
CAN $23.99
UK £15.99

9781119293460
USA $19.99
CAN $23.99
UK £15.99

9781119293590
USA $19.99
CAN $23.99
UK £15.99

9781119215844
USA $26.99
CAN $31.99
UK £19.99

9781119293378
USA $22.99
CAN $27.99
UK £16.99

9781119293521
USA $19.99
CAN $23.99
UK £15.99

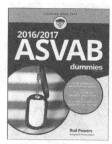

9781119239178
USA $18.99
CAN $22.99
UK £14.99

9781119263883
USA $26.99
CAN $31.99
UK £19.99

Available Everywhere Books Are Sold

dummies.com

dummies
A Wiley Brand

Small books for big imaginations

GETTING STARTED WITH Coding
Get Creative with Code!
Camille McCue, PhD

9781119177173
USA $9.99
CAN $9.99
UK £8.99

MODDING Minecraft
Build Your Own Minecraft Mods!
Sarah Guthals, PhD
Stephen Foster, PhD
Lindsey Handley, PhD

9781119177272
USA $9.99
CAN $9.99
UK £8.99

MAKING YouTube VIDEOS
Star in Your Own Video!
Nick Willoughby

9781119177241
USA $9.99
CAN $9.99
UK £8.99

DESIGNING Digital Games
Create Games with Scratch!
Derek Breen

9781119177210
USA $9.99
CAN $9.99
UK £8.99

GETTING STARTED WITH Raspberry Pi
Program Your Raspberry Pi!
Richard Wentk

9781119262657
USA $9.99
CAN $9.99
UK £6.99

EXPERIMENTING WITH Science
Think, Test, and Learn!

9781119291336
USA $9.99
CAN $9.99
UK £6.99

CREATING Digital Animations
Animate Stories with Scratch!
Derek Breen

9781119233527
USA $9.99
CAN $9.99
UK £6.99

GETTING STARTED WITH Engineering
Think Like an Engineer!
Camille McCue, PhD

9781119291220
USA $9.99
CAN $9.99
UK £6.99

WRITING Computer Code
Learn the Language of Computers!
Chris Minnick and Eva Holland

9781119177302
USA $9.99
CAN $9.99
UK £8.99

Unleash Their Creativity

dummies.com